THE PROTECTION OF TRADITIONAL KNOWLEDGE AT THE FRONTIERS OF DRUG DISCOVERY

This book concerns the often fractious interface between drug discovery and commercialisation, environmental degradation, the biodiversity crisis, the exploitation of Indigenous peoples and the destruction of their culture, the right to health, inequalities of power, and the ability of the law to protect knowledge.

For millennia, medicinal plants have provided a trove of treatments for human ailments, and the key to that treasure has been the traditional knowledge of the Indigenous peoples who have lived alongside these plants. More recently that knowledge has been taken, often without consent or recompense, by Western science as a springboard for the development of pharmaceutical agents. As a response to threats to biodiversity and Indigenous culture, international mechanisms have created, or are creating, enforceable rights for Indigenous peoples to control such knowledge.

With a background in pharmacology and molecular biology and significant experience as a lawyer in pharmaceutical and biotech patent litigation, the author brings a fresh perspective to understanding the difficulties of enforcing such rights and, in particular, examines whether there is a philosophically justifiable limit to the downstream scope of such rights.

This book is aimed at all those with an interest in the control of Indigenous genetic knowledge and the protection of Indigenous culture, whether academics, anthropologists or pharmaceutical researchers, and those seeking to make Indigenous rights work, as activists, legislators or practising lawyers.

The Protection of Traditional Knowledge at the Frontiers of Drug Discovery

Peter S Harrison

·HART·
OXFORD · LONDON · NEW YORK · NEW DELHI · SYDNEY

HART PUBLISHING

Bloomsbury Publishing Plc

Kemp House, Chawley Park, Cumnor Hill, Oxford, OX2 9PH, UK

1385 Broadway, New York, NY 10018, USA

29 Earlsfort Terrace, Dublin 2, Ireland

First published in Great Britain 2024

A catalogue record for this book is available from the British Library.

A catalogue record for this book is available from the Library of Congress.

Library of Congress Control Number: 2024940198

ISBN: HB: 978-1-50993-753-0
ePDF: 978-1-50993-754-7
ePub: 978-1-50993-755-4

Typeset by Compuscript Ltd, Shannon

ACKNOWLEDGEMENTS

Very many people have encouraged and supported me in the writing of this work. I have greatly appreciated the opportunity to discuss the project with academics from across the UK and internationally including, without limitation: Pamela Andanda, Tanya Aplin, TT Arvind, Abbe Brown, Robert Burrell, Patricia Covarubbia, Jane Cornwell, Graham Dutfield, Ben Farrand, Simon Halliday, Naomi Hawkins, Emily Hudson, Marta Iljadica, Marcel Jaspers, Phillip Johnson, Aisling McMahon, Duncan Matthews, Adoración Pérez Troya, Vicenç Ribas, Alison Slade, Lorraine Talbot, Karen Walsh, Andrea Zappalaglio and Sally Zhu. Of course, all errors and misunderstandings remain very much my own.

My thanks also go to the library staff at the British Library, Boston Spa; the Royal Horticultural Society Library, Harlow Carr, Harrogate; the York Minster Library; and the University of York Library.

Particular thanks go to: my Heads of School, Professors Caroline Hunter and TT Arvind for their continued moral support for this project; my ever-engaging students at York Law School; and, in particular, to research assistance from Lowri Beynon.

Finally, my thanks go to my wife Elinor, and sons Alasdair and Arthur, for their love and unwavering support throughout.

In memory of The Honourable Roger T Hughes, KC (1941–2024)

TABLE OF CONTENTS

Acknowledgements v
List of Figures xi
List of Tables xiii
Table of Cases xv
Table of Legislation xvii

1. Introduction **1**
I. The Aim of this Work 1
II. Claims of Misappropriation of TKAGR 4
III. The Problem of Downstream Use 7
IV. How Should We Seek to Address this Problem of 'Scope'? 10
V. Overview of the Structure of this Work 17

2. The International 'Solutions' to Claims of Misappropriation of TKAGR **19**
I. Introduction 19
II. The UN Route(s) 20
III. The WTO Route 31
IV. The WIPO Route 34
V. Conclusions 36

3. The Nature of the Positive Rights in TKAGR within the Nagoya Protocol **37**
I. Introduction 37
II. The Positive Protection Provisions of the Nagoya Protocol 37
III. What Does 'Access' to a Genetic Resource Mean? 38
IV. The Meaning of 'Genetic Resources' 39
V. The Products of Genetic Expression 41
VI. What Does 'Utilization of Genetic Resources' Mean? 43
VII. The Meaning of 'Biotechnology' and 'Derivatives' 47
VIII. Does the 'New' Definition of 'Derivative' Assist? 49
IX. What Is the Purpose of the Expanded Definition of 'Derivative'? 51
X. 'Isolated' Derivatives 54
XI. The Problem of 'Chemical Derivatives' 55
XII. Informational Linkages: 'Genetic Information' 58

XIII. Genetic Expression and Downstream Derivatives 69
XIV. The Right to Control 'Access' to TKAGR under Article 7.................70
XV. The Right to Benefit-Sharing under Article 5(5) 73
XVI. The 'General' TKAGR Provision at Article 12(1) 75
XVII. Special Considerations 76
XVIII. Conclusions: The Nature of the Nagoya Protocol Positive Right Over TKAGR 80

4. The Philosophical Justifications for Positive Rights in TKAGR.................82
I. Introduction..82
II. The 'Problem' of Intangibles 82
III. The 'Problem' of Knowledge 86
IV. High-level Justifications for the Protection of Knowledge 88
V. Is Traditional Knowledge Different?...89
VI. Deontological Justifications 91
VII. Consequentialist Justifications for Intellectual Property 121
VIII. Unjust Enrichment, Misappropriation and Restitution..................141
IX. Distributive Justice..143
X. Restorative/Corrective Justice ('Reparations')................................148
XI. Human Rights Justifications 150
XII. Indigenous 'Sovereignty' and 'Indigenous Intellectual Property' in TKAGR..154
XIII. Conclusions...176

5. The Landscape of Drug Discovery 179
I. Introduction..179
II. The Pharmacological Background..179
III. Looking for Crux Points – The Flow of Information and the 'Dilution' of Contribution..200
IV. The Nature of 'Serendipitous' Discoveries of New Uses..................203
V. Case Studies of Serendipitous Discoveries within Drug Discovery 204

6. The Application of Philosophical Justifications for Positive Rights in TKAGR to the Serendipitous Discovery of Second Uses 217
I. Introduction..217
II. Policy Options 217
III. Deontological Justifications 218
IV. Utilitarian Goals and the Scope of the Positive Right in TKAGR 232
V. A Rawlsian Distributive Justice Analysis 244
VI. Restorative/Corrective Justice ('Reparations')................................249
VII. Human Rights Justifications – The Indigenous Right to Self-determination..250
VIII. Conclusions...255

7. Synthesis of Findings and Further Analysis **257**
I. Introduction 257
II. How Might We Achieve Synthesis? 257
III. A Synthesis 263
IV. The Workability of a Limited Veto – Introduction 267
V. The Workability of a Limited Veto – Assessment of 'Contribution' 268
VI. The Workability of a Limited Veto – Serendipity and 'Retrospective Obviousness' 269
VII. The Workability of a Limited Veto – 'Coincidental' Second Uses 274
VIII. Conclusions 279

8. Conclusions **281**
I. Introduction – Aims of the Work 281
II. Application of Philosophical Justifications 283
III. Synthesis 285
IV. What is Serendipity? 285
V. Coincidental Discoveries 286
VI. Overall Conclusions 287

Bibliography *292*
Index *309*

LIST OF FIGURES

Figure 1 Simplified schematic of path taken by a piece of TKAGR within the drug discovery process.......8
Figure 2 'Family tree' of international responses to anti-misappropriation rights.......19
Figure 3 Schematic diagram of the factors influencing therapeutic efficacy.......190
Figure 4 Drug design cycle: lead structure identification (after Kubinyi).......199
Figure 5 Drug design cycle: lead structure optimization (after Kubinyi).......200
Figure 6 Schematic of the nature of serendipitous discoveries in biology.......203
Figure 7 Schematic representation of the biochemical mechanism of action of sildenafil citrate.......271

LIST OF TABLES

Table 1 Key elements of the Nagoya Protocol articles giving rise to positive rights. 22
Table 2 Rawls's maximin analysis 146
Table 3 Subtypes of acetylcholine receptors 181
Table 4 Some major ethnobotanically-derived medicines (after Cox) 186
Table 5 Phases of drug development 197
Table 6 Examples of serendipitously discovered second uses of plant-derived drugs. 205
Table 7 Application of Lockean justification to potential policy options 231
Table 8 Application of personality rights theories to potential policy options 232
Table 9 Comparison of utilitarian arguments versus potential policy options 239
Table 10 Indigenous group versus drug company maximin analysis 245
Table 11 Indigenous group versus drug company 'broader situation' maximin analysis 249
Table 12 Summary of the application of the Indigenous right to self-determination, UNDRIP and the communitarian claim to potential policy options 254
Table 13 Summary matrix of results from various approaches 258
Table 14 Summary matrix of results (without justifications based on Locke, Kant, Fichte and Hegel) 264

TABLE OF CASES

Canada

Beloit Canada Ltée v Valmet OY (1994) 55(3d) Canadian Patent Reports 385 (FCTD) 268
The Wellcome Foundation Ltd et al v Apotex (1999) 82(3d) Canadian Patent Reports 359 (FCTD) 268

European Court of Human Rights

Sunday Times v United Kingdom (1979) 2 EHRR 245 87

Court of Justice of the European Union

Case C-833/18 SI and Brompton Bicycle Ltd v Chedech /Get2Get [2020] ECLI:EU:C:2020:461 115

European Patent Office

Bayer G 6/88 [1988] OJEPO 4/90....202, 224, 226
Mobil (Friction Reducing Additive) G 2/88 [1988] OJEPO 4/90 ....202, 224–26
Eisai (Second Medical Indication) G 5/83 [1984] OJEPO 64.... 202, 225

United Kingdom

Baigent and another v Random House Group Ltd [2007] EWCA Civ 247, [2007] All ER(D) 456 16
Black Clawson International Ltd v Papierwerke Waldhof-Aschaffenburg AG [1975] AC 591 (UKHL)....87
Celanese International Corp v BP Chemicals Ltd [1999], RPC 203 (EWHC).... 15, 268
Coco v A N Clark (Engineers) Ltd [1969] RPC 41 (EWHC) 16
Hamilton v Mendes (1761) 2 Burr 1198 87

Philips Electronics NV v Ingman Limited, The Video Duplicating Company Limited [1999] FSR 112 (EWHC)........89
Pozzoli Spa v BDMO SA & Anor [2007] EWCA Civ 588, [2007] FSR 37........269
Redwood Music Ltd v Chappell and Co Ltd [1982] RPC 109 (EWHC)........268
Vallejo v Mendes (1774) 1 Cowp 143........87
Warner-Lambert Company LLC v Generics (UK) Ltd and Oths [2018] UKSC 56........226

United States

Graham et al v John Deere Co of Kansas City et al (1966) 383 US 1 (USSC)........269

TABLE OF LEGISLATION

United States

United States Code Title 35 91
§112 229
§284 16

United Kingdom

Patents Act 1977 (as amended)
Section 4A(1) 225
Section 4A(3) 225
Section 4A(4) 226
Section 48 26
Section 48A 26
Section 48B 26
Section 49 26
Section 50 26
Section 64 16

International Treaties

Convention on the Grant of European Patents (European Patent Convention) of 5 October 1973 as revised by the Act revising Article 63 EPC of 17 December 1991 and the Act revising the EPC of 29 November 2000
Article 53(c) 225
Article 54 270
Article 56 270
Article 84 145
Article 85 145
Article 123(2) 145, 270
Article 123(3) 145, 270

United Nations

Bonn Guidelines on Access to Genetic Resources and Fair and Equitable Sharing of the Benefits Arising out of their Utilization (2002) 21–22, 50, 167
Committee on Economic, Social and Cultural Right General Comment No. 17 (2005)....152
Convention on Biological Diversity (1993) 9, 19, 22, 26, 28, 30–36, 38, 40–42, 45, 48, 51–52, 54–55, 65–67, 157, 164, 167
Article 2 ....39–41, 44, 49–50, 53, 59
Article 8(j) 21, 24, 27, 73–74, 77, 120, 163
Convention on the Law of the Sea on the Conservation and Sustainable use of Marine Biological Diversity of Areas Beyond National Jurisdiction (2023)
Article 13 29
Article 14(1) 28, 67
Declaration on the Rights of Indigenous Peoples (2007).... 21, 25, 27, 91, 155, 168, 172, 174, 178, 254, 256, 265, 284, 289
Article 3 ....20, 169, 171
Article 11 .... 20, 24, 169–71, 173, 177, 251–52
Article 24 ....20, 171, 173
Article 28(1) 170
Article 31 .... 20, 169, 171, 173, 252
Article 46 173–74
Liepzig Declaration and Global Plan of Action on Genetic Resources for Food and Agriculture (1996) 29–30
Nagoya Protocol on Access to Genetic Resources and the Fair and Equitable Sharing of Benefits Arising from their Utilization (ABS) to the Convention on Biological Diversity (2010) 7, 9, 16–17, 19, 28, 30,33–35, 37–81
Article 2 ....43, 48, 50, 55, 59, 64
Article 5(1) 22–23, 25, 38, 43, 64, 69–70, 73
Article 5(2) 22–23, 25–26, 43, 64, 69–70, 73, 75
Article 5(5) 22, 24–26, 29, 70, 73–75, 80, 219
Article 6(1) 23–24, 38, 43, 72
Article 6(2) 23–26, 75
Article 7 .... 23–26, 29, 37, 70–75, 77, 80, 219
Article 8(a) 76–79, 238
Article 8(b) 76, 78–80, 238
Article 12(1) 74–76, 78, 80

International Treaty on Plant Genetic Resources for Food and Agriculture (1983) ... 29–30
Article 1.1 ... 30
Article 1.2 ... 30
Article 9 ... 30
International Covenant on Civil and Political Rights (1966) ... 173
Article 17 ... 151
Article 19(2) ... 151
Article 19(3) ... 151
International Covenant on Economic, Social and Cultural Rights (1966) ... 151, 169, 173
Article 15 ... 152–54
Kunming-Montreal Global Biodiversity Framework ... 25–27, 66–67, 157
Section K para 7(a) ... 171
Rio Declaration on Environment and Development (1993)
Paragraph 26 ... 164
Principle 22 ... 164
Vienna Convention on the Law of Treaties (1969)
Article 31(1) ... 45
Universal Declaration of Human Rights (1948)
Article 12 ... 151
Article 17 ... 151
Article 27 ... 151–52

World Intellectual Property Office

Berne Convention for the Protection of Literary and Artistic Works (1886)
Article 7(1) ... 219
Article 7*bis* ... 219

World Trade Organization

Trade Related Aspects of Intellectual Property Agreement (1994) ... 165, 238–39
Article 7 ... 31
Article 8 ... 31
Article 27.3(b) ... 31–32
Article 29 ... 33
Article 29*bis* ... 33, 35
Declaration on the TRIPS agreement and public health (Doha Declaration; 2001) ... 239
Paragraph 19 ... 31

Practice Guidance/Notices

European Patent Office

EPO Guidelines G-VII 5 (Case Law of the EPO Boards of Appeal I.D.2) 269
EPO Guidelines G-VII 5.1 (Case Law of the EPO Boards of Appeal I.D.3.1) 269
EPO Guidelines G-VII 5.2 (Case Law of the EPO Boards of Appeal I.D.4.1) 269

Swiss Federal Intellectual Property Office

Legal Advice from the Swiss Federal Intellectual Property Office (FIPO) of 30 May 1984 ....202, 225

United Kingdom Intellectual Property Office

UKIPO Practice Notice: Patents Act 1977-Second Medical Use Claims 226

World Health Organization

World Health Organisation Health Economics and Drugs TCM, "Remuneration guidelines for non-voluntary use of a patent on medical technologies" WHO/TCM/2005.1 268

1

Introduction

I. The Aim of this Work

The aim of this work is to examine the balance between respect for the justifications of rights holders and the liberty of the broader world in relation to a relatively new-born, and evolving, intellectual property right. Its aim is to determine where, if at all, any justifiable limit can be drawn to the downstream scope of positive rights of Indigenous peoples to control their traditional knowledge associated with genetic resources (TKAGR) when that knowledge is used within the search for new pharmaceutically active compounds (or new uses for such compounds) within drug discovery research. Such positive rights have been created (or are in the course of being created) as part of an international drive to preserve biodiversity and Indigenous culture by creating control over access to, and utilisation of, genetic resources and the traditional knowledge associated with such resources.

The concept of controlling the use of genetic resources may initially appear to be relatively straightforward. Taking a plant cutting, propagating it and growing it indisputably looks like the accessing and using of that plant. However, examination of the concept of a genetic resource rapidly reveals that, with the advent of biotechnological tools for manipulating the genome, any assumption of simplicity is misplaced – and we are led to question whether 'genetic information' such as a nucleotide sequence (or even the natural epigenetic modification of a genome) can be considered a genetic resource. Yet further complexities are encountered when considering whether the biochemical products of genetic expression (such as enzyme proteins and the products of enzymatic reactions – or even man-made chemical derivatives thereof) are to be included within the subject matter to be controlled.

Such problems of definition are further amplified when we come to consider TKAGR. This type of knowledge can take many forms and be held in many ways – of particular interest in the present work is knowledge of how a particular genetic resource can be used to influence a human disease state. However, due to the inherent malleability, mixability and easily reproduced nature of information, such traditional knowledge is perhaps harder even to define and delimit than 'genetic resources'. This is particularly true when one looks at the fate of such knowledge within the process of drug discovery. Unfortunately, the provisions of the extant (and proposed) international instruments relating to the protection of genetic resources and associated traditional knowledge are unclear with regard to this downstream scope. The rapidly developing advent of artificial intelligence (AI) and machine learning (ML) within the drug discovery process will further add to this lack of clarity.

Stimulated by these uncertainties, the core of this book is the examination of the justifiable downstream scope of a positive right in TKAGRs in the light of an empirical examination of the drug discovery process. This empirical examination highlights how any piece of information (including traditional knowledge) entering into a drug discovery process is subject to significant mixing with other information, leading to its dilution/attenuation. Such a piece of information may serve as the inspiration for further discoveries (alone, or mixed in with other information), and those discoveries may themselves serve as further stimulus for new research directions, or be used as part of more iterative development work. However it is used, the information will enter into a series of complex and overlapping discovery pathways, including 'dead-ends' and feedback loops. In many cases, any useful downstream discovery will (though always causally linked in fact to the original information) appear particularly distal or remote from the information which served as the original stimulus for the work.

This complex 'epistemic dilution' throws up a significant challenge: should we consider *any* downstream use (eg the development of a new drug) as constituting the use of the original inspiring piece of traditional knowledge, no matter how greatly that information has been diluted? The question is an important one – the efficient and non-wasteful exploitation behaviour and investment decisions of all parties affected by a right rely upon an informed and reliable appreciation of a right's scope.

There is, of course, one potentially simple answer to this problem of epistemic dilution: why do we not just say that *all* downstream uses which are caused *in fact* by the original inspiration provided by the traditional knowledge constitute use of that original knowledge? Such an approach would certainly save us looking into the complex causal continuum between inspiration and outcome to determine a point at which to limit the right to control downstream use. However, the problem with such a simplistic approach is that it ignores the interests of immediately affected third parties, in particular, and of the broader world in general. As will be discussed in this book, determination of a justifiable *legal* scope of a right requires a determination of causation *in law*, as opposed to a mere determination of causation *in fact*. That justifiable scope is dependent upon the reason(s) for the existence of the right – reasoning which must balance competing interests.

Established intellectual property law does not commonly consider such questions of scope as ones of causation as such. Instead, it relies on judgments of imitativeness and non-imitativeness. Inherent within such considerations of imitativeness is the concept of conflicting 'contribution' – intellectual property rights do not exist in a vacuum: one always has to consider conflicting claims between those seeking to assert the right and those properly seeking to avoid it.

In the present case, what a simple causation *in fact* test arguably ignores is a recognition of the contribution made by those pharmaceutical researchers who are developing (or have developed) the new information in which the original inspiration is being 'diluted'. This conflict between the contributions of the Indigenous peoples who have over time come to an understanding of the traditional knowledge which has inspired the work and those downstream researchers who have built upon that inspiration is at the heart of the current work.

Looking at the question of downstream scope through the lens of competing contributions we might argue that the scope should end where the accretion of downstream contributions somehow 'outweighs' the contribution made by the Indigenous 'originators'. However, we are still presented with the question of where such a 'tipping point' of competing contributions should be arrived upon. Comparing conflicting contributions is inherently difficult – it is not easy to measure a single contribution, or to summate a number of contributions. Indeed, the current work shows that when you empirically examine the drug discovery process you find that there are very few easily determined points at which one might obviously argue that such a tipping point has been reached and that a chain of causation *in law* has been broken. Perhaps what we require is some sense of a step change in the nature of the competing contributions. Of course, we do not have necessarily to reinvent the wheel here. We might ask whether any guidance can be taken from other intellectual property rights that have been forced to wrestle with questions of scope within the field of drug discovery. The field of patent law would appear the most obvious choice.

It should be stressed at the outset that the subject matter of established patent law is a distinctly different creature from that of positive rights in TKAGR. Accordingly, direct comparison between patent law and control over TKAGR is potentially misleading, and needs to be treated with a great deal of caution. However, patent law and the processes of drug discovery have had a long interaction, particularly with regard to questions of 'downstream' scope. Provided that the distinct differences of patent law are borne in mind, the history of this interaction may act as a source of putative concepts to be considered in the context of the scope of traditional knowledge in the present problem. One of the chief aspects of the interaction between patent law and drug development has been the recurrent question of whether a claim to one therapeutic use of a drug should extend the discovery of a second therapeutic (or other) use.

With such questions in mind (and in the light of this work's empirical analysis of the flow of information through the topography of drug discovery processes) the current work posits that 'serendipitous' discoveries of a new use of the subject of the traditional knowledge (what might be termed within patent law as the uncovering of an unexpected 'second use') might act as a putative point at which one might consider there to be a break in the causation *in law* link between the original stimulus and the useful outcome. Crucially, this is a point at which the competing contributions between the Indigenous peoples on the one hand, and pharmaceutical researchers on the other, is brought to a head. Here, one is forced to ask why the Indigenous 'discovery' of one therapeutic use should prevent third-party exploitation of a second, entirely unforeseen, use. As will be seen in this work, this is a question that takes us to the heart of what contribution *means* in this context.

As has already been stressed, although an understanding of existing types of intellectual property right may act as a source of inspiration for our thinking, the different nature of traditional knowledge means that the guidance found in those other rights can take us only so far. As such, in addressing normative problems in this area we are pushed back to first principles – we need to ask: what are the underlying philosophical reasons for the existence of these rights? As will be seen, such justifications roughly fall into two camps: those justifications based upon consequentialist goals; and deontological justifications based on concepts of duty. Both are considered in depth in this work. Accordingly, this work looks to apply the philosophical 'toolbox' of reasons for the existence of property rights in intangible concepts to the question of competing claims in relation to serendipitously discovered new uses and attempts to arrive at a synthesis of the results obtained from the application of each justification. The reader should be warned from the outset that this is not an area in which it is easy to arrive at definitive conclusions. The complexities and difficulties are both empirical and theoretical. They are as follows:

1. The complexity of the passage of TKAGR through the topology of the drug discovery process and the difficulty of identifying clear points within the movement of such information at which limits of control may be investigated.
2. The complexity of the epistemic dilution of the idea held within a piece of TKAGR through the drug discovery process and the complexity of competing contributions inherent within the entanglement of information in that discovery process.
3. The difficulty in the application of contribution-based reward justifications for the control of information in the light of a complicated plurality of types and sources of competing contributions and to specific examples of contribution and of competing contributions.
4. The complexity in determining the true nature of serendipity and second uses in the light of the nature of traditional knowledge.
5. The potential complexities wrought by the existence of a right to control information which, crucially, has no temporal limitation.

The remainder of this chapter is intended to give further introductory background to the problems considered in this book, to outline the analytical approaches taken to address that problem, and to provide the reader with a guide to the broad structure of this work.

II. Claims of Misappropriation of TKAGR

Many compounds that have pharmacological effects in humans are derived from living organisms. In some cases these compounds have been honed by hundreds of millions of years of evolution to have exquisite selectivity and potency in biological systems – indeed, some of these compounds are among the most toxic substances we know of.[1] In static plants and fungi which cannot easily escape from predators

[1] For example, the LD_{50} dose in humans of botulinum toxin from the bacterium *Clostridium botulinum* (ie, Botox, used in cosmetic treatments) has been estimated to be 1.3–2.1 ng per kg body weight by intravenous or intramuscular injection and 10–13 ng/kg when inhaled. SS Arnonet et al, 'Botulinum Toxin as a Biological Weapon: Medical and Public Health Management' (2001) 285(8) *Journal of the American Medical Association* 1059.

such compounds are used for defence. In predator organisms they are more often used as tools in the hunt for prey. In yet other organisms they are used in the drive to reproduce.[2] In some cases the biological effect produced by evolution has been harnessed by man to provide beneficial therapeutic effects and many currently approved drugs have their origin in plants and fungi,[3] or animal venom.[4] This is in no way only a historical phenomenon. In their analysis of 1,562 drugs approved internationally between 1981 to 2014, Newman and Cragg identified that the majority of these drugs were reliant on a natural product as their inspiration: 16 per cent were a biological macromolecule; 5 per cent were an unaltered natural product (or a mixture of such products); 21 per cent were direct chemical derivatives of natural products; and 25 per cent were synthetic drugs which were either a direct mimic of a naturally derived product or which otherwise reproduced the active structure ('pharmacophore') of a natural product.[5] Only 27 per cent of these approved drugs were synthetic drugs which were not reliant on a natural product as their inspiration.[6]

Often the Western understanding that a particular organism contained a compound of potential therapeutic benefit arose out of the knowledge of folk-healers or traditional medicine systems.[7] In many historical cases, those Western ethnobotanists and scientists accessing and using traditional knowledge have treated this knowledge as a non-rivalrous and non-excludable 'public good' and have treated the originators of this knowledge to be undeserving of recognition, or reward, for its subsequent use, and similarly undeserving of any degree of control over the use of the information.[8]

More lately, the interface between Indigenous knowledge and Western pharmacology has become an area of high emotions, polemics and political activism.[9]

[2] GVP Reddy and A Guerrero, 'Interactions of Insect Pheromones and Plant Semiochemicals' (2004) 9(5) *Trends in Plant Science* 253.

[3] PA Cox, 'The Ethnobotanical Approach to Drug Discovery: Strengths and Limitations' in DJ Chadwick and J Marsh (eds), *Ethnobotany and the Search for New Drugs* (Ciba Foundation Symp 185) (Chichester, John Wiley, 1994) 25, 27; NR Farnsworth, 'The Rôle of Ethnopharmacology in Drug Development' in *Bioactive compounds from Plants* (Ciba Foundation Symp 154) (Chichester, John Wiley, 1994) 2.

[4] GF King (ed), *Venoms to Drugs: Venom as a Source for the Development of Human Therapeutics* (Abingdon, Royal Society of Chemistry, 2014).

[5] DJ Newman and GM Cragg, 'Natural Products as Sources of New Drugs from 1981 to 2014' (2016) 79 *Journal of Natural Products* 629, 631.

[6] The remaining 6% were vaccines.

[7] See generally: CM Cotton, *Ethnobotany: Principles and Applications* (Chichester, John Wiley, 1996) 234; MJ Balick and PA Cox, *Plants, People, and Culture: The Science of Ethnobotany* (New York, Scientific American Library, 1997); L Schiebinger, *Plants and Empire, Colonial Bioprospecting in the Atlantic World* (Cambridge MA, Harvard University Press, 2004), B Laws, *Fifty Plants that Changed the Course of History* (Newton Abbott, David and Charles, 2010).

[8] P Schuler, 'Biopiracy and Commercialization of Ethnobotanical Knowledge' in JM Finger and P Schuler (eds), *Poor People's Knowledge* (Oxford, Oxford University Press, 2004).

[9] See generally: M Riley (ed), *Indigenous Intellectual Property Rights, Legal Obstacles and Innovative Solutions* (Lanham MD, Altamira Press 2004); D Wüger, 'Prevention of Misappropriation of Intangible Cultural Heritage Through Intellectual Property Laws' in JM Finger and P Schuler (eds), *Poor People's Knowledge* (Oxford, Oxford University Press, 2004); C Oguamanam, *International Law and Indigenous*

Shiva uses the term 'biopiracy' to include *all* aspects of the control by Western commercial interests of biological resources and biodiversity.[10] However, it is generally more common for biopiracy to be used to describe a narrower set of circumstances, namely the particular situation where a genetic resource (and information relating to that genetic resource) obtained from Indigenous peoples is used scientifically, or commercially, without their consent and/or without those Indigenous peoples having received any benefit from the 'downstream' use of said genetic resources and/or the related information.[11]

As will be described in more detail in chapter four, this history of claimed misappropriation eventually led to a movement to secure legal mechanisms by which Indigenous peoples would gain control over genetic resources and traditional knowledge such that misappropriation could no longer occur.[12] However, as will also be discussed further in this book, the particular nature of traditional knowledge is such that its protection is not easily achieved through the use of what might be termed 'established' intellectual property rights (such as copyright, patents, utility models, trade secrets, trade marks, plant variety protection or geographical indications), or through the law of confidence.[13] Attempts to protect traditional knowledge relating to genetic resources (and traditional knowledge and cultural expression more widely) have therefore focused on the creation of a set of sui generis rights which, independent of currently established intellectual property rights, would ensure that such genetic resources and related knowledge could be controlled by those originally holding the information.

The drive to prevent 'misappropriation' of genetic resources and related traditional knowledge has taken place, with significantly differing rates of progress, in a number of international fora. The key fora are as follows:

- World Trade Organization (WTO)
- United Nations (UN)
- World Intellectual Property Organization (WIPO)

The nature of the rights established under the current (and proposed) international solutions to countering misappropriation of genetic resources and traditional

Knowledge: Intellectual Property, Plant Biodiversity, and Traditional Medicine (Toronto, University of Toronto Press, 2006); SS Latha, 'Biopiracy and Protection of Traditional Medicine in India' (2009) 31(9) *European Intellectual Property Review* 465; see also: G Dutfield, 'Traditional Knowledge, Intellectual Property and Pharmaceutical Innovation: What's Left to Discuss?' in M David and D Halbert (eds), *The Sage Handbook of Intellectual Property* (Thousand Oaks CA, Sage, 2014) 649.

[10] V Shiva, *Biopiracy: The Plunder of Nature and Knowledge* (New York, South End Press, 1997) 3.

[11] See generally: G Dutfield, 'Protecting the Rights of Indigenous Peoples: Can Prior Informed Consent Help?' in R Wynberg et al (eds), *Indigenous Peoples, Consent and Benefit Sharing: Lessons from the San-Hoodia Case* (Dordrecht, Springer, 2009) 53, 55; DF Robinson, *Confronting Biopiracy; Challenges, Cases and International Debates* (London, Earthscan, 2012) 14.

[12] RJ Coombe, 'The Recognition of Indigenous Peoples' and Community Traditional Knowledge in International Law' (2002) 14 *St Thomas Law Review* 275.

[13] G Dutfield, *Intellectual Property Rights, Biogenetic Resources and Traditional Knowledge* (London, Earthscan, 2004) 101.

knowledge are set out in detail in chapter two and a 'family tree' of these approaches is described in Figure 2 in that chapter. The most developed amongst these international approaches is the 2010 Nagoya Protocol on Access to Genetic Resources and the Fair and Equitable Sharing of Benefits Arising from their Utilization to the Convention on Biological Diversity (Nagoya Protocol) which will be discussed in depth in chapter two.

III. The Problem of Downstream Use

A. The Dilution of Knowledge within Drug Discovery

The development 'trails' within drug development are often long and complicated, and the original contribution from a biological source or traditional knowledge is sometimes overestimated.[14] A piece of traditional knowledge can take many such routes within the drug discovery process – there are many pathways and feedback loops, the original information may be admixed to a greater body of existing information regarding the clinical problem, and there may be further admixture to the original information of discoveries derived from it and subsequent admixture to other parallel information which is not derived from it. In such a way, the original information is 'diluted' or 'attenuated'. Here we immediately see the conflict between the original contribution of the Indigenous peoples and contribution provided by those performing the research which lies at the heart of the current work – the dilution of knowledge throughout the drug discovery process is arguably accompanied by a concomitant dilution in contribution.

Chapter five of this work will look at the topography of the drug discovery research process in greater depth. However, for introductory purposes, Figure 1 is a much-simplified schematic showing some of the potential steps that a piece of TKAGR may take within a drug discovery process. For simplicity, this flow diagram suggests that the steps are fairly linear. However, the 'real life' drug discovery trail for a particular drug (or family of drugs) will rarely show such linearity. It is, of course, entirely possible that the scientific (and commercial) benefits of using a particular piece of original knowledge may be relatively proximal to that original knowledge, and the history of the science of pharmacology is full of the use of relatively simple plant extracts (or compounds directly purified from such extracts) to give a therapeutic benefit.[15] However, the extraction and testing of a biochemical constituent of a genetic resource is, within modern drug discovery,

[14] G Dutfield, 'A Critical Analysis of the Debate on Traditional Knowledge, Drug Discovery and Patent-Based Biopiracy' (2011) 33(4) *European Intellectual Property Review* 238.

[15] One can see this where particular endogenous toxins are simply extracted and used. One example is the use of the puffer fish toxin, tetrodotoxin, as a research tool. See eg CH Lee and PC Ruben, 'Interaction Between Voltage-Gated Sodium Channels and the Neurotoxin, Tetrodotoxin' (2008) 2(6) *Channels* 407.

far more usually merely the *beginning*, rather than the end, of a process of finding a safe and efficacious drug.[16]

Figure 1 Simplified schematic of path taken by a piece of TKAGR within the drug discovery process

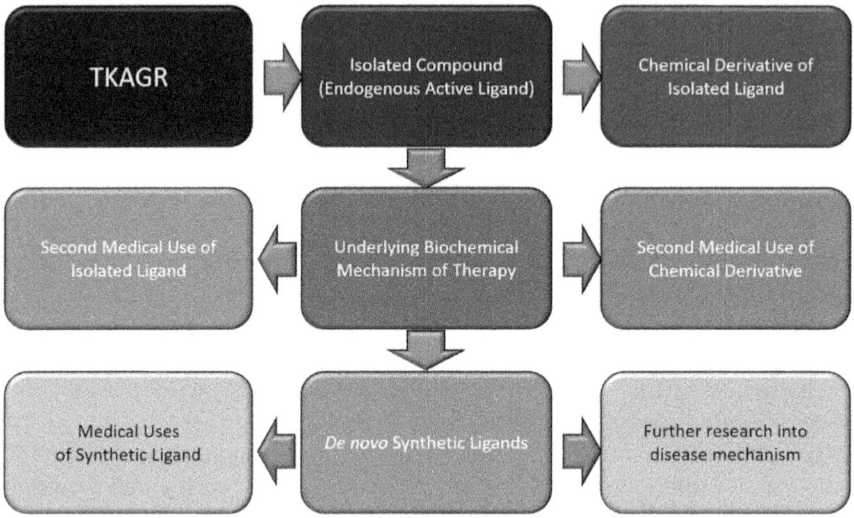

Evolution through natural selection can be improved upon in the search for a better drug, but such work has the additional advantage for those sponsoring the work of generating intellectual property 'space' relative to their competitors' efforts. Indeed, much research into chemical derivatives is also undertaken in the search for so-called 'me-too' (or, perhaps less pejoratively, 'follow-on') compounds which allow a competitor to enter a market without infringement of earlier patents covering the field (but which can also yield truly enhanced pharmacological chemical entities).[17] Such modification of compounds is but one element of the drug discovery process. The finding of a new pharmacologically active compound within a genetic resource may uncover an as-yet-unknown biological mechanism within humans (or at least previously unknown ways of affecting known systems) which can give rise to further lines of research, both in terms of new chemical entities and new therapeutic benefits.

Given the pharmaceutical industry's striving not only to improve on an original, but to seek out clear intellectual property space, it is highly likely that the scientific (and commercial) benefits of using a piece of original TKAGR will be significantly distal to a complex process of mixing and dilution of the original information.

[16] DG Grahame-Smith and JK Aronson, *Oxford Textbook of Clinical Pharmacology and Drug Therapy* (Oxford, Oxford University Press, 1992) 3; J Hall, 'The Drug Development Process' in ID Giovanna and G Hayes (eds), *Principles of Clinical Research* (Petersfield, Wrightson Biomedical, 2001) 1.

[17] A Hollis, 'Me-too Drugs: Is There a Problem?' (2004) www.who.int/intellectualproperty/topics/ip/Me-tooDrugs_Hollis1.pdf.

B. Where *Should* the Right End?

The core purpose of the Nagoya Protocol is to provide a set of *binding* mechanisms for implementing the access and fair and equitable benefits sharing (ABS) objectives of the Convention on Biological Diversity (CBD). As will be discussed in chapter two, it does this by creating what are essentially rights of veto over certain genetic resources and over specific traditional knowledge which relates to those genetic resources. However, when one looks at the real-world complexity of drug discovery research and the provisions of the Nagoya Protocol, we see a potential problem. It might be argued that much of the rhetoric in the argument for creating positive rights in traditional knowledge seems to take an uncomplicated view of the role of traditional knowledge in pharmaceutical discovery/development and tends, in particular, not to mention the more distal and remote research activities. It also tends to assume that all downstream uses of a piece of TKAGR, or another piece of traditional knowledge which relates to a therapeutic solution, are derived in a simple, linear, fashion from the original piece of knowledge. As we have seen, this is not necessarily the case.

The way in which certain articles of the Nagoya Protocol came to be drafted (and certain definitions came to be defined and incorporated into those articles) would appear to leave a degree of uncertainty over the scope of protection offered by the Nagoya Protocol in relation to the *downstream* use of biochemical constituents of genetic resources. These uncertainties stimulated the author to ask the following question (which is the core of the current work): given the potential dilution of the original TKAGR, is it justifiable to allow the 'owner' of the original knowledge to possess an absolute veto on all downstream activity, or are other solutions more supportable? This can be reframed as: (i) Does a broad, apparently unending, scope of veto on use constitute fair/justifiable protection for the holders of traditional knowledge regarding the therapeutic efficacy of genetic resources, even where the 'non-consensual' use, is extremely distal to the original knowledge? And (ii) If such a scope is unfair/unjustifiable, can we gain any certainty as to where the scope *should* end (which may be interpreted as an activity *not* constituting access/use)?

Although these questions were stimulated by the uncertainty of the Nagoya Protocol in this regard, (and may inform our understanding of the correct interpretation of the Nagoya Protocol), it is a more fundamental normative question whose solution (if there is one) is more broadly applicable to the protection which *should* be afforded to Indigenous peoples, whichever method of creating positive rights is promulgated within a jurisdiction (and indeed whatever solution is finally arrived at through the WIPO or the WTO routes).

It should be immediately noted that the key focus of this work is deliberately upon the right to *veto* downstream use, as opposed to a right merely to share in the fruits of a third party's existing, or intended, commercial exploitation. A right to veto is a significantly stronger right than a mere right to share benefits of exploitation in that it allows the right holder to choose whether the subject matter is exploited, how it is exploited, by whom and on what terms. A right to share in proceeds of exploitation that is not supported with a right to veto is a lesser right. Accordingly, questions of the justification and scope of the stronger veto rights fall first to consideration. As will be seen, however, the appropriateness of a mere compensation model relative to downstream vetoes and questions of determination of compensation based upon 'contribution' come to consideration within the context of proposed policy options (see chapter six).

IV. How Should We Seek to Address this Problem of 'Scope'?

Although the downstream use question set out above is relatively simple to formulate, it is one that is harder to answer. The current work addresses the overall question by essentially asking two related, and intertwined, questions:

1. How can one delineate the boundary of a right to control traditional knowledge?
2. What are the philosophical justifications for a veto right in TKAGR?

The work adopts two parallel analytical approaches to these questions:

1. Analogical reasoning which:
   (a) treats the involvement of a piece of TKAGR within a drug discovery process as a flow of information (a chain of causation) during which the original concept becomes diluted through the contribution of others; and (alongside that approach)
   (b) seeks to determine what justifiable parallels (if any) can be drawn with relevant existing categories of intellectual property rights, particularly in relation to the identification of putative boundaries and the handling of competing contributions.
2. The application of a 'toolbox' of philosophical justifications for property in intangible concepts to putative boundaries to the right.

Each of these questions, and analytical approaches, will be dealt with in turn.

A. Boundary/'Crux' Point Delineation

As will be dealt with in more detail in chapter four, trying to create exclusivity in an intangible (such as knowledge) is inherently wrought with problems. Ideas are, by their nature, non-exclusionary and non-rivalrous, and exclusivity in ideas can be only be created through the imposition of what Bentham styled the 'head of law'.[18] If one is (through a positive legal mechanism) to delineate an area that is to be excluded from the use of others, one needs to be able with reasonable certainty to identify the point at which third-party use of the idea is to be prevented. However, whereas the 'core' of an idea may seem easy to articulate, problems begin to arise when one seeks to determine the 'edges' of a concept. The uncertainty of such delineation is related to the nature of the type of information that one seeks to protect. Problems of delineation of both 'backward-looking' (subsistence) and 'forward-looking' (infringement) boundaries are (as will be discussed in chapter four) arguably more acute in relation to 'raw' ideas than when dealing with (relatively) more concrete *expressions* of such ideas. Traditional knowledge that tells us of the therapeutic benefit of a particular genetic resource is, arguably, information in its 'rawest' form.

In the current problem, the issues concerning boundary delineation are compounded by the complexity of the mechanisms by which a piece of traditional knowledge can be used within the field of drug discovery. It is this mix of the inherent breadth of the nature of traditional knowledge, teamed with the plurality and complexity of potential downstream uses, which makes the determination of justifiable limits to positive rights to control its use such a thorny problem. Thorny as it may be, if we are to get anywhere with finding a justifiable limit we need to identify some putative boundaries which can be taken on for further analysis. As will be discussed below, this work uses two approaches to seek such putative boundaries. The first is to identify parallels with concepts of breaks in chains of causation and to apply such concepts, where applicable, by analogy. The second seeks to identify potentially relevant concepts that have been used within the analysis of other intellectual property rights and to apply such concepts, where applicable, by analogy. It should be immediately noted that both approaches are used in parallel and inform one another.

B. Philosophical Justifications for a Veto Right

Attempts to delineate the putative edges of a right are crucial precursors to questions of scope and without such examination one is in danger of dealing merely in broad generic terms. However, such enquiries cannot, of themselves, answer the question of what is a *justifiable* limit to a particular right to exclude others from an activity. A determination of such justifiable limits can, by definition, only come from the application of the *philosophical* grounds for excluding others from an activity to a particular situation. As will be further discussed in chapter four, there is a rich body of higher-level philosophical principles (consequentialist, deontological and those not so easily categorised) which have been used for excluding third party use of what might be called intellectual products and thereby justifying

[18] J Bentham, *Manual of Political Economy* (1839) reprinted in W Stark (ed), *Jeremy Bentham's Economic Writings* (London, George Allen and Unwin, 1952) 263.

the existence of intellectual property rights in the light of opposing justifications for the preservation of a 'commons of ideas'. The present study will seek to identify and summarise these justifications and apply them to the question of the proper scope of positive protection over uses of TKAGR. However, simple rehearsal of the underlying opposing justifications is likely to provide only broad generic principles as to the limit of these rights. Where one is faced with a continuum, or greyscale, of putative 'infringements' (ie non-consensual uses), such a broad examination is unlikely, of itself, to provide more focused guidance as to whether certain forms of distal activity should constitute non-consensual use.

The power and usefulness of a philosophical position within a legal context comes from the ability to apply it to 'real-world' situations. As stated by Underkuffler, the adoption of a theoretical dimension means nothing without knowing to *what* this theory is to be applied.[19] In the present case the 'what' to which we are seeking to apply a theoretical dimension – ie our philosophical 'toolkit' – is the putative boundary delineation to the right identified through analogical reasoning.

C. Analogical Reasoning: Causation, Dilution and the Topography of the Drug Discovery Process

Intellectual property rights are often analogised as creating exclusivity over a 'field' of activity. The mental image conjured up is perhaps one of a two-dimensional area, or perhaps even a three-dimensional space. Such images can help us visualise a problem and they certainly assist in the drawing of two- or three-dimensional Euler diagrams. In this analogy, questions of scope are visualised as the determination of the (sometimes fuzzy) 'edges' of the area or space. However, analogies are simply that, and we need always to be aware of their limitations. What is used as a mental aid should not circumscribe our ways of thinking.

An outstanding feature of the present case is the sense of a 'flow' of information (TKAGR) through a series of pathways where one piece of knowledge stimulates a further downstream use. It is the nature of that information at any point in the pathway (and the use to which it is put) which provides path-dependency on the original inspiring knowledge. In such a case perhaps a more productive analogy is with a causal chain, rather than with an excluded area with edges. It is to this type of analogical reasoning that we will now turn.

We are concerned in this work with the question of whether a particular use is consensual or not. This would appear, on the face of it, to have a relatively straightforward binary outcome – consent is either granted or consent is not granted. In fact, the granting of consent, or otherwise, has many complexities: does the person giving (or denying) consent have the authority to grant/deny it? Is the consent (or denial) clear? Is the consent/denial contingent upon something else? These

[19] LS Underkuffler, *The Idea of Property: It's Meaning and Power* (Oxford, Oxford University Press, 2005) 21.

complexities are important (and given the way traditional knowledge may be held by Indigenous groups could be particularly problematic in relation to the granting of consent to use of such knowledge).[20] There is, however, a further question: is the consent properly *required*? In our present case we can ask: is the downstream use of a piece of knowledge within a drug discovery programme such that consent is required?

Our first approach may be to say that this question has a simple answer based upon a simple causation analysis: did the use in question *in fact* derive from the original piece of information? If so, consent is required. If we look (broadly) at the application of a causation *in fact* (or sine qua non) test to the situation in which a new drug has been developed on the basis of a piece of TKAGR, we would find that *but for* the original piece of TKAGR one would never have arrived at the final drug in the same way in which it was arrived at. One may have eventually arrived at that drug by other (path-independent) means (eg through random screening), but possibly less simply, quickly or cheaply as through the path-dependent means. Of course, with regard to the question of consent we are not concerned about such path-independent means – such means are, by definition, not dependent *in fact* upon the original information.

If causation in fact *alone* is sufficient to create liability, one might successfully argue that *any* downstream use, no matter how distal or remote (and no matter how changed, diluted and widely dissipated the original 'inspiration' has become) can be subject to a veto from the original holder of the information. Within the philosophy of scientific discovery there is a long tradition of recognition that new discoveries are based upon the work of those who have gone before. Newton's declaration that 'If I have seen further it is by standing on the sholders [*sic*] of Giants'[21] echoes (somewhat ironically, and perhaps deliberately) the earlier statement *nanos gigantum humeris insidentes* (dwarves on the shoulders of giants) attributed to Bernard of Chartres.[22] Although Hanson[23] acknowledges that all scientific discoveries have to be causally dependent *in fact* upon work that has gone before, he stresses that such causality is essentially a retrospective view which is taken once a discovery has been made – if one is still *within* a chain of discovery it does not, of itself, render the last step in the discovery trite or obvious, nor take us unerringly to the final conclusion *before* that discovery is made. Is such a strict causation *in fact* test correct in our present instance? Such 'but for' tests for causation give only a stark binary outcome, lack subtlety and could be taken to entirely

[20] See discussion on the ways in which TKAGR can be held at ch 4.XII.B.

[21] Letter from Newton to Hooke (5 February 1676) in HW Turnbull et al (eds), *The Correspondence of Isaac Newton*, vol I (Cambridge, Cambridge University Press, 1959) 416.

[22] 'Bernard of Chartres used to compare us to [puny] dwarfs perched on the shoulders of giants. He pointed out that we see more and farther than our predecessors, not because we have keener vision or greater height, but because we are lifted up and borne aloft on their gigantic stature.' John (of Salisbury, Bishop of Chartres) *The Metalogicon: A Twelfth-Century Defense of the Verbal and Logical Arts of the Trivium* (Oakland CA, California University Press, 1955) 167.

[23] NR Hanson, *Patterns of Discovery, An Inquiry into the Conceptual Foundations of Science* (Cambridge, Cambridge University Press, 1965) 50.

absurd extremes – there is undoubtedly a sine qua non link between a wrong turning taken by Leopold Lojka in Sarajevo on 28 June 1914 and the detonation of a nuclear device over Nagasaki 31 years and 42 days later and it is hard to imagine that the latter event would not have happened in the way that it did, but for the former.[24]

Other problems with a sine qua non test arise where one considers that causal chains are not only long, but that one event will be the 'result' of the interaction of a large variety of distinct efferent events or preconditions – a particular situation is often the outcome of multiple equilibria of causes. Following an empirical approach, much scientific experimentation will seek to control as many efferent factors as possible so as to isolate the causative factor of interest. However, such control is impossible where performing an ex post facto analysis of the historic causes of an event. In addition, multiple efferent events cause particular problems where there is duplicative causation (two efferent factors, each of which was sufficient alone to cause an event) or pre-emptive causation (when an intervening factor brings forward an event that would have happened anyway due to a prior, but delayed-action, cause).

These limitations of 'but for' tests in relation to determination of legal responsibility have given rise to a considerable amount of serious scholarship.[25] Simply put, a 'pure' sine qua non test encounters extreme difficulty when applied to legal problems. Hart and Honoré have argued the merits of a bifurcated analysis, in which an initial causation *in fact* test is subject to a second stage (causation *in law*) test in which we need to examine whether there is any policy reason that would preclude our treating a cause as a cause (or an intervening event as an intervening event).[26]

There are parallels in our present problem with the problems of remoteness seen in other torts. There is a rich tradition within the law more generally of using ideas of causation to examine remoteness and, although much of the focus of that analysis has been in relation to the law of negligence, it is certainly not limited to that tort.[27] However, the great majority of this examination relates to the remoteness of *loss*, whereas the remoteness in the current problem might be better described as remoteness of 'gain' or advantage. Although Hart and Honoré acknowledge that causation may be applied to questions of gain, they use the example of gains leading to reduction in a claimant's loss, rather than the enrichment of the defendant.[28] However, remoteness of 'gain' has been examined within the context of the assessment of the quantum of an account of profits where the contribution that the infringement made to overall enrichment of the infringer

[24] Hanson (ibid) cites the popular saying 'For the want of a nail a shoe was lost; for the want of a horse a rider was lost; for the want of a rider the battalion was lost; for the want of a battalion a battle was lost; for the want of a victory a kingdom was lost – all for the want of a nail.'

[25] See generally: RW Wright, 'Causation in Tort Law' (1985) 73 *California Law Review* 1735; MS Moore, *Causation and Responsibility, An Essay in Law, Morals and Metaphysics* (Oxford, Oxford University Press, 2009); R Goldberg, *Perspectives on Causation* (Oxford, Hart, 2011).

[26] HLA Hart and T Honoré, *Causation in the Law* (Oxford, Oxford University Press, 1985) 110.

[27] ibid 84.

[28] ibid 86.

is called to be determined.[29] There is, however, no reason to limit our analytical toolbox to causation principles considered within issues of apportionment alone.

If there *is* to be a difference in outcome between a strict causation *in fact* analysis and causation *in law* analysis on a particular set of facts, that difference in outcome must reflect the justifications underpinning the right that the putative claimant seeks to assert. The problem is that such justifications will often take the form of very broad principles. Without *specific* examples of 'remoteness' with which to test those principles the guidance they provide may seem very abstract and hard to apply. Accordingly, a thorough causation *in law* analysis requires us to have an understanding of the appropriate types of 'intervening event' which could break a particular chain of causation *in law*. In our present problem, the pharmaceutical development process is complex. Accordingly, determination of potential 'chain-breaking' types of interventions (or combinations of interventions) requires an empirical understanding of the processes by which drugs are discovered. This book will (in chapter five) therefore seek to understand the topography of pharmaceutical discovery (and development) process from the perspective of the journey of a piece of TKAGR through that process. It will seek to identify whether there are points in that process which, due to a notable feature in the nature of the mixing of the information at that point, may arguably stand in the way of a chain of causation *in law*. For consistency of terminology these putative 'chain-breaking' interventions in causation in law will be termed 'crux points' in the drug discovery process.

In parallel, and where necessary (and as discussed below), caveated guidance will be sought from approaches that have been taken within patent law when it has looked at the scope of patent rights within the drug discovery process.

D. Analogical Reasoning: Guidance from Established Intellectual Property Rights

Questions of 'distal'/'remote' use are not alien to the field of intellectual property, and the approaches used in examining the problem of remoteness/distality in other intellectual property rights may be assistance. However, before we can read across from the experience gained with more established intellectual property rights, or seek to apply other intellectual property approaches by analogy, we need to recognise how the subject matter of a positive right in traditional knowledge is similar to (and different from) that of those established rights.

Traditional knowledge (being a form of information) is inherently similar to the subject matter of a patent (ideas). However, the transgenerational nature of

[29] See eg: *Imperial Oil Limited et al v Lubrizol Corporation et al* (1996) 71 CPR (3d) 26, 30 (Canadian FCA); L Bentley, 'Accounting for Profits Gained by Infringement of Copyright: When Does it end?' (1991) *European Intellectual Property Review* 5, 10; *Celanese International Corp v BP Chemicals Ltd* [1999] RPC 203 (EWHC); AJ Stack et al, 'Accounting of Profits Calculations in Intellectual Property Cases in Canada' (2008) 17(2) *Canadian Intellectual Property Review* 405.

traditional knowledge and the historical nature of its discovery render it inappropriate for patent protection.

Patents (and other *registered* intellectual property rights) create so-called 'monopoly' rights which can be enforced against a third party, even where ideas developed by the infringing third party have not originated from the patentee.[30] The infringer may have generated the idea entirely independently of, and without any knowledge of, the patent and yet still infringe.[31] Patents allow what Attas calls a 'path-independent extension of the right in the idea'.[32] In marked contrast, the Nagoya Protocol positive rights in TKAGR envisage that the idea informing the infringing use will have originated from the protected traditional knowledge. The extension of the right in the misused information is therefore 'path dependent' (not path independent as is seen under patent law). Of course, it cannot really be otherwise; use of entirely independently arrived upon information cannot ever be a *misuse* of the traditional information. In this respect, at least, positive rights in traditional knowledge arguably more closely resemble a copyright, or a right in confidential information, both of which require a path-dependent infringement/breach of right. Despite this passing similarity, crucially copyright laws are not usually perceived as protecting ideas *as such*.[33] Equitable rights to prevent a breach of confidence (or to be compensated for such a breach) do allow for the protection of information *as such*, but differ significantly from Nagoya Protocol positive rights in TKAGR in that they require an *inequitable* breach of confidence on the part of the defendant.[34] Crucially, this requirement is absent in respect of the Nagoya Protocol positive rights. Although there will probably exist some situations in which traditional knowledge is held by a narrow group of individuals who are bound by a mutual obligation of confidence (and where disclosure to a third party could be argued to be in breach of such an obligation), there will be other (perhaps many other) situations in which the relevant information is held more broadly within an Indigenous group (or groups) and/or has long been passed to third parties. Here the information could never possess the requisite quality of confidence for the application of an equitable right based on breach of confidence. Limitation of protection to only that information which could be argued to be 'confidential' would severely curtail the quantity of Indigenous knowledge that could ever be eligible for protection and would place considerable evidential burdens upon those seeking to control its dissemination.

[30] The use of 'monopoly' in this context is to distinguish these types of rights from rights that restrict copying alone; there remains debate over whether such monopolies should be considered as true monopolies in an economic sense. See generally: RE Meiners and RJ Staaf, 'Patents, Copyrights, and Trademarks: Property or Monopoly?'(1990) 13 *Harvard Journal of Law and Public Policy* 911, 916.

[31] Although the infringer's knowledge of the patent may in some cases go to the damages recoverable by the patentee. See eg United States Code, Title 35 §284. Provisions can also exist for 'secret prior user' defences, See eg Section 64 UK Patents Act 1977 (as amended).

[32] D Attas, 'Lockean Justifications of Intellectual Property' in A Gosseries et al (eds), *Intellectual Property and Theories of Justice* (Palgrave Macmillan 2008) 29, 47.

[33] See eg *Baigent and another v Random House Group Ltd* [2007] EWCA Civ 247.

[34] See eg *Coco v A N Clark (Engineers) Ltd* [1969] RPC 41 (EWHC).

Given these fundamental differences, it is argued in this work that no *direct* guidance can be taken from these existing intellectual property rights. However, notwithstanding the identified differences between the subject matter for patent protection and TKAGR, there is a long history of interface between patent law and the drug discovery process – notably in relation to competing contribution. Provided that the relevant differences in the rights are appreciated, the considerations of patent law with respect to questions of scope within drug discovery may serve as a source of analogous concepts for consideration when examining downstream limits to the right to control TKAGR.

E. Application of High-Level Justifications to Determined 'Crux Points'

Both analogical approaches discussed above are, of course, merely tools for locating putative boundary delimitations to test against high-level philosophical justifications for control over intangibles. It should be immediately noted that the aim of the study is *not* to reconcile the fundamental differences between the conflicting high-level justifications. The author seeks to be deliberately agnostic as to the merits of the competing philosophies at the highest level (for example, the overarching validity of utilitarianism versus deontological justifications). The aim is to apply the justifications as 'tools' for determining the correct scope of the veto rights in TKAGR. In doing so, the validity of the justification as applied to the subject matter will be critically examined on a case-by-case basis. However, it is intended that application of the key (and indeed radically different) high-level justifications will illuminate different facets of the putative veto right. Whilst acknowledging the significant differences in approach between the diverse philosophical positions, the work will seek to arrive at a synthesis of the outcomes obtained from the application of each high-level justification.

V. Overview of the Structure of this Work

Having (in chapter two) described the provisions of the Nagoya Protocol within the context of the other international 'solutions' to the problem of misapproriation of TKAGR, the first exercise within this work (set out in chapter three) is to determine what the provisions of the Nagoya Protocol appear to say in respect of the scope of a positive right in TKAGR. As will be seen, the outcome of that analysis is that the downstream scope of such a right within the Nagoya Protocol is unclear. As has been discussed above, the determination of what the Nagoya Protocol says in this regard should not, of itself, impact on the outcome of the justificatory analysis based on first principles. However, notwithstanding that, an examination of the provisions of the Nagoya Protocol is highly instructive as it serves to introduce some key concepts of downstream use that will be engaged with later in this work. Crucial here is the disconnection between the concept of a genetic resource per se and that of traditional knowledge *associated with* that genetic resource.

Before the high-level justifications for rights in traditional knowledge can be brought to bear upon putative boundary limitations (the crux points discussed above) we must establish broadly what theoretical arguments have been used to justify the protection of knowledge and how such arguments can be applied more particularly to the protection of TKAGR. This is achieved in chapter four.

If, as is discussed above, we look to treat the involvement of TKAGR with the drug discovery process as a flow of information and a process of dilution of the original contribution, we need to understand the types of flows of information we might see – we need a sense of the topography of the drug discovery process. Accordingly, an empirical study of this process is set out in chapter five.

Within that study (and reflecting on analogies with patent law) the serendipitous discovery of second medical (and other) uses is identified as a potential point at which there is an arguable step change in the dilution of the original TKAGR contribution. As a result, the empirical study is further focused upon four case studies from the history of drug discovery in which various types of 'serendipitous' discoveries were made:

1. The identification of an anticoagulant effect of the anti-inflammatory agent acetylsalicylic acid (aspirin), a downstream derivative of the original compound (salicin) found in the genetic resource.
2. The identification of a local anaesthetic effect of cocaine (a compound directly found in the genetic resource but known to have psychoactive effects).
3. The discovery of the dye mauveine whilst attempting to synthesise quinine.
4. The discovery of antitumour effects of the vinca alkaloids (directly found in the genetic resource but believed to have antidiabetes effects).

Having identified serendipitous discoveries as a putative step change in contribution dilution, it is at this point that the two parallel streams of the study come together. In chapter six the key philosophical justifications for veto rights in TKAGR identified in chapter four are applied to the serendipitously discovery crux point identified in chapter five. It was anticipated that each high-level justification could provide a variety of different answers to the question of scope in relation to the identified crux point. Accordingly, the next step in the study (in chapter seven) is to determine to what extent (if at all) the answers provided through the application of high-level justifications to the identified crux point can be synthesised/reconciled. Part of this analysis brings us to the question of what a 'serendipitous' discovery actually is, and how one can be defined in practice. There is particular focus (within the latter part of chapter seven) on what the term serendipitous discovery means when both the second and the first therapeutic uses are elicited through effects on a shared physiological mechanism. The finding of this, and the other analyses, are brought together and summarised in the Conclusion in chapter eight.

2

The International 'Solutions' to Claims of Misappropriation of TKAGR

I. Introduction

As briefly introduced in chapter one, the drive to address claims of misappropriation of TKAGR has taken place, with differing rates of progress, in a number of international fora, principally the UN, the WTO and the WIPO. These international tracks are summarised in Figure 2 as a 'family tree' of international approaches to anti-misappropriation rights. In addition to these international approaches, there is a broad raft of anti-misappropriation legislation promulgated by individual jurisdictions. Much of that has followed (or is likely to follow) the routes taken by the multilateral routes under the UN CBD (or WTO or WIPO) and it is the aim of this work to focus on the broader multilateral approaches and the broader principles supporting positive rights to control over traditional knowledge, rather than to take a jurisdiction-by-jurisdiction approach. However, readers who are interested in the progress of the national implementation of the provisions on the Nagoya Protocol are directed to the online tool provided by the CBD Access and Benefit-sharing Clearing-House.[1]

Figure 2 'Family tree' of international responses to anti-misappropriation rights

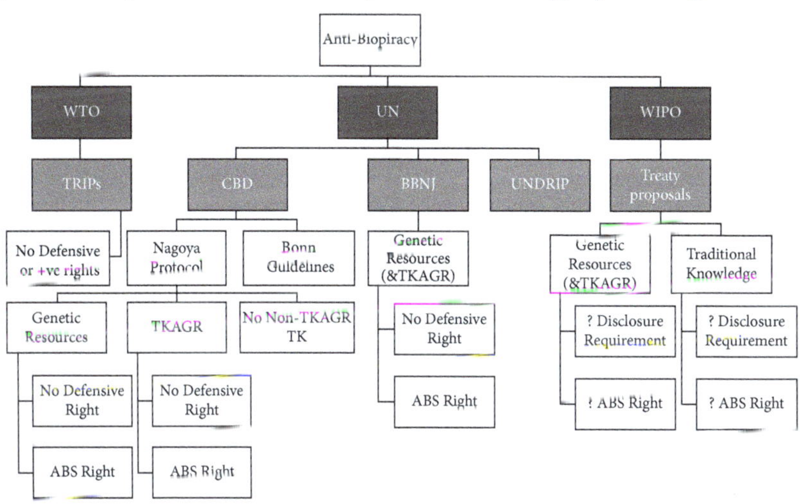

[1] www.cbd.int/abs/theabsch.shtml.

II. The UN Route(s)

The UN has addressed the question of rights in traditional knowledge through five distinct (but related) tracks and we will deal with each in turn.

A. The Declaration on the Rights of Indigenous Peoples

In September 2007 the General Assembly on the UN adopted the Declaration on the Rights of Indigenous Peoples (UNDRIP).[2] UNDRIP broadly addresses the rights of Indigenous people, stating at Article 3 that: 'Indigenous peoples have the right to self-determination. By virtue of that right they freely determine their political status and freely pursue their economic, social and cultural development.' However, there are three particular articles (11, 24 and 31) of specific relevance to the question of traditional knowledge (and related genetic resources): Article 11 states:

> Indigenous peoples have the right to practise and revitalize their cultural traditions and customs. This includes the right to maintain, protect and develop the past, present and future manifestations of their cultures, such as archaeological and historical sites, artefacts, designs, ceremonies, technologies and visual and performing arts and literature.
>
> States shall provide redress through effective mechanisms, which *may include restitution*, developed in conjunction with indigenous peoples, with respect to their cultural, intellectual, religious and spiritual property taken without their free, prior and informed consent or in violation of their laws, traditions and customs. [emphasis added]

Article 24 states:

> Indigenous peoples have the right to their traditional medicines and to maintain their health practices, including the conservation of their vital medicinal plants, animals and minerals …

Article 31 states:

> Indigenous peoples have the right to maintain, *control*, protect and develop their cultural heritage, traditional knowledge and traditional cultural expressions, as well as the manifestations of their sciences, technologies and cultures, including human and genetic resources, seeds, medicines, knowledge of the properties of fauna and flora, oral traditions, literatures, designs, sports and traditional games and visual and performing arts. They also have the right to maintain, *control*, protect and develop their intellectual property over such cultural heritage, traditional knowledge, and traditional cultural expressions.' [emphasis added]
>
> In conjunction with indigenous peoples, States shall take effective measures to recognize and protect the exercise of these rights.

[2] A/RES/61/295.

Additionally, Article 38 provides that States shall take appropriate measures, including legislation, to achieve the ends of UNDRIP. However, UNDRIP gives no specific detail on how these broad ends should be achieved. The likely meaning of these provisions of UNDRIP, its status and where it lies within our understanding of the broader concept of Indigenous 'sovereignty' (or an Indigenous right to self-determination) will be discussed in detail in chapter four, in section XII.A.

B. The Convention on Biological Diversity

As a UN declaration UNDRIP is not legally binding. Whilst it clearly has moral force in acknowledging broad Indigenous rights to the preservation of culture, arguably more substantial advances have been (progressively) made through the UN environmental mechanisms. On 5 June 1992 the CBD was opened for signature. It came into force (although again as a UN Declaration it is not legally binding on UN Member States) on 29 December 1993, having been ratified by 194 members of the UN.[3] The CBD is, first and foremost, a convention which looks to protect the biodiversity of the planet, ensuring sustainable use and fair and equitable sharing of the exploitation of biodiversity.[4] Towards that final end, Article 8(j) of the CBD requires that each contracting party shall 'as far as possible and as appropriate':

> Subject to its national legislation, respect, preserve and maintain knowledge, innovations and practices of indigenous and local communities embodying traditional lifestyles relevant for the conservation and sustainable use of biological diversity and promote their wider application with the approval and involvement of the holders of such knowledge, innovations and practices and encourage the equitable sharing of the benefits arising from the utilization of such knowledge, innovations and practices.[5]

In 2002, the sixth CBD Conference of Parties agreed a set of guidelines (the 'Bonn Guidelines on Access to Genetic Resources and Fair and Equitable Sharing of the Benefits Arising out of their Utilization' – hereafter the Bonn Guidelines) with the aim of providing guidance to legislators in implementing Article 8(j) of the CBD.[6] The Bonn Guidelines were entirely voluntary[7] and expressly did not seek to amend parties' obligations under the CBD[8] or further create or assign rights.[9] However, the sixth CBD Conference of Parties did explain that it considered these guidelines to be 'a useful first step of an evolutionary process in the implementation of

[3] www.cbd.int/information/parties.shtml.

[4] T Kiene, *The Legal Protection of Traditional Knowledge in the Pharmaceutical Field. An Intercultural Problem on the International Agenda* (Münster, Waxmann, 2012) 191, 198.

[5] www.cbd.int/convention/articles/default.shtml?a=cbd-08.

[6] CBD COP Decision VI/24.

[7] ibid Annex I(7).

[8] ibid Annex I(2).

[9] ibid Annex I(5) and I(6).

relevant provisions of the Convention related to access to genetic resources and benefit-sharing'.[10]

C. The Nagoya Protocol

The evolutionary progress under the UN environmental mechanisms reached a landmark with the adoption in October 2010 of the Nagoya Protocol. As at January 2024, the Nagoya Protocol has 141 ratifications, although both Australia and the United States remain as significant non-signatories.[11] The Nagoya Protocol came into force on 12 October 2014.[12]

The key aim of the Nagoya Protocol is to provide a set of *binding* mechanisms for implementing the ABS objectives of the CBD. However, the Nagoya Protocol is deliberately limited in its scope. It (and the Bonn Guidelines before it) originates from the CBD and accordingly its absolute focus is on the misappropriation of *genetic* resources, and the misuse of traditional knowledge related to a particular genetic resource, rather than attempting to create a broader positive right in traditional knowledge per se. As we will see, the protection of traditional knowledge more broadly has been taken up within the agenda of WIPO.

Broadly speaking, the Nagoya Protocol looks to apply two obligations (*access* subject only to prior informed consent and *use* subject to benefit sharing) to the users of two separate, but closely related, resources (genetic resources and TKAGR). The key operative provisions are summarised in Table 1.

Table 1 Key elements of the Nagoya Protocol articles giving rise to positive rights

Article	'Right holder'	Subject matter	Controlled activity	Condition
5(1)	Party	Genetic resources	Utilisation (including 'subsequent applications and commercialization')	Fair and equitable sharing upon mutually agreed terms
5(2)	Indigenous and local communities	Genetic resources	Utilisation	Fair and equitable sharing based on mutually agreed terms
5(5)	Indigenous and local communities	TKAGR	Utilisation	Fair and equitable sharing upon mutually agreed terms

(continued)

[10] ibid para 6.
[11] www.cbd.int/abs/nagoya-protocol/signatories/.
[12] www.cbd.int/doc/press/2014/pr-2014-10-12--protocol-en.pdf.

Table 1 ***(continued)***

Article	'Right holder'	Subject matter	Controlled activity	Condition
6(1)	Party	Genetic resources	Access for utilisation	Prior informed consent
6(2)	'Indigenous and local communities'	Genetic resources	Access	Prior informed consent or 'approval and involvement'
7	'Indigenous and local communities'	TKAGR	Access	Prior informed consent, or 'approval and involvement' and establishment of mutually agreed terms

In relation to access to genetic resources Article 6(1) states:

> In the exercise of sovereign rights over natural resources, and subject to domestic access and benefit-sharing legislation or regulatory requirements, access to genetic resources for their utilization shall be subject to the prior informed consent of the Party providing such resources that is the country of origin of such resources or a Party that has acquired the genetic resources in accordance with the Convention, unless otherwise determined by that Party.

And Article 6(2) states:

> In accordance with domestic law, each Party shall take measures, as appropriate, with the aim of ensuring that the prior informed consent or approval and involvement of indigenous and local communities is obtained for access to genetic resources where they have the established right to grant access to such resources.

In relation to the sharing of benefits arising out of use of genetic resources, Article 5(1) states:

> In accordance with Article 15, paragraphs 3 and 7 of the Convention, benefits arising from the utilization of genetic resources as well as subsequent applications and commercialization shall be shared in a fair and equitable way with the Party providing such resources that is the country of origin of such resources or a Party that has acquired the genetic resources in accordance with the Convention. Such sharing shall be upon mutually agreed terms.

And Article 5(2) states:

> Each Party shall take legislative, administrative or policy measures, as appropriate, with the aim of ensuring that benefits arising from the utilization of genetic resources that are held by indigenous and local communities, in accordance with domestic legislation regarding the established rights of these indigenous and local communities over these genetic resources, are shared in a fair and equitable way with the communities concerned, based on mutually agreed terms.

With regard to access to TKAGR, Article 7 states:

> In accordance with domestic law, each Party shall take measures, as appropriate, with the aim of ensuring that TKAGR that is held by indigenous and local communities is accessed with the prior and informed consent or approval and involvement of these indigenous and local communities, and that mutually agreed terms have been established.

With regard to sharing the benefits arising out of the use of TKAGR, Article 5(5) states:

> Each Party shall take legislative, administrative or policy measures, as appropriate, in order that the benefits arising from the utilization of traditional knowledge associated with genetic resources are shared in a fair and equitable way with indigenous and local communities holding such knowledge. Such sharing shall be upon mutually agreed terms.

Neither Article 6 nor 7 is drafted in what one might consider to be a classic way to create a positive intellectual property right. However, the key element to any positive intellectual property right is that certain identified activities are prohibited without the *consent* of the right holder (or put another way the right holder has a right to veto certain activities of third parties) and it is (usually) for the right holder alone to determine under what circumstances the consent will be given (or the veto on use will be lifted).[13] Taking that approach, Article 6(1) by requiring prior informed consent from a party (meaning here a nation state) clearly creates a positive (veto) right over that access.

However, the position of Articles 6(2) and Article 7, relating to Indigenous peoples (rather than nation state parties) is somewhat less clear. Article 6(2) *either* requires prior informed consent from Indigenous and local communities holding the knowledge *or* 'approval and involvement' from those Indigenous and local communities which have the 'established right to grant access to such resources'. Article 7 *either* requires prior informed consent from Indigenous and local communities holding the knowledge *or* 'approval and involvement' from those Indigenous and local communities with, in either case, a further requirement that 'mutually agreed terms' should be established.

In neither Article 6(2), nor Article 7, is it clear how, if at all, such approval and involvement is materially different from prior informed consent. Morgera et al[14] suggest that whereas the term 'approval and involvement' is derived from Article 8(j) of the CBD, the 'prior informed consent' language seen in both articles is derived instead from Article 11 of UNDRIP. They further suggest that the use of 'approval and involvement' as an alternative to 'prior informed consent' may reflect the reluctance of some parties to fully endorse within the Nagoya Protocol

[13] Such rights can be subject in some cases to compulsory licensing regimes.

[14] E Morgera et al, *Unravelling the Protocol: A Commentary on the Protocol on Access and Benefit Sharing to the Convention on Biological Diversity* (Leiden, Brill/Nijhoff, 2014) 152, 175.

a human rights (ie UNDRIP) standard of Indigenous control over resources. They further suggest that such reluctance may stem from governmental sensitivities regarding the grant of rights to Indigenous communities and that the alternative 'consent' versus 'approval' language provides for flexibility in implementation. Savaresi also identifies the different sources of language,[15] but suggests that if a difference does in effect exist, then parties' overriding obligations to respect the primacy of human rights law should, in any event, ensure that they seek to follow the UNDRIP-derived approach.[16] Whilst acknowledging the different origins of each phrase, it seems difficult to realistically argue that the operative effect of 'consent' should be any different from 'approval' considering the overall context of the Nagoya Protocol.[17] This is particularly true of Article 7, in which both 'approval' and 'consent' are both allied to a further requirement that access should be subject to 'mutually agreed terms'. We will come back to this point when looking at the provisions of the 2022 Kunming–Montreal Global Biodiversity Framework (in chapter two, section II.D) which seem to support the argument that 'consent' and 'approval' should not be given different interpretations.

Whatever degree of consent is required, we need also to understand the nature of the activity which is subject to that control. In both Articles 6(2) and 7 this activity is the *accessing* of the subject matter of the right. The question as to whether this 'access' means a first-time physical apprehension, continued physical apprehension, first-time conceptual apprehension or continued conceptual apprehension is moot, and will be dealt with in detail further in this chapter.

Assuming that Articles 6(2) and 7 *do* create a positive veto right, we see that broadly they work in tandem to control access to a genetic resource and to the traditional knowledge which will give that genetic resource value or enhanced value. We should note, however, that both contain a (different) qualification. In Article 6(2) control (approval or consent) is limited to those Indigenous and local communities that 'have the established right to grant access to such resources'. The Article 7 right is significantly less qualified, requiring merely that relevant traditional knowledge is 'held' by Indigenous and local communities.

Articles 5(1), 5(2) and 5(5) of the Nagoya Protocol are perhaps less clear in creating positive (veto) rights. They require that the benefits arising out of *use* should be shared in a 'fair and equitable' way and that such sharing should be on 'mutually agreed terms'. Arguably this requirement for fair and equitable sharing does not, of itself, create an unambiguous *veto* right. Indeed, one might imagine that a third-party user of a resource may be permitted to simply continue with

[15] A Savaresi, 'The International Human Rights Law Implications of the Protocol' in E Morgera et al (eds), *The 2010 Protocol on Access and Benefit-Sharing in Perspective: Implications for International Law and Implementation Challenges* (Leiden, Martinus Nijhoff, 2012) 53, 70.

[16] It is worth noting here that it is questionable whether UNDRIP does in fact provide support for an injunctive remedy rather than merely compensatory relief (see ch 3 below).

[17] Morgera *Unravelling the Protocol* (n 14) 153; GS Nijar, *The Protocol on ABS: An Analysis* (Kuala Lumpar, CEBLAW, 2011), 26.

their use of the resource without hindrance from the right holder, provided that a 'fair and equitable' share is provided to that right holder. One might further imagine that the quantum and terms of a 'fair and equitable' share could be determined by an ex post facto binding determination (whether through court or tribunal proceedings, or through mediation or arbitration). Such an approach would, in many ways, echo the compulsory licensing regimes seen in numerous intellectual property systems.[18] Of course, this type of approach would not, of itself, permit an *absolute* veto over use. However, how should we interpret the requirement that benefit sharing is on *mutually agreed terms* in the light of the 'fair and equitable' sharing requirement? What if the mutual agreement is not on fair and equitable terms; is the agreement rescindable/voidable? In that situation, who is to say what is fair and equitable? More importantly, with regard to consent, it would appear on the face of the language in Article 5 that, even if the terms of the potential agreement are perfectly 'fair and equitable', the party having the right to require sharing (Indigenous people or party as appropriate) must surely have a right to refuse to agree – if they did not have that right it could not be a truly free, *mutual* agreement. If this is correct, the right to refuse to agree (even on what an external observer might consider to be objectively fair terms) should be interpreted as a right to refuse consent (ie a veto right) similar to that (more clearly and expressly) set out in Articles 6(2) and 7.

We need to note that Article 5(2) – dealing with control over genetic resources – contains a similar qualification to that seen in Article 6(2), in that its provisions only apply to 'genetic resources that are held by indigenous and local communities in accordance with domestic legislation regarding the established rights of these indigenous and local communities over these genetic resources'.

Mirroring the position seen with Article 7, Article 5(5) – dealing with traditional knowledge relating to genetic resources – is much less qualified, requiring only that the knowledge is 'held' by the relevant Indigenous or local community.

D. The Kunming–Montreal Global Biodiversity Framework

In December 2022, as part of the general UN drive towards achievement of its Sustainable Development Goals[19] the Parties to the CBD adopted the Kunming–Montreal Global Biodiversity Framework (GBF) and its associated decisions.[20] In relation to the Nagoya Protocol, the GBF has one goal (Goal C) and one target (Target 13). Goal C intends to ensure that

> the monetary and non-monetary benefits from the utilization of genetic resources *and digital sequence information on genetic resources*, and [TKAGR], as applicable, are

[18] See eg ss 48, 48A, 48B, 49 and 50 UK Patents Act 1977 (as amended).
[19] www.sdgs.un.org/goals.
[20] CBD/COP/DEC/15/4.

> shared fairly and equitably, including, as appropriate with indigenous peoples and local communities, and substantially increased by 2050, while ensuring traditional knowledge associated with genetic resources is appropriately protected, thereby contributing to the conservation and sustainable use of biodiversity, in accordance with internationally agreed access and benefit-sharing instruments.[21]

Target 13 looks to ensure that parties look to 'take effective legal, policy, administrative and capacity-building measures at all levels, as appropriate' to achieve Goal 3.[22] Much of the immediate impact of the GBF will be in relation to capacity building and a determination of current practices.[23] From an interpretation perspective, the key point to note from the GBF is the inclusion in Goal 3 of the language relating to 'digital sequence information on genetic resources'. The impact of the inclusion of this language will be discussed in chapter two (section II.E).

The other point to note is that within its considerations for implementation (at Section C paragraph 7(a)) the GBF 'acknowledges the important roles and contributions of indigenous peoples and local communities as custodians of biodiversity and as partners in its conservation, restoration and sustainable use', and that in the implementation of the GBF Parties must ensure that

> the rights, knowledge, including traditional knowledge associated with biodiversity, innovations, worldviews, values and practices of indigenous peoples and local communities are respected, and documented and preserved with their free, prior and informed consent, including through their full and effective participation in decision-making, in accordance with relevant national legislation, international instruments, including the United Nations Declaration on the Rights of Indigenous Peoples, and human rights law.[24]

This wording is not surprising in the light of the language in UNDRIP and Article 8(j). However, for this author one of the most interesting elements of this statement is actually hidden in a footnote to it. This footnote states that: 'In this framework, free, prior and informed consent refers to the tripartite terminology of "prior and informed consent" or "free, prior and informed consent" or "approval and involvement"'.[25] This seems like an unusual place to put such a potentially important clarification for the meaning of free, prior and informed consent within the context of the CBD. Although it is perhaps not definitive in relation to the interpretation of the Nagoya Protocol, it is strongly supportive of the conclusion reached above that the terms 'consent' and 'approval and involvement' as used within the Nagoya Protocol should not be given different interpretations, and that 'prior informed consent' means 'free prior and informed consent'.

[21] ibid Goal 3 (emphasis added).
[22] CBD/COP/DEC/15/4.
[23] www.cbd.int/abs/gbf.shtml#tab=0.
[24] CBD/COP/DEC/15/4 Annex para 7(a).
[25] Footnote 6 to CBD/COP/DEC/15/4 Annex para 7(a).

E. The BBNJ Treaty

The ocean serves as a vast reserve of genetic material and is increasingly the subject of large metagenomic surveys.[26] It is also the potential source of a huge range of biologically active substances which may be useful as the starting point for drug discovery.[27] Where such resources fall within the sea area belonging to a State, such genetic resources (and relevant TKAGR) will fall within the ambit of Nagoya Protocol. However, outwith such jurisdiction, where the genetic resource is obtained from the so-called 'High Seas', the provisions of the Nagoya Protocol would cease to apply. Accordingly, on 19 June 2023, the UN adopted an Agreement under the UN Convention on the Law of the Sea on the Conservation and Sustainable use of Marine Biological Diversity of Areas Beyond National Jurisdiction (BBNJ Treaty), which came into effect in January 2024. The broad aim of the BBNJ Treaty is to better address the conservation and sustainable use of marine biological diversity in those areas of the seas that fall outwith the jurisdiction of nation states. It seeks to do this in two broad ways. The first is to establish Marine Protected Areas of the High Seas. The other is to ensure that marine genetic resources from areas beyond national jurisdiction (ABNJ) will be utilised in a way that provides financial support for the conservation and sustainable use of marine biological diversity of areas beyond national jurisdiction. Article 14(1) of the BBNJ Treaty states that:

> The benefits arising from activities with respect to marine genetic resources and digital sequence information on marine genetic resources of areas beyond national jurisdiction shall be shared in a fair and equitable manner in accordance with this Part and contribute to the conservation and sustainable use of marine biological diversity of areas beyond national jurisdiction.

Although the BBNJ Treaty (perhaps surprisingly) makes no mention of the CBD or of the Nagoya Protocol, the definitions of 'Marine genetic resources', 'Utilization of marine genetic resources' and 'Biotechnology' closely resemble the equivalent definitions within the Nagoya Protocol (which will be discussed in detail in chapter three) and there is no reason to believe that they should be interpreted differently from the Nagoya Protocol. However, the BBNJ Treaty does include a provision relating to benefits arising from activities with respect to 'digital sequence information on marine genetic resources'. Why that term is there, and its significance, will be examined in detail at chapter three (section XII).

[26] See eg E Laiolo et al, 'Metagenomic Probing Toward an Atlas of the Taxonomic and Metabolic Foundations of the Global Ocean Genome' (2024) 1 *Frontiers in Science* 1038696.

[27] See generally: WH Gerwick and BS Moore, 'Lessons from the Past and Charting the Future of Marine Natural Products Drug Discovery and Chemical Biology' (2012) 19(1) *Chemistry and Biology* 85; R Blasiak et al, 'The Ocean Genome and Future Prospects for Conservation and Equity' (2020) 3(8) *Nature Sustainability* 588.

With regard to traditional knowledge, Article 13 of the BBNJ Treaty states that:

> Parties shall take legislative, administrative or policy measures, where relevant and as appropriate, with the aim of ensuring that traditional knowledge associated with marine genetic resources in areas beyond national jurisdiction that is held by Indigenous Peoples and local communities shall only be accessed with the free, prior and informed consent or approval and involvement of these Indigenous Peoples and local communities. … Access to and use of such traditional knowledge shall be on mutually agreed terms.

Again, the language of this article mirrors the equivalent language of the Nagoya Protocol and there is no reason to believe that it should be interpreted any differently from the Nagoya Protocol. However, the situations in which the provisions of Article 13 will apply are not entirely clear on the face of the Treaty. Presumably traditional knowledge can take the form of navigational information to direct those seeking to access marine genetic resources in ABNJ as well as information pertaining to the use of marine genetic resources that will unlock their usefulness. In addition, it is worth noting that the BBNJ does not require that the relevant indigenous peoples and local communities are resident within an ABNJ – indeed, to do so would be absurd, as this is clearly not where Indigenous people live. If (as is likely) the relevant Indigenous people reside within a nation state, and given that in Articles 7 and 5(5) of the Nagoya Protocol the relevant TKAGR does not appear to be tied to the geographic presence of the genetic resource within a nation state, the interface between Article 13 BBNJ and the TKAGR provisions of the Nagoya Protocol is unclear.

F. The International Treaty on Plant Genetic Resources for Food and Agriculture

Although the focus of this work is on the use of TKAGR within drug discovery, for completeness it is worth mentioning the traditional knowledge protection mechanisms that exist within the UN International Treaty on Plant Genetic Resources for Food and Agriculture (ITPGRFA). At its 1983 Rome conference, the UN Food and Agriculture Organization (FAO) adopted the International Undertaking on Plant Genetic Resources.[28] This was the first comprehensive international agreement on plant genetic resources used in food and agriculture.[29] Years of negotiation within the FAO eventually led to the adoption in 1996 of the FAO Liepzig Declaration and Global Plan of Action on Genetic Resources for Food and

[28] FAO Resolution 8/83.

[29] D Matthews, *Intellectual Property, Human Rights and Development: The Role of NGOs and Social Movements* (Cheltenham, Edward Elgar, 2011) 57.

Agriculture. Adoption of this Global Plan (together with the adoption of the CBD in 1993) drove the eventual adoption in 2001 of the ITPGRFA (which came into effect on 29 June 2004). For our current purposes, the key provision of ITPGRFA is in relation to so-called 'Farmers Rights' at Article 9. This states that:

> [Each] Contracting Party should, as appropriate, and subject to its national legislation, take measures to protect and promote Farmers' Rights, including:
>
> (a) protection of traditional knowledge relevant to plant genetic resources for food and agriculture;
>
> (b) the right to equitably participate in sharing benefits arising from the utilization of plant genetic resources for food and agriculture; and
>
> (c) the right to participate in making decisions, at the national level, on matters related to the conservation and sustainable use of plant genetic resources for food and agriculture.

No detail is given with the ITPGRF as to the nature of these rights and they are clearly much more loosely described than under the Nagoya Protocol. In addition, the ITPGRF is relatively scant on definitions. In particular, it contains no definition of 'traditional knowledge' or of 'Farmer's Rights' or indeed of what a 'farmer' is. The ITPGRF definition of 'Genetic material' and of 'Plant genetic resources for food and agriculture' mirrors the equivalent definitions in the CBD, and there is no reason to suspect that their meaning was intended to be different (other than the limitation to food and agriculture). Indeed, this is supported Article 1.1 ITPGRF which states that:

> The objectives of this Treaty are the conservation and sustainable use of plant genetic resources for food and agriculture and the fair and equitable sharing of the benefits arising out of their use, in harmony with the Convention on Biological Diversity, for sustainable agriculture and food security.

And at 1.2 ITPGRF that:

> These objectives will be attained by closely linking this Treaty to the Food and Agriculture Organization of the United Nations and to the Convention on Biological Diversity.

The key point to note from the ITPGRF is its limitation to food and agriculture. It is also worth noting that the Nagoya Protocol does *not* exclude genetic resources for food and agriculture (or TKAGR for food and agriculture). Therefore, it is highly likely that in relation to genetic resources for food and agriculture there will be many situations in which *both* the Nagoya Protocol and ITPGRF should apply. In fact, in relation to TKAGR for food and agriculture, this is likely to be the majority of situations – for a farmer in possession of TKAGR for food and agriculture to not fall within the terms of the Nagoya Protocol they would somehow have to fall outwith the definition of Indigenous peoples and local communities and it seems reasonable to assume that most farmers in possession of TKAGR would, at the very least, constitute part of a relevant 'local community'.

III. The WTO Route

A. Positive Rights

The Trade Related Aspects of Intellectual Property Agreement (TRIPS) is an agreement between WTO Member States to establish minimum standards for the regulation of various forms of intellectual property.[30] As it currently stands, TRIPS is silent as to the protection of Indigenous peoples' rights to control TKAGR and genetic resources (or traditional knowledge or folklore more broadly) and, as Matthews has highlighted, there is an 'absence of coherence' between TRIPS and the CBD which 'both address the relationship between genetic resources and intellectual property in different but overlapping ways'.[31] However, many WTO members in the Global South consider that the discouragement of biopiracy should be a key part of any new TRIPS provision.[32] Indeed, the lack of interface between TRIPS and the CBD was reflected in paragraph 19 of the 2001 Doha Declaration.[33] This instructed the Council for TRIPS to examine the relationship between the TRIPS and the CBD and consider the protection of traditional knowledge and folklore in any future review of TRIPS.[34] It additionally adds that the TRIPS Council's work on this topic must take development issues fully into account and should be guided by the TRIPS Agreement's objectives (at Article 7) that

> intellectual property rights should contribute to the promotion of technological innovation and to the transfer and dissemination of technology, to the mutual advantage of producers and users of technological knowledge and in a manner conducive to social and economic welfare, and to a balance of rights and obligations.

And the principles (at Article 8) namely that:

1. Members may, in formulating or amending their laws and regulations, adopt measures necessary to protect public health and nutrition, and to promote the public interest in sectors of vital importance to their socio-economic and technological development, provided that such measures are consistent with the provisions of this Agreement.
2. Appropriate measures, provided that they are consistent with the provisions of this Agreement, may be needed to prevent the abuse of intellectual property rights by right holders or the resort to practices which unreasonably restrain trade or adversely affect the international transfer of technology.

However, the fraught story of the attempt to build mutual supportiveness between TRIPS and the CBD is one in which the relatively rapid progress in the maturity

[30] www.wto.org/english/tratop_e/trips_e/trips_e.htm.
[31] Matthews (n 29) 63.
[32] Kiene (n 4) 191.
[33] www.wto.org/english/thewto_e/minist_e/min01_e/mindecl_e.htm.
[34] Either under a review of Art 27.3(b) or of the whole of the TRIPs Agreement under Art 71.1.

and enforceability of the ABS provisions of the CBD has been matched by significant disagreement and delay within the TRIPS decision-making processes.[35] Negotiation within the processes of the WTO has centred on the redrafting of Article 27.3(b). This article allows signatory countries to exclude from patentability 'plants and animals other than micro-organisms, and essentially biological processes for the production of plants or animals other than non-biological and microbiological processes'. Of course, this provision also allows other signatories to allow patents for such processes. At the time of signature, the whole concept of patenting life forms was (and still is) controversial,[36] and a requirement that the provisions of the subparagraph be reviewed was built in to the subparagraph from the outset.[37] Whereas the majority of TRIPS is not open to easy renegotiation, the review provisions of Article 27.3(b) have served as a focal point for those seeking broader TRIPS amendment. Of course, if one were seeking to ensure that the protection of Indigenous peoples' rights to control TKAGR and genetic resources was incorporated into TRIPS, this review provision could be seen as a useful opening and this is exactly what has happened.

In 2003, the African Group of nations made a proposal that rights relating to traditional knowledge should be protected and include, in relation to any local community or traditional practitioners, the right for such community or practitioner to: (i) have respect for their will and decisions on whether or not to commercialise their knowledge; (ii) respect and honour any sanctity they attach to their knowledge; (iii) give prior and informed consent for any access and any intended use of their knowledge, (iii) full remuneration for their knowledge; and (iv) prevent third parties from using, offering for sale, selling, exporting and importing their knowledge and any article or product in which their knowledge is input, unless all the consent requirements have been met.[38] In 2010 Bolivia submitted a further proposal that TRIPS should protect the 'rights of indigenous communities and prevent any private monopolistic intellectual property claims over their traditional knowledge'.[39] Despite these steps, neither proposal for positive rights has developed a strong momentum within the TRIPS mechanism, and progress has stalled.[40]

B. Disclosure Requirements

As opposed to moving towards developing *positive* rights, the predominant focus of debate within the TRIPS Council has been on the fact that, as it currently stands,

[35] Matthews (n 29) 67.

[36] M Hussain, 'Patenting of Life Forms: Reflections on Some Legal and Ethical Issues' (2014) 4(2) *IUP Law Review* 7.

[37] 'The provisions of this subparagraph shall be reviewed four years after the date of entry into force of the WTO Agreement' TRIPS Art 27.3(b).

[38] IP/C/W/404.

[39] P/C/W/545.

[40] South Centre, Health, 'Intellectual Property and Biodiversity Programme Matrix of Key Issues in the WTO Trips Council June 2023', www.southcentre.int/wp-content/uploads/2023/07/TRIPS-Matrix-June-2023-rev2.pdf.

TRIPS contains no provision to prevent a patent applicant from claiming patent rights on an invention based on a genetic resource, or TKAGR, and does not require a patent applicant to disclose the origin of genetic resource or TKAGR used in a claimed invention. To fix what to some advocates of Indigenous rights looked like a glaring omission, in 2006 Brazil, India, Pakistan, Peru, Thailand and Tanzania proposed that Article 29 of TRIPS be amended.[41] TRIPS Article 29 contains the details of the various information that an applicant for a patent needs to disclose to obtain a valid patent. The proposal was that a new Article 29*bis* be inserted into TRIPS which would additionally require (a) mandatory disclosure of the country or source of origin of genetic resources or TKAGR used in an invention, and (b) evidence of compliance with prior informed consent and access and fair and equitable benefit sharing as required by the national legislation of the country providing the genetic resources and/or associated traditional knowledge (ie the country of origin of such resources, or a country that has acquired the genetic resources and/or associated traditional knowledge in accordance with the CBD). In 2008 a 'draft modality' text was submitted with the support of an 'unprecedented coalition' of 108 countries.[42] This included, inter alia, that the TRIPS Council should discuss the insertion of a disclosure of origin requirement and proof of prior informed consent and benefit sharing into Article 29. However, the proposal stalled at that point as some WTO members did not want to 'complicate' the negotiation of other aspects of the WTO with intellectual property matters.[43]

In 2011, following the adoption of the Nagoya Protocol in 2010 a new decision text (revised to be consistent with the Nagoya Protocol) was proposed by Brazil, China, Colombia, Ecuador, India, Indonesia, Peru, Thailand, the ACP Group (African, Caribbean and Pacific countries) and the African Group.[44] Whilst this proposal received broad support from Global South countries, some members from the Global North have refused discussion on the proposal within TRIPS Council, noting that the issue is being discussed within the WIPO processes.[45] Whilst many Global South countries maintain the WIPO and WTO processes are mutually supportive and do not overlap, progress within the TRIPS mechanism has become glacial,[46] and the momentum in the development of *defensive* disclosure of origin requirements is being more effectively taken forward within the ambit of WIPO.

[41] Draft Decision to Enhance Mutual Supportiveness Between the TRIPs Agreement and the Convention on Biological Diversity (IP/C/W/474).

[42] TN/C/W/52; Matthews (n 29) 67.

[43] JC Medaglia, 'Study on the Relationship Between the ABS International Regimen and Other International Instruments Which Govern the Use of Genetic Resources: The World Trade Organization (WTO); the World Intellectual Property Rights Organization (WIPO); and the International Union for the Protection of New Varieties of Plants (UPOV)' (2009) *Comments of UPOV for the Secretariat of the Convention on Biological Diversity*, 7 www.upov.int/export/sites/upov/about/en/pdf/upov_comments_medaglia_study_final.pdf.

[44] TN/C/W/59.

[45] South Centre, Health, 'Intellectual Property and Biodiversity Programme Matrix of Key Issues in the WTO Trips Council June 2023', www.southcentre.int/wp-content/uploads/2023/07/TRIPS-Matrix-June-2023-rev2.pdf.

[46] ibid.

IV. The WIPO Route

A. Positive Rights

The WIPO Intergovernmental Committee (IGC) on Intellectual Property and Genetic Resources, Traditional Knowledge and Folklore (GRTKF) is currently working on text-based negotiations to establish an international legal instrument that will seek to protect of traditional knowledge, traditional cultural expressions and genetic resources through positive rights. Although there may eventually be a single treaty document, traditional knowledge, traditional cultural expressions and genetic resources are being treated as three separate negotiating strands, each with its own GRTKF subcommittee. Compared to the relatively rapid advancement of the Nagoya Protocol under the CBD, historic progress under the WIPO strands has been 'painfully slow'[47] – the draft documents within each stream contain many (often contradictory) proposals which reflect the (often contradictory) aims of the negotiating parties.[48] Although representatives of Indigenous groups have been encouraged by the IGC to participate in the WIPO processes, much of the work of the GRTKF subcommittees has continued without contribution from Indigenous groups. Some of this may stem from an inherent scepticism with the intellectual property system in general and problems with how Indigenous groups accredited with the IGC can fully engage in a process which is at its heart intergovernmental.[49] There has also been some reluctance by countries in the Global North to engage with the process.[50] Some reluctance may come from a perception that, in relation to genetic resources and TKAGR at least, much of the substantive work in this space has been done within the context of the CBD and that little more is to be gained through a WIPO intergovernmental treaty. The WIPO GRTKF website[51] seems remarkably coy about the progress of the processes to formulate positive rights for TKAGR. There has, however, been relative progress within the ambit of the IGC in securing a disclosure requirement on patentees in relation to the origin of genetic resources and TKAGR. This is, of course, something that would be difficult to achieve within the mechanism of the CBD itself.

B. Disclosure Requirements

In July 2022, the WIPO General Assembly voted to convene a Diplomatic Conference (to be held no later than 2024) with the aim of concluding an

[47] Center for International Environmental Law Geneva, 'The Gap Between Indigenous Peoples' Demands and WIPO's Framework on Traditional Knowledge' (2007) 2 www.wipo.int/export/sites/www/tk/en/igc/ngo/ciel_gap.pdf.
[48] WIPO/GRTKF/IC/28/4; WIPO/GRTKF/IC/28/5; WIPO/GRTKF/IC/28/6.
[49] Matthews (n 29) 73.
[50] Center for International Environmental Law (n 47) 4.
[51] www.wipo.int/tk/en/.

International Legal Instrument Relating to 'Intellectual Property, Genetic Resources and Traditional Knowledge Associated with Genetic Resources'. The current WIPO draft does not create a formal mechanism for enforcing positive rights in genetic resources or TKAGR, such as those created under the CBD.

In contrast, the focus of the current GRTKF working draft on genetic resources considered by the committee in Special Session (September 2023) focuses a creating a defensive 'disclosure requirement' only. The espoused aim of the draft is to 'enhance the efficacy, transparency and quality of the patent system with regard to genetic resources and traditional knowledge associated with genetic resources', and 'prevent patents from being granted erroneously for inventions that are not novel or inventive with regard to genetic resources and traditional knowledge associated with genetic resources'. It aims to create a twofold requirement.

The first is a requirement that where the claimed invention in a patent application is (materially/directly) based on genetic resources, the patent applicant must disclose: (a) the country of origin of the genetic resources, or (b) in cases where that information is not known to the applicant, the source of the genetic resources. The second is a requirement that where the claimed invention in a patent application is (materially/directly) based on TKAGR, the patent applicant must disclose: (a) the indigenous peoples or local community that provided the TKAGR, or (b) in cases where that information in is not known to the applicant, the source of the TKAGR. Although under the September 2023 draft the phrase 'materially/directly based on' remains for open discussion, the draft suggests that it should mean that 'the genetic resources and/or TKAGR must have been necessary or material to the development of the claimed invention, and that the claimed invention must depend on the specific properties of the genetic resources and/or TKAGR'. What 'necessary or material' means in this context is not clarified.[52]

Although this disclosure requirement will probably provide evidential support those looking to assert genetic resource and TKAGR rights, the narrowness and conservative nature of the approach needs to be recognised. Firstly, the disclosure requirements apply only to *patent* applicants, not to those looking to apply for other intellectual property rights. Secondly, there is (perhaps surprisingly) no requirement on applicants to provide evidence of compliance with the prior informed consent and benefit-sharing requirements created under the Nagoya Protocol.[53] In addition, although signatory states must put in place 'appropriate, effective and proportionate legal, administrative, and/or policy measures to address an applicant's failure to provide the information required' and may 'provide for post grant sanctions or remedies where there has been fraudulent intent in regard to the disclosure requirement', the draft specifically provides that no Contracting Party shall 'revoke or render unenforceable a patent solely on the basis of an applicant's

[52] WIPO/GRTKF/IC/SS/GE/23/4.

[53] This is in marked contrast to the draft Art 29*bis* of TRIPs (TN/C/59) which requires that a patent applicant should provide relevant information regarding compliance with prior informed consent and access and fair and equitable benefit in accordance with the CBD.

failure to disclose the information specified' – thereby removing what would appear to have been the major sanction for non-compliance.

V. Conclusions

As has been seen in this chapter, efforts to protect Indigenous peoples' rights over TKAGR have been made across a broad range of fronts. The degree, and rates, of success within the different international mechanisms has been extremely mixed. Clearly progress within the CBD mechanism has been by far the most successful – this is probably the result of the CBD mechanism being relatively focused. Other contentious issues and positions have not been thrown into the negotiation 'melting pot' as particularly appears to be the case for the WTO process. Of course, this narrow focus means that there are certain elements of the broader protection of Indigenous peoples' rights over TKAGR which cannot, easily, be achieved through the CBD mechanism. Creating requirements that patent applicants need to disclose the origin of genetic resources and TKAGR in their applications is one such element. This is something that can most easily be brought into effect through WIPO processes, and after significant delay it now looks like such a requirement will be in place within a relatively short timeframe (perhaps even within two to three years). Even here, however – perhaps reflecting inherent conflicting positions between the parties – the current proposals are highly conservative and there is unlikely in the near future to be a requirement for patent applicants to demonstrate compliance with ABS provisions. The relative conservatism within the WIPO process is also evidenced by the glacial nature of developments to protect traditional knowledge and traditional cultural expression more broadly.

3

The Nature of the Positive Rights in TKAGR within the Nagoya Protocol

I. Introduction

As explained in chapter one of this work, the question of whether (in the light of the potential dilution of the original traditional knowledge related to a genetic resource within the drug discovery process) it is justifiable to allow the 'owner' of the original knowledge to possess an absolute veto on all downstream activity was originally stimulated by the uncertainty of the Nagoya Protocol in this regard. It was also explained that the answer to this normative question of competing contributions between Indigenous peoples and pharmaceutical researchers could only lie in the application of high-level philosophical doctrines to the problem, notwithstanding the actual provisions of the Nagoya Protocol (or indeed of any future WIPO or WTO treaty in this regard). However, it is extremely useful to understand what the sui generis rights in TKAGR (and the related provisions relating to the protection of genetic resources alone) created by the Nagoya Protocol purport to do, and determine whether the veto rights apparently set out there can be interpreted as extending to *all* path-dependent downstream uses arising out of such original traditional knowledge.[1]

II. The Positive Protection Provisions of the Nagoya Protocol

As has been discussed above (in chapter two, section I.C), Articles 5, 6 and 7 of the Nagoya Protocol purport to create rights to control access to, and utilisation of, genetic resources and in particular TKAGR. The subject matter, controlled activity and conditions for use were summarised there in Table 1. As can be seen in that table, the condition being placed upon the 'controlled activity' varies according to the controlled activity being regulated. Where the controlled activity is 'access' to

[1] An earlier (and less complete) analysis of these provisions of the Nagoya Protocol has been published by the author as PS Harrison, 'Grasping Frankenstein's Monster: Uncertainty in the Downstream Scope of the Nagoya Protocol' (2019) 1 *Intellectual Property Quarterly* 61.

the relevant subject matter the condition is prior informed consent (or 'approval and involvement'). Where the controlled activity is 'utilization' of the relevant subject matter, the condition is 'fair and equitable sharing based on mutually agreed terms'. Article 6(1) is different in this regard in that the controlled activity is 'access for utilization' and under Article 5(1) the benefits arising out of 'subsequent applications and commercialization' are to be subject to fair and equitable sharing based on mutually agreed terms. However, as we will see, the particular provisions in relation to the scope of protection given to 'traditional knowledge associated with genetic resources' cannot be read in isolation from the broader provisions of the Nagoya Protocol. Clearly our first point for understanding the scope of these provisions of the Nagoya Protocol is to understand what is meant by the key terms 'access', 'genetic resources' and 'utilization'.

III. What Does 'Access' to a Genetic Resource Mean?

Notwithstanding the importance of the term, 'access' is not defined within the CBD or the Nagoya Protocol. In relation to a *physical* resource, it is clear that accessing that resource could simply mean taking *physical* possession of the resource. An ethnobiologist being given plant samples by a group of Indigenous people (or a government department) is clearly 'accessing' those samples. However, is a geneticist who is later given that plant by the ethnobiologist, and goes on to extract DNA from it, equally 'accessing' that material? 'Access' could conceivably mean the first-time physical apprehension of a physical resource or the *continued* physical apprehension of a physical resource. Whether access refers to the first accessing or to a continued/ongoing access is important. If it is the latter, one could see access as extending beyond mere *physical* access within the jurisdiction in which the genetic resources are held, to a broader concept of *legal* access – this being a permission for the continued holding of a genetic resource that would be otherwise be prohibited. The debate on this point is far from settled and has been the subject of some polemic debate.[2]

Although one dictionary definition of the verb 'access', 'the action of going or coming to or into, coming into the presence of or into contact with',[3] gives a strong emphasis on the first movement toward something, it is certainly not inconceivable to see the word within the context of the Nagoya Protocol as meaning a *series* of different 'accessings', with each accessing occurring each time something new is done to the resource.

[2] See eg: P Du Plessis, 'Disclosure of Origin of Biological Resources and Potential Effects of the Protocol' (2011) 40(5) *Chartered Institute of Patent Attorneys Journal* 331; T Roberts, 'CBD and Nagoya – A Rejoinder' (2011) 40(6) *Chartered Institute of Patent Attorneys Journal* 403; P Du Plessis, 'CBD and Nagoya' (2011) 40(7) *Chartered Institute of Patent Attorneys Journal* 466.

[3] *The Compact Oxford English Dictionary* (Oxford, Oxford University Press, 1979) 52.

During the negotiation of the Nagoya Protocol the view of many genetic 'user' countries was that genetic resources are 'accessed' when a biological sample crosses a national boundary. The view of genetic 'provider' countries was that access occurs when biological material is *used* – regardless of whether it crosses a national boundary.[4] If this broader interpretation of access, encompassing subsequent activity, is not correct, then the requirement for consent/approval from the rights holders would arguably be restricted solely to the *very first* occasion upon which the subject matter of the rights in question were acquired. At first sight this may seem unduly limited. However, one has to appreciate that the Nagoya Protocol does, within Article 5, contain other provisions ensuring that the 'utilization' of the resource is subject to mutually agreed terms. This narrow interpretation is arguably also consistent with the overriding objective of the Nagoya Protocol set out at Article 1:

> The objective of this Nagoya Protocol is the fair and equitable sharing of the benefits arising from the utilization of genetic resources, *including by* appropriate access to genetic resources and by appropriate transfer of relevant technologies, taking into account all rights over those resources and to technologies, and by appropriate funding, thereby contributing to the conservation of biological diversity and the sustainable use of its components. [emphasis added]

Indeed, if anything, Article 1 could be said to envisage 'access' as something of a narrower subset of broader 'utilization', rather than being required to be coterminous with it. However, even if we do take a broader interpretation – wherein Article 6 envisages a positive right controlling some sort of *ongoing* legal access – we are left with the question: what is it access *to*? Does it relate only to use of genetic material containing DNA, the DNA alone, or does it envisage something yet further, such as 'access' to other chemical compounds found within an organism – for example, a plant-derived, therapeutically active ligand? To address that question we need to look to the meaning of 'genetic resources'.

IV. The Meaning of 'Genetic Resources'

The concept of 'genetic resources' is clearly at the heart of the Nagoya Protocol. It is the subject matter which is 'utilized', 'accessed' and 'accessed for utilization'. Given the importance of the term, the definition provided within the Nagoya Protocol is surprisingly brief. Indeed, the definition of 'genetic resources' is taken in its entirety from the definition provided in Article 2 of the CBD. During negotiation of the CBD there was little discussion of the meaning of 'genetic resources' and (due to time pressures) a 'lowest common denominator' definition, legally

[4] MW Tvedt and OK Fauchald, 'Implementing the Protocol on ABS: A Hypothetical Case Study on Enforcing Benefit Sharing in Norway' (2011) 14(5) *Journal of World Intellectual Property* 383.

ambiguous, but acceptable to the majority, was decided upon.[5] That definition is as follows: '"Genetic resources" means genetic material of actual or potential value', where '"Genetic material" means any material of plant, animal, microbial or other origin containing functional units of heredity.'[6]

The first point to note is that the definition of 'genetic resources' is not coterminous with that of 'genetic material' but is 'genetic material of actual or potential value'. It is not entirely clear what this limitation to 'actual or potential value' achieves. One might ask what is meant by 'value' and indeed further ask: 'actual or potential value' to whom? However one answers these questions, it is arguable that the definition is flexible enough to provide for changes in what constitutes actual or potential value as science and technology develop.[7]

The term 'functional units of heredity' is not defined in either the Nagoya Protocol or the CBD itself. However, on the face of it, a functional unit of heredity would seem to refer to a gene; the *Merriam–Webster Dictionary* defines a gene as:

> A specific sequence of nucleotides in DNA or RNA[8] that is located usually on a chromosome and that is the *functional unit of inheritance* controlling the transmission and expression of one or more traits by specifying the structure of a particular polypeptide and especially a protein or controlling the function of other genetic material. [emphasis added][9]

In its very narrowest sense, 'material of plant, animal, microbial or other origin containing functional units of heredity' could refer solely to DNA extracted from the cells of an organism (this being the part of the original organism which contains functional hereditary units) whether that DNA encodes for the entire genome of the organism, or encodes for only a subset of genes of interest. However, one might additionally argue that the term 'material' could more broadly refer to an entire organism (or any part of an organism) which contains 'functional units of heredity'. If this were the case, 'genetic material' of an organism would include *any* element of the organism that would enable it to be propagated – which in a plant would include either a cutting, a seed or a spore. Such a definition of 'genetic material' would also appear to be broad enough to encompass eukaryotic cells (such as erythrocytes) containing only mitochondrial DNA (arguably a 'functional unit of heredity', if only of the mitochondrion itself).[10]

The CBD does go on to provide a, potentially helpful, separate definition of 'Biological resources' which: 'includes genetic resources, organisms or parts

[5] CM Correa, 'Implications for BioTrade of the Protocol on Access to Genetic Resources and the Fair and Equitable Sharing of Benefits Arising from their Utilization' (2012), paper prepared for the BioTrade Initiative on UNCTAD (UNCTAD/DITC/TED/2011/9).

[6] CBD Art 2.

[7] T Greiber et al, *IUCN Explanatory Guide to the Protocol on Access and Benefit-Sharing* (IUCN Environmental Policy and Law Paper No 83, 2012) 64.

[8] Ribosenucleic acid.

[9] 'Gene', www.merriam-webster.com/dictionary/gene.

[10] See generally FJ Iborra et al 'The Functional Organization of Mitochondrial Genomes in Human Cells' (2004) 2 *BioMed Central Biology* 9.

thereof, populations, or any other biotic component of ecosystems with actual or potential use or value for humanity'.[11] This separate definition of 'biological resource', which includes 'genetic resources' within a broader definition, alongside separate mention of 'organisms or parts thereof', would seem to suggest that the narrower (DNA-only) interpretation of 'genetic resources' is correct. There otherwise seems little additional work for a broader (part of organism) definition of 'genetic material' to do (other than to distinguish parts of organisms which do not contain units of heredity such as structural proteins, although this is a small subset of the parts of an organism). This narrow interpretation is supported by Correa[12] who notes that it is consistent with the prevailing thinking in the early 1990s (when the CBD was agreed) that manipulation of large or small sections of DNA would be the crucial element in exploitation of genetic resources.

V. The Products of Genetic Expression

Genes (the CBD's 'functional units of heredity') are the way in which an organism encodes the instructions for making the proteins which make up the structural components of cell and tissues, and which regulate and catalyse reactions within the cells. For all (non-viral) organisms, when a particular gene is expressed the relevant portion of DNA within a chromosome is 'transcripted' into a strand of messenger RNA (mRNA) in which the sequence of base pairs in the DNA is reflected in the sequence of base pairs in the mRNA. That strand of mRNA itself serves as a template for the synthesis of a polypeptide chain in which the order of the amino acids making up that chain is itself determined by the sequence of nucleic acid bases within the mRNA. In this way the nucleic acid base sequence in the mRNA is 'translated' into the amino acid sequence. That polypeptide chain is subjected to post-translational modification which 'folds' the chain into a functional protein.[13] Where such protein is an enzyme, it will (subject to regulatory messages) catalyse the conversion of other biochemicals within the cell.[14] In this way the (non-DNA) biochemical components of an organism are an *expression* of the genetic material of the cell, even if they are not *themselves* functional units of heredity.

The question of whether 'non-DNA' biological components of an organism fall within the scope of 'genetic resources' for the purpose of the Nagoya Protocol is an important one. If they did not, potentially important substances found within an organism – including the biologically active ligands which have

[11] CBD Art 2.
[12] Correa (n 5).
[13] As will be seen in the discussion of digital sequence information below, this explanation is relatively simplistic in that it does not take account of the natural regulatory processes of alternative gene splicing and mRNA editing seen in eukaryotes, but it is sufficient for present purposes.
[14] See CK Mathews et al, *Biochemistry* (San Francisco, Benjamin Cummins, 2000) 875.

biological effects in other organisms (such as the prokaryotic and eukaryotic toxins from which many medicines or pharmacological tools are derived) – would arguably be excluded from the access and benefit-sharing provisions of the Nagoya Protocol.

If one takes a narrow interpretation of 'genetic resources' to include only the DNA of an organism, then one might argue that 'use' of that DNA will, of necessity, include only those techniques in which that piece of DNA itself is manipulated. These might include taking the entire genome of an organism (which could be expressed in its entirety through nuclear transfer cloning) or a subset of genes of interest which can be spliced into the genome of another organism.[15] Such a subset of genes could be used to provide the recipient (genetically modified) plant, animal, fungus or microorganism with a beneficial advantage (eg drought, pest or herbicide resistance) or to stimulate the recipient organism to synthesise a particular molecule (which molecule itself may be used to provide a therapeutic benefit). Although these are undoubtedly powerful and commercially important techniques, they do not include 'use' which takes a product of genetic expression (such as a protein or a metabolite produced through enzyme catalysis) as a starting point.

The fear that such products of genetic expression would be excluded from the access and benefit-sharing provisions of the Nagoya Protocol was a major driving force for the advocates for the 'provider' countries at the negotiations of what would become the Nagoya Protocol.[16]

Aubertin and Filoche report that provider country negotiators argued that the creation of wealth does not take place as result of the use of DNA or genes themselves, but in 89 per cent as a result of research and development regarding biochemical components (which include not only natural molecules, but also synthetic products which copy a natural molecule) and that a Nagoya Protocol dealing only with the use of genetic resources in the strict sense of the term, and not derivatives, would be meaningless.[17] Correa reports that the result of the negotiation was the addition to the Nagoya Protocol of the concepts of 'utilization', 'biotechnology' and 'derivative' which were not present in the CBD, and states that 'the common understanding among all parties was that the definition of

[15] Including (but certainly not limited to) CRISPR/Cas9 gene editing technology; see: F Zhang et al, 'CRISPR/Cas9 for Gene Editing: Progress, Implication and Challenges' (2014) 23 *Human Molecular Genetics* R40; PD Hsu et al, 'Development and Applications of CRISPR for Gene Engineering (2014) 157(6) *Cell* 1262.

[16] Correa (n 5) 14; Greiber (n 7) 63; EC Kamau et al, 'The Protocol on Access to Genetic Resources and Benefit Sharing: What Is New and What Are the Implications for Provider and User Countries and the Scientific Community?' (2010) 6(3) *Law, Environment and Development Journal* 246, 251; E Morgera et al, *Unravelling the Protocol: A Commentary on the Protocol on Access and Benefit Sharing to the Convention on Biological Diversity* (Leiden, Brill/Nijhoff, 2014) 66.

[17] C Aubertin and G Filoche, 'The Nagoya Protocol on the Use of Genetic Resources: One Embodiment of an Endless Discussion' (2011) 2(1) *Sustentabilidade em Debate – Brasília* 51.

"Utilization of genetic resources" held the key to determining whether the scope covered derivatives or not'.[18] Greiber et al also report that:

> Late in the Nagoya Protocol negotiations, it became clear that many of the contentious technical issues could be solved if there were a clear understanding of the concept of utilization. … the Parties included Subparagraph (c) defining the term 'utilization of genetic resources'. This definition helps to provide legal certainty through specific indicators that make a clear test for determining when the Nagoya Protocol governs a particular activity and when it triggers the obligation to share benefits.[19]

So, it is to the definition of 'utilization of genetic resources' that we must now turn. As will be seen, some of the confidence in the clarity of the definition shown in the last quote is, for this author, optimistic.

VI. What Does 'Utilization of Genetic Resources' Mean?

Throughout the Nagoya Protocol genetic resources is used in tandem with the term 'utilization'. Article 3 of the Nagoya Protocol, which deals with scope, adds little. It merely states:

> This Nagoya Protocol shall apply to genetic resources within the scope of Article 15 of the Convention and to the benefits arising from the utilization of such resources. This Nagoya Protocol shall also apply to traditional knowledge associated with genetic resources within the scope of the Convention and to the benefits arising from the utilization of such knowledge.[20]

Article 5(1) refers to the sharing of benefits 'arising from the utilization of genetic resources as well as subsequent applications and commercialization', Article 5(2) refers to benefits arising from the 'utilization of genetic resources' and Article 6(1) refers to access to genetic resources for their 'utilization'. So, what does 'utilization' mean here? The relevant definitions are provided in Article 2 of the Nagoya Protocol:

> (b) 'Utilization of genetic resources' means to conduct research and development on the genetic and/or biochemical composition of genetic resources, including through the application of biotechnology as defined in Article 2 of the Convention; …
> (d) 'Biotechnology' as defined in Article 2 of the Convention means any technological application that uses biological systems, living organisms, or derivatives thereof, to make or modify products or processes for specific use.
> (e) 'Derivative' means a naturally occurring biochemical compound resulting from the genetic expression or metabolism of biological or genetic resources, even if it does not contain functional units of heredity.

[18] Correa (n 5) 14.
[19] Greiber (n 7) 63.
[20] Art 3 Nagoya Protocol.

Our starting point for analysis is the term 'research and development on the genetic and/or biochemical composition of genetic resources'. Research and development on the 'genetic composition of genetic resources' would seem relatively clear – meaning analysis of the DNA sequences found within the particular genetic resource. What, though, does research and development on the *biochemical* composition of genetic resources mean? As we have seen above, the definition of 'genetic resources'/'genetic material' in the Nagoya Protocol (via Article 2 of the CBD) is rather scant. As is also highlighted above, the 'material … containing functional units of heredity' within the definition of 'genetic resources' can possibly be interpreted in two ways:

(a) functional units of heredity *alone*; or
(b) more broadly as 'material' of the organism in question that contains 'functional units of heredity'.

If one assumes for the moment that the first (functional units of heredity *alone*) interpretation is correct, this leaves us with a difficult question over the meaning of research and development on the *biochemical* composition of genetic material/resources. If we reasonably assume that 'genetic composition' means the nucleotide sequence within a strand of DNA, then we are left looking for *other* biochemical elements of the DNA strand(s) which may be the subject for investigation. What could these be?

Within eukaryotic organisms, nuclear DNA is wrapped around structural proteins called histones to form a composite material called 'chromatin'. These structures (together with non-histone chromosomal proteins) are used to assist the organised coiling of DNA within a chromosome, protecting it, ensuring it fits within the nucleus and regulating gene expression.[21] Modification of histone[22] (together with DNA methylation)[23] are mechanisms for bringing about long-lasting heritable (so-called 'epigenetic') changes to the way in which the genome of an organism is expressed that are distinctly separate from modification of the nucleotide sequence.[24] The examination of chromatin structure (and the changes to such structure brought about through epigenetic modification) could arguably meet a narrow definition of research on 'units of heredity' that was not focused on

[21] See Mathews (n 14) 1075; See generally AM Lesk, *Introduction to Genomics* (Oxford, Oxford University Press, 2012) 10.

[22] T Jenuwein and CD Allis, 'Translating the Histone Code' (2001) 293 *Science* 1074; T Kouzarides, 'Chromatin Modifications and their Function' (2007) 128 *Cell* 693; see generally CD Allis et al (eds), *Epigenetics* (Cold Spring Harbor, NY, Cold Spring Harbor Laboratory Press, 2009) 36.

[23] J D Lewis et al, 'Purification, Sequence, and Cellular Localization of a Novel Chromosomal Protein that Binds to Methylated DNA' (1992) 69 *Cell* 905; X Nan et al, 'Transcriptional Repression by the Methyl-CpG-Binding Protein MeCP2 Involves a Histone Deacetylase Complex' (1998) 393 *Nature* 386; NL Adkins and PT Georgel, 'MeCP2: Structure and Function' (2011) 89 *Biochemical Cell Biology* 1.

[24] N Carey, *The Epigenetics Revolution. How Modern Biology Is Rewriting our Understanding of Genetics, Disease and Inheritance* (Icon Books, London, 2012) 178; see generally: A Bird, 'Perceptions of Epigenetics' (2007) 447 *Nature* 396; G Felsenfeld, 'A Brief History of Epigenetics' in CD Allis et al (eds), *Epigenetics* (Cold Spring Harbor, NY, Cold Spring Harbor Laboratory Press, 2007) 15.

the nucleotide sequence alone. However, (although this is a very important area for study in its own right) in the light of broader concerns over the scope of 'utilization of genetic resources', it would seem perverse to give the term 'research and development on the biochemical composition of genetic resources' such a narrow interpretation.[25]

In contrast, if we interpret 'genetic material' not to be limited to DNA (with or without histones), but to include more broadly that 'material of plant, animal, microbial or other origin' which contains the 'functional units of heredity' (that is, *any* part of an organism which contains genetic material), it would logically follow that research and development on the *biochemical* composition of genetic resources would appear to mean research on the biochemical composition of such 'material of plant, animal, microbial or other origin containing functional units of heredity'.

Since the DNA nucleotide sequence element of the resource would appear to be dealt with by the first part (genetic composition) of the definition, the reference to 'biochemical composition' could arguably mean all those *other* biochemical elements present in the material which are created through genetic expression. For this author, this interpretation seems by far the more realistic – even though the narrow interpretation of 'genetic resources' (as is discussed above) would seem to be the correct one when looking at the CBD *alone*. Indeed, examining the meaning of 'research and development on genetic resources', Correa follows a similar line of reasoning:

> Interestingly, this definition [of utilization] alludes to research and development on the 'biochemical composition' of genetic resources, that is, the arrangement of the chemistry of the compounds of living tissues and the processes in a living organism, and not to research and development on biochemical compounds as such. It may be understood, however, that any study of a 'biochemical composition' may include that of the individual components.[26]

Such a broad interpretation is supported by the 2008 Report of the Meeting of the Group of Legal and Technical Experts (GLTE) on Concepts, Terms, Working Definitions and Sectoral Approaches, which sets out a non-exhaustive list of the kinds of research and development that could be included as utilisation.[27] This list is instructive. Although most activities are equally consistent with a DNA-only interpretation of 'genetic resources', the GTLE suggestion of 'Propagation and cultivation of the genetic resource in the form received' is clearly more consistent with a broader 'part of organism' interpretation, as this would clearly include

[25] This approach is consistent with the rule of interpretation set out in Art 31(1) of the 1969 Vienna Convention on the Law of Treaties namely: 'A treaty shall be interpreted in good faith in accordance with the ordinary meaning to be given to the terms of the treaty in their context and in the light of its object and purpose.'

[26] Correa (n 5) 14.

[27] Report of the Meeting of the Group of Legal and Technical Experts on Concepts, Terms, Working Definitions and Sectoral Approaches, UN Doc UNEP/CBD/WG-ABS/7/2 (12 December 2008) www.cbd.int/doc/meetings/abs/abswg-07/official/abswg-07-02-en.pdf

propagation of seeds, spores or cuttings of plants. With significantly more confidence, Kamau et al state that:

> The provider states were successful concerning the extension of benefit sharing to benefits from biochemical compounds resulting from genetic expression or metabolism of biological or genetic resources. Biochemicals that do not contain hereditary traits clearly do not fall under the term 'genetic resource'; they are hence not subject to sovereign rights of provider states and, more specifically, to the [prior informed consent]. They can however – and were now indeed – be captured by the term 'utilisation of genetic resources'. This term triggers benefit-sharing duties.[28]

Within the European Union, the provisions of the Nagoya Protocol were brought into effect through Regulation 511/2014 of 16 April 2014 (the ABS Regulation). Since the ABS Regulation, in part, mirrors the Nagoya Protocol, and given the lack of clarity in the Nagoya Protocol, in August 2016 the EU Commission issued its guidance on the scope and meaning of terms within the ABS Regulation through Notice 2016/C313/01 (the Commission Notice). Of interest to our analysis, the Commission Notice seeks to provide some explanation for the positions taken. In relation to 'utilisation of genetic resources', the Commission Notice states that the Nagoya Protocol definition is 'quite broad and covers various activities relevant for many sectors, without providing for a list of specific activities to be covered … so as not to pre-empt changes in the rapidly evolving knowledge and technology in this domain'.[29]

The Commission Notice appears to see the definition of 'research and development' as being key to understanding the scope of the Nagoya Protocol.[30] Noting that these are not defined in the Nagoya Protocol, the Commission states that interpretation of these terms 'should be based on their ordinary meaning in the context they are used and in the light of the purpose of the Regulation'.[31] The Commission appears to be particularly concerned that so-called 'upstream' activities (such as the maintenance and management) of a genetic collection for conservation purposes should not be caught.[32] However, in relation to 'downstream' activities the Commission Notice is arguably less clear, but proposes that researchers use a 'litmus test' whereby users should ask themselves whether what they are doing with the genetic resources 'creates new insight into characteristics of the genetic resource which is of (potential) benefit to the further process of product development. If this is the case, the activity … should be considered research and therefore falls under the term "utilisation"'.[33]

[28] Kamau (n 16).
[29] Commission Notice 2016/C313/01, para 2.3.3.
[30] ibid.
[31] ibid.
[32] Indeed this was a major concern of industry actors during the consultation period of the Commission Notice. See E Morgera and M Geelhoed, 'Consultancy on the Notion of "Utilisation" in the Nagoya Protocol and the EU ABS Regulation for the Upstream Actors', ec.europa.eu/environment/nature/biodiversity/international/abs/pdf/ABS%20Final%20Report%20upstream%20users.pdf.
[33] Commission Notice (n 29) para 2.3.3.

VII. The Meaning of 'Biotechnology' and 'Derivatives'

As stated above, given the overall context, a reading of 'conduct research and development on the biochemical composition of genetic resources' to include non-DNA biochemicals appears to be the interpretation that avoids outcomes which seem counter to the overall spirit of the Nagoya Protocol. Morgera et al[34] suggest that 'biochemical composition of genetic resources' in Article 2(c) does not, in fact, clarify the object of the utilisation 'self-evidently', but go on to state that the combined reading of Article 2(c) with the other 'new' definitions provided in the Nagoya Protocol, 'in particular that of derivatives', leads to the conclusion that utilisation of genetic resources includes research on the products of genetic expression.

As will be seen below, for this author the definition of 'derivatives' falls far short of providing clarity. (Although as will be explained, since that lack of clarity is found in a non-limiting example it arguably does not actually serve to effectively limit the scope of the definition of 'utilization of genetic resources'.) If one performs a simple 'de-nesting' of the nested definitions found within 'utilization of genetic resources' one arrives at the following:

> 'Utilization of genetic resources' means to conduct research and development on the genetic and/or biochemical composition of genetic resources, including through the application of [any technological application that uses biological systems, living organisms, or [naturally occurring biochemical compounds resulting from the genetic expression or metabolism of biological or genetic resources, (even if they do not contain functional units of heredity)] thereof, to make or modify products or processes for specific use]]. (NB: the square brackets show the nesting of the definitions)

The complexity, and lack of clarity, is obvious.

'Biotechnology' is provided as a (non-limiting) example of one of the means *by which* to conduct research and development on the genetic and/or biochemical composition genetic resources; that is, it is described as a mechanism or *tool*. The general understanding of biotechnology as a technique is broad and such technology has a long history. Dutfield identifies three 'generations' of biotechnology:

(a) traditional technologies such as brewing and bread making (in which yeasts are used to effect chemical transformations);
(b) microbial fermentation (including tissue culture and modern plant and animal breeding); and
(c) technologies dependent upon the transference of DNA from one organism to another to develop transgenic organisms.[35]

[34] Morgera (n 16) 65.

[35] G Dutfield, *Intellectual Property Rights, Biogenetic Resources and Traditional Knowledge* (London, Earthscan, 2004) 14.

Peters takes a similar broad approach, again highlighting the genesis of biotechnology in prehistoric plant and animal breeding, in the use of yeast in breadmaking and brewing, and in the use of bacteria to make yoghurts and cheeses. She distils the meaning of biotechnology to be as follows: 'In its purest form, the term "biotechnology" refers to the use of living organisms or their products to enhance human health or the human environment.'[36] However, notwithstanding the different means used, one of the recurring similarities of all types of biotechnology is the production of a final 'product', whether that be a disease-resistant crop, a monoclonal antibody, an antibiotic, a beer or a Stilton cheese. This focus on products is, of course, reflected in the definition originally provided in the CBD: 'A technological application that uses biological systems, living organisms, or derivatives thereof, to *make or modify products or processes* for specific use' [emphasis added].[37]

If we assume that the original CBD definition of genetic material intended to capture DNA alone, we can see that the definition of 'biotechnology' was entirely consistent with that narrow interpretation. It would be consistent the use of transgenic whole organisms ('living organisms') whose genome has been modified by the insertion of particular genes to manufacture particular proteins (or downstream products from those proteins where those proteins are enzymes). It would certainly include (but not be limited to) the application of 'In vitro nucleic acid techniques, including recombinant deoxyribonucleic acid (DNA) and direct injection of nucleic acid into cells or organelles'.[38]

However, if we assume that 'genetic material' should be read as (also) meaning 'parts of organisms which contain functional units of heredity', then in terms of 'conducting research and development on the *genetic* composition' such an interpretation would be consistent with techniques that do not specifically seek to move DNA through in vitro nucleic acid techniques, but rather attempt the '[f]usion of cells beyond the taxonomic family, that overcome natural physiological reproductive or recombination barriers and that are not techniques used in traditional breeding and selection'.[39] Such techniques could include the production of monoclonal antibodies through the creation of hybridoma cell lines made by fusing B-lymphocytes with a myeloma cell line.[40]

In both the examples above, one might argue that the 'Biotechnology' is being used to exploit the *genetic* composition of the 'genetic resource', rather than being part of the research and development on the (non-chromatin) *biochemical* composition of the 'genetic resource'. If this is correct, how then might these 'biotechnology' applications be used in the research and development of the

[36] P Peters, *Biotechnology A Guide to Genetic Engineering* (Dubuque, IA, Wm C Brown, 1995) xi.

[37] Protocol Art 2.

[38] Art 3(i) (a), Cartagena Protocol on Biosafety to the Convention on Biological Diversity.

[39] ibid.

[40] C Milstein, 'The Hybridoma Revolution: An Offshoot of Basic Research' (1999) 21(11) *BioEssays* 966.

biochemical of the genetic resource? As we have seen, the understanding of biotechnology extends beyond what the Cartagena Nagoya Protocol on Biosafety to the Convention on Biological Diversity calls 'Modern Biotechnology'[41] (essentially in vitro nucleic acid techniques and cell fusion techniques) and the definition within the CBD is certainly not so limited.[42] Such research into the biochemical composition of genetic resource would certainly include the use of cell and tissue cultures using *unmodified* organisms to assist in the making of a greater amount of the substance in question.

In practice, however, there is no split in the use of biotechnology techniques as between *genetic* and *biochemical* composition – *all* biotechnology techniques are available for research on the (non-DNA) biochemical composition of a resource, notably the use of genetically modified bacteria, or eukaryotic cell lines, to produce a sufficient quantity of a substance for analysis and study. One might imagine here the production of human interferon through the use of transgenic bacteria.[43]

To conclude, the unamended definition of 'Biotechnology' in the CBD is entirely consistent with a broad interpretation of 'genetic resources' to mean 'parts of an organism containing functional units of heredity' and 'biochemical composition of genetic resource' to include the non-DNA products of genetic expression. It is, however, equally consistent with a narrower chromatin-only interpretation of 'genetic resource' or a chromatin-only interpretation of 'research and development on the biochemical composition of the genetic resource'.

VIII. Does the 'New' Definition of 'Derivative' Assist?

As we have seen, the Nagoya Protocol introduces a definition of 'Derivative':

> a naturally occurring biochemical compound resulting from the genetic expression or metabolism of biological or genetic resources, even if it does not contain functional units of heredity.[44]

In itself, the definition of 'Derivative' is clear. Had it been inserted as an expansion of the definition of 'genetic material' at Article 2 of the CBD it would have unambiguously expanded that term to include any protein (such as an enzyme) produced through genetic expression or any naturally occurring compound produced through enzyme-catalysed metabolism within the organism in question.

[41] Art 3(i), Cartagena Protocol on Biosafety on Biosafety to the Convention on Biological Diversity.

[42] Indeed the presence of a narrower definition for 'Modern Biotechnology' within the Cartagena Protocol on Biosafety to the Convention on Biological Diversity supports a broader interpretation for 'biotechnology' within the CBD and Protocol.

[43] D Riesenberg et al, 'High Cell Density Fermentation of Recombinant *Escherichia coli* Expressing Human Interferon Alpha 1' (1990) 34(1) *Applied Microbiological Biotechnology* 77.

[44] Nagoya Protocol Art 2(e).

This is not, however, how the phrase is used. Indeed, it is not used as a capitalised defined term *anywhere* within the Nagoya Protocol.[45] Instead it is arguably used as what appears to be a clarificatory example of the term 'Biotechnology'.

As we will see, the way in which 'Derivative' entered into the Nagoya Protocol is complex. However, if we understand the mention of 'derivatives' within the Article 2 of the CBD (and Article 2 of the Nagoya Protocol) definition of Biotechnology as being a reference to 'Derivative' as a defined term within Article 2(e) of the Nagoya Protocol, then its effect is (arguably) to amend the definition of Biochemistry to the following:

> any technological application that uses biological systems, living organisms, or *[naturally occurring biochemical compounds resulting from the genetic expression or metabolism of biological or genetic resources, (even if they do not contain functional units of heredity)]* thereof, to make or modify products or processes for specific use. [italicised text denotes substitution]

With the substitution in place, it is not entirely clear what work the 'thereof' is performing in that sentence. Reference to a derivative (undefined) of biological systems or living organisms suggests that the system or organism has been manipulated is some way. Genetic manipulation of such systems or organisms to make products or processes is, of course, 'classic' biotechnology. Here the 'thereof' seems sensible. However, once one makes the substitution of 'derivative' with its new definition, the presence of the 'thereof' becomes more confusing. The substituted definition makes reference to 'genetic expression or metabolism of biological or genetic resources' so why does that need to further particularised to be 'of' biological systems or 'of' living organisms? Such further particularisation is arguably otiose. It certainly does not enhance clarity. One might charitably conclude that the presence of the 'thereof' is vestigial – having been left behind during a rushed negotiation. As will be discussed below, the reality is more complex.

With or without the 'thereof', one might argue that what is being described is the use of a 'naturally occurring biochemical compound resulting from the genetic expression or metabolism of biological or genetic resources' within a technical application used in research upon genetic resources. This interpretation is incomplete – as we saw above, the underlying constant of 'Biotechnology' is that it is a *process* for producing product and this requirement is still present within the definition. However, putting that requirement to one side for the moment, we need to recognise that the application of a 'naturally occurring biochemical compound' here is a description of the *actor* upon a *subject*, rather than a description of the *subject itself*.

[45] It is interesting to note that 'derivatives' may have been used in this way in the indicative list of typical mutually agreed terms set out at para 44(i) of the pre-Protocol (non-binding) Bonn Guidelines: 'Provisions regarding the sharing of benefits arising from the commercial and other utilization of genetic resources and their derivatives and products' (COP 6 Decision VI/24 'Bonn Guidelines', Part D, para 44(i)). However, even here it is not really evident what is meant by a 'derivative' of a genetic resource in this context.

If this use as a *tool* was the intention of the negotiators of the Nagoya Protocol, then the definition of 'Derivative', and where it is inserted, works relatively clearly. There are, indeed, very many such 'naturally occurring biochemical compounds resulting from the genetic expression or metabolism of biological or genetic resources' which are used as tools in the conduct of research upon the 'genetic and/or biochemical composition of genetic resources'. There does not appear in these definitions to be a requirement that the genetic resources from which the tool is taken has to be the *same* genetic resource upon which the tool is being used. As such, the definition would include the use of DNA probes taken from other organisms, dyes and stains derived from plants, animals, fungi and microbes, inhibitors of intracellular metabolism, and ligands at intracellular or extracellular receptors. Nor is there, of course, any restriction on using a tool obtained from one organism ('genetic resource') upon the biochemical composition of *the same* genetic resource – one might imagine here the (admittedly narrow) use of tetrodotoxin obtained from a *Tetraodontidae* puffer fish to examine voltage-gated sodium channels in the same species of puffer fish.[46]

Although the definition of 'Derivative' as a tool clearly works in this (limited) way, it hardly seems a necessary clarification, given that the use of such compounds has long been a mainstay of biological research techniques. In addition, such a detailed explanation hardly seems 'in character' given the other, rather sparse, definitions provided within the CBD and Nagoya Protocol.

We also have the remaining problem that in the definition of 'Biotechnology' the application using the 'naturally occurring biochemical compound' should 'make or modify products or processes for specific use', which is clearly not the case with all biological research tools. So, what then is the purpose of the expanded definition of 'Derivative'?

IX. What Is the Purpose of the Expanded Definition of 'Derivative'?

During the negotiation of the Nagoya Protocol, developing nations sought to ensure that the Protocol included specific reference to 'derivatives', arguing that this is where the main interest of modern biological research lies.[47] In contrast, (perhaps for the same reason) some developed nations sought to ensure that the provisions of the Nagoya Protocol merely applied to functional units of heredity (ie DNA).[48] As a result of this impasse, the term 'derivative' did not find its way

[46] CH Lee and PC Ruben, 'Interaction Between Voltage-Gated Sodium Channels and the Neurotoxin, Tetrodotoxin' (2008) 2(6) *Channels* 407.

[47] Morgera (n 16) 66.

[48] M Buck and C Hamilton, 'The Protocol on Access to Genetic Resources and Benefit-sharing Arising from their Utilisation to the Convention on Biological Diversity' (2011) 47 *Review of European Community and International Environmental Law* 56.

into the operative terms of the Nagoya Protocol but it was understood that by way of compromise the term 'utilization of genetic resources' would include the 'notion' of derivatives.[49]

As we have seen, the word 'derivative' was already present in the existing (1992) CBD definition of 'Biotechnology', namely: 'any technological application that uses biological systems, living organisms, or *derivatives* thereof, to make or modify products or processes for specific use' [emphasis added].

As discussed above, what appears to be referred to here is derivatives of biological systems or living organisms (which have most likely been created through modification of the genetic material within them), rather than to the biochemicals produced through translation of genes into proteins. Notwithstanding that (very) distinctly different use, the presence of the word 'derivative' at that position appears to have acted as an easily negotiated route for insertion of the new definition of 'Derivative', without the parties becoming involved in a potentially fractious confrontation over a new definition of 'Biotechnology'.

For this author, using a strict doctrinal interpretation, the taking of that route has left us with the rather limited effect of 'Derivative' as a non-limiting example of a tool to be used on genetic resources (and a strange hangover requirement to directly produce a product or process as would be the case with a Biotechnology application). The result is certainly difficult to untangle. Morgera et al refer to this outcome as 'puzzling'.[50] Notwithstanding this, they state that the relevance of the definition of 'Derivative' to the interpretation of 'utilization of genetic resources' can be argued on two grounds:

(a) 'utilization' *implicitly* refers also to research and development through the application of biotechnology *on* derivatives' [emphasis added]; and
(b) 'The definition of 'utilization' makes reference to the 'biochemical composition of genetic resources' which arguably relates to the reference to compounds in the definition of 'derivatives' as it is only the latter that provides the necessary elements to circumscribe this otherwise vague concept'.[51]

With regard to point (b), Morgera et al appear to suggest that the term 'biochemical composition of genetic resources' is unclear. Although understandable, as discussed above, this author believes one can interpret that term clearly enough when one broadly interprets 'genetic material' to include the cells of an organism which contain 'functional units of heredity'. However, even assuming uncertainty in this regard, given that 'Derivative' is used as an example of a tool ('Biotechnology') used to act *upon* the subject of 'biochemical composition of genetic resources' it is hard to see how one can easily use the reference to 'biochemical compound' in the definition of 'Derivative' to guide us as to the overall meaning of 'biochemical composition of genetic resources'.

[49] R Kosaka, *The Negotiating History of the Protocol on ABS: Japanese Perspective* (2012) www.ipaj.org/english_journal/pdf/9-1_Kohsaka.pdf.
[50] Morgera (n 16) 66.
[51] Morgera (n 16) 67.

This use of 'derivative' as somehow clarificatory of, or integrated within, 'genetic resources', notwithstanding rules of interpretation, is prevalent. Vogel et al are highly critical of this approach.[52] They state that despite the introduction of 'derivative' in Article 2 (e), 'derivative' is not incorporated into Article 3 which defines the scope. They go on to say that notwithstanding that, many delegates and scholars are not 'disheartened' since they have inferred 'derivative' in the phrase 'utilization of such sources'. Vogel et al's fear is that such an inference is not obvious and would morph 'utilization of such sources' into 'a 'panchrestron', Garrett Hardin's neologism for something that signifies everything and therefore means nothing.[53]

Morgera et al's point (a) is, at first sight at least, the stronger. They suggest that if your understanding of 'biotechnology' is a narrow one, meaning merely the use of organisms to make products following manipulation of their genetic material, then such an understanding would not be entirely consistent with research on the products of genetic expression found within a genetic resource. They suggest that expanding the meaning of biotechnology to include the use of 'Derivatives' (as newly defined) is consistent with 'biotechnology' meaning a broader range of activities and, in particular, including research on the products of genetic expression found in a genetic resource.

At first blush, this may seem a reasonable interpretation. Indeed, as we have seen the original definition of 'Biotechnology' in Article 2 of the CBD (without the expansion of the term 'derivative') appears to refer only to the use of biological systems or of living organisms (which have most likely been created through modification of the genetic material within them) *to make products*. However, although that interpretation is certainly consistent with a narrower understanding of biotechnology, as was discussed above, the use of those 'narrow' techniques is still entirely consistent with a broad interpretation of 'genetic resources' and a broad interpretation of 'research and development on the genetic or biochemical composition'.

In addition, the inclusion of the new definition of 'Derivatives' within the definition of 'Biotechnology' is consistent with a broad understanding of the term biotechnology and with research on the products of genetic expression found within the cells of a genetic resource. However, if this were the aim of the inclusion of a specific definition of 'Derivative', it seems a relatively imprecise way of achieving the end, and we are still left with the problem of reconciling the need for the application to directly produce or modify a product or process.

Although concluding that the operative effect of the new definition of 'derivative' is to further clarify that research and development on 'naturally occurring biochemical compounds resulting from genetic expression or cellular metabolism and not containing DNA' can fall within 'utilization of genetic resources',

[52] JH Vogel et al, 'The Economics of Information, Studiously Ignored in the Protocol on Access to Genetic Resources and Benefit Sharing' (2011) 7(1) *Law, Environment and Development Journal* 52.
[53] G Hardin, 'Meaninglessness of the Word Protoplasm' (1956) 82(3) *Scientific Monthly* 112.

Morgera et al are (unsurprisingly) concerned that 'the unfortunate drafting may raise doubts in interpreters and as a consequence lead to variations in national legislation implementing the Nagoya Protocol'.[54]

Overall we might broadly conclude that the new definition of 'Derivative', although, in itself, clear, is poorly placed within the definitions provided within the CBD and the Nagoya Protocol. As part of the definition of 'genetic material' or 'genetic resource' it would have provided welcome clarification. As part of the definition of 'Biotechnology' (which is itself merely a non-limiting example of research and development) perhaps all we can really say with regard to the use of the term 'Derivative' is that it is at least not inconsistent with the definition of 'biochemical composition of genetic resources' including naturally occurring products of genetic expression.

X. 'Isolated' Derivatives

Morgera et al raise the problem of what they refer to as an 'isolated derivative', that is, a derivative 'acquired and utilised without physical access to genetic resources, such as those isolated from their natural environment and available ex situ'.[55] Although they argue that such compounds fall within the scope of 'utilization of genetic resources' they are concerned that there may be variations in national legislation implementing this aspect of the Nagoya Protocol.

This author sees no realistic difficulty in interpreting 'research and development on the genetic and/or biochemical composition of genetic resources' as encompassing work on such an isolated derivative. The mere fact that a naturally occurring compound has been physically isolated from its genetic resource source makes it no less a constituent part of biochemical composition and in vitro (or indeed in silico) study of it no less study of the biochemical composition of genetic resource source. Correa is in agreement:

> A 'biochemical compound' is any chemical compound naturally occurring in living organisms. It may be used without separation from the biological resource to which it belongs (eg dried plants) or isolated and even synthesized. Currently available techniques allow researchers to precisely detect, isolate and structurally characterize bioactive natural compounds. 'Naturally occurring' may be interpreted in this context as meaning that a biochemical compound is the result of processes at the cellular level, unaltered by human intervention, that have taken place in vivo or in vitro. This would include, hence, compounds obtained at laboratories or production facilities.[56]

In contrast Greiber et al state:

> The definition of 'utilization' however, refers to research and development on the biochemical composition of genetic resources. This linkage between biochemical compounds and genetic resources has led to some different interpretations, especially

[54] Morgera (n 16) 68.
[55] ibid.
[56] Correa (n 5).

as to whether biochemicals must be accessed simultaneously with access to genetic resources. Therefore, there is no consensus on the situation of 'isolated derivatives' (eg, an extract from a plant stored in a lab) that have not been accessed simultaneously with the genetic resources.[57]

Some of this confusion would appear to derive from an unnecessary conflation of the idea of 'access' with that of 'utilisation'.

XI. The Problem of 'Chemical Derivatives'

The analysis provided above would appear to strongly suggest that research and development on the naturally occurring biochemical compounds resulting from genetic expression (or cellular metabolism of a genetic resource) falls within the scope of 'utilization of genetic resources' for the purposes of the benefit-sharing provisions of Article 5 of the Nagoya Protocol. However, as is shown in Figure 1 (and discussed in detail in chapter four, section I), the identification and isolation of such a compound (though often of great importance) is often merely the beginning of a research and development trail aimed at the production of chemicals, which though based upon the original compound, are structurally modified such as to enhance their biological efficacy and bioavailability, and reduce their side-effect profile, relative to the original compound. Within the field of biochemistry such compounds are referred to as chemical derivatives (or more simply as just 'derivatives') of the original biochemical.[58]

One might suggest that, in the light of the very long-standing use of the term 'derivative' within the field of biochemistry, the use of the term 'Derivative' within the Nagoya Protocol is unfortunate and potentially confusing.[59] Notwithstanding this potential confusion, we need to be absolutely clear; the reference to 'Derivative' within the Nagoya Protocol is *not* a reference to human-made chemical derivatives, but (as we have seen) has a very specific given meaning in the Nagoya Protocol, being: 'a naturally occurring biochemical compound resulting from the genetic expression or metabolism of biological or genetic resources, even if it does not contain functional units of heredity'.[60]

By definition, then, the meaning of the phrase 'naturally occurring' excludes any human-made, non-naturally chemical derivatives. However, we should not be confused into believing that this limitation could assist us in the broader question of whether chemical derivatives fall within the scope of Article 5. The operative effect of the term 'Derivative' has been examined above, and, as this term is used within Article 2 of the Nagoya Protocol (as a non-limiting example

[57] Greiber (n 7) 67.

[58] Derivative: 'a chemical substance related structurally to another substance and theoretically derivable from it' (www.merriam-webster.com/dictionary/derivative).

[59] Although as we have seen, it was perhaps originally used for an entirely different purpose within the CBD.

[60] Nagoya Protocol, Art 2(e).

of 'Biochemistry'), it would not operate to extend the scope of the meaning of research and development on genetic resources. Crucially, however, neither would its limited scope (of itself) operate to limit the scope of meaning of research and development on genetic resources to research and development upon naturally occurring compounds alone.[61] The answer to this question of interpretation (if there is one) has to lie in the definition of 'utilization of genetic resources' and particularly the phrase 'research and development on the biochemical composition of genetic resources'.

Assuming 'biochemical composition of genetic resources' to mean the products of genetic expression, we can be reasonably confident that the following broad classes of substances created by the metabolism of a genetic resource would fall within the provisions of Article 5:

(a) a naturally occurring RNA strand produced directly from the transcription of the DNA of the organism;
(b) a naturally occurring protein produced from the transcription/translation of the DNA of the organism;
(c) glycosylated protein (such as a functional enzyme) produced from the metabolism of the protein produced in (b) above; and
(d) biochemical compound ('X') whose synthesis was catalysed by the enzyme in (c) above.

Clearly, a chemical derivative of the biochemical 'X' above is not a member of the set of endogenous compounds which are naturally produced within a cell by genetic expression and it would not be part of the 'biochemical composition' of the genetic resource. Could, however, the production of a chemical derivative of 'X' (called hereafter 'X-A') be considered to be part of the 'research and development' on X? The use of chemical derivatives of an endogenous biochemical can be used to enhance our understanding of the interaction between X and the intra- or extracellular target through which X has a biological effect. Is this sufficient to constitute research on the *original* substance? Although Correa is comfortable that a broad definition of 'research and development' would mean that the benefit-sharing obligations of the Nagoya Protocol would encompass work upon a naturally occurring biochemical compound, he states that 'the extent to which it would apply to downstream products derived, in turn, from such compounds is less clear'.[62] Aubertin and Filoche are somewhat more certain, and state:

> By presenting derivatives as nothing more than a biochemical compound from a living organism, claims relating to synthetic molecules with a structure similar to a natural

[61] Although the operative effect of the definition of 'derivative' does not assist us in this regard, we can at least note that if the broad aim of introducing the term 'derivative' had been (as Morgera et al. (n 16) suggest) to ensure that compounds naturally produced within a cell by genetic expression were caught within the access and benefit-sharing provisions of the Protocol, the concept of derivative would not include a chemical derivative.

[62] Correa (n 5).

> substance fall outside the scope of the Nagoya Protocol. It would therefore appear that a natural molecule which has been synthesized and altered does not fall within the scope of the Nagoya Protocol, even if it was 'inspired' by nature.[63]

As discussed above, the GTLE arrived at a non-exhaustive list of 'typical uses' of genetic resources.[64] Amongst that long list there was one use that could arguably be construed as encompassing a chemical derivative namely: 'Use of genetic material as a "factory" to produce organic compounds, such as: Active compounds for pharmaceutical production' However, since the list of organic compounds to be manufactured concludes with 'Other naturally occurring compounds' it would appear that the active compounds envisaged are *naturally occurring* rather than human-made derivatives. Overall, the uses are entirely focused on work on naturally occurring substances. A similar approach is taken in respect of a discussion on the meaning of 'derivatives'. So, although an opportunity was there for the drafters of the Nagoya Protocol to specifically identify human-made *chemical* derivatives of the biochemical composition of genetic resources, the opportunity was not taken.

In relation to 'derivatives', for this author the Commission Notice glosses over the doctrinal problems outlined above. It states that:

> through the concept of 'biotechnology', the definition of utilisation is interlinked with the definition of 'derivatives' in Article 2(e) of the Nagoya Protocol, which clarifies that 'derivative' means 'a naturally occurring biochemical compound resulting from the genetic expression or metabolism of biological or genetic resources, even if it does not contain functional units of heredity.[65]

The Commission go on to conclude that: 'research and development on derivatives (whether or not containing functional units of heredity) is within scope where they are derived from genetic resources accessed under the Nagoya Protocol'.[66] It is, however, clear from the examples set out by the Commission that the derivatives they refer to are *naturally* occurring products of genetic expression, not human-made chemical derivatives thereof.

Overall, therefore, one has to conclude that the question of whether 'utilization' within the meaning of the Nagoya Protocol includes work on *human-made* chemical derivatives of naturally occurring biochemicals remains entirely unclear. So, if it is unclear whether the Nagoya Protocol directly covers human-made chemical derivatives, we need to consider whether more indirect *informational* linkages will lead to downstream use of such derivatives falling within the scope of the Nagoya Protocol. It is to those informational linkages that we will now turn.

[63] Aubertin and Filoche (n 17).
[64] UNEP/CBD/WG-ABS/7/2.
[65] Commission Notice (n 29) para 2.3.3.
[66] ibid.

XII. Informational Linkages: 'Genetic Information'

The discussion above demonstrates that there remain significant uncertainties over what constitutes 'research and development' on 'genetic resources'. However, one clear constant in the discussion on 'utilisation' set out above is that the research is done on DNA or on biochemicals that have physically originated *from the genetic resource itself*. What if, however, the subject for research and development did not *physically* originate from the genetic resource itself but was independently synthesised using *information* gained from the original genetic resource? Relatively recent advances in synthetic biology allow the de novo synthesis of genetic material, so-called 'synthetic DNA', without the need for a primer or template which is *physically* derived from a genetic resource.[67] New DNA strands are built from a digital database of the required base-pair sequences. Once generated, these synthetic DNA molecules work in an identical fashion to those created from a physical template and can be used in gene cloning, or even in the generation of entire synthetic genomes.[68]

This section will look at whether, on a doctrinal (and technical) analysis, the Nagoya Protocol ABS rights cover the downstream use of *information* gained from the original genetic resource. If they do not, there is an arguable case that the use of synthetic biology techniques would create an effective mechanism for evading the ABS provisions of the Nagoya Protocol. This section will go on to briefly describe the current discussion within the Nagoya mechanism(s) for addressing the issue of genetic information.

A. Genetic Information 1: Is Synthetic DNA Covered within the definition of 'Genetic Resources'?

Until relatively recently, the most common technique for generating DNA strands was to generate so-called complementary DNA (cDNA). Here DNA is synthesized from an mRNA template obtained from a cell. The mRNA template is itself generated by transcription from DNA genes of the original organism. As such there is a clear chain of causation from the *original* genetic material to the cDNA, via the mRNA template. The cDNA thus generated is most often used for gene cloning or probes.[69]

Another technique used alongside cDNA is polymerase chain reaction (PCR). PCR allows the amplification of a small DNA template called a DNA

[67] See generally JC Venter, *Life at the Speed of Life, From the Double Helix to the Dawn of Digital Life* (London, Abacus, 2013) 250.

[68] DG Gibson et al, 'Creation of a Bacterial Cell Controlled by a Chemically Synthesized Genome' (2010) 329(5987) *Science* 52.

[69] See generally E-L Winnaker, *From Genes to Clones, Introduction to Gene Technology* (Weinheim, VCH, 1987) 32.

oligonucleotide or DNA primer. The template has, to date, been obtained from an organism and there is, again, a chain of causation from the original organism to the DNA created by PCR.[70] However, new technology now allows a DNA strand to be created de novo – without the need for a primer or template. Oligonucleotide strands are built from a digital database of the required base-pair sequences and annealed together to make longer DNA strands. Once generated, these synthetic DNA molecules can work like those created from a template and can be used in gene cloning or even in the generation of synthetic genomes.[71] Although this technology may enable production of de novo human-designed genes that do not appear in nature, much work will focus on the synthesis of (or adaptations of) known genes that currently exist in nature. However, to synthetically replicate a naturally occurring functional DNA strand or gene, knowledge of the nucleotide sequence of that DNA strand or gene will be required. That nucleotide sequence will have been generated by research on the original organism. Certainly without the information on the base-pair sequence of the original DNA the synthetic copy would be very unlikely to replicate the specific functionality of the original. Can the use of a naturally originating nucleotide sequence from a genetic database be considered to be 'accessing' or 'utilising' genetic material even if there is no physical access to physical genetic material?

i. 'Accessing'

It is worth looking again at the definition of genetic resources at Article 2 of CBD (and Article 2 of the Nagoya Protocol) namely that: 'Genetic resources' means *genetic material of actual or potential value*, where 'Genetic material' *means any material of plant, animal, microbial or other origin containing functional units of heredity*. Clearly synthetic DNA contains functional units of heredity (indeed self-replicating organisms containing synthetic DNA have been produced).[72] However, is it of plant, animal, microbial or other *origin*? The *Oxford English Dictionary* defines 'origin' as meaning:

> 1. The act of fact of arising or springing from something; derivation; rise; beginning of existence in reference to its source or cause. 2. That from which anything arises, springs or is derived.[73]

Arguably *the beginning of existence* of a copy synthetic strand of DNA *in reference to its source or cause* is the original genetic sequence – in the sense that 'but for'

[70] See RK Saiki et al, 'Primer-Directed Enzymatic Amplification of DNA with a Thermostable DNA Polymerase' (1988) 239(4839) *Science* 487.

[71] See HG Khorana et al, 'Studies on Polynucleotides. 103. Total Synthesis of the Structural Gene for an Alanine Transfer Ribonucleic Acid from Yeast' (1972) 72(2) *Journal of Molecular Biology* 209.

[72] Gibson (n 68); JF Pelletier et al, 'Genetic Requirements for Cell Division in a Genomically Minimal Cell' (2021) 184(9) *Cell* 2430.

[73] *The Compact Oxford English Dictionary* (Oxford, Oxford University Press, 1979).

the existence of the original naturally occurring genetic sequence the synthetic copy in that form could not exist. However, although the information originates from the original organism, does the *material* originate from that organism? This is very far from clear.

Du Plessis (a negotiator at the Nagoya summit on behalf of Namibia) has stated that: 'DNA sequences are information, written in chemicals and that using such information without [prior informed consent] and benefit sharing is tantamount to theft, in the same way that copying CDs would be.'[74] However, Du Plessis gives no explanation as to how the wording of the Nagoya Protocol achieves this aim. Morgera et al[75] address the question of access to/utilization of genetic information as part of a broader concern for the impact of 'bioinformatics' on the Nagoya Protocol. They conclude that the Nagoya Protocol is unclear with regard to the question of whether genetic information falls within the definition of 'Genetic Resources' and indeed that the Nagoya Protocol was conceived without consideration of bioinformatics. However, they also determine that this is an area which needs to be determined if the Nagoya Protocol is not to become obsolete within 'a few years' time.' Focusing further on the definition of 'Genetic Resources' they paraphrase Tvedt and Shei's argument[76] that

> functional [units of heredity] could refer to both the genetic structure per se and to the information encapsulated in the DNA sequence that can be screened and transferred electronically and become functional in a new digital form. In that light, it has been argued that the biological *origin* rather than the biological *form* of the information matters for falling under the definition of the utilisation of genetic resources.

This focus on *functionality* may appear at first sight to be a reasonable purposive interpretation of the definition of genetic materials. It is, of course, the functionality of the 'functional units of heredity' which gives purpose and potential value to the genetic component of genetic material. If such a purposive approach were not taken, it would allow a party to reproduce the functionality of a naturally occurring gene by producing a synthetic DNA copy of it and thereby take the benefit/functionality of that gene whilst avoiding the access provisions of the Nagoya Protocol. However, in considering this question of functionality we need to be careful of oversimplification – only a small fraction (1.5 per cent in humans) of eukaryotic DNA directly codes for proteins (in the form of 'exons'),[77] the remainder takes the form of intragenic DNA ('introns' – non-coding DNA which sits within a gene) and intergenic DNA (non-coding DNA which sits between genes).

[74] P Du Plessis, 'Disclosure of Origin of Biological Resources and Potential Effects of the Protocol' (2011) 40(5) *Chartered Institute of Patent Attorneys Journal* 331.

[75] Morgera (n 16) 70.

[76] MW Tvedt and PJ Schei 'The Term "Genetic Resources": Flexible and Dynamic while Providing Legal Certainty?' in S Oberthür and GK Rosendal (eds), *Global Governance of Genetic Resources: Access and Benefit Sharing after the Protocol* (London, Routledge, 2014) 18.

[77] TG Wolfsberg et al, 'Guide to the Draft Human Genome' (2001) 409 *Nature* 824.

Although such non-coding DNA was originally given the name 'junk DNA', it is increasingly clear that it (in combination with histones) plays a key role in chromosome structure, gene expression and epigenetic heredity.[78] Some intergenic DNA codes for RNA that is not translated into proteins, but has a structural role (eg ribosomal RNA) or regulatory function (miniRNA) within the cell. Other non-coding DNA comprises 'pseudo-genes' (fossil genes that have lost their ability to be expressed), non-expressed viral genes, telomeres (which protect against chromosomal degradation during cell division), and 'conserved' non-coding sequences (which show a high degree of evolutionary conservation and may be involved in gene regulation).[79] The ENCODE consortium has reported that: 'The vast majority (80.4%) of the human genome participates in at least one biochemical RNA and/or chromatin associated event in at least one cell type.'[80]

In the light of this, limiting the definition of 'functional units of heredity' merely to expressed genes (exons) seems overly narrow. However, bringing non-coding DNA within the ambit of the access/utilisation requirements of the Nagoya Protocol may present its own, significant, difficulties. For example, in relation to highly conserved non-coding sequences, these sequences may have been preserved across aeons and taxonomic groupings – just because the original sequence was determined from a sample taken from a liana from a megadiverse nation does not mean that the same sequence could not have been equally determined from a yeast, a mouse or an elephant. We need to ask: in what way is the code from the liana unique or special such that a right to control access is justifiable?

The same (difficult) question can also be raised in relation to those *expressed* portions of DNA which are wholly, or closely, conserved: '75% of our expressed genetic make-up is the same as a pumpkin, 57% the same as a cabbage'.[81] Why should a particular nation (or Indigenous group) have a right to control 'access' to a nucleotide sequence which has been determined from an organism (say a liana) which was found within a certain nation state (say Ecuador) when it could have as easily been determined from brewing yeast in Burton-on-Trent?[82]

If the nucleotide sequence is entirely conserved across taxonomic groups, then what would happen if the 'accessor' of the nucleotide sequence argued in their defence that the sequence information actually used by them had originated not from the Ecuadorian liana but from the defendant's independent determination from the genome of the Burtonian yeast? In this case would control over the sequence reside in the party that controls the resource from which the nucleotide sequence information was *first* determined – akin to a path-independent

[78] E Pennisi, 'Genomics. ENCODE Project Writes Eulogy for Junk DNA' (2012) 337(6099) *Science* 1159, 1161.

[79] The ENCODE Project Consortium; I Dunham et al. 'An Integrated Encyclopedia of DNA Elements in the Human Genome' (2012) 489 (7414) *Nature* 57.

[80] ibid.

[81] GK Ferguson, *The Human Genome: Poems on the Book of Life*, www.thehumangenome.co.uk/THE_HUMAN_GENOME/Primer.html.

[82] An English town famous for its concentration of breweries.

monopoly right to the sequence? Or is there an *originality* requirement (akin to copyright) according to which independent (non-path dependent) determination of the sequence constitutes a defence to 'infringement'? It would seem extraordinary within its overall context if the Nagoya Protocol had created the first (path-independent) right, so the latter path-dependent approach appears the more feasible. However, with 'copy-rights' there is often a continuum of complexity and a middle ground – what if the defendant (although truly independently sequencing the nucleotide sequence) had been in some way directed toward that gene by an understanding of functionality of sequence by work done on the liana? What if the nucleotide sequence were not entirely conserved across species – how similar would the 'copied' sequence need to be to be considered an 'accessing' of the original sequence, or would it in some way rely upon Tvedt and Shei's 'functionality' and how would one determine or compare such 'functionalities'?

Although this is something of an extreme (though plausible) example, in practice claims over a right to control access are more likely to focus on a situation in which the nucleotide sequence (or sequences) encodes for something that is distinctive to the organism from which the sequence was determined. One might imagine here that our Ecuadorian liana contains exons which encode for an enzyme which catalyses the synthesis of a compound which is found to have anti-cancer properties. Where those exons are *only* to be found in that particular species of liana, then unique control to access may arguably be more easily justified. Of course, it may be that the sequences encoding for the production of that particular anti-cancer compound are found within a genus of liana (or that a family of very closely related compounds is found in that family). We might ask, does control over access extend to the entirety of the genus or to the entirety of the class of compounds? What degree of distinctiveness over other sequences and compounds is required? One reasonable definition of gene 'functionality' is the effect that the presence or absence of a gene has on the phenotypic characteristics of the host organism. In some cases that may be simple; in others it could be far less determinable.[83]

A related, but more granular, definition of functionality could mean the ability of a gene to make a protein which then goes on to perform a particular function. That function may, in turn, be to synthesise a further (non-protein) molecule which goes on to have a downstream function within the biochemistry of the cell. According to that definition, the claim to a particular genetic sequence would be rooted in the biochemical 'product' produced by expression of the sequence (and potentially the biological effect of that product).

Unfortunately, gene expression (in eukaryotes) is rarely simple. There are many levels of gene regulation, and the same string of genetic code on a chromosome can, through the process of alternative splicing of the DNA, code for a number of different protein isoforms. In this way the 'mere' 20,000 or so genes in the human

[83] Particularly where the phenotype is the result of the interaction of a number of separate genes.

genome can code for the very much greater number different proteins found in a human.[84] In humans it may be that around 95% of multi-exon protein-coding genes produce alternatively spliced protein variants.[85] In some cases, the different parts of a protein are even coded for on entirely different chromosomes.[86]

The correlation between protein amino acid sequence and the gene coding for it is yet further complicated (in both prokaryotes and eukaryotes) by the process of mRNA 'editing'. Here the nucleotide sequence in the mRNA is altered *before* protein synthesis, such that the amino acid in the final protein will differ from that which would ordinarily have been predicted from the nucleotide sequence in the encoding gene.[87]

Given sufficient understanding of the relevant genome–proteome linkage, reading back from the biochemical 'product' to the code is perhaps not impossible. However, the complexity, and required level of understanding of the relevant gene expression–protein linkage may well significantly complicate claims to a particular piece of genetic information. In particular, since many different proteins can be manufactured from the same gene, claims over genetic information based upon protein functionality may give rise to multiple separate (and perhaps competing) claims over a single gene.

Yet further complication may arise where third parties claim a degree of difference in the functionality and structure of 'their' protein relative to that found in the claimed genetic resource. As between different species (say the liana and the yeast), even where the primary peptide sequence of a protein is identical, there would very likely be a difference in the types and nature of post-translational modification/glycosylation of the protein,[88] which in itself can be a major determinant of functionality.[89] Essentially, although they would appear *similar*, they would not be identical and they may have subtle differences in function. How much functional similarity would be required for the protein in the yeast to be considered the same as that in the liana?

These are not insurmountable difficulties when looking at, say, medicines regulation (for example, see the treatment of 'biosimilars' by medicines regulatory agencies),[90] or indeed in patent litigation. However, in both cases, the definition of the required functionality has been established by the regulatory applicant,

[84] Carey (n 24) 53; see also K Kampourakis, *Making Sense of Genes* (Cambridge, Cambridge University Press, 2017) 75.

[85] Lesk (n 21) 8.

[86] S Schoenfelder et al, 'Preferential Associations Between Co-regulated Genes Reveal a Transcriptional Interactome in Erythroid Cells' (2010) 42 *Nature Genetics* 53. See also Kampourakis, (n 84) 77.

[87] Lesk (n 21) 9.

[88] See eg G Walsh and R Jefferis, 'Post-translational Modifications in the Context of Therapeutic Proteins' (2006) 24 *Nature Biotechnology* 1241.

[89] See eg LH Zhai et al, 'Proteomic Characterization of Post-translational Modifications in Drug Discovery' (2022) 43 *Acta Pharmacologica Sinica* 3112.

[90] See, for example, such treatment by the European Medicines Agency: www.ema.europa.eu/ema/index.jsp?curl=pages/medicines/general/general_content_001832.jspandmid=WC0b01ac0580bb8fda.

or patentee, in *very* detailed terms and that detail forms part of the basis of the grant of exclusivity to the right holder. It is not at all clear how such a requirement could be accommodated within the Nagoya Protocol as it stands. Moving from control over *physical* genetic resources to *informational* genetic resources will likely require an appreciation of concepts of 'firstness' and detailed claims to functionality – concepts more at home within the ambit of patent law and apparently not envisaged (and certainly not currently legislated for) within Articles 6 and 5(1) and (2) of the Nagoya Protocol.

No doubt as studies on the regulatory and other roles of non-coding DNA proceed, it may be that the interaction between non-coding regions of DNA and coding DNA (and with histones) becomes better understood. These findings may then be argued to be an important part of the information concerning the functionality of the 'functional units of heredity' and subject to access requirements. Some of the interactions may be found to be common across taxonomic groups and the question of why such generic interplays should be controlled under an ABS right will arise. The same problem will probably arise in relation to findings within the field of epigenetics.

Where the interaction between non-coding DNA and coding DNA is unique to a species, unique control to access over that interaction may be more easily justified. One should note here that the genetic control over the degree to which a particular gene or set of genes is expressed can be a crucial aspect of an organism. One example is the cinchona tree. Different strains of cinchona produce different quantities of quinine (and related alkaloids), a fact that has been responsible for significant examples of industrial espionage, geopolitics and military strategy.[91]

ii. 'Utilization'

Beyond the question of 'access', the synthetic DNA 'problem' also gives rise to questions concerning benefit sharing under Article 5 of the Nagoya Protocol. As we have seen above, the definition of 'utilization of genetic resources' at Article 2 of the Nagoya Protocol means to conduct research and development on the genetic and/or biochemical *composition* of genetic resources. So, does the use of a nucleotide sequence determined from an endogenous gene to generate a synthetic DNA strand constitute 'research' on the *composition* of original genetic resource and so pull that strand of synthetic DNA within the benefit-sharing provisions of Articles 5 regardless of the *physical* origin of the DNA molecule(s)? We saw in relation to the question of 'accessing' a genetic resource that making the leap from considering the resource to be an *informational* resource (rather than merely a *physical* resource) required an appeal to the purpose of the access requirements, something that could be assisted by reference to the 'functionality' of the functional

[91] MJ Balick and P Cox, *Plants, People, and Culture: The Science of Ethnobotany* (New York, Scientific American Library, 1997) 28; E Raviña, *The Evolution of Drug Discovery: From Traditional Medicines to Modern Drugs* (Weinheim, Wiley-VCH, 2011) 129.

unit of heredity.[92] One might sensibly argue that such interpretative strategies are not required where one is looking at research and development upon a genetic resources – research and development is inherently more about *information* than is the concept of access. However, although we may not have the question of what functionalities are required (and how we compare competing functionalities) we still have the significant questions over entitlement, 'originality' and 'substantive copying' with regard to sequences that are conserved across taxonomic groups – all concepts to which the Nagoya Protocol gives no guidance.

As with the question of access, it is again difficult to limit this definition of 'research' to that (exonic) DNA which is expressed as a protein alone without taking account of intragenic and extragenic non-coding DNA and epigenetics.

iii. 'Digital Sequence Information' vs Genetic Information

The potential ability of synthetic biology to potentially undermine the genetic ABS provisions of the Nagoya Protocol has provoked significant debate amongst parties to, and commentators on, the Nagoya Protocol. Indeed, the Commission Notice takes a robust position that: 'as the reference to Derivatives in the Nagoya Protocol is to *naturally occurring* biochemical compounds the definition does not cover material such as synthetic gene segments'.[93] In addition, they go one to state that: 'the Nagoya Protocol deals with access to and utilisation of genetic resources *as such* and therefore does not regulate issues concerning digital information obtained from genetic resources'.[94]

The question of the control over genetic information was identified at the Thirteenth Conference of the Parties (COP) to the UN CBD in December 2016 as being one that required very detailed investigation.[95] In February 2018, the COP's Ad Hoc Technical Expert Group (AHTEG) on 'Digital Sequence Information' (DSI) of Genetic Resources presented a detailed report[96] on the concerns raised under consultation, and this report was considered at the Fourteenth COP in November 2018.[97] This Fourteenth COP adopted Decision 14/20 which noted the wide divergence of views of parties on this matter and decided to establish a science- and policy-based process, which included the convening of an extended AHTEG.[98] In 2020 the AHTEG published a yet further detailed report on the meaning and implications of DSI.[99] This incorporated an analysis by Houssen,

[92] PJ Schei and MW Tvedt '"Genetic Resources" in the CBD: The Wording, the Past, the Present and the Future' (Fridtjof Nansen Institute Report 4, 2010) www.fni.no/docandpdf/FNI-R0410.pdf; Tvedt and Schei (n 77) 18.
[93] Commission Notice (n 29) para 2.3.3.
[94] ibid.
[95] CBD/COP/DEC/XIII/16.
[96] CBD/DSI/AHTEG/2018/1/4.
[97] CBD/NP/MOP/3/1.
[98] CBD/COP/DEC/14/20, 30 November 2018.
[99] CBD/DSI/AHTEG/2020/1/3.

Sara and Jaspars.[100] For this author, that analysis provides one of the most rigorous, in-depth, technical analysis of what the term 'DSI' means and the problems inherent in containing the threat posed by synthetic biology within the limits of the CBD. It is worth noting that although the term 'DSI' has become very widely used amongst parties to, and commentators on, the Nagoya Protocol, it is itself a highly contested term. Houssen et al note that: '[DSI] is widely acknowledged as a placeholder term for which no consensus on a replacement or precise definition exists to date.'[101]

Houssen et al examine the very wide range of terminologies that have been used to capture the wide variety of 'genetic informations' that exist within the CBD-related discussions. Amongst the broadest terminologies described by Houssen et al are 'Dematerialised Genetic Resources' (DGR) and 'Genetic Information'. As described by Houssen et al, DGR refers to

> the informational aspects of genetic resources. It includes the acquisition, digitalization, storage and dissemination of DNA sequences from genetic resources. The separation between the provider of the genetic resource and the eventual user as well as the digital nature of the data prompts the use of the word 'dematerialized'. This information can then be 're-materialized' through gene synthesis and incorporation in living modified organisms (genetic modified organisms). This may only cover the DNA and RNA sequences of these genetic resources, but the word 'dematerialized' may include all types of information relating to the genetic resources.

For Houssen et al, 'Genetic Information' is a 'collective term used to refer to information derived from genetic resources, plant materials and viruses. It is a catch-all term used in discussions around the information under the CBD and the Nagoya Protocol.' Due to its arguably greater breadth, the term Genetic Information will be used throughout this work.

Discussions on the inclusion of DSI within the ABS regime of the Nagoya Protocol remain ongoing.[102] At the 2022 Fifteenth CBD COP, Decision 15/9 was adopted.[103] This again recognises the divergent views on DSI on genetic resources with regard to its scope under the CBD but seeks to ensure that the parties 'develop a solution for the sharing of benefits arising from the use of digital sequence information on genetic resources'. It is worth noting that alongside this decision the Fifteenth COP also concluded the Kunming–Montreal GBF.[104] As was stated at

[100] W Houssen et al, 'Digital Sequence Information on Genetic Resources: Concept, Scope and Current Use' (2020) Annex to CBD/DSI/AHTEG/2020/1/3.

[101] ibid.

[102] C Lawson et al, 'The Future of Information Under the CBD, Nagoya Protocol, Plant Treaty, and PIP Framework' (2019) 22 *Journal of World Intellectual Property* 1; JC Medaglia, 'Digital Sequence Information (DSI) and Benefit-Sharing Arising from its Use: An Unfinished Discussion.' (2020) 69(6) *GRUR International* 565; F Rohden and AH Scholz, 'The International Political Process Around Digital Sequence Information Under the Convention on Biological Diversity and the 2018–2020 Intersessional Period' (2022) 4(1) *Plants, People, Planet* 51.

[103] CBD/COP/DEC/15/9, 19 December 2022.

[104] CBD/COP/DEC/15/4, 19 December 2022.

chapter two, section II.D, Goal C of the GBF states that benefits from the utilisation of genetic resources and *digital sequence information on genetic resources*, and of traditional knowledge associated with genetic resources, should be shared fairly and equitably. DSI is not defined within the GBF and the framework itself affirms that, amongst others, Decisions 15/9 is of equal standing to the GBF itself. So, although Goal C is clearly highly aspirational in relation to the inclusion of 'digital sequence information on genetic resources' within ABS provisions of the CBD instruments, it does not help our understanding of its meaning.

Whilst the debate on the treatment of synthetic DNA continues within the CBD processes, as has been described at chapter two, section II.E, the UN has separately finalised the 2023 BBNJ Treaty adopted to address the conservation and sustainable use of marine biological diversity of areas beyond national jurisdiction. Article 14(1) of the BBNJ Treaty states that: 'The benefits arising from activities with respect to marine genetic resources and *digital sequence information on marine genetic resources* of areas beyond national jurisdiction shall be shared in a fair and equitable manner in accordance with this Part' [emphasis added].

It is noticeable that 'digital sequence information on marine genetic resources' is here not being used as a contested 'place holder' – it has been deliberately inserted as an operative term. Indeed, it is a term that appears at thirty places throughout the BBNJ Treaty. However, at no place is DSI defined within the treaty (even though the treaty does make an effort to define 'Biotechnology', 'Marine genetic resources' and 'Utilization of marine genetic resources' very much in line with the wording of equivalent terms within the CBD and the Nagoya Protocol). How 'digital sequence information on marine genetic resources' will be interpreted within the context of the BBNJ Treaty is at present unclear. However, the BBNJ Treaty is the first biodiversity treaty to be concluded after the signing of the Kunming–Montreal GBF and it clearly follows the aspirations of Goal C of that framework. Not providing a definition of 'digital sequence information on marine genetic resources' is for some commentators a deliberate policy, and perhaps the intention is that during the implementation of the BBNJ Treaty the understanding of that term will be informed by the decisions arising out of the CBD deliberations and the overall purpose of the CBD.[105]

B. Genetic Information 2: Are 'Biomimetics' Covered within the Definition of 'Utilization of Genetic Resources'?

In addition to genetic information relating to genetic material (in its many diverse forms) there is, arguably, a second type of genetic information which is accessed/

[105] P Oldham et al, 'Digital Sequence Information in the UN High Seas Treaty: Insights from the Global Biodiversity Framework-Related Decisions' (LSE Law-Policy Briefing Paper, 2023) 53, papers.ssrn.com/sol3/papers.cfm?abstract_id=4343130.

utilised when an exact chemical copy of the endogenous biochemical found within the genetic resource is created by de novo synthesis, what will be termed here a 'biomimetic'.

Let us assume that a compound of potential interest ('X') has been isolated from the Ecuadorian liana discussed above. As has been discussed in detail above, it is likely that 'utilization of a genetic resource' would encompass research and development on compound X (if not, perhaps, a downstream chemical derivative of compound X). Part of that research would almost certainly be to characterise the chemical structure of that compound through analytical chemistry. Once the structure of X is characterised it can be set out in a structural formula. That information could be taken by a synthetic chemist whose task is to perform a de novo synthesis of X. If that task is successful, the synthetic chemist would have created a compound – termed here X^S – which although an *exact* copy ('biomimetic') of X was not *physically* derived from the Ecuadorian liana: the only connection between X^S and X that is physically derived from the Ecuadorian liana (termed here X^O) is a link of *information* – the knowledge of the structure of X, knowledge that has been derived from studying the original genetic resource.

If we take the approach of those who believe that the term 'Derivative' expands the meaning of 'genetic resource', we might ask whether biomimetics are actually 'a naturally occurring biochemical compound resulting from the genetic expression or metabolism of biological or genetic resources'. Clearly, in one narrow sense they are not, in that they have not *physically* been produced by the genetic expression or metabolism of the particular organism in question. However, where X^S is (as is entirely possible) chemically indistinguishable from X^O, one might argue that it has still *resulted* (in a broader causal sense) from genetic expression or metabolism of biological or genetic resources; our knowledge of its structure would not exist *but for* the genetic expression or metabolism of biological or genetic resources.

If one places no importance on the term 'Derivative' (other than merely to serve to define the tool by which the research and development is conducted), then one is forced back to looking at the definition of 'utilization' more broadly. As has been argued above, 'utilization' is likely to encompass research on the products of genetic expression or metabolism in any event. One might argue that where there is no physical difference between X^S and X^O, there is no practical difference in performing research upon X^S as on X^O. Also as above, it was the knowledge of the structure of X^O that allowed us to synthesise X^S in the first place. Excluding X^S from control would seem here like a relatively easy way to avoid the provisions of the Nagoya Protocol, given that the compound differs only in that it was made in a laboratory de novo, as opposed to being extracted from the organism.

However, just as was the case for synthetic DNA, we encounter a dilemma. Where one severs the direct *physical* causal link between the genetic resource and X^O, the causal route to X^S has to pass through an indirect *information* stage. In the case of synthetic DNA we looked at the position where a conserved exonic gene sequence found in an Ecuadorian liana could have equally been found in our Burton-on-Trent yeast. What if we apply that example to the product (our compound X) of the gene sequence? Here X^O can be as equally found in the liana as in the yeast.[106] In this sense there is nothing special about the genetic resources of the *liana* – other than that X was discovered in the liana first.

A control over utilisation of the information concerning the structure X – such that control could be exercised over the use of X^S would here be based upon 'first-ness' – was again not a concept apparently envisaged (or legislated for) within Articles 6 and 5(1) and (2) of the Nagoya Protocol.

XIII. Genetic Expression and Downstream Derivatives

Does the concept of 'genetic information' discussed above give us any further guidance in relation to the question of whether the scope of Article 6 and Article 5(1) and (2) of the Nagoya Protocol encompasses man-made chemical derivatives of the products of genetic expression?

If a genetic resource (which can incorporate the products of expression of the genes within the resource) can be interpreted not only as a *physical* resource but as an *informational* resource, might one argue that if the informational causal chain can extend to the reproduction of nucleotide sequences (or to the reproduction of biomimetic copies (X^S of X^O)), it could also extend to an X-A downstream chemical derivative of or X^O (or X^S)?

As we saw above, it is unclear on a doctrinal analysis of the Nagoya Protocol whether it clearly covers downstream chemical derivatives. As with our biomimetic, once one moves into an informational (rather than physical) causal chain the potential causal reach becomes greater. One might very successfully argue that it was the knowledge of the existence of compound X (found within the Ecuadorian liana) which led to the synthesis of X-A (or indeed of X-B or any other combination). However, allocating a right to control downstream use of *information* where that compound could have equally been found expressed by the genome of an organism in a different taxonomic group comes to rely on an idea of firstness and 'copying'. These are certainly difficult concepts to deal with in relation to a genetic resource per se – in a sense the right in information only comes into existence once the scientific information (nucleotide sequence or biochemical structure) has been 'harvested' by someone from the genetic resource – it is difficult to envisage how such a right in the information can exist in the genetic resource in an inchoate form *before* such discovery.

Although reliance upon an informational causal link is problematic with regard to genetic resources per se (and was perhaps not fully envisaged by the formulators of the Nagoya Protocol), the move from a physical causal link to an *informational*

[106] This would be true for a small molecule. For proteins, even where the primary peptide sequence is identical, there is likely to be a difference in the post-translational modification/glycosylation of the protein as between the liana and the yeast.

causal link is the key element of the protections given in Articles 7 and 5(5) of the Nagoya Protocol. It is possible therefore that the scope of protection offered by these provisions will be significantly more flexible than the protections offered by Article 6 and 5(1) and (2) (and quite clearly some informational link was entirely intended by the formulators of the Nagoya Protocol), and it is to these positive protections that we will now turn.

XIV. The Right to Control 'Access' to TKAGR under Article 7

As we have seen, Article 7 of the Nagoya Protocol requires 'the prior and informed consent or approval and involvement of these indigenous and local communities, and that mutually agreed terms have been established' before TKAGR can be 'accessed'. As with the access right under Article 6, it is difficult to see this requirement for prior consent/approval as creating anything other than a positive right, although the right is not formulated as one might a classical intellectual property right. Again, however, we are left with the question of what 'access' means in this context. The Nagoya Protocol itself gives us no guidance.

When we examined the meaning of 'access' as it relates to genetic resources per se we saw that access could mean merely the first physical access of the resource or, as was argued by the provider countries, a broader concept of ongoing 'access' wherein new permissions were required for new 'accessings' of the resource. Similar arguments can apply in relation to the Article 7 right although taking into account the markedly different subject matter.

TKAGR has no internationally accepted definition.[107] However, in relation to potentially useful genetic resources it is perhaps best described as the knowledge (however held, whosoever held by, and however widely) that tells us that any type of genetic resource may be useful and the ways it can used and prepared to give that usefulness. Of course, the usefulness of a genetic resource (and the information associated with it) may not relate to a therapeutic benefit – one might imagine here a plant with particular drought-, pest- or disease-resistance. Similarly there is an entire body of traditional knowledge that is *not* limited to useful organisms. Within this body is subset of traditional knowledge which relates to therapeutic benefits (or purported benefits) which are *not* linked to genetic resources (these might include therapies related to variants of acupuncture or cupping or body modification (such as tattoos), or variants of body manipulations such as reflexology, osteopathy and chiropractic). There will also be traditional knowledge which relates to neither therapeutic benefits nor genetic resource per se; this will include traditional cultural expression and other knowledge such as presence of mineral and water resources, animal migration and climate patterns. Of course, it

[107] Commission Notice (n 29) para 2.3.2.

is the intersection between the subsets of therapeutic traditional knowledge and TKAGR that is likely to be of most interest to those seeking to develop 'novel' pharmaceutical ligands. However, we need to note that the very nature of traditional knowledge held within Indigenous groups means that many of these subsets are, in practice, artificial and would probably not correspond to how the Indigenous peoples, themselves, perceive such knowledge. The knowledge may have unclear edges and overlaps within a particular customary activity – for example, where a plant (or mixture of plants) is used to induce euphoria/hallucination within a broader ceremonial activity.[108]

Notwithstanding these classifications, crucially (and obviously) traditional knowledge is not a *physical* resource but an *informational* one and this changes the very nature of how it can be accessed. Access in the form of mere physical acquisition cannot apply; although traditional knowledge can be recorded in physical form, it is certainly not limited to such form. The 'acquisition' here is instead conceptual and the acquiring of the concept could certainly be argued to be access to the information. However, does this mean that it is only the *first* acquisition of the concept from the holders of the information which is the 'accessing' event? One might imagine here that an ethnobiologist obtains the first disclosure from a particular Indigenous group in Ecuador of the anti-tumour effects of ground-up liana seeds. It is hard to argue that such an event is other than an 'accessing' for the purpose of Article 7. However, what about the case where our ethnobiologist publishes her findings and a third-party uses them to find the appropriate liana for anti-cancer research purposes – is the initial reading the accessing or the acting upon that reading to source the liana?

Given the overall purpose of the Nagoya Protocol (and the access provisions of Article 6) it would seem perverse to limit access to the very *first* accessing event – a 'one-off' event, a single dipping into the 'well' of Indigenous information, after which all further use of the information is permitted. Indeed, given the overall context of the Nagoya Protocol, it would seem more consistent that each new user should require consent to access (and that for each user continued 'access' to a piece of TKAGR requires *continual* ongoing consent from the holders of the traditional knowledge for use of the knowledge). If this were not the case the provisions of Article 7 would be limited and easily evaded.

However, where one creates a requirement for ongoing consent to 'access' in relation to something as intangible as an idea, the potential is there for the scope of control to be very broad indeed. Does the reference to prior informed consent here mean that that consent must encompass all continued usage of (alternatively put as continued 'access' to) the information and that *any* new use of the information, howsoever remote, requires permission? What about the pharmacologist who tests the liana extract against tumour cells? What about the

[108] For example, see the use of *ayawasca* by the indigenous peoples of the Amazonian Basin. See DJ Campos, *Shaman and Ayahuasca – Journeys to Sacred Realms* (San Francisco, Divine Arts, 2011).

synthetic chemist who makes a chemical derivative of that extract, and so on? When is the information no longer being *used*? The Nagoya Protocol is silent as to these questions.

When examining the meaning of 'access' as it applies to 'genetic resources' under Article 6 we saw that (provided there was physical causal link between the source of the subject matter being controlled and access) the scope of control was relatively easily determined (subject to questions over chemical derivatives). However, we also saw that with extension of control into synthetic DNA and biomimetics there was a decoupling from physical causation to an *informational* causal link which was dependent upon detailed knowledge of a particular nucleotide sequence or chemical structure. We also saw that where the physical causal link became decoupled we came to rely more on questions of 'firstness' and 'discovery' or 'originality' to identify the party who should have control.

At this point we need to be clear that the Nagoya Protocol has no requirement that the Indigenous peoples have to have any understanding of the biological mechanism by which the organism to which they are referring has its effect. Indeed, any such requirement would render the provisions of Article 7 essentially useless. One might imagine a situation in which an Indigenous people mistakenly believed a therapeutic benefit was derived from a fruit, whereas in fact the effect was created by a mould growing within the fruit of which they were unaware. It is hard to imagine that such a mistaken belief would render the Indigenous group's Article 7 right of control over the information as in some way invalidated by this error. However, as we shall see later in this work (in chapter six) there may be an impact on the scope of control where the 'errors' are of a different nature.

In relation to a right to control access under Article 7 there appears to be no requirement that a piece of traditional knowledge should be connected to a *specific* physical sample of genetic resource – indeed such a requirement would be overly restrictive, and would (again) clearly lead to the Article 7 right being easily evaded.

Article 7 also contains no express requirement for the information to be used in any particular way. There is no requirement within Article 7 (unlike Article 6(1)) that the genetic resource with which a piece of traditional knowledge is associated should simultaneously be 'utilised' as seems to be the case Article 6(1). If this were the case, then one successfully might argue that the scope of Article 7 would be curtailed by the definition of 'utilization of genetic resources' (whatever that actually means).

However, in the absence of such an express link there seems little basis to assume that Article 7 is so restricted. Therefore, TKAGR can realistically only mean information that relates to the characteristics and properties of a 'genetic resource' more generally. 'Genetic resource' here, of course, means material of plant, animal, microbial or other origin containing functional units of heredity that are of actual or potential value. Presumably, *any* information relating to a particular plant, animal, microbe or other organism (presumably also covering fungi) containing functional units of heredity will be covered.

XV. The Right to Benefit-Sharing under Article 5(5)

Article 5(5) of the Nagoya Protocol states that:

> Each Party shall take legislative, administrative or policy measures, as appropriate, in order that the benefits arising from the utilization of traditional knowledge associated with genetic resources are shared in a fair and equitable way with indigenous and local communities holding such knowledge. Such sharing shall be upon mutually agreed terms.

As discussed in relation to the sharing of benefits under Articles 5(1) and (2), although the requirement for fair and equitable sharing of benefits does not, of itself, create a right to control use, the requirement that such sharing should be on mutually agreed terms arguably creates such a right.

The key term in relation to understanding the scope of such a right is clearly 'utilization of traditional knowledge associated with genetic resources'. Unlike 'utilization of genetic resources', this term is not expressly defined within the Nagoya Protocol or the CBD. As with 'access' to TKAGR under Article 7, it is clear that such use does not have to relate to a specific *physical* sample of a genetic resource. Morgera et al[109] suggest that 'utilization of traditional knowledge associated with genetic resources' needs to be understood 'by combining different elements of the Nagoya Protocol' and that the term can be 'interpreted along similar lines to the definition of utilization of genetic resources'. However, as we have seen in the analysis above, the meaning of 'utilization of genetic resources' (and also 'access to genetic resources') is far from clear, particularly where the purported causal link is *informational* rather than physical. We should also note that although there is no doubt that the provisions of Article 7 and Article 5(5) should work together with Article 6 and Article 5(1) and (2) where appropriate, the meaning of 'utilization of traditional knowledge associated with genetic resources' does not seem to be expressly linked to, or restricted by, the definition of 'utilization of genetic resources', nor is there any requirement that 'utilization of genetic resources' should occur alongside the 'utilization of traditional knowledge associated with genetic resources' (although there will, of course, be many occasions when both will happen concurrently).

What Morgera et al actually go on to imply is something distinctly different from (and broader than) 'utilization of genetic resources', suggesting that where the traditional knowledge 'serve[s] as lead information for the utilisation of genetic resources, it can be understood as hinging on the same intent (research and development) as genetic resources'.[110] Here Morgera et al reflect the view of the Ad Hoc Open-Ended Inter-Sessional Working Group on Article 8(J) and Related Provisions of the Convention on Biological Diversity which states that: 'In essence, traditional knowledge that sparks the process or provides the lead

[109] Morgera (n 16) 74.
[110] Morgera (n 16) 74.

to the properties of a genetic resource although it may not be reflected in the end-product remains associated to that product.'[111] They also reflect the view of the Group of Technical and Legal Experts on Traditional Knowledge Associated with Genetic Resources in the Context of the International Regime on Access and Benefit-Sharing, which stated:

> traditional knowledge often provides the lead to genetic resources with potential properties, even if the traditional knowledge does not match the end product. Thus it should nevertheless be covered by the International Regime. Although the traditional knowledge used for the final product may not match the body of traditional knowledge, traditional knowledge adds value to genetic resources by providing a massive increase of efficiency in identifying genetic resources with potential properties. Traditional knowledge can therefore be considered as an indicator of the potential properties of a genetic resource. At the same time, it was noted by some that traditional knowledge does not always provide useful leads to genetic resources.[112]

The work of these UNEP expert groups was not incorporated as clarification into the operative provisions of the Nagoya Protocol.[113] However, what they seem to envisage is something decidedly broader than utilisation of genetic resources per se. If this position were incorporated into our understanding of the right created by Article 5(5), it would allow the right to encompass a situation where a piece of traditional knowledge serves as a 'lead' (or inspiration) to research workers to investigate the properties of the genetic resource to which the traditional knowledge relates – essentially giving a reason to look at this particular resource in a particular way, rather than others. The position also acknowledges that the information could attach itself to a downstream product that did not necessarily 'match' or 'reflect' the original traditional knowledge. This broader understanding of 'utilization of traditional knowledge associated with genetic resources' would appear to be consistent with the overall context of the Nagoya Protocol and of Article 8(j) of the CBD. However, we cannot determine from these positions whether the scope of Article 5(5) should extend to *all* downstream products, in *all* circumstances.

Before concluding this analysis of the nature of the Nagoya Protocol positive right over TKAGR Article 5(5) and Article 7, it is necessary to understand the effect of two other articles of the Nagoya Protocol which are both important in understanding the way in which a right to control TKAGR could be used in practice. The first is the 'General' TKAGR provision at Article 12(1) and the second are the special considerations under Article 8, and it is to those that we will now turn.

[111] Report of the Sixth Meeting of the Ad Hoc Open-Ended Inter-Sessional Working Group on Article 8(J) and Related Provisions of the Convention on Biological Diversity, Conference of the Parties to the Convention on Biological Diversity Tenth Meeting Nagoya, Japan, 18–29 October 2010, 36, www.cbd.int/doc/meetings/cop/cop-10/official/cop-10-02-en.pdf.

[112] Report of the Meeting of the Group of Technical and Legal Experts on Traditional Knowledge Associated with Genetic Resources in the Context of the International Regime on Access and Benefit-Sharing, Montreal, 9–15 November 2009 (UNEP/CBD/WG-ABS/8/2) 8, www.cbd.int/doc/meetings/abs/abswg-08/official/abswg-08-02-en.pdf.

[113] United Nations Environmental Program.

XVI. The 'General' TKAGR Provision at Article 12(1)

Article 12(1) of the Nagoya Protocol contains an overarching provision that:

> In implementing their obligations under this Nagoya Protocol, Parties shall in accordance with domestic law take into consideration indigenous and local communities' customary laws, community Nagoya Protocols and procedures, as applicable, with respect to traditional knowledge associated with genetic resources.

Although the provision has been described as an 'unprecedented recognition of legal pluralism in international treaty law',[114] Morgera et al comment that this provision gives a considerable degree of discretion to parties in that it requires only that parties 'take into consideration' customary laws, community protocols and procedures of Indigenous and local communities rather than to formally recognise or apply such customary law.[115] Therefore, it may, at a minimum, require parties to identify and understand the relevant customary laws, community protocols and procedures, even if we cannot be certain how such customary laws will impact on a party's implementation of the Nagoya Protocol.[116]

What is the effect of this 'general' provision? The first point to note is that it clearly applies to *all* provisions of the Nagoya Protocol, including to access and benefit sharing of genetic resources. The second point to note is that it requires *only* that parties take into consideration Indigenous and local communities' customary laws, community protocols and procedures that relate respect to TKAGR. Given the stronger rights provided to Indigenous peoples to control TKAGR (under Articles 7 and 5(5)), then where an Indigenous group is in possession of TKAGR, it is difficult to clearly determine what further benefits Article 12(1) would provide to it.

Of course, Article 5(2) of the Nagoya Protocol gives Indigenous groups the ability to control the 'utilization' of *genetic* resources that are 'held' by Indigenous and local communities, in accordance with domestic legislation regarding the 'established rights of these indigenous and local communities over these genetic resources', and Article 6(2) provides for an Indigenous group to control access to a genetic resource where that group has an 'established right to grant access to such resources'. It is unclear what such 'holding' or 'established right to grant access to such resources' means in this context. It is also difficult to easily envisage where such rights over genetic resources (as such) would exist entirely without the involvement of some aspect TKAGR. So, it may be here (in the application of Articles 5(2) and 6(2)) that the general provisions of Article 12(1) as to the 'taking account of' TKAGR-related customary law may apply. Such situations, and

[114] K Bavikatte and DF Robinson, 'Towards a People's History of the Law: Biocultural Jurisprudence and the Nagoya Protocol on Access and Benefit Sharing' (2011) 7 *Law, Environment and Development Journal* 35, 45.

[115] Morgera (n 16) 217.

[116] ibid.

the relevant customary laws, are likely to be very case specific, so it is difficult to come to general conclusions. However, the broad applicability of Article 12(1) may serve to prevent the creation of case-specific lacunae that would disadvantage Indigenous holders of TKAGR.

XVII. Special Considerations

In considering the downstream scope of the TKAGR provisions of the Nagoya Protocol it is worth considering that the prior informed consent and benefit-sharing requirements set out within the Nagoya Protocol may not be entirely absolute. At Article 8 the Nagoya Protocol requires that each party shall in the development and implementation of its access and benefit-sharing legislation or regulatory requirements:

> Article 8(a)
>
> Create conditions to promote and encourage research which contributes to the conservation and sustainable use of biological diversity, particularly in developing countries, including through simplified measures on access for non-commercial research purposes, taking into account the need to address a change of intent for such research; and
>
> Article 8(b)
>
> Pay due regard to cases of present or imminent emergencies that threaten or damage human, animal or plant health, as determined nationally or internationally. Parties may take into consideration the need for expeditious access to genetic resources and expeditious fair and equitable sharing of benefits arising out of the use of such genetic resources, including access to affordable treatments by those in need, especially in developing countries.

A. The Effect of Article 8(a)

For Morgera et al[117] Article 8(a) is clearly designed to ensure that the Nagoya Protocol should not hamper scientific research into conservation and the sustainable use of biological diversity since the underlying rationale for the Nagoya Protocol is that it should not restrict the other aims of the Convention, being the 'conservation of biological diversity and the sustainable use of its components'.[118] Morgera et al suggest that the types of research covered by Article 8(a) would include 'taxonomy, microbial systems and ecology, ecosystem research, genomics and metagenomics', although this clearly far from an exhaustive list.[119] However,

[117] Morgera (n 16) 179.
[118] Nagoya Protocol, Art 1.
[119] Morgera (n 16) 180.

the key element of this provision is that the envisaged (and undefined) 'simplified measures' will apply only to work done for non-commercial purposes. This clearly acts as a major limitation of this relaxation. In a world in which there is significant commercial involvement in the funding (or partial funding) of even 'blue-sky' research, it may be difficult for research work to properly fall within Article 8(a). As Morgera et al highlight, problems may arise in properly falling within Article 8(a) where a research team uncovers a potential commercial use for the results of their previously non-commercial work, or if results or specimens obtained from non-commercial research are used by unrelated third parties to develop commercial products.[120] If the commercial purposes bar did not apply to those types of activity, then Article 8(a) would serve as a significant circumvention of the implementation of the ABS provisions of the Nagoya Protocol.

However, what is the position where research is originally done for the purposes of conservation and sustainable use of biological diversity and the results are used for further research used outwith these fields? For example, what happens if results were fed into biomedical research and drug discovery? Should we consider that to be within the field of 'sustainable use of biological diversity'? The Nagoya Protocol is silent on that point. Presumably if such work were non-commercial, then it would be unlikely to be too offensive to the spirit of the Nagoya Protocol. However, of course, within biomedical science research and drug discovery the divide between commercial and non-commercial research is particularly permeable.

Morgera et al note that the first element of Article 8(a), that Parties should 'create conditions to promote and encourage research which contributes to the conservation and sustainable use of biological diversity, particularly in developing countries', will apply to *both* non-commercial and commercial research although what this would mean in practice is unclear.[121]

It is also important to note that Article 8(a) mentions only 'simplified measures' on *access* (rather than in relation to benefit sharing). Article 8(a) also does not distinguish between access to genetic resources and TKAGR. Morgera et al note that this would suggest that in relation to the promotion and encouragement of commercial research on conservation and sustainable use of biological diversity, the prior informed consent provisions of Article 7 will apply in full (which is complementary to Article 8(j) of the CBD).[122] However, in relation to non-commercial research on conservation and sustainable use of biological diversity, the prior informed consent provisions of Article 7 would be subject to the 'simplified measures on access' relaxation (whatever that may be).

We should note, however, that the 'simplified measures on access' to both TKAGR and genetic resources under Article 8(a) would presumably be subject

[120] ibid.
[121] ibid 183.
[122] ibid, 184.

to the broader overarching requirement at Article 12(1) of the Nagoya Protocol that parties should 'take into consideration indigenous and local communities' customary laws, community Nagoya Protocols and procedures, as applicable, with respect to traditional knowledge associated with genetic resources'. As is discussed in section XVI above, the broad effect of Article 12(1) is unclear and any particular application of it would likely be very case-specific. Therefore, it is difficult to come to any certain view of what a party's 'taking into consideration' under Article 12(1) would look like when applied to in Article 8(a) in general.

B. The Effect of Article 8(b)

How are we to read the effect of Article 8(b)? Its drafting could certainly be clearer. For Wilke, its aim is that parties 'ensure that public health objectives can be met and are indeed supported by access as well as benefit sharing rules'.[123] As Morgera et al highlight, the first point to note is that it does not require parties to 'create conditions' (as per Article 8(a)) merely to 'pay due regard' to health emergencies.[124] It also not does require 'simplified access' but requires merely 'expeditious' access to 'genetic resources' and 'expeditious fair and equitable sharing of benefits arising out of the use of such genetic resources'. What such expeditious access or benefit sharing means in practice is, again, unclear. Morgera et al suggest that it does not mean a suspension of access and benefit-sharing rules, but merely that parties should 'fast track' access to ensure that their usual processes do not cause undue delay during an emergency.[125]

When would such a requirement for 'expeditious' access to 'genetic resources' and 'expeditious fair and equitable sharing of benefits arising out of the use of such genetic resources' come into effect? Article 8(b) states that it requires 'present or imminent emergencies that threaten or damage human, animal or plant health, as determined nationally or internationally'. For Wilke, the wording is sufficiently broad to encompass emergencies that pose a threat not only to human and animal health, but also to biodiversity.[126] The reference to international emergency would certainly cover such a declaration by the WHO, but for Morgera et al it would also include similar declarations under the International Plant Protection Convention and the World Organisation for Animal Health.[127] The reference to national emergency certainly provides for a wide range of flexibility on the part of a state.

[123] M Wilke, 'A Healthy Look at the Nagoya Protocol – Implications for Global Health Governance' in E Morgera et al (eds), *The 2010 Protocol on Access and Benefit-sharing in Perspective: Implications for International Law and Implementation Challenges* (Leiden, Martinus Nijhoff, 2012) 123, 126.

[124] Morgera (n 16) 185.

[125] ibid 187.

[126] Wilke (n 123) 128–30.

[127] Morgera (n 16) 186.

What type of genetic resources are we talking about here? On the face of the wording of Article 8, it would certainly seem to include the genetic resource that was the cause of the crisis, for example, a pathogen such as a virus or bacterium. Wilke mentions the 2006 avian flu crisis in which the government of Indonesia had, for surveillance and research purposes, shared samples of the H5N1 virus found in Indonesia with the WHO.[128] Having discovered that an Australian company had developed a vaccine based on that H5N1 sample (and was applying for a patent for the technology), Indonesia stated that its supply of a sample to WHO did not incorporate consent for that sample to be used for development of a commercial product and that this commercial use was in violation of the Indonesia's sovereignty over its genetic resources.[129] Presumably Article 8(b) would have operated in this situation not to have entirely suspended Indonesia's rights over its genetic resources set out in the Nagoya Protocol but to have required Indonesia's 'expedition' of access and benefit-sharing processes.

What about a situation in which a genetic resource is utilised to produce an endogenous substance that treats a condition that has been declared an international or national emergency? Such a situation is perhaps less likely to occur than the pathogenic genetic resources example presented above; however, it is certainly not impossible. This chapter has discussed in detail whether use of endogenous substances (or downstream drugs) fall within the definition of utilisation of a genetic resource and that will not be rehearsed here – we will assume for current purposes that use of an endogenous substance is utilisation of a genetic resource. It is worth noting in that regard that Article 8(b) refers to the broader term genetic 'resource' rather than the narrower genetic 'material'. Presumably in such a situation when an emergency has been called the effect of Article 8(b) will be to require 'expedition' of access and benefit-sharing processes relating to the endogenous substance.

However, for the current purposes of this work the crucial observation in relation to Article 8(b) is that it expressly refers to expediting access and the benefit-sharing process in relation to genetic resources *only*. It does not expressly mention TKAGR or speak generally of access and benefit sharing (as does Article 8(a)). This suggests that the TKAGR provisions of the Nagoya Protocol are intended not to be affected by Article 8(b) and so would continue to apply even in a present or imminent health crisis. Morgera et al highlight that 'there might be situations in which a conflict arises between international human rights ie the rights of indigenous and local communities over their traditional knowledge and the right to health of the general population', This a key point to which we will return (see chapter six, section IV.C).

[128] Wilke (n 123) 121.

[129] See generally ER Sedyaningsih et al, 'Towards Mutual Trust, Transparency and Equity in Virus Sharing Mechanism: The Avian Influenza Case of Indonesia' (2008) 37 *Annals of the Academy of Medicine Singapore* 486.

The operation of Article 8(b) is potentially complicated given that the expedition of processes required under Article 8(b) would presumably be subject to the broader overarching requirement at Article 12(1) of the Nagoya Protocol that parties should 'take into consideration indigenous and local communities' customary laws, community protocols and procedures, as applicable, with respect to traditional knowledge associated with genetic resources'. However, as discussed in section XVI above, the broad effect of Article 12(1) is unclear and any particular application of it would likely be extremely case-specific. However, if Article 8(b) essentially applies to genetic resources that are not subject to the access and benefit-sharing provisions relating to TKAGR, and Article 12(1) relates to, inter alia, customary laws relating to TKAGR, it is hard to imagine exactly what type of expedition of access and benefit-sharing process would be subject to Article 12(1), but not fall within the TKAGR access and benefit-sharing provisions of Article 7 and Article 5(5).

XVIII. Conclusions: The Nature of the Nagoya Protocol Positive Right Over TKAGR

What we can conclude from the above analysis is that what seems to be missing from the 'positive' rights in relation to TKAGR under Article 5(5) and Article 7 of the Nagoya Protocol is any principle or guidance for determining a balance which combines fair protection for the traditional knowledge/genetic resources rights holders with a reasonable degree of legal certainty for third parties. Where such knowledge serves as a research 'lead' for subsequent development, the Nagoya Protocol itself gives no guidance as to how far that knowledge can have any 'reach through effect' into new scientific discoveries, or at what point a downstream researcher could consider themselves free of the traditional knowledge right.

However, beyond the determination of the scope of the provisions of the Nagoya Protocol, a more fundamental point highlighted by the current analysis is the disconnection between the concept of a genetic resource per se and that of traditional knowledge *associated with* that genetic resource. This disconnection might appear relatively obvious on initial examination if one equates a genetic resource only with its physical embodiment. However, when examining the meaning of 'genetic resource' we see that there is an argument that it extends beyond the mere *physical* embodiment of the resource to include a concept of genetic *information* which incorporates DNA sequences and even epigenetic code. If such genetic information is excluded from being considered a 'genetic resource', there would be substantial scope for evading a positive right to control the use of the genetic resource.[130] It is also argued in this chapter that a biochemical produced

[130] Although it is also noted that this could create some strange anomalies where a gene sequence is conserved across a wide range of taxonomic groups, some of which might be as easily accessed from countries other than the biodiverse Global South.

by the expression of the genome of a genetic resource should also be considered a component of a genetic resource (although the coverage of downstream chemical derivatives of such a component is less clear).

What is clear, however, is that, although traditional knowledge *associated with* a genetic resource is a species of information, it is of an unrelated type to the informational component of a genetic resource. Traditional knowledge *associated with* a genetic resource (though it may serve as a gateway to their study) is not related to DNA or epigenetics. Accordingly, arguments that are applied to extend the definition of a genetic resource cannot properly be used to extend the definition of TKAGR. Equally, however, the definition of a genetic resource does not delimit the meaning or scope of TKAGR and, in principle, the downstream scope of a right to control such traditional knowledge cannot be curtailed by considerations which would apply in relation to genetic 'information'. In this respect the TKAGR is a broader (and far less proscribed) concept than the informational component within the genetic resource.

4

The Philosophical Justifications for Positive Rights in TKAGR

I. Introduction

As was stated in chapter one, to understand the justifiable scope of a positive right to TKAGR we need to examine the theoretical underpinnings for the existence of rights to control the use of ideas (and their expression) in general, and then apply those theories to the case for the existence of a positive right in TKAGR in particular. This chapter will follow that approach. The first step, however, is to identify the special difficulties that the protection of intangible concepts present as these problems very much underlie the ways in which the theoretical underpinnings are brought into practical effect.

II. The 'Problem' of Intangibles

The power and value of an intellectual property right resides in its ability to limit the freedom of those who do not own the right to engage in certain activities. The degree to which it does this, and the exact activities that are curtailed, will depend on the exact nature of the right. However, at their heart all intellectual property rights confront a problem: they are an attempt through positive law (and the enforcement of that positive law) to create exclusivity in intangible goods that would otherwise be inherently difficult to control.[1]

A purely tangible object is (usually) relatively easily defined – its physical limits circumscribe the boundary of the thing itself. Similarly, use of a purely tangible object is rivalrous (or subtractable)[2] – this means that use by one person cannot help but deprive others of that particular use of the object (or subtract that use from the use of others). Its use can also (in theory, if not necessarily always in practice, and often subject to considerable cost) be excluded through physical

[1] C May, *The Political Economy of Intellectual Property Rights*, vol 1 (Cheltenham, Edward Elgar, 2010) x.

[2] C Hess and E Ostrom, 'Introduction' in C Hess and E Ostrom (eds), *Understanding Knowledge as a Commons: From Theory to Practice*. (Cambridge, MA, MIT Press, 2007) 3, 9; V Ostrom and E Ostrom, 'Public Goods and Public Choices' in ES Saras (ed), *Alternatives for Delivering Public Services: Toward Improved Performance* (Boulder, CO, Westview Press, 1977).

possession or physical control of access. As such, exclusivity in that tangible thing is relatively easily achieved. However, this is not the case for ideas, or for the varied ways in which an idea may be expressed.

The field of epistemology, what an idea *is* or how we can classify (or be certain of) knowledge, has been the subject of philosophical discourse for millennia.[3] For present purposes, however, we need to acknowledge that knowledge and ideas, and their expression, are at heart merely information. In distinct contrast to tangible objects, the use of information is non-rivalrous – my use of a piece of information cannot deprive another (or indeed many millions of others) from identical use of that information. Similarly, in contrast to tangible objects, information is physically unexcludable – it is easily copied, disseminated, adapted, mixed with other information and the mixed information can be further copied, disseminated, adapted and mixed, ad infinitum.[4]

However you seek to classify it, whether as an idea, an instruction, a concept, an algorithm, a behaviour or a meme,[5] once the intellectual product of a mind is first conveyed out of the mind of its author its ready amenability to imitation and adaptation allows it take on a 'life of its own', entirely independent of its author. In the absence of a legal mechanism to constrain downstream use by others, the original author cannot but lose control over their intellectual product. As was (more poetically) stated by Jefferson: 'If nature has made any one thing less susceptible than all others of exclusive property, it is the action of the thinking power called an idea, which an individual may exclusively possess as long as he keeps it to himself.'[6]

However, the problems with controlling the use of intellectual products do not end with the non-rivalrous and non-excludable nature of their use. Unlike a purely tangible object, there is also the significant problem of *defining* an intangible. If I am seeking to assert control over information through a legal mechanism, my first task is to understand *what* the information is – that is, *how* the intangible is defined. Given the inherent malleability and adaptability of information, it is important that I understand the 'boundaries' of what is to be protected. However, the boundaries I need to consider are 'multi-dimensional'. The first, and perhaps most obvious, dimension relates to my understanding of the point at which the initial information has become so changed, or is so different, that it no longer represents, or is a part of, that which was originally conceived. Attas has referred to this as the problem of 'individuation' of ideas which he divides into three areas:

(a) the problem of distinguishing between an idea in its first expression and the many secondary expressions it might stimulate;
(b) the problem of distinguishing between a general and more abstract idea and the specific details that are required to put it into practice; and

[3] J Garvey and J Stangroom, *The Story of Philosophy: A History of Western Thought* (London, Quercus, 2012) 179.
[4] Hess and Ostrom (n 2).
[5] S Blackmore, *The Meme Machine* (Oxford, Oxford University Press, 1999) 4.
[6] Thomas Jefferson, letter to Isaac McPherson, 13 August 1813, 13 *Writings* 333 (press-pubs.uchicago.edu/founders/documents/a1_8_8s12.html).

(c) the problem of extension of protection of an idea to cover the same idea which has been independently conceived.[7]

We might for current purposes call these the 'forward-looking' boundaries of the intangible.

The second dimension relates to my understanding the boundaries between what I have conceived (and seek to protect) and the field of the ideas/information of others who have gone before me. Attas has called this the problem of 'origination' and identifies the difficulty of considering a newly minted concept as being in some way separate from the multitude of previously existing concepts which have acted as the backdrop and/or stimulation for the concept under consideration.[8] Gibson uses the term 'origination' to describe the process of identifying and individuating the creator of a work, the origin of a work and the 'presumption of a finite, concluded and indeed lifeless material form'.[9] For current purposes we might call these the 'backward-looking' boundaries of the intangible.

It is worth noting here that Gibson coins a useful term within this context. As we will see, philosophical justifications for the existence of rights to control ideas often require some degree of 'contribution' by the author in the form of originality, inventiveness and/or novelty – that is, a sense in which the subject matter of protection is not imitative of something else. Gibson describes this state as 'in-imitativeness'.[10]

From an epistemological standpoint, we can see the very close links between individuation and origination. Indeed, all forms of established intellectual property right have grappled, and continue to grapple, with both boundary dimensions. Determination of the forward-looking (individuation) boundaries is most commonly couched in the language of infringement – does a third-party use of the protected intangible fall within the scope of the protected intangible? In contrast, the backward-looking (origination) boundaries are most commonly encountered when looking at questions of validity or subsistence – is the intellectual product sufficiently different from the intellectual products that have gone before to warrant protection? In most cases there will be a complex interplay between both boundary dimensions. When defendants argue that their (allegedly infringing) use of a purportedly protected intellectual product is a mere repetition of that which was understood before the conception of the asserted intellectual product, putative rights holders can find themselves navigating with difficulty between the Scylla of asserted validity and Charybdis of asserted infringement.

Given the inherent nature of information, both types of boundaries are rarely distinct. With regard to the backward-looking boundary, there will very likely

[7] D Attas, 'Lockean Justifications of Intellectual Property' in A Gosseries et al (eds), *Intellectual Property and Theories of Justice* (London, Palgrave Macmillan 2008) 29, 49.

[8] ibid 41.

[9] J Gibson, *Community Resources: Intellectual Property, International Trade and Protection of Traditional Knowledge* (Farnham, Ashgate, 2005) 81.

[10] ibid.

be a continuum between that which went before and that which is sought to be protected, and with regard to the forward-looking boundary, a continuum between that which is sought to be protected and that which is adapted by others from that information. The question of where to draw a definitional line within these continua goes to the very heart of the existence of the right in the intangible.

Sometimes a party seeking exclusive use of information will seek to define a piece of information by reference to a tangible product which is created out of that information. This may seem to give a reassuring foothold, but it is in some cases erroneous and care must be taken – although the tangible product may be *one* embodiment of a broader piece of information, it may not represent the entirety of the information, or indeed all the potential embodiments which could flow from the information. That said, the degrees of uncertainty along the forward-looking and backward-looking dimensions will vary as between the types of intellectual product to be protected – the protection of 'pure' ideas per se being subject to the greatest degree of uncertainty and the protection of the more concrete expressions of an idea being subject to less uncertainty. The narrower the embodiment of the idea, then, by definition, the less uncertainty will surround its definition in both dimensions. Accordingly, where a party chooses only to protect a narrow embodiment of an idea, they will likely encounter fewer problems with asserting validity and infringement. The choice between the certainty (and potential lesser commercial reward) provided by asserting a narrow embodiment and the potentially greater commercial gains (but increased uncertainty) through assertion of a broader embodiment is a perennial difficulty for intellectual property owners (and, indeed, their advisors). However, why should we be concerned if the boundaries of that which I am seeking to assert control over are indefinable? What mischief comes from my 'woolly' boundaries?

Of course, my control over a piece of information inherently requires others to curtail their utilisation of that information. If I assume, as a general point, that it is correct that I should only prevent others from an activity with some justification, then it would seem right that the boundary of my control should only extend to that which is supported by that justification (whatever that justification may be). Any control that extends beyond this is, by definition, unjustifiable. Any such analysis is, of course, based on an assumption that it is in some sense improper to place limitations on others, but is otherwise focused upon the argument of the person asserting the right. We need to be aware that such assertions of right are rarely made into a justificatory 'vacuum'. Hohfeld highlighted the correlative nature of rights versus duties – granting a right to one has the correlative effect of imposing duties upon other.[11] Following such an Hofeldian approach, Waldron states that:

> Since legal duties are hard things for people to have – since they constrain conduct and in that sense limit freedom – we should expect the realm of duties to be the testing

[11] WN Hohfeld, 'Some Fundamental Legal Conceptions as Applied in Judicial Reasoning' (1913) 23 *Yale Law Journal* 16, 30; WN Hohfeld, 'Fundamental Legal Conceptions as Applied in Judicial Reasoning' (Faculty Scholarship Series, Paper 4378, 1917).

> ground for claims of right. The realm of duties – the propositions about duty that a given claim of right entails – is where we should expect the problems with the right (if there are any) to surface.[12]

Whether one sees questions of what duties should be borne by others as some sort of background into which rights are asserted, or as direct opposing arguments for the existence of a right, or whether one perceives the imposition of a right as in some way curtailing inherent rights of others, the question of the justification for the existence or scope of a right might be considered as a 'justificatory equation'. Such an equation would pit the justification(s) for the existence of the right on one side of the equation against justification(s) for the non-existence of the right on the other side of the equation. However, this is not in any way a 'zero sum' arithmetic equation. We need to immediately note that the scope of a particular right may be supported by more than one (and potentially many) justifications. Further, not all such justifications may be of equal validity or merit, and differing justifications may give rise to differing justifiable limits. Altogether, it is unlikely that the 'set' of scopes supported by these varied justifications will be co-terminous. Similarly, it is unlikely that the opposing justifications would create a co-terminous set of counter-scopes, or indeed that each counter-argument would be fully aligned with each 'pro' argument. However, as will be seen, problems of non-alignment are usually addressed by the narrower, specific, arguments for the existence of a right being countered by broader, general counter-arguments based upon inherent individual liberty.[13]

III. The 'Problem' of Knowledge

Assuming for the moment that control should be limited by justification, is there an argument that the position is particularly acute in respect of the control of knowledge? Is knowledge in some way *special*? There is a long tradition that a restriction on the use of ideas per se cannot be justified at all, a tradition in part captured in the medieval, rhyming aphorism, *scientia donum Dei est, Unde vendi non potest* (knowledge is a gift from God and should not be sold),[14] and developed in the writings of Kant, Fichte and Hegel (as will be discussed later in this chapter). Notwithstanding this thinking, it is not an overstatement to say that the transfer and adaptation of information has been, and continues to be, at the very heart of

[12] J Waldron, 'From Authors to Copiers: Individual Rights and Social Values in Intellectual Property' (1993) 68 *Chicago Kent Law Review* 841, 842.

[13] H Breakey, 'User's Rights and the Public Domain' in *Intellectual Liberty – Natural Rights and Intellectual Property* (Farnham, Ashgate, 2012) 75.

[14] G Post et al, 'The Medieval Heritage of a Humanistic Ideal: Scientia donum Dei est, unde bendi non potest' (1995) 11 *Traditio* 195, 197; see also L Hyde, *Common as Air: Revolution, Art and Ownership* (London, Union Books, 2010) 20.

the development of human civilisation – indeed one might ask what *is* human civilisation without knowledge? For Bronowski:

> Man is distinguished from other animals by his imaginative gifts. He makes plans, inventions, new discoveries, by putting different talents together; and his discoveries become more subtle and more penetrating, as he learns to combine his talents in more complex and intimate ways.[15]

Given this, it might be argued that the freedom to use information is not one that should be interfered with lightly. As a result, a restriction of the right of others to use knowledge might (at the very least) be understood to be one where:

(a) a particularly high justificatory threshold is required, and
(b) there is a need to be highly cognisant of not improperly restricting the action of third parties.

Here the inherent uncertainty in defining the boundaries of a piece of information adds a further layer of concern. Such uncertainties (combined with the inherent imperfections in any legal mechanism) may give us a high (perhaps unavoidable) probability that any mechanism which grants rights of control over information will result in some third parties being improperly prevented from doing that which they would otherwise be free to do. Is this risk a price too high to pay? That question cannot be addressed within this work, but certainly an appreciation of the danger caused by the inherent uncertainty of the boundaries to information must be carefully considered when looking at the 'justificatory equation' for imposing any control over information.[16]

Notwithstanding any such justificatory equation, it would seem reasonable that the formulators of intellectual property rights (and those tasked with making them work) should, in any event, be particularly sensitive to the balance of conflicting interests between the justifications for granting protection to an intellectual product and the right of the broader world to work freely, and ensure that a careful framework of rules (and guidance for their interpretation) is in place to reduce the danger of improper curtailment of third-party activity. Indeed, support for a clear framework of rules also derives from a closely related source. Bingham identified a requirement that 'law is accessible, and so far as possible, clear and predictable' as one of his principles underpinning the rule of law.[17] Indeed, the importance of clarity and predictability in law has a long history,[18] and has been cited by senior appellate courts in a variety of jurisdictions.[19] Whatever the

[15] J Bronowski, *The Ascent of Man* (London, Book Club Associates, 1977) 20.
[16] See generally PS Harrison, 'A Good Idea Gone Bad. Can We Still Justify Patent Monopolies?' in A Johnston and L Talbot (eds), *Great Debates in Commercial and Corporate Law* (London, Red Globe Press, 2020) 62.
[17] T Bingham, *The Rule of Law* (London, Penguin Law, 2011) 37.
[18] *Hamilton v Mendes* (1761) 2 Burr 1198, 1214; *Vallejo v Mendes* (1774) 1 Cowp 143, 153.
[19] *Black Clawson International Ltd v Papierwerke Waldhof-Aschaffenburg AG* [1975] AC 591 [UKHL] 638; *Sunday Times v United Kingdom* (1979) 2 EHRR 245, 271.

justification for controlling the use of intellectual products, it is hard to envisage why the principle of clarity and predictability in law (and in its application) should not apply to understanding the limitations to the scope of an intellectual property right.

Accordingly, ensuring that any intellectual property right framework provides a mechanism for determining with a reasonable degree of certainty what is (and what is not) protected or permitted is not only of immense practical significance to those seeking to operate the law, but is an element in securing the proper rule of law. Of course, the inherent uncertainties of defining information do not make providing such a 'reasonable degree' of certainty easy. However, these inherent uncertainties might be argued to place a heavy burden on the formulators and adjudicators of intellectual property laws to give due care to questions of scope of protection.

IV. High-level Justifications for the Protection of Knowledge

The key high-level philosophical justifications for the existence of intellectual property rights protecting knowledge (or its expression) are most commonly divided into consequentialist claims or deontological approaches.[20]

Within the consequentialist group of justifications, positive law is created in an attempt to meet a perceived societal need or collection of such needs. As is the case with any consequentialist approach, the most contentious question is how we choose (and justify) the consequences that should be sought. In relation to the existence of intellectual property rights, the most commonly expressed consequentialist goal is a desire to incentivise artistic, social and technological development (though this essentially utilitarian motivation is often presented as a desire to achieve positive 'economic' outcomes).[21] This is a justification which has been particularly applied to the protection of inventions through a patent system.[22]

[20] See generally: P Drahos, *A Philosophy of Intellectual Property* (Aldershot, Dartmouth, 1996); G Dutfield and U Suthersanen, *Global Intellectual Property Law* (Cheltenham, Edward Elgar, 2008) 47; E Derclaye, 'Patent Law's Role in the Protection of the Environment – Re-assessing Patent Law and its Justifications in the 21st Century' (2009) 40(3) *International Review of Intellectual Property and Competition Law* 249; A Moore, *Stanford Encyclopedia of Philosophy* (2011), plato.staford.edu/enties/intellectual-property.

[21] MA Lemley, 'Ex Ante versus Ex Post Justifications for Intellectual Property' (2004) 71(1) *University of Chicago Law Review* 129; SV Shiffrin, 'The Incentives Argument for Intellectual Property Protection' in A Gosseries et al (eds), *Intellectual Property and Theories of Justice* (London, Palgrave Macmillan, 2008) 29.

[22] See eg: F Machlup and E Penrose, 'The Patent Controversy in the Nineteenth Century' (1950) 10(1) *Journal of Economic History* 1; V Denicolo and LA Franzoni, 'The Contract Theory of Patents' (2003) 23 *International Review of Law and Economics* 365; M Fisher, 'Classical Economics and Philosophy of the Patent System' (2005) 1 *Intellectual Property Quarterly* 5.

The deontological approaches are based on natural rights, human rights or other matters of 'duty'. The natural rights justifications essentially fall into two mains camps:

(i) 'labour-desert' based on the concept that we own ourselves and by mixing our labour with the world we gain ownership in that we have mixed our labour with; and
(ii) rights based on freedom of personality and the extension of individual personality.

It should be stressed, however, that although all intellectual property rights have the key similarity in that they seek (to varying degrees) to exclude third parties from engaging in certain 'intellectual' or commercial activities, the range of subject matter covered by intellectual property rights is so broad that certain of the philosophical justifications for 'intellectual property' often seem to sit more comfortably for some rights than for others.

Advocating a pluralistic approach to the justification of intellectual property, Resnik highlights that different rights require different balances of 'competing moral values in the light of the particular facts and circumstances'.[23] Mr Justice Laddie (of the High Court of England and Wales), in a more Orwellian vein, put it thus:

> It seems to me to be strongly arguable that not all intellectual property rights are equal. Some are more equal than others. It is convenient and conventional to treat copyright, designs, topography rights, moral rights, confidential information, patents and trade marks as a group. But there are substantial differences between them.[24]

Accordingly, we will find in the present analysis that not all the philosophical justifications that have been provided to justify the existence of intellectual property rights will necessarily comfortably justify the control of TKAGR (indeed some, arguably do not support it at all), whereas with others the struggle is not so great.

V. Is Traditional Knowledge Different?

Before we look to the various justifications for protection of TKAGR, we need first to address whether the application of what could be argued to be essentially 'Western' intellectual concepts of property (and of the self) are appropriate to the protection of something (traditional knowledge) which is radically different in nature from the usual subject matter of Western intellectual property law. As we will see, some of the problems with the application of Western philosophical

[23] DB Resnik, 'A Pluralistic Account of Intellectual Property' (2003) 46(4) *Journal of Business Ethics* 319, 319.

[24] Laddie J in *Philips Electronics NV v Ingman Limited, The Video Duplicating Company Limited* [1999] FSR 112, 134 [EWHC].

approaches arise from the way in which traditional knowledge is 'developed' (that is, in general in an ad hoc way across generations) and held within Indigenous groups. These are, however, problems that can be dealt with on a case-by-case basis and do not (of themselves) necessarily undermine the entire process of bringing an 'alien' Western philosophy to bear upon this subject matter.[25]

A greater potential criticism is that in many cases the ways in which traditional knowledge is respected and conceived by Indigenous peoples are not founded upon formalised Western notions of self and (particularly) of property.[26] (See also the discussion below at section XII.B.) Notwithstanding this, we have to consider that the positive rights to control genetic resources (and TKAGR) established within the Nagoya Protocol (or perhaps to be created in any other mechanism within a Western paradigm, such as the WTO or WIPO) are a function of *positive law* created within what is a Westernised legal philosophical framework. Accordingly, there is an argument for saying (whether or not such an approach is appropriate or otherwise to the subject matter) that such rights need to be assessed on essentially Western philosophical terms. As a heuristic tool, this work will assume this to be the case, and will use Western philosophical approaches where assessing situations in which those rights will be interacting, and conflicting, with third-party intellectual property rights (and concepts of freedom) whose justifications are themselves rooted within the Western tradition.

In any event, critics of the protection of traditional knowledge (perhaps at some time in the future a pharmaceutical or biotechnology company seeking to avoid a veto over downstream use) are most likely to root their arguments in the Western philosophical tradition and such criticisms are likely to be most effectively countered with arguments arising out of the same philosophical paradigm.

Although ideas of distributive justice have long played a significant part in the debate concerning the ownership of property, they have only more recently being applied to questions of the rightness of control over ideas – most commonly to examine the imposition of Western intellectual property regimes in the Global South.[27] This work will therefore also look to consider the extent to which distributive justice (particularly a Rawlsian *maximin* analysis) can be applied to the question of scope of positive rights in TKAGR. We will see in this analysis that

[25] Although they may of course create difficulties in bringing traditional knowledge within the framework of existing intellectual property rights.

[26] J Githaiga, 'Intellectual Property Law and the Protection of Indigenous Folklore and Knowledge' (1998) 5(2) *E Law: Murdoch University Electronic Journal of Law* para 18, www.murdoch.edu.au/elaw/issues/v5n2/githaiga52.html; J Gibson 'Community and the Exhaustion of Culture. Creative Territories in Creative Cultural Expressions' in F Macmillan and K Bowrey (eds), *New Directions in Copyright Law*, vol 3 (Cheltenham, Edward Elgar, 2006) 21; J Gibson (n 9) 82; A Rahmatian, 'Neo-colonial Aspects of Global Intellectual Property Protection' (2009) 12(1) *Journal of World Intellectual Property* 40.

[27] M Chon, 'Intellectual Property from Below: Copyright and Capability for Education' (2007) 40 *UC Davis Law Review* 803; K Aoki, 'Distributive Justice and Intellectual Property: Distributive and Syncretic Motives in Intellectual Property Law (with Special Reference to Coercion, Agency, and Development)' (2007) 40 *UC Davis Law Review* 717; A Chander and M Sunder, 'Is Nozick Kicking Rawls's Ass? Intellectual Property and Social Justice' (2007) 40 *UC Davis Law Review* 563.

there are some philosophical approaches, notably restorative/corrective justice,[28] which (though Western concepts) are less commonly used to justify intellectual property rights per se, but may have a particular role in the justification of rights to control TKAGR.

The question of whether there is a human right to intellectual property is complex. However, as will be discussed below at section XII, many advocates for Indigenous rights have advanced an argument for the protection of TKAGR (and traditional knowledge more generally) that is based upon concepts of Indigenous sovereignty or a right to self-determination (which has, in part, been acknowledged through UNDRIP). Whilst discussion of such a right is not one of the 'classic' justifications for intellectual property, as we will see it has been a vital component of the discourse surrounding the existence of positive rights in TKAGR.

VI. Deontological Justifications

A. Lockean Desert-Based Justifications

i. Locke's Theory of Property

John Locke's *An Essay on Concerning the True Original, Extent, and End of Civil Government* was published in 1689 (the so-called 'Second Treatise' of Locke's *Two Treatise of Government*).[29] This was in Britain, and elsewhere, a period during which the absolute power of monarchs was the subject of fierce debate, to (and well beyond) the point of revolution. Locke's views on absolute monarchs, the origins of a sovereign's authority and the need for separation of powers informed much of the thinking of revolutionary political philosophers and lawyers thereafter, including those involved in drafting the US Declaration of Independence and Constitution.[30]

A key element of Locke's thesis, the justification for the ownership of property in private hands, is found at Chapter V (entitled 'Of Property') of the *Second Treatise*.[31] There is no denying the historical importance of this approach. For Ferguson there is an argument that Locke's theories on property set the course for the foundation of a widely distributed private property rights and broad-based democracy in the British colonies in North America, Australia, New Zealand,

[28] SR Munzer, 'Corrective Justice and Intellectual Property Rights in Traditional Knowledge' in A Lever (ed) *New Frontiers in the Philosophy of Intellectual Property* (Cambridge, Cambridge University Press, 2012) 58.

[29] Although there is argument over the date of the composition of the work. See P Laslett, *Locke, Two Treatise of Government* (Cambridge, Cambridge University Press, 1988) 45.

[30] AC Grayling, *Towards the Light: The Story of the Struggles for Liberty and Rights that Made the Modern West* (London, Bloomsbury, 2007) 114.

[31] Laslett (n 29) 285.

and in the United States.[32] However, there is also a serious argument that Locke's theory of property formed a part of the philosophical bedrock of colonial exploitation and misappropriation of land held by Indigenous peoples.[33] This theory has also become an important element in the academic analysis of the justification for intellectual property rights. Locke's thesis can be summed up as follows:

(a) At some point in an indeterminate past (but at least before the advent of a monetary economy) mankind existed in a 'State of Nature' governed by the 'Law of Nature'.
(b) Within that State of Nature the World and all therein had been granted by God to Mankind to be held in common. This combined holding of the resources of the world is referred to as 'the Common'.
(c) Within this State of Nature the number of humans inhabiting the planet is small in comparison to the essentially inexhaustible resources of the Common. The Common can provide for all.
(d) To be useful to humans the resources of the Common need to be harvested in some way, whether it be foraging, hunting or fishing.
(e) Every man has property in his own person, similarly the labour of his body and the work of his hands belong to that person.
(f) When a person removes a resource from the Common he mixes his *labour* with it. That person owns his *labour* and by mixing it with the resource he joins to the resource something which is his own which makes the resource part of his own property.
(g) In so doing the resource is removed from the Common for the exclusive use of that person.[34]
(h) In applying labour to a resource such as to remove a resource from the common a '*property*' is '*begun*' in the resource.
(i) At the time of removal of the resource from the common there is no requirement that there be any consent from the other commoners (essentially the broader community) for the 'property' to begin.
(j) For a 'property' to begin, however, there is a requirement that there is '*enough, and as good left in the common for others*'. This has come to be known as the 'enough and as good' proviso.
(k) The removal of the resource cannot be to an extent that would result in the spoiling of unused resource.[35] This has come to be termed the 'waste' exception or 'non-waste' requirement.
(l) These principles apply not only to fruit, game and other resources, but to the land itself. The improvement of untamed land to enhance the resources that can be created on it will begin a property in that parcel of land. This

[32] N Ferguson, *Civilization, The West and the Rest* (London, Allen Lane, 2011) 107.
[33] See eg OU Ince, *Colonial Capitalism and the Dilemmas of Liberalism* (Oxford, Oxford University Press, 2018) 44.
[34] Laslett (n 29) 288 (Locke, ch V, para 28).
[35] ibid 290 (Locke, ch V, para 31).

accumulation of a right in land is subject to the same exceptions as other resources. If the land is unused it returns to the common and may be appropriated by another who will work and improve the land.[36]

(m) It is the application of labour which gives value to something whether it be food, resources or land. The greater the application of labour to a thing or land, the greater the value developed in that thing or land.

(n) Where a man harvests more than he can make use of without the harvest decaying, but uses the excess to barter for something else that he needs, or does not perish (such as precious metals or diamonds), that would not fall foul of Locke's waste exception. This is beginning of a monetary economy. Locke states: 'And thus came in the use of Money, some lasting thing that Men might keep without spoiling, and by mutual consent Men would take in exchange for the truly useful, but perishable Supports of Life.'[37]

(o) The use of money uncouples the amount of land that a person may properly own without breaching the waste exception. Where a man can accumulate wealth through accumulation of non-perishables (such as gold, silver or diamonds) then he can accumulate more land than can immediately support his family without 'wasting' the Common – as would happen with perishables.[38]

(p) Such non-perishables are not of themselves of value, as they do not of themselves contribute to feeding, clothing and transporting a man. Their value arrives only from the consent of the community.[39]

(q) As societies developed, the initial ownership of property under the Law of Nature, created through the application of labour, became recognised through tacit acceptance of the community and eventually formalised through positive laws of an organised government.

It should be stressed that within Locke's thesis the tacit acceptance of the value of imperishable metals or money (and which allows the development of unequal holdings without breaching the waste exception) remains separate from the tacit acknowledgement of holdings in land.

If Locke's theory is to be accepted as correct, in toto, then it has a major implication which was identified by Locke himself. Where peoples are considered *not* to be mixing their labour with the land, then the land itself and the natural produce which it creates remain part of the Common. If such land is in the Common, then it is free to be brought into private ownership by the application of labour to it. Even where labour *is* being applied to the land, in the absence of a monetary economy the waste exception would apply such that any holding could only be justified if it were small enough to support a family without causing waste to

[36] ibid 294 (Locke, ch V, para 36).

[37] ibid 300 (Locke, ch V, para 46).

[38] See SH Marguerat, *Private Property Rights and the Environment: Our Responsibilities to Global Natural Resources – Palgrave Studies in Environmental Policy and Regulation* (London, Palgrave Macmillan, 2019) 311.

[39] Laslett (n 29), 302 (Locke, ch V, para 50).

the Common. Locke refers a number of times to the uncolonised portions of the Americas as an example of a continuation of the State of Nature where the land and its resources remain in the Common. Of course, at the time of Locke's writing (1689) the east coast of North America was progressively being developed by English and French colonies which were converting the supposedly unused forest to farmland.[40] Accordingly, writers such as Shiva consider Locke's theories on property to be part of the philosophical underpinning to Western ideas justifying the exploitation of 'vacant' land, a way of thinking which she describes as legitimising colonial exploitation within the British Empire and the United States and as a justification for the dispossession of Indigenous peoples across the globe.[41] Locke was, in fact, involved with the drafting of the constitution of one British colony (Carolina) and it would seem at least likely that a philosophy which would provide direct legitimisation for the British colonists' expropriation of land from Indigenous hunter-gatherer peoples was within his contemplation.[42]

Locke did not visit the Americas. Had he done so, he may have realised that the land of the north-east coast of North America, described by settlers (and himself) as being unused, was in fact already used by the Indigenous peoples who cultivated parcels of land to augment a diet derived from hunter-gathering, fishing and forest management (such as the harvesting of maple sap). There is a very deep irony here. The English 'Pilgrim Father' settlers who travelled to America on the *Mayflower* and established the Plymouth Colony in 1620 would appear to have been saved from starvation by their introduction of traditional farming techniques taught to them by the Indigenous Wôpanâak (or Wampanoag) people.[43] The settlers learnt the technique of cultivating maize, squash and climbing beans (known as the 'three sisters' by the Wôpanâak), which grow in the poorer soils of New England where the rye, barley and wheat which the settlers had brought with them from England would not. The Wôpanâak (and other Indigenous peoples of the north-east coast) had learnt that maize, squash and beans, when grown as part of a companion planting system in a 'three sisters mound', would create a fertile soil: climbing beans are nitrogen fixers; maize provides the climbing beans with support on which to grow; and the wide leaves of the squash grown at the foot of the maize assist with water retention and weed control. The beneficial effect of these crops on poor soils was enhanced by the Wôpanâak use of wood ash and fish as plant fertilisers.[44]

[40] L James, *The Rise and Fall of the British Empire* (London, Abacus, 1995) 3; D Gillmor and P Turgeon, *Canada, A People's History*, vol 1 (London, McClelland and Stewart, 2000) 76; N Ferguson, *Empire* (London, Penguin, 2003) 55.

[41] V Shiva, *Biopiracy: The Plunder of Nature and Knowledge* (New York, South End Press, 1997) 3.

[42] Against: R Ashcraft, *Revolutionary Politics and Locke's Two Treatises of Government* (Princeton, NJ, Princeton University Press, 1986) ch 9; but see J Waldron, *God, Locke, and Equality: Christian Foundations in Locke's Political Thought* (Cambridge, Cambridge University Press, 2002).

[43] DJ Silverman *This Land Is Their Land: The Wampanoag Indians, Plymouth Colony, and the Troubled History of Thanksgiving* (London, Bloomsbury, 2019).

[44] J Mt Pleasant, 'The Science Behind the Three Sisters Mound System: An Agronomic Assessment of an Indigenous Agricultural System in the Northeast' in JE Staller et al (eds), *Histories of Maize:*

Locke's theory of property has formed the basis of a libertarian, Neo-Lockean school of thought. Perhaps foremost amongst these 'Neo-Lockeans' is Robert Nozick, who argues that justice in property holdings relies upon a just *initial* acquisition of the property from the Common and a just chain of transfers thereafter.[45] Where a transfer in the chain is in some way improper Nozick allows for a 'rectification' of title – what Radin calls a theory of 'corrective justice'.[46]

ii. The Lockean Justification for Intellectual Property

The Lockean theory that one can gain property over the Common through the application of one's labour has been applied to the creation of an exclusive property right in ideas – ideas that were (until they were conceived of) in a 'Common' of yet to be had ideas. By analogy with Locke's theory of property over tangible goods, here it is the application of 'labour' (that is, the work done in conceiving the idea) that is sufficient to wrest the idea out of the imagined 'Lockean Common' and into private ownership. This concept has been looked at in considerable length by Hughes, who considers the Lockean justification in many ways more appropriate for intangible ideas than for tangible property.[47] Hughes believes that the propertising of ideas under the Lockean model can be justified if three propositions can be met. These propositions are:

(a) The production of ideas requires a person's labour;
(b) These ideas are appropriated from a Lockean Common which is itself not significantly devalued by the ideas removal from it (in compliance with the 'enough and as good' proviso); and
(c) The ideas can be made property without breaching the non-waste condition.

Hughes states that Locke's theory of property can be interpreted in two ways:

(i) Society rewards labour with property on *instrumental* grounds. Society *must* give a reward or no one will provide their labour; or
(ii) On a normative basis, labour *should* be rewarded with property.

(a) Labour – Avoidance

Taking the first point, Hughes states that in the Lockean model a person's handiwork becomes their property because the work of an individual's hands and 'the energy, consciousness, and control that fuel their labour' is their own.

Multidisciplinary Approaches to the Prehistory, Linguistics, Biogeography, Domestication, and Evolution of Maize (London, Academic Press, 2006).
[45] R Nozick, *Anarchy, State and Utopia* (New York, Basic Books, 1974) 175.
[46] MJ Radin, *Reinterpreting Property* (Chicago, University of Chicago Press, 1993) 106.
[47] J Hughes, 'The Philosophy of Intellectual Property' (1988) 77 *Georgetown Law Journal* 287.

Hughes asks the question whether the act of conceiving ideas can indeed be referred to as a 'labour' in the Lockean sense. Labour is most often thought of as physical 'sweat of the brow' activity. Hughes suggests that many might suppose that the work of producing ideas is preferable to manual labour. However, Hughes suggests that even if this is correct in some cases, even those working on developing ideas may in fact prefer to be doing something less onerous – creation being for most people less fun than recreation. Hughes refers to this as the 'avoidance' view of labour. He suggests that there are two distinct strands to this avoidance approach: a normative proposition of Locke's labour theory (the very unpleasantness of labour justifies a reward) and an instrumental argument (that no one would perform labour without reward – a position itself based on a utilitarian foundation that the product of labour generally enhances the public good). Hughes suggests that Locke had the utilitarian position in mind when he stated that 'he who appropriates land to himself by his labour, does not lessen but increase the common stock of mankind'.[48] Hughes feels that the instrumental argument has dominated case law and judicial announcements and where the normative 'labour deserves reward' position has emerged, it is has more often been used an adjunct to the instrumental position.[49]

(b) 'Labour-Desert' or 'Value-Added' Theory

Hughes also examines the 'value-added' or 'labour desert' interpretation of Locke's labour justification. This approach is not based on the unpleasantness of labour – indeed Hughes states that this understanding of property does not, in fact, require an understanding of the concept of labour per se. Hughes comments that labour per se, no matter how arduous, could potentially create nothing of value to broader society, or something which was only of value to the labourer himself. What is important in the value-added approach is that the labour expended produces something *of value* to society – something beyond what morality requires the individual to produce. Hughes suggests that judicial or legislative statements that fuse the normative and instrumental elements of the labour avoidance justification are probably based, unknowingly, on the value-added theory. Hughes goes on to say that although the value-added theory is often thought to be an instrumentalist approach – inventors/creators will be incentivised to add value to the Common provided they have some personal gain – there is a normative proposition that such inventors/creators *should* be rewarded if they have enhanced the commonweal, even if personal gain was not what actually incentivised them to enhance the Common.

[48] Laslett (n 29) 294 (Locke, ch V, para 37).
[49] Hughes (n 47) 304.

(c) The 'Enough and As Good' Requirement

In Locke's theory during the early days of the Common it is thought of as being essentially inexhaustible. The acquisition of a part of the Common through the application of labour by one family does not in practice remove part of the Common from anyone else. A second family can always seek their farmstead over the next hill. In this way there is no moral reason why the first labourer should not acquire property over the subject of his labour – his acquisition is non-competitive. Of course, in reality the tangible Common is not truly inexhaustible. In relation to tangible property, the period during which a labourer could acquire property in the Common in a truly non-competitive manner would be short lived – the Common would not have 'enough and as good' for very long.

By propertising an idea out of the Common of potential ideas is the inventor/creator exhausting that Common? Once propertised, that particular idea is now outwith that Common. However, Hughes suggests that there is in fact an inexhaustible supply of 'enough and as good' ideas remaining in the Common. There are always new ideas out there and we have, so far, not run out. Hughes suggests that the idea of the effectively inexhaustible Common applies more properly to intangibles than to tangible property. Indeed, other than in extraordinary circumstances (and even then only for a very short time) the concept of the inexhaustible Common can *only* apply to the Common in ideas.

(d) 'Enough and As Good' and the 'Permanent Common'

Even assuming the apparent 'inexhaustibility' on the ideas Common, we need to ask ourselves whether there are certain areas of the Common (essentially certain ideas) which should never become propertised? Hughes believes that the prevention of private propertisation of certain central ideas allows intellectual property law to avoid the inequitable control of core resources that can be present in physical property systems. Returning to the idea of a tangible Common for a moment, he asserts that even in vast wilderness there are certain areas which an individual should not be permitted to claim because to do so would not leave 'as good and as many' for the remaining individuals. He states that:

> The 'New World' prior to its colonization may have been as close to a Lockean common as human history records,[50] yet it is easy to make a list of things which the society could not allow to be appropriated as private property: the Amazon, St Lawrence and Ohio Rivers, the Cumberland Pass, or the St George's Bank fisheries.[51]

What ideas might we consider as being beyond propertisation? Hughes considers that there are two broad classes of idea that should not be subject to propertisation: 'everyday ideas' and 'extraordinary ideas'. In respect of everyday ideas (such

[50] Although, as discussed above, such a position ignores the presence and activities of its indigenous occupants.

[51] Hughes (n 17) 320.

as washing the car, taking the dog for a walk), allowing for their propertisation would breach the 'enough and as good' proviso since they are so fundamental to everyday existence that their removal from the Common would unavoidably deplete the Common. In respect of 'extraordinary' ideas, Hughes sees these as falling into two categories: those that are important because they reveal fundamental information about the functioning of the universe (such as mathematical concepts and algorithms and scientific discoveries), and those that, although initially amenable to property ownership, become with time and use increasingly important to the functioning of society and accordingly become 'depropertized' – akin perhaps to the genericisation of trade marks. Hughes sees the spectrum of protectable ideas as sitting between the two extremes of common and extraordinary ideas. However, he identifies that ideas related to the two extremes can be protectable. Car washing per se is unprotectable; a new car washer can be. Integral calculus per se is unprotectable, whereas a new notation to express it can be. Hughes concludes that, subject to these limits, the Lockean 'enough and as good' requirement probably only holds true for the concept of a Common of ideas and 'That may mean that Locke's unique theoretical edifice finds it firmest bedrock in the common of ideas.'[52]

(e) The Non-waste Condition

As mentioned above, the aspect of Locke's theory of property which has the most logical difficulty is the non-waste condition and the allowance for enhanced land holding through the acquisition of non-perishable metals and 'jewels'. Hughes believes that many intellectual property systems do not embody, or require, a non-waste condition. The core component to his argument is that ideas do not 'spoil' in the way that natural produce may. He argues that although some may say that ideas are perishable (in that stories become old, literature styles become outdated, technologies become obsolescent), there is in fact no *real* deterioration in the idea and the loss is only seen against the social background and may (dependent on trends in fashion or technology developments) be reversible.[53] Hughes does not believe that the lack of requirement for a non-waste condition is fatal to the application of the Lockean theory of property to intellectual property (particularly given the rapidity with which Locke moves away from the non-waste condition with the advent of imperishable assets/monetary economy).

Although, in conclusion, Hughes believes that elements of a Lockean argument to justify intellectual property are powerful, he does not believe that a pure Lockean solution is complete. As he states: 'Those who try to apply Locke to all modern property end up multiplying distinctions like pre-Copernican astronomers calculating celestial orbits with their Ptolemaic epicycles. At some point it becomes easier to reorient one's universe.'[54]

[52] ibid 329.
[53] ibid 328.
[54] ibid 330.

(f) Post-Hughes Analysis

Attas takes a substantially less charitable approach to the Lockean justification than Hughes.[55] Attas particularly tackles the question of Locke's positive method of private appropriation. Locke provides in the 'mixing' of a labourer's own labour with the Common a 'mechanism' by which a previously commonly owned aspect of the Common comes into the private ownership of the labourer. Attas highlights Nozick's point that even if labour can be 'owned' in any real sense, why should its mixing with the Common allow ownership in an aspect of the common rather than vice versa?[56] Attas also quotes Shiffrin who argues against a Lockean basis for intellectual property on the grounds that something which originates in our own mind (though 'owned' whilst an idea in our own heads) cannot be used to control others once it has been dissipated into the public domain.[57] Attas's principle critical focus is, however, on what he terms the 'problem of origination': if Locke's positive method of private appropriation, whereby an individual acquires a prima facie exclusive claim to previously commonly held resources, is to operate, one has to be able to identify with certainty the ideas which are to be appropriated. Attas argues that any ideas can be either discoveries, inventions or artistic creations. However, regardless of its type, no idea is created in a vacuum. All ideas arise out of the societal background of their time. New discoveries rely upon previous discoveries, new inventions incorporate previous technology, and artistic creations whether musical, dramatic or in the visual arts incorporate styles, patterns and concepts from previous work. One cannot with any absolute certainty determine the 'origination' of the idea from that which went before. Attas argues that within a formalised intellectual property system one can develop mechanisms by which one can determine (for the sake of a particular right) where the old ideas stop and where new ideas begin. However, for Attas this approach is one of *convention* not one of Lockean *natural* law.

Attas also looks at Locke's third proviso: the negative requirement that others' interests would not be harmed by appropriation (whether through the 'enough and as good' requirement or the 'non-waste' requirement). Attas's key argument under the head of 'non-harm to others' is in relation to what he describes as the 'individuation' of ideas. The problem relates to defining the boundaries of what you seek to individuate. Attas acknowledges that there can be difficulties in defining the boundaries of a tangible object and quotes Nozick's question: 'If a private astronaut clears a place on Mars, has he mixed his labor with (so that he comes to own) the whole planet, the whole uninhabited universe or just a particular plot?'[58] Although part of the individuation problem can be addressed by the fact

[55] Attas (n 7), 29.
[56] Nozick (n 45).
[57] SV Shiffrin, 'Lockean Arguments for Private Intellectual Property' in SR Munzer (ed), *New Essays in the Legal and Political Theory of Property* (Cambridge, Cambridge University Press, 2001) 165.
[58] Nozick (n 45), 174.

labour is purposive and this defines the extent of the object laboured upon, for Attas, many discoveries and inventions are merely serendipitous and such chance discoveries cannot be defined by the purpose of the inventor. Attas's view is that defining the boundary of an idea is more difficult than for tangible property and can be 'baffling'.[59]

Attas also briefly looks at questions of imitation, parody and inspiration and the question of where an idea 'ends'. He is also concerned about the difference between a general abstract idea and the specific details that are required to put the general idea into practice and the question of whether such specifics are caught within the general.

However, difficult as these questions are, most troubling for Attas is the question of whether ownership of an idea: (a) should extend to ownership of an *identical* idea even where such an idea is arrived at independently by a third party (as is the case with patents), what Attas calls a 'path-independent extension of the right in the idea'; or (b) should allow for free ownership of an independently conceived idea provided there is no copying nexus back to the original idea (as is arguably the case with copyright), what Attas terms 'a path-dependent extension of the right in the idea'. Attas accepts that positive law can handle these types of problems, making 'reasoned and principled justifications for intellectual property in some cases and rejecting it in others'.[60] As with the problem of origination, his argument is that the uncertainty leads one to conventional approaches based upon a consequentialist analysis, rather than a Lockean *natural* law justification.

For Attas, the difficulty with regard to certainty and being able to draw a *natural* line is enhanced by the 'squeeze' between certainty in origination and certainty in individuation. He states that for clear origination you need to reject background and contributory influences. For clear individuation you may need to include offshoots and derivatives of the ideas. The two positions are, in Attas's view, contradictory. Attas states:

> [I]t appears that the more we are willing to recognise the owner as the originator of the idea, brushing aside inputs of preceding ideas, the less we are able consistently to recognise offshoots of the idea as within it. That is to say, the narrower we individuate the intellectual product. For we cannot have it both ways: that the idea owes nothing to its predecessors yet its successors are wholly indebted to it.[61]

The problems of origination and individuation are significant difficulties for the practical application of the Lockean account (as will be seen below when we seek to use it in the determination of the justifiable scope of positive rights in TKAGR). Although Dutfield and Suthersanen are highly sensitive to these problems (stating that Locke's theory of property might be considered as being 'too

[59] Attas (n 7) 47.
[60] ibid 52.
[61] ibid 53.

basic and outdated' at its core) they highlight that it does at least serve to identify the inherent conflict which sits at the heart of an intellectual property right. They state that:

> since the beginning there have been two competing stakeholders: the labourer (inventor, author, investor, entrepreneur) and the 'commons' (which can be other labourers or competitors within the market or societal welfare sector such as health or education).
>
> Hence, Locke's theory is useful in urging us to consider the need for the existence and maintenance of a 'public domain' (as opposed to several private domains) or an intellectual commons (as opposed to intellectual property).[62]

iii. The Lockean Model as Applied to Traditional Knowledge

How might one apply a purely Lockean model to TKAGR? We might look in the first place to the following scenario: an Indigenous group uncover (through serendipity or deliberate and iterative 'trial and error' or a combination of both) a useful characteristic of a particular plant. Such information may have been determined within one generation, or added to by serendipity/trial and error over a series of generations. As Hughes would apply Locke's model, it is the application of 'labour', the process of discovering the information (which previously resided in the idea Common), which would entitle the group to claim rights to control the information.

Although they approach the question in relation to the creation of artistic works rather than TKAGR, Munzer and Raustiala have provided a detailed and systematic analysis of the justifications for intellectual property with respect to the question of traditional knowledge.[63] They examine the justification of an intellectual property right in traditional knowledge under the Lockean principle of desert based on labour. They have no conceptual objection to a traditional knowledge right residing in a *group* – for them it is open to groups to obtain rights based on a joint contribution. However, they identify a problem with a right in traditional knowledge: the original 'investigators/creators' are '*by definition*' dead. They question whether (even if such originators were entitled to rights commensurate with their labour) it is correct that the originator's 'desert' should extend to their distant descendants or unrelated inhabitants of a region who have subsequently come to know of the knowledge. Surprisingly, they do not seek to apply (or criticise) Nozick's neo Lockean entitlement theory approach[64] that where property has been justly acquired (appropriated from the Common) in the past (and where subsequent transfers are just), then the claim of title to the property *in the present* can be justified.

[62] Dutfield and Suthersanen (n 20) 55.

[63] SR Munzer and K Raustiala, 'The Uneasy Case for Intellectual Property Rights in Traditional Knowledge' (2009) 29 *Cardozo Arts and Entertainment Law Journal* 39.

[64] Nozick (n 45) 151.

At this point Munzer and Raustiala also consider that where the Indigenous group have endeavoured to keep a piece of traditional knowledge secret, that the group should have a right to control access to that information and bring an action for misappropriation for a breach of confidentiality. However, they give no real reason why, or indeed how, such reasoning fits into an analysis of a Lockean justification for rights in traditional knowledge.

Munzer and Raustiala examine the Lockean justification further under the concept of 'firstness'. They state that firstness (being the first to make, obtain or occupy the property) does not, of itself, provide a strong general, or specific, justification for property rights but does provide a particular justification where 'disputes over desert or incentives prove very difficult or costly on other grounds'.[65]

Munzer and Raustiala briefly examine the Lockean case for intellectual property. Munzer and Raustiala conclude (without any strong justification) that provided one looks at the Lockean Common of future ideas as one which is an 'open-access common' rather than one in which the idea resources are owned in common, then a firstness argument may have merit. Notwithstanding this, Munzer and Raustiala's principal difficulty with the firstness argument is similar to that raised by them in relation to labour desert. Even *if* firstness matters, the current holders of the traditional knowledge were *not* in fact the first to make the discovery (or to individualise the idea out the Common to use the Lockean analogy) and Munzer and Raustiala do not see why the descendants should be entitled to a right which may be justified only to their remote ancestors. Again, perhaps surprisingly, they do not seek to apply, or criticise, Nozick's just entitlement approach.

Munzer and Raustiala imagine a situation in which traditional knowledge rights are asserted in a centuries-old traditional dance and look at the incremental changes in that dance with time. Their analysis is as follows:

(i) Perhaps the 'originators' of the dance in fact borrowed elements from other long-lost dances of their ancestors or from other groups. We cannot know.
(ii) Looking at incremental changes may give separate 'layered' rights to the individual increments, but not to the *entirety* of the dance.
(iii) Enquiries into firstness would probably be very fact specific and in fact entirely indeterminate in the absence of written records.

Can such an argument be flawed because it is actually a trans-temporal 'group' which has progressively developed the dance and it is this 'group' which can lay claim to the traditional rights rather than the membership of that group from time to time? Whilst Munzer and Raustiala accept that such a claim may weaken their 'remote descendant' critique (but do not say why), they revert back to the argument that firstness does not, in any case, provide a justification for specific or particular intellectual property rights. They also add that the trans-temporal group claim requires an *indefinite duration* of the right in the dance to allow the bundle

[65] Munzer and Raustiala (n 63) 62.

of rights in the dance to develop and amalgamate. However, they believe this is counter to the need to balance private property rights against the public interest (which has driven the development of limited durations for intellectual property rights) but give no philosophical rationale for why traditional knowledge should, or should not, be time limited.

Munzer and Raustiala's concern about the difficulty in identifying the source of the traditional knowledge right seems to echo Attas's broader concern about the problem of origination (and the problem of individuation). However, is their problem actually a subcategory of Attas's broader philosophical concern? Munzer and Raustiala's concern appears predominantly to be in relation to the practical *evidential* problems envisaged in finding the source of the information.

Although they do not mention it, Munzer and Raustiala's observation of the potential complexity seen in determining the origin and scope of a particular piece of knowledge does seem to provide further evidence in support of Attas's argument that it is hard to see a *natural law* justification for intellectual property rights in general.

It would also suggest that Attas's reasoning can comfortably be extended to a traditional knowledge right (which, understandably, Attas himself did not address) and may suggest that traditional knowledge (particularly where the information is of a trans-generational and/or of an inseparably amalgamated nature) is an area in which the problems of origination and individuation can be particularly difficult – not unlike questions of jointly originated artistic works.

B. Personality-Based Justifications for Intellectual Property – Introduction

Personality-based justifications have long sat at the heart of the deontological arguments for rights in property (and intellectual property). Broadly speaking there are three related arguments under this head. The first is Kant's limited, but interesting, arguments against pirated books based on the concept of 'authorial personality'. The second is based on Fichte's ideas of rights based on personality. The third is based on Hegel's broad metaphysical system. Each will be dealt with in turn.

C. The Kantian Justification

i. Kant on Property Ownership

As we have seen, the Lockean-desert account for intellectual property rights relies upon an extension of Locke's original views relating to the first ownership of a piece of tangible property (land or the produce of land) to claims to ownership over a portion of the supposed terra nullius of 'as yet to be had ideas'. This account is grounded in Locke's key principle of self ownership, a self-ownership that serves as the fount of ownership of things extrinsic to the self. Kant's justification of ownership of property, though similarly deontological, is founded on a radically different basis – namely the individual's *innate* right to freedom. For Kant, the right to ownership of property in things is *not* an inherent natural law right, but is merely derivative upon a person's inherent right to control his affairs.[66] Accordingly, in his *Metaphysics of Morals* of 1797, Kant defines property in this way: 'that is rightfully mine … with which I am so connected that another's use of it without my consent would wrong me'.[67]

The most direct way in which a person can be connected with something is by *physical* possession, what Kant describes as 'sensible' possession. However, if free beings are to be able to realise their inherent freedom by using objects for their freely chosen purposes one cannot reasonably require that they retain physical possession of them at all times. So for Kant, 'something external would be mine only if I may assume that I would be wronged by another even though I am not in possession of it'.[68] Mere physical possession is not, of itself, sufficient to create ownership of an object. Therefore, the possession required to give effect to individual freedom is 'intelligible possession' where the owner is deprived by the action of a third party on the owner's property even if the property is spatially separate from the owner and even if the owner is unaware of the actions of the third party. Of course, having 'intelligible possession' of a particular object requires all other free beings to respect that possession and refrain from using that object. The unilateral declaration of intelligible possession would impact on the freedom of others and interfere with the universality of the right to freedom. However, universality can be maintained if all free beings agree to respect other's claims to intelligible possession. The mutual obligation to respect property rights can only exist within a society – a civil condition – which provides a mechanism to acknowledge and police such ownership and to determine competing claims. Indeed, for Kant, the creation of a condition in which the property is respected and protected is one of the reasons why free individuals are obligated to work towards the achievement of a civil state.

This theory addresses how existing claims to ownership are respected. How, though, are *initial* claims to ownership treated? In Chapter 2 of the *Metaphysics of Morals* Kant describes a stepwise process by which an object comes into the ownership of an individual through original acquisition.[69] It is a process that is consistent with his categorisation of sensible and intelligible possession:

(i) *Possessio phaenomenon* – the apprehension of an object by taking possession of the object in space and time provided it belongs to no one (or else it

[66] AD Rosen, *Kant's Theory of Justice* (Ithaca, NY, Cornell University Press, 1993) 19; P Guyer, *Kant on Freedom, Law and Happiness* (Cambridge, Cambridge University Press, 2000) 236; AW Wood, *Kantian Ethics* (Cambridge, Cambridge University Press, 2008) 197.

[67] Immanuel Kant, *The Metaphysics of Morals* [1797] 6.245, in MJ Gregor (trans, ed), *Immanuel Kant, Practical Philosophy* (Cambridge, Cambridge University Press, 1996) 401.

[68] ibid.

[69] ibid 411.

would conflict with another person's freedom in accordance with universal laws); followed by

(ii) *Declaratio* – the giving a sign to others of your possession of the apprehended object and of your intention to exclude everyone else from it; followed by

(iii) *Appropriatio* – appropriation as the act of the general will of the community giving an external law through which everyone is bound to agree with your choice of acquisition.[70]

Under this process, where one has a true terra nullius of land the individual is free to seek to acquire land. However, this initial acquisition – what Kant refers to as 'taking control' or *occupatio* – gives rise only to a 'provisional' ownership which requires confirmation by the consent of others. Obtaining this provisional ownership requires that the acquirer give a signal to the wider world that she is making a claim to it and wants to exclude others from it – for example through a 'keep out' sign or a fence. The turning of the provisional ownership into a finalised ownership requires broad consensus that the acquirer is the owner of the property – indeed, it is only once *all* have consented to our acquirer's ownership that it becomes truly valid. To get to this stage requires 'negotiation' with others which is supervised and policed by those in authority within society. Kant is unclear as to the exact process for resolving conflict over disputed claims, but is clear that the parties have a duty to arrive at settlements which tend to secure a fully civil condition for society. Alongside this, property claims in general grow more finalised as society advances to a fully civil condition.[71]

ii. *Kant and Intellectual Property*

Can this philosophy of ownership be extended to ownership over intangibles such as ideas? There is a glaring problem. The key to Kant's *occupatio* phase of acquisition is that the prospective owner must have the wherewithal to *physically* defend her acquisition against all comers. As mentioned at the beginning of this chapter, tangible objects, whether these be land or the fruit of that land, are rivalrous and physically excludable. Intangible things, such as ideas, are just the opposite – in the absence of a formal mechanism securing protection they are non-rivalrous and non-excludable. No physical mechanism of acquisition or defence is possible.

As we have seen Locke's natural right theory is arguably amenable to a logical leap into the realm of the terra nullius of 'as yet to be had' ideas – it does not rely on physical defence of the acquired property. In contrast, the extension of Kant's *occupatio* into this sphere is significantly more problematic. Kant himself states that: 'Original acquisition of an external object of choice is called taking control of it (*occupatio*), and only corporeal things (substances) can be acquired originally.'[72] Indeed, there is further evidence that Kant would never have intended

[70] ibid.
[71] M Verhaegh, 'Kant and Property Rights' (2004) 18(3) *Journal of Libertarian Studies* 11, 12.
[72] Gregor (n 67) 412.

such an extension of his account for the acquisition of property into the realm of intangibles.[73] In 1785, Kant published his essay *Of the Injustice of Counterfeiting Books* in which he proposed a sui generis right of 'authorial' personality. According to Pievatolo,[74] Kant saw this authorial right as a *ius personale* (a right to compel others to do things) rather than an invention of a new *ius reale* (right in property). In doing so, Kant saw himself as following the Roman law tradition in which only tangible objects – *res quae tangi possunt* – are amenable to ownership.

As Dutfield and Suthersanen highlight, at the time of Kant's writing *Of the Injustice of Counterfeiting Books*, the Holy Roman Empire was a complex mosaic of independent states.[75] With no consistent overarching law controlling the printing and selling of books the situation was rife for cross-border trade across the Empire in pirated books. Kant was seeking a justifiable mechanism for preventing this piratic trade. Kant divided a book into three theoretical elements:

(i) a mere physical commodity – bound pages with writing on;
(ii) as a means for conveying thoughts; and
(iii) as a 'speech'

In relation to (i), when the purchaser purchases a book she purchases *that* book and owns *that* object and may dispose of it as she wishes. However, save for lighting fires and propping up tables, that book has little value without the input of the author. In relation to (ii), reprinting of books cannot prevent the original author from conceiving her thoughts – ideas cannot be stolen as they are not property.[76] Accordingly, neither element (i) nor element (ii) will give a right to prevent reprinting of books. Indeed, as *ius reale* can only apply to things and not to ideas, the purchaser of a book may reproduce the work for themselves as they are merely doing something with their private property.

To find a justification for preventing commercial reprinting, Kant had to invoke a separate, *ius personale*, mechanism. Accordingly, Kant sees a book as a 'speech' or an 'action' by the author – an *opera* – which (in 1785) could only be conveyed to a wider audience through the medium of the book. As Dutfield and Suthersanen put it: 'To Kant, the author retains the opera or speech. It is not a commodity to be sold and bought. The book as opus is merely the mute instrument which holds the book as opera.'[77] Why should this focus on the concept of a book as speech matter? Pievatolo puts it thus:

> To speak in the name of another without his authorization is like engaging in a relationship with another without his consent. As personal rights, according to Kant, concern relations among free beings, they can arise only from expressed agreements.

[73] MC Pievatolo, *Freedom, Ownership and Copyright: Why Does Kant Reject the Concept of Intellectual Property?* (2010) ssrn.com/abstract=1540095.
[74] Pievatolo (n 73).
[75] Dutfield and Suthersanen (n 20) 56.
[76] Pievatolo (n 73) 3.
[77] Dutfield and Suthersanen (n 20) 57.

> Hence the unauthorised printer is like the unauthorized spokesperson, who produces a relation to the author with the public without being entitled to do it.[78]

Clearly Kant in some respects anticipates the ideas of modern copyright in that there is a concept of a right in the work which sits separately from the vessel in which the work resides (be it a book, magnetic tape or digital format). However, his idea of *opera* in a work is not, as we have seen, a *property* right. It is arguably a good deal closer to the concept of a moral right in a work, but it is more than a right to attribution or a right to prevent derogative treatment. Neither apparently does it include a right to prevent creation of derivative works (perhaps as it cannot interfere with the creation of ideas). Kant's concept of *opera* is certainly very narrow and does not extend to other art forms.[79] For Pievatolo, Kant's deliberately narrow approach to controlling piracy is consistent with his overall philosophy. She concludes that Kant holds to the Roman Law tradition (that *ius reale* cannot apply to intangibles) not because of conservatism, but because of Enlightenment – liberty of speech is an important part of the innate right of freedom and cannot be suppressed without suppressing freedom itself.[80]

iii. Kant and Traditional Knowledge

To what extent can Kant's ideas on the protection of property, and his limited right to authorial personality, assist with the question of the justification for a right to veto use of TKAGR? Kant's theory of acquisition of property expressly excludes ownership in intangibles – an exclusion that is consistent with his concept of a narrow scope of protection offered by a right to authorial personality. Any attempt at application of Kant's account for property to the present question requires us to go back to first principles. Traditional knowledge, even TKAGR, and even knowledge with the most practical of applications, remains a body of intangible ideas. According to Kant there can be no ownership in such ideas.

We might seek to suggest that where Indigenous peoples have (through the use of secrecy, social structure and of taboos) sought to exclude third parties from appropriating a particular piece of knowledge they have placed a clear *declaratio* to the world that the information was theirs and that they thereby sought to derive 'provisional' ownership over the information. However, for Kant, since no *possessio phaenomenon* is possible in respect of an intangible, any attempt to seek such provisional ownership must fail. Notwithstanding this failure, can we seek to apply Kant's concept of 'authorial personality' to the question? Authorial personality as described in *On the Injustice of Counterfeiting Books* is, as we have seen, deliberately limited. It will not create any sort of property in ideas. However, it does argue that anyone who seeks to act as a 'spokesperson' for an author will require their

[78] Pievatolo (n 73) 3.
[79] ibid 4.
[80] ibid 7.

consent to do so. In *On the Injustice of Counterfeiting Books* it is the reprinting of a book – the 'retelling' as it were of the *opera* inherent in the original book (without the consent of the author) that is amoral, since it creates a relationship between the author and the reprinter without the author's consent.

Can we say that a group of Indigenous peoples is in a sense an 'author' for these purposes? The Kantian authorial personality account is strongly reliant on the innate freedom of *the individual*. No matter how close knit, it might be difficult to describe a group of Indigenous people as the single individual that Kant envisaged. Of course, the closer knit, and less dispersed the group, the closer they may approximate to an individual. However, there will be a continuum of closeness of relationships across varying Indigenous groups and it is impossible to say with any certainty what the requisite 'closeness' to create an authorial identity should be. Even if, for the sake of argument, we assume that a close-knit Indigenous group *can* have the requisite authorial personality, does unauthorised use of the information created by the group within (say) a pharmaceutical research process constitute an unauthorised 'retelling' of the *opera* – the 'speech' of the Indigenous group in the information? It is hard to say whether a piece of information can be considered a 'speech' as such. On the one hand, Kant does not provide us with a de minimis definition below which the subject matter of a book is in some way unworthy of being a speech. On the other hand, it is hard to envisage that the oral divulgement of a piece of information by one or more members of an Indigenous group to (say) an ethnobotanist, constitutes authorial 'speech' in the way that Kant envisaged.

Assuming, again for the sake of argument, that misuse of a piece of information does constitute unauthorised 'retelling' of the speech within the information, we need to remind ourselves that the mischief Kant sought address relied upon the presence of two (or more) competing publishers, one authorised, the other not. We need also to note that Kant's proposed solution was that the unauthorised publisher would pay damages to the authorised publisher. Kant does not propose any form of *injunction* or veto preventing the unauthorised publisher from publishing (enforceable by the author or the rightful publisher). Such an approach would seem consistent with Kant's view that property rights (giving the right to *exclusive* use) cannot exist in intangibles. His solution, though compensating the rightful publisher, still allows the ideas within the work to continue to be disseminated subject to compensation. Following Kant's 'authorial personality' approach closely (and for the moment accepting the many assumptions made above), it might appear that if the Indigenous group were to give consent to one pharmaceutical company to utilise a piece of TKAGR, the group would not have a power of *veto* over unauthorised use by a second pharmaceutical company, but the authorised user might have a right of *compensation* from the unauthorised user.

Do we, though, need these competing 'publishers' for Kant's approach to apply? Is there some broader principle within Kant's approach which will allow us to examine misuse in the absence of an authorised 'publisher'/user? As discussed above, Kant's theoretical basis for the right to authorial personality relies upon the innate freedom of the individual to enter into relationships only with consent and the 'relationship' with the unauthorised publisher is created by the unauthorised publisher without the author's consent. Kant himself makes a 'universal observation'[81] that includes reference to the relationship between the author and his editor. He states: 'the editor transacts his business of editor not merely in his own name, but in the name of another (namely the author) and without consent cannot transact [it] at all'.[82]

This highlights the importance which is seen throughout the essay on the 'name' of the author (which is of course closely linked to the personality of the author). Later in his universal observation, Kant clearly expresses that works of art may be imitated and are to be seen as distinct from the written word as they are not the 'speech' of a named author:

> But the writing of another is the speech of a person (opera); and whoever publishes it can speak to the public only in the name of this other, and say nothing more of himself than that the author makes the following speech to the public through him.[83]

Crucially Kant allows the production of derivative works as they are no longer the speech of the original author:

> When one in the meantime alters (abridges or augments or retouches) the book of another, so that it would now be wrong even to give it out under the name of the author of the original; then the retouching in the proper name of the publisher is no counterfeit, and therefore not prohibited. For here another author transacts through his editor another business than the first, and consequently seizes this in his business with the public not a bit; he represents not that author, as speaking through him, but another. Likewise, the translation into another language cannot be held to be a counterfeit; for it is not the same speech of the author, though the thoughts may be exactly the same.[84]

The right envisaged by Kant therefore seems to sit more closely to a right to protect goodwill and reputation than one that controls *ideas* – it is in many ways a form of unfair-competition provision in favour of *named* authors.

Can we apply this general principle to our Indigenous group holding TKAGR? Even assuming a sufficient degree of closeness such that the group can be considered an 'author', the information they hold seems much closer to mere information than to Kant's envisioned 'speech'. Downstream use of TKAGR is very likely to be divorced from the 'name' of the Indigenous group, and in any event much will be akin to the derivative works, which, according to Kant's account, are free to use.

[81] I Kant, *Of the Injustice of Counterfeiting Books* (1785) 7, staffweb.hkbu.edu.hk/ppp/fne/essay3.html.
[82] ibid.
[83] ibid.
[84] ibid.

To conclude, attempting to 'shoehorn' the Kantian concept of authorial personality into service as a justification for protecting TKAGR is fraught with difficulties. In fact, the clearest message that we get from Kant's theory of property, which is consistent with his concept for authorial personality, is that ideas cannot ever be prevented from being used. Even Kant's remedy for breach of authorial personality was *compensatory* rather than a right to veto use. Kant's approach therefore appears to militate against any right veto on the non-consensual use of TKAGR.

D. The Fichtean Justification

i. Fichte and Intellectual Property

Johan Gottlieb Fichte outlines his justification for the protection of intellectual property in his essay *The Illegality of the Unauthorised Reprinting of Books*, published in 1793 (eight years after the publishing of Kant's *Of the Injustice of Counterfeiting Books*).[85] Fichte's philosophy broadly follows that of Kant, in being based on the inherent freedom of the individual. However, in looking at the protection of authors he arrives at a somewhat different outcome.[86] As we have seen, Kant's justification for preventing the unauthorised reprinting of books is based on the relationship between the author and the public (and publishers), and the concept that a book incorporates the 'speech' of the author. Unlike Kant, who rejects outright the ownership of ideas, Fichte accepts that there can be some ownership of intangibles. For Fichte a book consists of the physical, tangible elements (paper, bindings, etc) with which a purchaser of the book can do as she likes, and separate 'non-physical' elements. These non-tangible elements can be divided into the following:

(i) the ideas in the book (the 'material' or 'content'); and
(ii) the expression of the ideas (the 'form').

In relation to the ideas in a book, Fichte believed that once ideas are published by an author they are placed into the public domain. Mayeda[87] gives two reasons why Fichte believed this should be the case:

(a) the acquisition of ideas entails no interference with the thoughts or physical person of the author; and
(b) in producing a work for public consumption, the author must have wished to communicate the ideas and share them with others.

[85] G Mayeda 'Commentary of Fichte's "The Illegality of the Unauthorised Reprinting of Books: An Essay on Intellectual Property During the Age of the Enlightenment"' (2008) 5(1,2) *University of Ottawa Law and Technology Journal* 141, 171.
[86] ibid; Pievatolo (n 73) 4.
[87] Mayeda (n 85) 151.

In marked contrast with this position in relation to ideas, Mayeda goes on to explain that in Fichte's account;

> The right to appropriate and use the form in which the ideas are expressed is not transferred to the purchaser. The form of expression is a creation of the author; it is a unique expression of her personality. It follows that any use or appropriation of form entails a violation of the personality of the author.[88]

Interestingly this clear divide in the treatment of an idea per se and the form in which the idea is expressed would appear to foreshadow modern copyright law.

ii. Fichte and Traditional Knowledge

Fichte's support for the protection of the individual means by which an author chooses to express her ideas seems to be based upon the traditional idea of an author producing a work. To what extent can we apply this rationale for protection to the situation of an Indigenous group holding TKAGR? Again we encounter a significant problem (as we had with Kant's approach) in apportioning a personality to a group. However, even assuming a sufficient degree of closeness such that the group can be considered an 'author' for these purposes, we must stress that the TKAGR held by the group is much closer to being an idea per se than to an expression of that idea. As we have seen, Fichte does not have an objection to the protection of ideas based on any inherent difficulty with 'owning' an intangible (as was the case with Kant) – his exclusion of ideas per se is, to some degree, based on the intention of the author to share her ideas with the world. In relation to TKAGR held by an Indigenous group, the question of whether they are seeking/have sought to share such knowledge will clearly depend on the circumstances in which the information is divulged. However, the difficulty with the protection of ideas per se within Fichte's account is inherent within the way he sees authors connecting with ideas; it is the way in which ideas and their connections are communicated to others through words and mental images – how there are *expressed* – that are unique to the author and give rise to the personality right.

To the extent that the TKAGR is held in some form which embodies a group *expression* of the idea, that expression could fall within the ambit of Fichte's right based on personality. However, any downstream use of the information within drug discovery is very unlikely to be using any particular 'form' in which the information is originally held. Any 'form' will likely to have been jettisoned early in the passage of the traditional knowledge through the research process. Downstream use will likely be use of pure information, eg 'plant A is useful for treating disease X'. It is difficult to see how such pure information could be the subject of Fichte's right protection *expression*. Accordingly Fichte's approach (as did Kant's) militates against any right of veto over the non consensual use of TKAGR.

[88] ibid 152.

E. The Hegelian Justification

i. The Hegelian Justification for Property

Hegel's *Elements of the Philosophy of Right* was published in Berlin in 1821. It includes his discussion of the role of and justification for property rights. Hegel's broader philosophy has attracted (very) substantial criticism. Warburton summarises many views thus:

> That question 'What does it mean?' is one that readers of Hegel's work ask themselves a lot. His writing is fiendishly difficult, partly because, like Kant's, it is mostly expressed in very abstract language and often used terms that he has himself invented. No one, perhaps not even Hegel, has understood all of it.[89]

and

> Hegel irritated many philosophers. Some philosophers even treated his work as an example of the risk of using terms imprecisely. Bertrand Russell came to despise it, and AJ Ayer declared that most of Hegel's sentences expressed nothing at all. For Ayer, Hegel's writing was no more informative than nonsense verse and considerably less appealing.[90]

However, although Russell came to believe that almost all Hegel's doctrines to be false, he did see his work as retaining an importance which is not merely historical, describing it as the 'best representative of a certain kind of philosophy which, in others, is less coherent and less comprehensive'.[91]

For Hughes, Hegel's justification for property is rooted in his general philosophy – the individual's will is at the core of an individual's existence and is constantly seeking actuality (*Wirklichkeit*) and effectiveness in the world.[92] Personality is related to the will's struggle to actualise itself, and a person must translate his freedom into an external sphere in order to exist as an 'Idea'. Dutfield and Suthersanen state that: 'Hegel declared that property is the initial and final embodiment of freedom and individuality. Indeed, to fail to have a sphere of property in one's own life is to fail to attain self-conscious knowledge of oneself as a free person.' They go one to say that, for Hegel, for someone to achieve a personality (and to be a person) an individual must control his external and internal environment and control his resources and that this control (as well as actualisation of one's will) is 'best achieved by a set of property rights'.[93] Hughes states that Hegelian assertion of the self alone is not sufficient to create a property right, any claim to property must be acknowledged and approved. Through such acceptance, the will's possession of an object (through 'occupation' or

[89] N Warburton, *A Little History of Philosophy* (New Haven, CT, Yale University Press, 2011) 126.
[90] ibid 127.
[91] B Russell, *History of Western Philosophy* (London, Routledge Classics, 2004) 667.
[92] Hughes (n 47) 331.
[93] Dutfield and Suthersanen (n 20) 58.

'embodiment') becomes property.[94] Hughes believes that although Hegel seems to support a 'first possession' or labour theory, this is not what Hegel means by 'occupation'. Although the will can only occupy something that is a virgin object (or something that has been abandoned by another), this first occupation is, in itself, insufficient. A property right is only retained so long as the will in some way manifests itself in the object; the will must continue to *want* the object and is required to *continually reaffirm* this desire. Accordingly, the property right can be lost through a failure to reaffirm, or by active withdrawal. Hughes states that although application of 'labour' to an object may denote occupation it is not a necessary prerequisite – one may equally manifest will in a natural object to which one has become *emotionally* attached. Hughes further states that *use* of an object is not a requirement for occupation.[95] He also states that marking or imposing a form on an object or keeping the object in close spatiotemporal proximity to an individual can all be helpful indicia of the individual's will, but again these are not *requirements* for occupation. Similarly abandonment of an object depends on the will's desire to possess an object, and does not require external indicia.[96]

ii. The Hegelian Justification for Intellectual Property

Application of Locke's property theory to the field of intellectual property requires something of a theoretical stretch with the imagining of a 'Common' of putative ideas and the acquisition of parts of that Common through the application of labour. Hegel's concept of property is, perhaps, not as intuitively easy to grasp as Locke's. However, its application to the realm of intellectual property (particularly in artistic works) arguably requires less of an intellectual stretch. In fact, as Hughes states, for Hegel, intellectual property does not need to be justified by analogy to physical property, and indeed, for Hughes, the analogy to *physical* property distorts the Hegelian relation between personality, mental traits and the will.[97]

Hegel identifies that people may be hesitant to call intellectual attainments which are created by the mind 'things'. However, in paragraph 68 of his *Elements of the Philosophy of Right*, Hegel outlines *why* intellectual property rights should exist. The paragraph is instructive, particularly in the way in which it appreciates the non-rivalrous nature of intangible intellectual products:

> The distinctive quality of intellectual production may, by virtue of the way in which it is expressed, be immediately transformed into the external quality of a thing, which may then in turn be produced by others. In acquiring it, the new owner may thus appropriate the thoughts which it communicates or the technical invention which it embodies, and it is this possibility which at times (as with literary works) constitutes the sole purpose of such things and their value as acquisitions; in addition, the new owner at

[94] Hughes (n 47) 334.
[95] ibid.
[96] ibid.
[97] Ibid. 333.

> the same time comes into possession of the *universal ways and means* of so expressing himself and of producing a multiplicity of such things.[98]

Hegel notes that the creation of such proprietorship is not 'without utility':

> The purely negative, but most basic, means of furthering the sciences and arts is to protect those who work in them against *theft* and to provide them, with security for their property, just as the earliest and most important means of furthering commerce and industry was to protect them against highway robbery.[99]

The Hegelian justification for property (and intellectual property rights) has been subject to significant criticism. First, we have to appreciate that Hegel was seeking to develop an entire (and distinct) metaphysical system and one arguably needs to be careful not to use elements of his philosophy in a 'pick-and-mix' manner outwith the context of his metaphysic system of the self. Indeed, Harris states that some Hegelian apologists regard it as an 'impertinence' to seek to quarry justice reasons at all from Hegel's writings.[100]

However, even assuming that Hegel's overall metaphysical system is not flawed, and that elements are not taken out of context, commentators have identified particular difficulties *within* the Hegelian property theory as it specifically applies to intellectual property. There are two key points: the question of alienation of the self and the question of what type subject matter is actually covered by Hegel's concept of intellectual property.

(a) Alienation

Whereas Hegel believes that one can alienate most 'real' property when one no longer wishes to occupy it, one of the basic tenets that underlie his philosophy is that one cannot alienate (or surrender) any universal element of one's self. Hughes, Moore, and Dutfield and Suthersan identify Hegel's concern in relation to whether this inalienability can be applied to intellectual products: does the giving away (or selling) of an item which embodies the expression of an idea act as an alienation of the ownership of that expression?[101] For Dutfield and Suthersanen, the 'crux' of Hegel's justification for intellectual property is given in paragraph 69 of his *Elements of the Philosophy of Right*:[102]

> Since the person who acquires such a product[[103]] possesses its entire use and value if he owns a *single* copy of it, he is the complete and free owner of it as an individual item. But the author of the book or the inventor of the technical device remains the

[98] AW Wood (ed) and HB Nisbet (trans), *GWF Hegel, Elements of the Philosophy of Right* (Cambridge, Cambridge University Press, 2003) 98 (emphasis original).
[99] ibid 99 (emphasis original).
[100] JW Harris, *Property and Justice* (Oxford, Oxford University Press, 1996) 232.
[101] Hughes (n 47) 320; Moore (n 20) 8; Dutfield and Suthersanen (n 20) 58.
[102] Dutfield and Suthersanen (n 20) 59.
[103] This is a product embodying an expression of the author of a thing.

> owner of the *universal* ways and means of reproducing such products and things, for he has not immediately alienated these universal ways and means as such but may reserve them for himself as his distinctive mode of expression.[104]

Here Hegel identifies one of the crucial characteristics of most intellectual property (with the exception, perhaps, of artists' resale rights),[105] namely that the right exists separately from a *particular* thing incorporating the right. Here also perhaps can be seen the beginning of the doctrine of exhaustion of rights (or first sale doctrine), namely that in selling a particular item incorporating the right the owner of the right can only control the initial sale, but not subsequent sales.

(b) Subject Matter

What type of intangible intellectual product is the subject matter of Hegel's extension of the personality? We saw above that neither Fichte, nor Kant, gave justifications for the control of information as information per se. Paragraph 69 of Hegel's *Elements of the Philosophy of Right* (set out above) appears to have a focus on the 'expression' of an individual as the basis for the existence of the right. As Hughes highlights, there exists a spectrum of intellectual products that demonstrate varying degrees of personality of the author of the work: from (at one end) works of art which arguably contain a substantial embodiment of the author's personality, through to (at the other end) computer programs, chip topography masks, client lists and industrial patents.[106] Hughes posits that the higher the degree of technical constraint within an object or problem, the less opportunity there is for *personal* expression. Generally speaking, an artist is constrained only by her materials and her opportunity for expression is accordingly very large. Hughes believes that at some point the technical constraints will become so large that any meaningful expression of the personality is impossible.[107] He stresses, however, that even creation of a highly technical intellectual product may still provide some limited mode of expression of the personality of the creator – there may be many ways to achieve a similar technical end but the creator can choose between them, and in doing so expresses her personality. In addition, a creator may become known for a particular solution, even if that solution style is acknowledged only within a small coterie.

Hughes points out that this analysis refers only to *one* variety of expression, namely one in which the intellectual work becomes the *conduit* for the expression personality. He points out that another potential Hegelian property claim exists where the creator claims the property in order to *create* (rather than *express*) a particular persona. Hughes believes such a claim has limits – one cannot simply

[104] Wood and Nisbet (n 98) 99 (emphasis original).
[105] See eg UK Artists Resale Rights Regulation 2006.
[106] Hughes (n 47) 344.
[107] Similar arguments have been raised with regard to the subsistence of copyright in technical objects. See eg CJEU decision in C-833/18 *SI and Brompton Bicycle Ltd v Chedech / Get2Get* [2020].

seek to be associated with a thing without there being some *internal* connection. He points out that it is true that certain inventors become associated with their inventions (Hughes refers to Doppler, Edison and Bell but there are, of course, many others). However, those relationships arise in time as a result of the invention, not necessarily due to an *initial* assertion of personality.

Although his writing is far from clear, Hegel himself seems to give guidance (within paragraph 69) that his concept of property in intangible concepts should extend only to the control of ideas which are embodied in a particularly *form*. He accepts that those who are made aware of an idea may themselves be entitled to rights where that idea is put into a new form:

> Besides, the destiny of a product of the intellect is to be apprehended by other individuals and appropriated by their representational thinking, memory, thought, etc. Hence the mode of expression whereby these individuals in turn make what they have learned … into an alienable thing will always tend to have some distinctive *form*, so that they can regard the resources which flow from it as their property, and may assert their right to reproduce it.[108]

It would appear, therefore, that Hegel's concept of intellectual property (though covering the *physical* embodiment of technical concepts) follows the thinking of Fichte and Kant in not extending to the protection of ideas per se.

iii. Hegel and Traditional Knowledge

At first blush, Hegel's idea of the self (and actualisation of the will) seems a long way from ideas of group ownership of traditional knowledge by Indigenous peoples. However, can we apply Hegel's justification for intellectual property to an Indigenous group holding TKAGR?

Papadopoulou is of the view that a 'plausible' justification for the introduction of property rights to TKAGR could be that it is an expression of an Indigenous people's 'common personality' and that the application of Hegel's personality theory to TKAGR would mean that Indigenous peoples 'as individuals, expressed their will on genetic resources, by using them, seizing them or marking them' and that 'the expression of their will on the resources is decisive in their process of self-determination, and lays the ground for their property right to TKAGR'.[109] There is an intuitive appeal to this approach. However, Papadopoulou suggests that there is a problem in applying Hegel's personality theory as it is a 'justification for the establishment of private property rights of individuals, but not collective rights owned by a community'.[110]

[108] Wood and Nisbet (n 98) 100.

[109] F Papadopoulou, *The Protection of Traditional Knowledge on Genetic Resources* (Cheltenham, Edward Elgar, 2018) 288.

[110] ibid.

Whilst Munzer and Raustiala do not directly address a Hegelian personality-based justification for a right in traditional knowledge, they approach something that is arguably similar under the head 'Moral Right of the Community'.[111] They consider the question of whether a 'moral right' of an Indigenous community in relation to a piece of traditional knowledge should give rise to an intellectual property right in that knowledge. They state that the concept of moral right (or rights) as arising in the civil law tradition and point to the French *droit moral* and German *Urheberpersönlichkeitsrecht* ('originator's personality right') as examples. They state that although the rationale for such rights is disputed, most often its basis is said to be the idea of personality or personhood developed by Kant, Fichte and Hegel. They also highlight that these rights, which include a right of attribution and a right to prevent derogatory treatment of a work, are essentially *non-economic* in nature.

Munzer and Raustiala believe that for such moral rights to apply to an Indigenous group one would have to envisage that that group in some way acted together as an 'author' since it is the personality (or personhood) of the author which is central to the idea of a moral right. When asking how one might ascribe 'personhood' to a community they highlight that: 'stereotypes are to be resisted, in part because they subsume all members of a group under one image. We do not say that these questions lack a non-stereotypical answer. However, we fail to see a clear path to satisfactory answers.'[112] Munzer and Raustiala ask whether the moral right of the community may potentially form the basis of a *sui generis* right of *indefinite* duration because:

(a) citing Tsosie,[113] as Indigenous peoples face a special threat to their culture they should have a right to control 'who can tell their stories and who can use their designs and symbols'; and
(b) since the actual creator and the moment of creation (or fixation) of the traditional knowledge cannot be determined, no other form of intellectual property could be available.

Munzer and Raustiala argue against such a justification. The moral right argument is strongest for them if one can assume that the Indigenous people who are claiming the right approximate as closely as possible to a single 'personality' – for example, they lived in a tight-knit group in one location and their language, culture and practices remain virtually constant. Although they accept that this may exceptionally be the case, they argue that in the great majority of situations this situation is disrupted by migration of individuals (in and out), intermarriage of individuals from other linguistic/cultural groups, and the adoption of

[111] Munzer and Raustiala (n 63) 68.
[112] ibid 71.
[113] R Tsosie, 'Reclaiming Native Stories: An Essay on Cultural Appropriation and Cultural Rights' (2002) 34 *Arizona State Law Journal* 299, 310.

external cultural ideas and practices, a process they describe as cultural 'hybridization' or 'blending'. Whilst stating that such hybridisation is in general a 'good thing' they note that it provides a problem for a traditional knowledge based on group personality: 'across the span of history, every cultural group has possessed [traditional knowledge]. … This raises the question why indigenous people's [traditional knowledge] ought to receive protection that other group's knowledge lacks.'[114]

They further argue that although it might be logically consistent to extend indefinite, group-related protection to all folklore (wherever it may be found) this would be disproportionate. Munzer and Raustiala believe that a proportionate response, based on moral right, would be:

(a) *divulgation* the right to make an item of their traditional knowledge known to the world and in this respect 'public' but to retain the power to keep that item from being used in any way by others – and therefore out of the public domain in a different respect; and
(b) *attribution*: the right to prevent attribution of the knowledge to any other group.

Given Munzer and Raustiala's general opposition to a sui generis positive right in traditional knowledge on other grounds, this does appear to be a major concession. In fact, their concept of 'divulgation' right looks very close to a positive right in all but name. It is strange that they support this, because, by their own argument, there remain significant problems to attributing a Hegelian (or Kantian, or Fichtean) personality to an Indigenous group both in terms of the containment of its membership and in temporal aspects (when is the personality meant to exist? – when the traditional knowledge was developed, or evolved, or 'fixed' by contact with the West?).

The problem in apportioning a personality to a group is clearly difficult. However, even if we can assume within a particular situation that there is a sufficient degree of 'closeness' such that the group can be considered an 'author' for the purposes of justifying a Hegelian (or Kantian, or Fichtean) personality right there is a greater problem. As was identified above, TKAGR is much closer to being information per se. There seems no reason, then, to suggest that Hegel's justification should not encounter the same difficulties as seen with the application of Fichte's justification. If the basis for a right is based upon *expression* of an idea, that justification will fail to support a justification for a right in information per se. Accordingly, for this author, Hegel's approach (as did Kant's and Fichte's) militates against any right of veto on the non-consensual use of TKAGR where such knowledge is an *idea* rather than the expression of an idea.

[114] Munzer and Raustiala (n 63) 72.

(a) Taubman's Right to Protect a Collective Persona

Although he does not directly address the philosophies of Kant, Fichte or Hegel, it is interesting to note that Taubman envisages that traditional communities can have a 'collective' personality.[115] Taubman highlights the so-called 'right of personality' that is seen in some (most notably civil) jurisdictions.[116] He argues that such a right includes the entitlement to 'choose what face is presented to the public, unless the public interest trumps private interests' and states that 'it is a right not to have a public personality imposed upon one, but to retain control over one's public identity'. Taubman argues that in a parallel way Indigenous communities claim control over their 'collective cultural persona' as a form of self-determination and that protection of a community's collectively held traditional knowledge and traditional cultural expressions

> does not mean simply closing off links with other cultural communities or the commercial domain, but about choosing what aspects of the collective identity may be used and disseminated beyond the community, and on what terms – including the recognition of customary law constraints on the use of elements of a community's cultural identity.[117]

Milius identifies difficulties with this account.[118] He argues that the conceptual problem with such a move is that the essence of distinctive characters is their identifiable variable for personhood, and that combining a large number of individuals into a collective does not 'alter the separateness of their individual autonomy associated with their individual personhoods', meaning

> that the whole cannot be considered the sum of its parts in the gaze of the law, but really as various collective superseding qualities of the whole (in this case having to do with traditional values and customs) which generally prevail over individual noise in the mix.[119]

To the extent that Taubman's 'collective persona' applies to the protection of cultural *expression* there very are clear echoes of the thinking of Kant, Fichte and Hegel in relation to the protection of the persona. However, Taubman also sees Indigenous collective personality as encompassing not only the way in which a collective persona, or its outward expression, is represented but to the control of traditional knowledge per se:

> There are external and internal aspects to the sense of violation that arises when traditional personality is appropriated. External exploitation of [traditional knowledge]

[115] A Taubman, 'Is There a Right of Collective Personality?' [2006] *European Intellectual Property Review* 485.

[116] G Brüggemeier et al (eds), *Personality Rights in European Tort Law* (Cambridge, Cambridge University Press, 2010).

[117] Taubman (n 118) 490.

[118] D Milius, 'Justifying Intellectual Property in Traditional Knowledge' [2009] *Intellectual Property Quarterly* 184, 196.

[119] ibid.

> and [traditional cultural expressions] is seen as misappropriation – a taking, theft or even conversion – of cultural or intellectual property; but it is also sensed as intrusion on the community itself.[120]

Clearly, the question of whether 'information' as such should be properly considered to be part of the collective external persona of an Indigenous group remains moot and will vary from group to group. Although, we might say that the closer knit the body holding the knowledge arguably, the stronger a personality basis for an intellectual property right in such knowledge, we also need to note that (as will be discussed in section XII of this chapter and has been stressed by Oguamanam)[121] the ways in which such knowledge is held is in no way uniform and Indigenous peoples have in some cases evolved complex structures for access and use of knowledge. In addition, as highlighted by Gupta, the contribution of different Indigenous community members to innovation and conservation is unlikely to be equal.[122]

How, then, should we treat Taubman's concept of the protection of the 'collective persona'? Although the idea has echoes of a Hegelian right of personality it also has strong echoes both of the 'utility through control' justification discussed in this chapter (in section VII.D) and an Indigenous right to self-determination (discussed in section XII.A) including to Gibson's communitarian justification (discussed in section XII.E) in which a right to control traditional knowledge arises out of the right of a community to manage its affairs. Indeed, if Taubman's protection of collective personality can encompass protection of information per se, it might perhaps be more properly treated as a part of a self-determination/communitarian, or a utility through control, justification rather than being seen as within the 'rights based on personality' philosophy of Kant/Fichte or Hegel. Indeed, such a treatment also addresses Milius's concern with regard to the difficulty of pooling individual identities.

What is the relationship between Taubman's concept of an Indigenous community's right to claim control over their 'collective cultural persona' and an 'Indigenous intellectual property right' to control traditional knowledge derived from an inherent right to self-determination (as discussed in section XII below)? It seems realistic to say that the former is essentially a clarification of an element of latter. The right of an individual to retain control over how one one's public identity is presented is clearly an important subset of a broader right to individual self-determination. Likewise, control over the 'collective cultural persona' of an Indigenous group can reasonably be seen as a subset of an Indigenous group's inherent right to self-determination.

[120] Taubman (n 115) 487.

[121] C Oguamanam, *International Law and Indigenous Knowledge* (Toronto, University of Toronto Press, 2006) 158.

[122] A Gupta, 'Getting Creative People, Individuals and Communities Their Due: Framework for Operationalizing Articles 8(j) and 10(c)' (paper submitted to the Secretariat of the Convention on Biological Diversity, 1996) 120.

VII. Consequentialist Justifications for Intellectual Property

The consequentialist justifications for intellectual property tend to be those most commonly expressed by intellectual property practitioners, judges and politicians and in the preambles to intellectual property legislation, whilst (for Merges) 'often intoning one of a few stock passages penned in a spare moment by Thomas Jefferson'.[123] Such justifications for intellectual property generally start from the broadly utilitarian perspective that intellectual creativity and innovation per se, and the betterment of society though the resultant enhanced intellectual and economic wealth that arises from these activities (and their commercialisation), are things which enhance the 'greater happiness of society'. This enhancement is to be achieved through the adoption of policies which encourage and support the creation of intellectual products. Moore sums up the theory in the following terms:

(i) society in general ought to attain an optimum of social utility;
(ii) as part of this aim, society should seek to optimise the amount of intellectual works being produced;
(iii) a necessary condition for promoting the creation of valuable intellectual works is granting limited rights of ownership to authors and inventors;
(iv) without certain guarantees as to the control of production of copies, authors and inventors might not engage in producing intellectual works;
(v) although the success of such policies cannot be ensured, failure is inevitable if those who incur no investment costs can seize and reproduce the intellectual effort of others; and therefore
(vi) the adoption of systems of protection (such as copyright, patent, and trade secret) yields an optimal production of intellectual production, and a corresponding optimal amount of social utility.[124]

Shiffrin states that the consequentialist justification argument: 'contends that intellectual property protections must be given to creators in order to give them the incentive to create their work', and that: 'In theory that incentive operates to stimulate creation of some work by promising the power to prevent other similar works from being produced or distributed.'[125] In fact, the consequentialist argument could be said to rely on two related, but distinct, incentives: the incentive to innovate and the incentive to commercialise. Such incentives-based approaches are closely linked to economic approaches to the analysis of intellectual property. Broadly speaking these approaches seek to determine conditions in which markets operate at optimal efficiency.[126]

[123] RP Merges, *Justifying Intellectual Property* (Cambridge, MA, Harvard University Press, 2011) 4.
[124] Moore (n 20) 10.
[125] Shiffrin (n 57) 94.
[126] See generally Dutfield and Suthersanen (n 20) 49.

A. Criticisms of Incentives-Based Justifications for Intellectual Property

The criticisms of the incentives-based justifications are wide ranging and the commentary here will be kept deliberately brief to allow a focus on how this justification relates to the protection of traditional knowledge.

The first key criticism is that market efficiency approaches are based upon an overly simplistic notion that the efficiency of the market is the principal desirable outcome of a set of positive laws. Even where one takes a purely Benthamite approach, that is, assuming that the enhancement of the *total* utility of a society is key (without reference to the distribution of social utility within that society), the utilitarian support for the desire to achieve an efficient market is based upon a simplistic 'efficient economy leads to more and better goods leads to more general happiness' causal chain. As will be discussed below, even this approach takes little account of any Millian 'quality' of utility concerns.[127] Where one rejects a total utility approach and places importance on problems of distribution, and demands of personal liberty, such a simplistic equation becomes still less viable.[128]

The second key criticism is that we cannot actually tell that providing intellectual property rights *does actually* serve to incentivise innovation. Moore suggests that empirical questions about the costs and benefits of intellectual property in encouraging innovation and its commercialisation are difficult to determine and have not been conclusive.[129] Shiffrin expresses further concerns that one cannot actually know whether the works incented under the law are superior in some respect (perhaps quantity or quality) to those that have been deterred by the law.[130]

Other commentators have gone further in their criticism, arguing that a proliferation of intellectual property rights creates a 'tragedy of the anti-commons' which has the effect of stifling the very innovation and commercialisation that it was intended (under the consequentialist account) to be incentivised.[131] Within this criticism is the argument that inventors will invent in any case, even in the absence of incentives. Shiffrin points out that many authors/inventors will be driven to create works (even in the absence of any formal incentivisation through intellectual property rights) through a desire to develop, inter alia, their art, reputation and for the general good of society.[132] She argues that to justify a 'strong'

[127] A Sen, *The Idea of Justice* (London, Penguin Books, 2010) 311.

[128] ibid 310; See generally A Sen, 'The Possibility of Social Choice' (1999) 89 *American Economic Review* 178.

[129] Moore (n 20).

[130] Shiffrin (n 57) 94.

[131] See eg MA Heller, 'The Tragedy of the Anticommons: Property in the Transition from Marx to Markets' (1998) 111 *Harvard Law Review* 621; see eg: MA Heller and R Eisenberg, 'Can Patents Deter Innovation? The Anticommons in Biomedical Research' (1998) 280 *Science* 698; DL Burk and MA Lemley, 'Policy Levers in Patent Law' (2003) 89 *Virginia Law Review* 1575; MA Lemley, 'Property, Intellectual Property, and Free Riding' (2005) 83 *Texas Law Review* 1031; S Leung, 'The Commons and Anticommons in Intellectual Property' (2010) 16 *UCL Jurisprudence Review* 16.

[132] Shiffrin (n 57) 94.

intellectual property regime the incentives argument must advance beyond what she calls

> the modest claim that creators need the funding available from intellectual property rights to recoup creation and labour costs; and that given the ability of competitors to make cheap copies, the funds creators need may exceed what would be available through unprotected release of their products and creations on the market.[133]

Although, as stated, here is not the place to fully explore these arguments, it is worth pointing out that the validity of an incentives-based justification for an intellectual property right will vary substantially in relation to both the intellectual property right in question and the field of activity which is arguably incentivised/deincentivised.[134]

B. Consequentialist Arguments for a Positive Right in TKAGR – An Introduction

What consequentialist arguments can be marshalled in support of a positive ABS right in TKAGR? As we will see, the key utilitarian goals for a positive ABS right in TKAGR are the preservation of Indigenous culture and of a biodiverse environment. We will look at how such a positive ABS right in TKAGR might effectively (or otherwise) achieve these ends. However, we will first address the extent to which the 'classic' 'incentive to innovate' and 'incentive to commercialise' utilitarian justifications for intellectual property rights support a positive ABS right in TKAGR.

i. *The 'Incentive to Innovate' Argument*

For Munzer and Raustiala Indigenous people may require a right to prevent others from using the traditional knowledge without providing compensation, but for Munzer and Raustiala this (and presumably any stronger right) cannot be defended on the basis of an incentive to innovate since no incentive in the form of intellectual property rights was required for *extant* traditional knowledge to be developed: 'The innovation has already occurred: at most we might use incentives to justify possible incremental improvements to existing [traditional knowledge]'.[135] Such a criticism relies on a very static view of the development of traditional knowledge. In contrast, Dutfield and Suthersanen suggest that such innovation in traditional knowledge is a live and ongoing process.[136] Indeed

[133] ibid 96.
[134] See generally Harrison (n19).
[135] Munzer and Raustiala (n 63) 74.
[136] Dutfield and Suthersanen (n 20) 73.

Mazzocchi refers to this ongoing evolution of traditional knowledge as 'traditional science'.[137] However, Munzer and Raustiala add that the more an Indigenous group looks to innovate some piece of shared knowledge, the less 'traditional' that knowledge appears. If a group (or an individual) do develop some new aspect of the traditional knowledge such information would, they argue, be justified protection on the basis of innovation, and indeed, such a development may well be the valid subject matter of an existing, 'classical' form of intellectual property. For them, however, that new innovation should not form the basis for a sui generis right in traditional knowledge.[138]

ii. The 'Incentive to Commercialise' Argument

Munzer and Raustiala contrast the incentive to commercialise with that to innovate. For them this incentive to commercialise justification is not subject to the 'innovation has already happened' criticism that they directed at the incentive to innovate ground. Any incentive to commercialise is directed at taking an existing piece of traditional knowledge and encouraging its commercial exploitation with the aim of bringing the information to a wider market and stimulating investment. Munzer and Raustiala believe that this 'consequentialist argument has some force' but point out the following limitations:

(i) It is not a justification for protection of traditional knowledge that the Indigenous group seek to retain within their group – for example, sacred knowledge;
(ii) 'any plausible extent of legal protection will not include indefinite duration' (although no reason is given for this); and
(iii) 'unless the extent of legal protection is exquisitely calibrated, and unless indigenous peoples know the extent of that protection – each of which is difficult to secure – they may well under-invest or over-invest in commercializing their [traditional knowledge]'.[139]

Munzer and Raustiala point out that any such over-investment would be problematic for Indigenous peoples as it would lead them to spend resources that they do not have. For example, they may become embroiled in unsuccessful enforcement activities which could lead to destruction of the value of the intellectual asset (once it was realised that the key element of the asset was free to use).[140]

[137] F Mazzocchi, 'Western Science and Traditional Knowledge: Despite Their Variations, Different Forms of Knowledge Can Learn from Each Other' (2006) 7(5) *EMBO Reports* 463.
[138] Munzer and Raustiala (n 63) 74.
[139] ibid.
[140] ibid.

iii. A Further Utilitarian Approach – 'Ensuring Stability'

Munzer and Raustiala point to a utilitarian justification for property rights based on a desire to ensure 'stability, security of expectations and the smooth functioning of society and the economy',[141] and examine whether such utilitarian model provides a justification for intellectual property right in Indigenous traditional knowledge. They cite the WIPO *Composite Study on the Protection of Traditional Knowledge*[142] as an example of such an argument. The composite study states that:

> [A] clear, transparent and effective system of TK protection increases legal security and predictability to the benefit not only of TK holders, but also of society as a whole, including firms and research institutions who are potential partners of TK holders. These benefits go beyond the promotion of innovation as such, given the argument that IP forms of protection of TK are unnecessary since the innovation will have taken place without IP protection.[143]

Munzer and Raustiala agree that stability and certainty are desirable as a general aim, but state that having such a desire does not, of itself, inform how one particularly achieves that aim through the formulation of positive laws. They state (somewhat mischievously in this author's view) that certainty could equally be arrived at through an announcement that no rights existed in traditional knowledge. Although that may well, in a very narrow sense, be correct, such a position would, of course, completely ignore any other justification for the existence of such rights.[144]

iv. Utilitarian Goals: The Preservation of Culture

Although they do not it put as such, Munzer and Raustiala's 'stability' head may actually be pointing to a further, broader, utilitarian argument for a positive right in traditional knowledge, namely preventing an impoverishment of Mill's concept of 'greater happiness'.[145] Dutfield and Suthersanen, in looking at traditional knowledge as an emerging right, propose that a positive traditional knowledge right would improve the lives of the traditional knowledge holders and communities.[146] They point to the fact that many examples of traditional activity are in decline, and many modes of traditional cultural expression are being lost.[147] One

[141] ibid. 66.
[142] WIPO Intergovernmental Committee on Intellectual Property and Genetic Resources, Traditional Knowledge and Folklore, Composite Study on the Protection of Traditional Knowledge WIPO/GRTKF/IC/5/8 (2003).
[143] ibid 14, para 35.
[144] Munzer and Raustiala (n 63) 66.
[145] JS Mill, *Utilitarianism, Liberty and Representative Government* (London, JM Dent and Sons, 1910).
[146] Dutfield and Suthersanen (n 20) 329. See also G Dutfield, *Intellectual Property Rights, Biogenetic Resources and Traditional Knowledge* (London, Earthscan, 2004) 97.
[147] Dutfield (n 146) 97.

might argue that, from a utilitarian prospective, an incentive not to *lose* is equivalent to an incentive to *gain*. An incentive to 'commercialise' and make a financial gain from existing traditional knowledge could potentially serve as an incentive to retain knowledge and cultural forms that would otherwise not be valued and could potentially be lost in the face of the ongoing spread of 'Western' cultural and scientific norms and market economies. Dutfield also points to a potential benefit to the national economies in which a particular piece of traditional knowledge originates as a consequentialist justification for providing a positive right to traditional knowledge.[148]

As has been discussed in the introduction to this work (and will be further discussed in chapter five) the contribution of traditional knowledge to pharmaceutical (and food) products can be high. Without positive rights, this value would not be captured and would not enter into the (usually poor) originator economy. Dutfield highlights, however, that the economic potential of traditional knowledge should not be overestimated as much of it will have no commercial application at all.[149]

The achievement of this utilitarian goal through the creation of positive ABS rights in TKAGR will be discussed in further detail (in sections VII.C and D) below.

v. Utilitarian Goals: Preservation of the Environment

Closely linked to the preservation of Indigenous culture, Dutfield additionally points to conservation of the environment from which traditional knowledge originates as a further consequentialist justification for providing a positive right to traditional knowledge.[150] Some traditional knowledge directly relates to methodologies of agricultural or forest management. If plants and the traditional knowledge associated with them are perceived as having potential commercial value, then the incentive to preserve them and the environment in which they are found may be enhanced, particularly in the face of external infrastructure development, mining, logging, plantation and ranching pressures.

Again, the achievement of this utilitarian goal through the creation of positive ABS rights in TKAGR will be discussed in further detail (in sections VII.C and D) below.

C. Exploring 'Preservation Through Valorisation'

The 'preservation through valorisation' approach to the maintenance of Indigenous culture and of the natural environment by giving value to traditional knowledge

[148] ibid 98.
[149] ibid.
[150] ibid 99.

(and to the genetic resources to which that traditional knowledge relates) requires examination in terms of:

(a) what utilitarian goals are served by the policy;
(b) how the positive laws create the desired value; and
(c) whether that value serves to meet the utilitarian goals identified.

As we will see, this analysis eventually brings us to a potential 'utilitarian paradox' at the interface between the preservation of the biodiverse environment and Western market economy at which the traditional rights justification operates.

i. What Utilitarian Goals Are Served by the Policy?

The basis of a rule-utilitarian justification is that as a result of a particular policy (or positive legal rule) the overall utility of a society is enhanced.[151] However, it has long been a matter for debate amongst utilitarians as to how one might actually seek to determine whether that policy has had the desired effect of enhancing overall the utility of a society.[152] Can one really perform a *felicific calculus* (or calculation of happiness) of an entire society? Can one examine with any certainty whether a particular policy has had an impact on that calculus?

Given the complexity of a modern (and even a premodern) society, the analysis of the impact of policy is, of necessity, more commonly focused on the effect on the perceived mischief to which the policy is directed (and the spillover effects into related areas), rather than looking at the *global* utility within a society. However, even if one *were* somehow able to quantify the global happiness of a society, we need to ask whether it is really the 'amount' of happiness in society that is important, or whether the *quality* of happiness is also important.

The question of what *types* of happiness should inform a model for living life, and whether we are obligated to do more than pursue pleasure for its own sake, has a very long history, and formed a key part of the (Stoical and other) criticism of the philosophy of Epicurus,[153] and part of the search for the definition of an objective well-being within a *eudaimonic* life.[154] The question of difference in *quality* of social utility was rapidly identified by utilitarians and Bentham's broad definition of happiness[155] was challenged by Mill, who held that 'higher' forms of happiness, arising from intellectual achievements, gave greater utility than 'baser'

[151] RB Brandt, *Ethical Theory* (Hoboken, NJ, Prentice-Hall, 1959); RB Brandt, 'Toward a Credible Form of Utilitarianism' in H-N Castañeda and G Nakhnikian (eds), *Morality and the Language of Conduct* (Detroit, MI, Wayne State University Press, 1963) 107.

[152] See eg J Garvey and J Strangroom, *The Story of Philosophy: A History of Western Thought* (London, Quercus, 2012) 286.

[153] ibid, 128; Russell (n 91) 231.

[154] A MacIntyre, *A Short History of Ethics: A History of Moral Philosophy from the Homeric Age to the Twentieth Century* (Oxford, Routledge Classics, 2002) 77; N Stewart, *Ethics: An Introduction to Moral Philosophy* (Cambridge, Polity Press, 2009) 61.

[155] J Bentham, *The Principles of Morals and Legislation* (1789) 1.

forms. Mill famously stated: 'It is better to be a human being dissatisfied than a pig satisfied; better to be Socrates dissatisfied than a fool satisfied.'[156] Progressive as Mill was (for his time), this approach does reflect something of a high-Victorian view of culture, and of the world. However, even if one does not follow such a strict Millian approach, the idea that there are differing qualities of happiness/utility does not seem unreasonable, and is certainly reflected in our own experience of life. However, in looking at such questions of quality of utility one is immediately confronted by substantial problems of subjectivity. We all have our own personal interests, values, and concerns: one women's happiness cannot simply be another's (although Harris has argued that there are some *fundamental* things which all (non-pathological) humans perceive as important to happiness and contribute to what should universally be accepted as a good life.[157] This is an approach which echoes the view of Rawls, and of Honderich, that one can specify the 'primary goods' which are necessary preconditions for well-being.[158]

Even if one could advance beyond this problem of subjectivity, how might you even arrive at an *objective* calculation of any difference in utility? As Blackburn states:

> [A]lthough we might judge that this year's holiday was better than last year's, we are not apt to think it makes sense to say it was twice as good, or that it generated half as many units of utility as (say) a lifetime's consumption of chocolate.[159]

Accordingly, when engaging in any utilitarian analysis we need to acknowledge throughout the problems posed by quantity, quality, subjectivity and lack of objective calculation.

Perhaps the simplest utilitarian account for preservation of traditional knowledge is that the existence of such knowledge provides a social utility *in itself* in that it is part of the 'patrimony of mankind'. Although Mill argued that high Western art (say Michelangelo's painting of the vault of the Sistine Chapel or the Bach *St Matthew Passion*) generated significant utility, he accepted that utility could be found in the appreciation of a broad range of achievements: 'art, the imaginations of poetry, the incidents of history, the ways of mankind, past and present, and their prospects in the future'.[160] Whether Mill's concept of human achievement would have, in fact, extended to traditional knowledge per se (rather than the utility generated by the Western scholarly examination of it) is unclear, but it would in the current century seem perverse not to extend a Millian utility to the art, forms of living and knowledge of Indigenous peoples (even where that knowledge cannot be readily defined as 'artistic' according to Western mores).

[156] Mill (n 145) 9.

[157] S Harris, *The Moral Landscape: How Science Can Determine Human Values* (London, Black Swan, 2010) 28.

[158] J Rawls, *A Theory of Justice* (Oxford, Oxford University Press, 1972) 78; T Honderich, 'The Question of Well-being and the Principle of Equality' (1981) xc *Mind* 481.

[159] S Blackburn, *Oxford Dictionary of Philosophy* (Oxford, Oxford University Press, 1996) 388.

[160] Mill (n 145) 15.

ii. Narrow Utility

To this contribution to the utility of all mankind might also be added a more particular sense of 'happiness' which arises where a society of Indigenous peoples are free to live a life that allows them to feel spiritually fulfilled by following their traditional religious beliefs and customary norms. This narrower utilitarian goal is naturally specific to a smaller group than that of all mankind. Of course, where one is pursuing a 'greatest happiness for the greatest number' rule-utilitarianism, one will encounter difficulties in promoting a specific utility for one group in conflict with a broader utility for a greater number. One is possibly left here attempting to balance the 'narrow' enhanced social utility of an Indigenous group 'living in peace' (perhaps to 'enjoy' their traditional knowledge) against a potential enhanced utility of a broader society brought about through (say) infrastructure development leading to rainforest destruction. Such complexities are far from thought experiments. The Tren Maya (Tsiímin K'aák) Project, the building of a 1,525-kilometre inter-city train network across the Yucatán peninsula of Mexico, will facilitate tourist visits to the Mayan archaeological remains (some of whom at least one would expect will be experiencing 'Millian' utility through the appreciation of ancient Maya culture) whilst bringing rainforest and environmental destruction which has been opposed by the extant Indigenous Maya people of the region.[161] Such utilitarian conflicts are not easily resolved, but do highlight the importance of determining the set of utilities that are intended to be produced (or at least incentivised) by one's proposed positive law.

The discussion above focuses on the quality of happiness. This debate can be taken further into the question of whether 'happiness' alone is a sufficient determinant for governing consequentialist policy. There is a long and rich history in philosophy in assessing whether the true determinant of utility should be the broader 'well-being' of individuals.[162] The question extends further into what determines what constitutes well-being – for example an idea of objective eudaimonic human flourishing or a more subjective test?[163] One might consider that 'well-being' is a less subjective marker than mere 'happiness' and that this relative objectivity could allow one to reduce well-being or welfare into something empirically measurable and amenable to the arithmetic balancing of summed welfare measures.

Derclaye and Taylor[164] have suggested that the rule-utilitarian justification for intellectual property has been misapplied by the Chicago 'law and economics'

[161] BA Camargo and Mario Vázquez-Maguirre, 'Humanism, Dignity and Indigenous Justice: The Mayan Train Megaproject, Mexico' (2021) 29(2–3) *Journal of Sustainable Tourism* 372.

[162] P Walsh, 'Well-being' in T Honderich (ed), *The Oxford Companion to Philosophy* (Oxford, Oxford University Press, 1995) 908.

[163] CCW Taylor, 'Eudaimonia' in T Honderich (ed), *The Oxford Companion to Philosophy* (Oxford, Oxford University Press, 1995) 252.

[164] E Derclaye and T Taylor, 'Happy IP: Replacing the Law and Economics Justification for Intellectual Property Rights with a Well-being Approach' (2015) 37(4) *European Intellectual Property Review* 197.

school such that an enhancement in societal wealth (as evinced by such economic markers as gross domestic product) acts as the sole proxy for greater societal well-being – a flawed process that serves to ignore wider concepts of human well-being. They suggest that other 'markers' for human well-being should be applied when looking to justify intellectual property rights:[165]

Marker 1	Happiness or more accurately 'positive affect'.
Marker 2	Health – including all aspects of physical health: not only freedom from disease and injury, but also adequate nutrition. It would also include mental health.
Marker 3	Life-satisfaction – a complementary notion to happiness: the two are combined in the construct of 'subjective well-being'.
Marker 4	Success in realising central life goals/values: the extent to which a person succeeds in securing the things they most care about, whether these be goals to which they aspire or aspects of their lives that matter to them.
Marker 5	Supportive personal relationships including marriage, relationships with family members, friendships and even relationships with others such as neighbours and work colleagues, insofar as these can be regarded as supportive.
Marker 6	Personal development: the development, improvement and exercise of various mental and physical aspects of our natures as human being, including the development of intellectual skills and the acquiring of knowledge, typically through education.
Marker 7	Leisure: the opportunity to spend time relaxing and to pursue interests and activities beyond those required by work, or by the need to secure the essentials for human existence.
Marker 8	Adequate income/resources: sufficient resources to enable certain other markers of well-being, such as good health (which implies adequate nutrition) and achievement of personal goals, to be secured. Those resources, in most societies, will typically be in the form of income or wealth but need not necessarily be so in all circumstances.
Marker 9	Rewarding employment: predominantly as an enabler of other markers (provided that the employment relationship is not abusive).[166]

If we apply Derclaye and Taylor's 'well-being' markers to the Indigenous sphere, we can see that what is described above as the 'narrower' utility of allowing Indigenous peoples to feel spiritually fulfilled by following their traditional

[165] E Derclaye and T Taylor, 'Happy IP: Aligning Intellectual Property Rights with Well-being' (2015) 2015(1) *Intellectual Property Quarterly* 1.
[166] ibid 2.

religious beliefs and customary norms would seem to particularly echo with Derclaye and Taylor's Marker 1 (happiness), Marker 3 (life-satisfaction/ 'subjective well-being') and Marker 4 (success in realising central life goals/values). Although Derclaye and Taylor do not specifically highlight Indigenous communities within their description of Marker 5 (supportive personal relationships), when we look at how traditional knowledge is held within a close Indigenous community (see section XII.B below) it is likely that this marker would be a strong element in an individual's well-being. It is also likely that this marker of well-being would be particularly enhanced through the ability of the individuals within a group to follow their traditional religious beliefs and customary norms.

iii. Environmental Utility

However, even such broader markers of 'well-being' remain, by definition, anthropocentric. A further, and distinctly separate, utilitarian account is that the preservation of a biodiverse environment is a 'utility' in itself. Singer divides the potential utility of preservation of the environment into two values: *intrinsic* value based upon the value of the thing itself, and *instrumental* value based upon the thing's ability to contribute to other utilitarian ends.[167] It is, of course, possible that a single thing may have overlapping intrinsic and instrumentalist values to varying degrees. However, is important to appreciate from where the contributions to overall utility are made – particularly where one is seeking to influence that utility through positive law.

For Singer the intrinsic value of preserving the environment can itself take two forms.[168] The first of these is that we as humans (today and in the future) are culturally and/or spiritually enriched by the act of living within in a biodiverse environment (and hence our happiness is enhanced). This enrichment is again a highly subjective appreciation, both as between persons and between cultures. For example, modern Western concepts of the aesthetics of nature have arguably been shaped by romantic, 'Burkean' concepts.[169] As with the utility found in enjoyment of traditional knowledge per se, one might also posit that Indigenous peoples gain a specific utility in the enjoyment of their ancestral environment (although as we will see that may be subject to conflicting Western-orientated utilities). The second intrinsic value is based on the view that we should extend our view of utility to encompass not only *human* 'happiness' but a broader, non-anthropocentric, concept of *environmental* well-being (sometimes referred to as 'deep ecology').[170]

[167] P Singer, *Practical Ethics* (Cambridge, Cambridge University Press, 1999) 274.

[168] ibid 276.

[169] See eg D Jamieson, *Ethics and the Environment* (Cambridge, Cambridge University Press, 2008) 158.

[170] See generally: A Leopold, *A Sand County Almanac* (New York, Oxford University Press, 1949); A Naess, 'The Shallow and the Deep, Long Range Ecology Movements: A Summary' (1973) 16 *Inquiry* 95; W Devall and G Sessions, *Deep Ecology: Living as if Nature Mattered* (Salt Lake City, UT, Gibbs M Smith, 1985); P Singer, *Animal Liberation* (New York, Harper Collins, 2002).

Outwith these broader (somewhat Millian) concepts, there is a more practical (and perhaps more Benthamite) aspect – a biodiverse landscape has *instrumental* value to humans in supporting their other endeavours and even the quality of their existence. In some cases this may be through a moderating effect on local (or even global) climate, soil and watercourse protection. In others, it may be through the provision of plant species which can be used for food, fibres, or as the basis for drug discovery and of genetic materials which may form the basis for the development of disease-, pest- or drought-resistance. Indeed, this role as a store of genetic resources may also be seen as an 'insurance policy' against future uncertainty, which would again provide a social utility in itself. As Atkins puts it: 'One anthropocentric but important concern about the extinction of species is that it wipes our sources of intricate molecules that have taken millions of years to emerge.'[171]

The degree of 'usefulness' (or instrumental value) of a particular biodiverse landscape will depend on the landscape in question, and will also vary according to whom the landscape is being useful. Global climate effects, and acting as a genetic bank, will be useful to a larger population of people, although the effect may seem remote. In contrast, local climate effects will be more immediately useful to a narrower group of people who actually live within, or next to, the affected landscape.

We need to note that although such intrinsic and instrumental utilitarian benefits arising out of the preservation of a biodiverse environment would arguably be greater within an environment which is in something approaching a 'pristine' state, often this supposedly pristine state is illusory and is in fact the product of long interaction between people and nature. For example, much of what has been considered 'virgin' rain forest has been actively managed by Indigenous peoples over generations, including selective clearance, plant selection and planting of 'forest gardens'[172] Notwithstanding this, Indigenously managed forests preserve a significant body of indigenous flora and are likely always to be a greater contributor to the environmental side of our utilitarian 'equation' than would be the entirely cleared alternative.[173]

To summarise, we have a number of utilitarian goals which may be served by creating value in traditional therapeutic associated with genetic resources:

1. Spiritual/cultural ('Millian'/intrinsic):
   (a) Traditional knowledge is part of the 'patrimony of mankind' and provides utility its own right;

[171] P Atkins, *What Is Chemistry?* (Oxford, Oxford University Press, 2013) 13.

[172] Dutfield (n 146) 99.

[173] KF Wiersum, 'Forest Gardens as an "Intermediate" Land-Use System in the Nature–Culture Continuum: Characteristics and Future Potential' (2004) 1 *Advances in Agroforestry* 123; JA McNeely, 'Nature vs Nurture: Managing Relationships Between Forests, Agroforestry and Wild Biodiversity' in PKR Nair et al (eds), *New Vistas in Agroforestry. Advances in Agroforestry*, vol 1 (New York, Springer, 2004).

(b) The spiritual fulfilment of Indigenous peoples by following traditional religious beliefs and customary norms;
(c) Humans broadly (and Indigenous peoples more specifically) are culturally and/or spiritually enriched by existing in a biodiverse environment; and
(d) Utility encompasses not only *human* 'happiness' (anthropocentric utilitarianism) but a broader non-anthropocentric concept of the well-being of the environment *itself*.

2. Practical ('Benthamite'/instrumental):
   (a) Biodiversity itself provides utility through its support of other human endeavours (through a moderating effect on local (or even global) climate, soil and watercourse protection or the provision of plant species which can be used for food, fibres, or as the basis for drug discovery and of genetic materials which may form the basis for the development of disease-, pest- or drought-resistance); and
   (b) An 'insurance policy' against future uncertainty (the environment acting as a store of potential treatments for plant and animal diseases, and of pest- and drought-resistant properties).

To the extent that any of these utilities do not conflict, might there be an argument for conflating these fractionated utilities into a single pooled environmental/cultural utility? As early as 1988, the Declaration of Belém stated that there was an 'inextricable link between cultural and biological diversity'.[174] There is an increasing academic awareness of the concept of 'biocultural diversity' which suggests that there is often a close interlinking between the preservation of Indigenous culture and of the environment, and recognises that in many ecosystems the activities of the Indigenous people help maintain the existing biodiversity and the existing biodiversity helps to sustain Indigenous ways of life in mutually supportive ways.[175]

One might envisage that there is little potential conflict within the class of Millian/intrinsic utilities described above and within the class of Benthamite/instrumental utilities. Generally speaking, there may also seem little scope for conflict between the two classes: third-party instrumental 'enjoyment' of traditional knowledge per se is unlikely to conflict with the intrinsic utilities described save (importantly) with an intrinsic 'utility through control' of traditional knowledge. Given the potential for some conflict, and the likelihood that positive rights/valorisation will affect each utility to varying degrees, as a heuristic tool each

[174] 1988 Declaration of Belém, Preamble; see DA Posey and G Dutfield, *Beyond Intellectual Property: Toward Traditional Resources Rights for Indigenous Peoples and Local Communities* (Ottawa, International Development Research Centre, 1996) 7.

[175] See generally: L Maffi, 'Biocultural Diversity for Sustainability' in J Pretty et al (eds), *The SAGE Handbook of Environment and Society* (Los Angeles, SAGE, 2007) 269; L Maffi and E Woodley, *Biocultural Diversity Conservation: A Global Sourcebook* (Abingdon, Earthscan, 2010).

utility will be examined separately in the following analysis. However, the potentially close 'biocultural' interaction between the preservation of the environmental and of traditional knowledge utilities will continue to be acknowledged.

D. The Achievement of Utilitarian Goals Through Valorisation

How, then, does creating value in TKAGR achieve the utilitarian goals of preservation of the biodiverse environment or of traditional knowledge per se (or a conflation of the two)? How is this value created in the first place?

It is crucial to note that the preservation of the environment (and of culture) relies on the *behaviour* of relevant actors responding to economic factors (including conflicting values), whether they be the Indigenous peoples themselves, or those external agents responsible for making business or planning decisions. However, although some economic theories can apply an objective value to a commodity, it has long been recognised within economics that for most individual economic actors the determination of value (which will drive behaviour) is subjective – and this subjective value is derived from individual's *perception* of the importance of an item.[176] This perceived value of an asset is the function of many factors.[177] These will include desirability (based in part on the amount of money that may be made from the asset), ease of resale and, crucially, rarity/accessibility: Taylor states:

> Valuation is always directed toward a definite quantity of a particular good or service. Choices and decisions are not concerned with the whole supply of a certain good or service. This marginal orientation was lacking in the classical economists' groping with the so-called paradox of value. They were unable to resolve the intriguing question of why diamonds had a higher price per unit than water when everyone knew that water was more useful and valuable than diamonds. Only through the principle of diminishing marginal utility could this conceptual dilemma be eliminated. Each additional unit of a particular good is devoted to a use that is less important and urgent than the use to which the preceding unit was applied.[178]

If you were dying of thirst in a desert you would clearly value water over a diamond. Perception based on situation and *relative position* is important. However, when looking at availability of an asset we need to recognise that since intangible property is (as was discussed at the beginning of this chapter) both non-rivalrous and non-excludable, exclusivity can only be created through the imposition of positive law.

[176] TC Taylor, *An Introduction to Austrian Economics* (Auburn, AL, Ludwig von Mises Institute, 1980) ch 4 (mises.org/austecon/chap4.asp).

[177] At least in respect of monetary value – we should note here that people can value an object in other, non-monetary, ways.

[178] Taylor (n 176).

The 'classic' intellectual property argument for creating value runs as follows: a requirement on third parties that they require prior consent from the rights holder before they can use information creates an (artificial) scarcity in the information which enhances its commercial value. In the absence of a right to control, there may be value to third parties in the subject matter but since free-riders will be free to use the subject matter as they wish, value will not attach to the information in the hands of its originators. However, if we acknowledge that subjective perception is crucial in creating value we need to understand that value is a more complex concept than merely creating artificial scarcity in something. Such a model only works where there is some actual, or potential, use for the information – control over the use of something inherently useless is highly unlikely to create any value. In addition, the terms of exclusivity established by positive law – such as certainty of definition and ease of enforcement – become crucial in determining the subjective value of the right.

i. *Preservation of the Environment*

There are many economic threats to biodiverse environments including logging, mining, the clearing of forest for animal pasture, plantations, infrastructure projects and the growth of urban areas. Many of these will be driven by *immediate* profit motives and economic concerns. One may be sceptical of the ability of a broadly enhanced value of genetic resources (and traditional knowledge associated with them) to successfully counter the powerful and immediate economic drivers for destroying biodiverse environments. Indeed, one can easily imagine a scenario where there is a significant disconnection between the value of genetic resources and traditional knowledge on the one hand, and the preservation of a biodiverse environment on the other. It is, of course, entirely conceivable that one could profit from the Western use of a genetic resource (and traditional knowledge associated with that resource) in the absence of the environment from which it originated – perhaps the genetic resource has already been collected (and could be propagated elsewhere) and/or the relevant knowledge (whether nucleotide sequence, biochemical structure or traditional knowledge) has already been already 'collected' and preserved. This would leave the land from which the genetic resource originated 'free' for other uses to generate a monetary return. This is an admittedly extreme case, but it highlights that the linkage between the value of a genetic resource/traditional knowledge in general and the preservation of the environment is in reality most likely based on the *promise* of (as yet unknown) genetic resource/TKAGR combinations which may provide value in the future. Of course, much of the promise of genetic resources 'in the bush' is just that – a promise. Some genetic benefits will be entirely unknown, others may be directed through Indigenous knowledge. However, the full realisation of their likely true value to Western science and commerce is something of a distant probability when compared to the near certainty of the monetary return to be that can be achieved from, say, the clear-cutting a forest to create animal pasture to produce hamburger meat or to plant a palm-oil plantation. Even taking account of these very different relative probabilities of making a monetary return in the long run, Western economics and accountancy practice additionally places significantly greater value to a potential profit to be made *today* versus a profit that may be made *tomorrow* – simply because of the cumulative effect of a rate of return on money invested today.[179]

Even with some scepticism in the overall efficacy of the valorisation approach, the perception amongst all the concerned actors in this sphere is that the creation of *some* value in genetic resources and in traditional knowledge associated with those resources (created through the existence of a right to control use) must be better than *no* perceived value whatsoever (which might well be the case in the absence of a right to control use).

ii. Preservation of Traditional Knowledge for its Own Sake

Outwith the preservation of the biodiverse environment, we identified a separate utilitarian justification for a positive right in traditional knowledge in the preservation of traditional knowledge for its own sake (either as part of the 'patrimony of mankind' or as part of the spiritual life of a specific Indigenous people). Here one might see the valorisation of traditional knowledge as having a more direct effect on preservation in a world where traditional knowledge is threatened by the encroachment of Western values. Where traditional knowledge (including that associated with genetic resources) can become a source of actual (or potential) wealth one could expect the creation of an economic drive which would act towards the preservation of the source of that wealth in the face of competing cultural pressures. Of course, there is an irony here that one is using a Western market economic mechanism to counter a problem which has essentially been caused by the introduction of the Western market economy.

Again, we need here to recognise that information *can* exist away from the environment in which it was created even more easily than can a genetic resource. Let us imagine that a huge ethnobotanical survey (akin to an emergency archaeological dig) could achieve the end of collecting all the relevant Indigenous information in an area before it was lost. Might that not, in itself, serve the utilitarian goal of preserving part of the 'patrimony of mankind' more easily than creating a body of rights that might (or might not) have their eventual effects through value created by market-economic forces?

It is here perhaps that taking a somewhat reductionist utilitarian approach might lead us astray. Our imaginary survey, even if it could in some way entirely reliably capture all the appropriate information, would preserve only one facet of the information. Information about genetic resources, no matter how accurate, becomes of mere historical interest in the absence of the genetic resource to which

[179] Singer (n 167) 270.

it is related. Of course, our imaginary survey could potentially be extended to encompass the collection of *all* genetic material related to the traditional information. Would this again serve to fulfil our 'patrimony of mankind' utilitarian goal without reliance on positive rights? In a purely reductionist sense the answer may be 'yes', but again reductionism leads us astray. Few people would say that watching animals in a zoo is as spiritually satisfying as seeing them in the wild. Similarly, knowing that genetic material is safely preserved in the Royal Botanic Gardens Millennium Seed Bank or the Svalbard Global Seed Vault[180] (and is thereby fulfilling a crucial instrumentalist utility) is arguably not as spiritually satisfying as knowing that the plants are growing 'in the wild'.

Realistically it makes sense in this instance to conflate the 'patrimony of mankind' and 'preservation of biodiverse environment' utilitarian goals, rather than treat them as separate entities – both elements arguably enhance the other (particularly within traditionally managed environments). We can see that even our imaginary 'perfect' ethnobotanical survey is not a substitute for a rights mechanism that aims to preserve both elements.

Notwithstanding its (intrinsic if not instrumentalist) utilitarian 'failure', our imaginary ethnobotanical survey is in any case just that – in reality no survey can be wholly truly comprehensive. No doubt some captured information and genetic resource is better in an emergency situation that no information or no genes at all, but it cannot be a substitute for the preservation of information and genetic resource in situ in a social environment in which information and genes will be preserved.

We have, however, identified above an additional utilitarian goal: that traditional knowledge is preserved for its own sake *as part of the spiritual life of Indigenous peoples.* Clearly here the reductionist approach taken, and criticised, above in relation to preservation of the 'patrimony of mankind' is even less sustainable. The spiritual life of the Indigenous peoples is closely linked to the biodiverse environment, and to the use of genetic resources *within* their social, customary and religious context. It makes even less sense to talk here of 'databases' and 'gene banks' than it did above – the preservation of information here is still more closely linked to the utilitarian goal of preservation of the biodiverse environment. It is also here that, arguably, a Western market economy mechanism seems at its most alien.

iii. Utility Through 'Control'

It is at this point that we should identify that the requirement that prior informed consent is required before a third party may use TKAGR might not only have its utilitarian benefit through valorisation of the information. Such a requirement

[180] www.kew.org/science-conservation/collections/millennium-seed-bank; www.regjeringen.no/en/topics/food-fisheries-and-agriculture/agriculture/svalbard-global-seed-vault/id462220/.

may also go *directly* to the 'well-being' of Indigenous peoples (notably Derclaye and Taylor's Marker 4 – success in realising central life goals/values, and Marker 5 – supportive personal relationships). The requirement for prior informed consent needs to encompass the right to say 'no' or it is not true consent. This right to exclusively consent to the use of information may, of itself, go to spiritual fulfilment of Indigenous peoples – for example, if their traditional religious beliefs and/or customary norms direct that sacred or special information should be maintained within the Indigenous group. Milius describes it thus:

> [T]he power to maintain control over one's traditional knowledge might confer a very real and cultural/spiritual sense of independence and self-reliance where that knowledge is used to the benefit of the community. Even where the knowledge is held by a small circle of practitioners, those who belong to that community at large and who benefit from the particular [traditional knowledge] through membership may also feel the real sense of autonomy that group self-reliance brings, and in not having to depend on outsiders for their technological knowledge and expertise.[181]

Although this may be an entirely justifiable basis for having a right to control access, its applicability will be case-dependent, rather than the broader applicability which applies to the valorisation of traditional knowledge. We need also note that the 'utility through control' goal is reliant, in the long term at least, on the broader preservation of the culture and environment which supports the appropriate traditional religious beliefs and/or customary norms. We also need to note that the absolute exercise of a veto over use of traditional knowledge in achievement of a 'utility through control' goal may in certain cases play against the creation of value in that knowledge which might otherwise be achieved through consensual commercial exploitation.

E. A Utilitarian Paradox?

On first examination the preservation of a biodiverse environment, and traditional knowledge per se (for all the reasons set out above), would seem to be an unarguable 'good'. However, the actual utilitarian landscape is more complex than can be captured in such a simplistic approach. A Western market-economy, profit-motivated ethos (at least in those cases where it treats biodiverse landscapes as an expendable, and limitless, resource for exploitation) is arguably at odds with many of the pro-biodiversity principles previously outlined. Much of the threat to biodiverse environments, the genetic resources within them and the traditional knowledge relating to them comes from an increasing 'Westernisation' of the human societies which live on and/or exploit the land on which the biodiverse environment in question is found. In a society in which the importance of Western consumer items/services increases, it is conceivable that things previously

[181] Milius (n 118) 198.

considered to be part of the 'wealth' of the pre-Westernisation society may lose value and consequently be lost. It is certainly possible that in a diminution of the value of the 'old ways', therapeutic knowledge (particularly that held by a relatively small group of people), cultural expression and language is liable to be lost. Dutfield cites the 1997 IUCN Inter-Commission Task Force on Indigenous Peoples.[182] This states that:

> Cultures are dying out faster than the peoples associated with them. It has been estimated that half the world's languages – the storehouses of people's intellectual heritages and the framework for their unique understandings of life – will disappear within a century.[183]

However, if we are to acknowledge that human happiness comes in many forms, we need consider that, in many respects, the Western market economy could, of itself, be said to bring an amount, if a different *type*, of social utility to the overall utilitarian calculus.

It has been argued that 'pre-Western' Indigenous existence was arguably always closer to the 'poor, nasty, brutish, and short' life envisaged by Hobbes than the more optimistic ideas of Rousseau (or indeed Marx).[184] Ferguson has described the life of the hunter-gatherer in Hobbesian terms, emphasising the violent and competitive nature of that life, and asserts that in many cases where hunter-gatherers encounter Western 'comforts' they relatively rapidly abandon their previous life.[185] This is undoubtedly an oversimplification. The history of the interface between Western society and Indigenous peoples is beyond the scope of the present work, but we must acknowledge that the bringing of Indigenous peoples within, or close to, the ambit of Western society has been heavily influenced throughout history by war, disease, slavery, forced and unforced religious conversions, and government policy (whether deliberately hostile, indifferent or guided by a misplaced paternalistic/pastoral concern) including change in environmental use, inward migration and forced resettlement. Much of this is not by any means confined to the depths of history – Allen reports on the efforts of the government of Indonesia to discourage the activities of the *kerei* medicine men of the animist Mentawai peoples living off the coast of Sumatra,[186] a group still subject to policies that conflict with their cultural identity.[187]

Even if not seeking deliberately to destroy Indigenous ways of life, the approach of many Western governments (and indeed of some governments in the Global South) has often been to discount the utility provided by Indigenous culture and

[182] Dutfield (n 146) 97.

[183] IUCN Inter-Commission Task Force on Indigenous Peoples (1997) 60.

[184] T Hobbes, *Leviathan* [1651] (London, JM Dent and Sons, 1940) 63 (ch XIII); J-J Rousseau, *Discourse on the Origin and Basis of Inequality Among Men* [755]; N Ferguson, *The Ascent of Money: A Financial History of the World* (London, Allen Lane, 2008) 18; Garvey and Strangroom (n 152) 247.

[185] Ferguson (n 184) 18.

[186] B Allen, *Last of the Medicine Men* (London, BBC Worldwide, 2000) 13.

[187] A Irwandi and R Taufik 'Cultural Identity in the Shackles of Modernization: The Case of Mentawai Indigenous Peoples' (2023) 9(2) *Jurnal Sosiologi Andalas* 211.

society when compared to the perhaps more easily measured utilities provided by Western-style economic development. Indeed, as has been touched upon above, Western-style economic theory is predicated on the value of economic development *today* over long-term values such as preservation of something (whether traditional knowledge or the environment) for the future (even where an allocation of value could be made). Singer suggests that application of an accountancy 'discount rate' to future goods means that: 'values gained one hundred years hence rank very low in comparison with values gained today; and values gained one thousand years in the future scarcely count at all'.[188]

However, although the 'advantages' of Western development (whether it be the availability of consumer goods or the advent of Western surgery and medicine) can be very poorly distributed within developing economies, they do add an element of social utility that cannot be easily excluded from our felicific calculus for the affected community. The impact of Ferguson's Western 'comforts' cannot be easily ignored. Here we might look at the move by the Inuit of Arctic Canada from a self-sustaining, self-reliant (though occasionally highly precarious)[189] hunter-gatherer community to one reliant on the cash economy. This occurred, in part, through the abandonment of reliance on dog-sled teams following the introduction of the snowmobile or 'metal-dog'. Snowmobiles are faster, more powerful and in many senses far more convenient than a dog team.[190] However, whereas a dog-team can run on meat obtained from hunting and fishing, snowmobiles run on petroleum products and require new mechanical parts – inevitably bringing their users into the cash economy. However, even here we need to acknowledge that this abandonment was a process actively encouraged by the Canadian government (and supported by other government policies, including the settlement of the previously nomadic Inuit into fixed towns and villages,[191] and even the deliberate culling of sled dogs by government authorities).[192]

So when we look to the utilitarian landscape surrounding the preservation of the environment we see a complex picture: on one hand we can argue that there is a social utility (both instrumental and intrinsic) to be gained from the preservation of the biodiverse environment per se, preservation of traditional knowledge per se and Indigenous ways of life for their own sake; on the other hand we might argue that the growth of Western market economy (which appears to threaten the existence of the biodiverse environment and forms of Indigenous society) provides its own species and quantity of utility.

[188] Singer (n 167) 270.

[189] R Harrington in E Carpenter (ed), *Padlei Diary, 1950: An Account of the Padleimiut Eskimo in the Keewatin District West of Hudson Bay During the Early Months of 1950* (New York, Rock Foundation, 2000).

[190] The author is the possessor of a dogsled proficiency certificate.

[191] J Houston, 'Fifty Years of Thinking it Over' in M von Finckenstein (ed), *Celebrating Inuit Art 1948–1970* (Toronto, Key Porter Books, 1999) 36; S Lührmann, 'Arctic' in CF Feest (ed), *The Cultures of Native North Americans* (Cologne, Könemann, 2000) 30, 44.

[192] P Goldring, 'Historians and Inuit: Learning from the Qikiqtani Truth Commission, 2007–2010' (2015) 50(3) *Canadian Journal of History* 492.

The question of how one might assesses the quantity, and quality, of these competing contributions to the overall calculation of total social utility (and indeed whether the two sides of the utilitarian calculation actually conflict one another in all circumstances) is again beyond the scope of this study. However, we need to acknowledge the irony that sits at the heart of the approach of giving commercial value to traditional knowledge as a way of protecting the biodiverse environment – the 'incentivisation through valorisation' approach seeks to operate through an effect *within* the Western market economic framework, rather than operating within the framework of traditional Indigenous ways of living.

There has been substantial criticism of this use of a Western-market-economy-based approach – along the lines that such Western methods are unsuited to the protection of something so alien from the market economy as traditional knowledge.[193] However, in contrast to this position, we might argue that since the threat to traditional knowledge arises *out of* Western market economic forces, an approach which affects those forces is a pragmatic solution that addresses a broader utilitarian aim. Indeed, one might say that the valorisation approach addresses *both* sides of the 'environment versus market economy' utilitarian conflict identified above.

VIII. Unjust Enrichment, Misappropriation and Restitution

Munzer and Raustiala define these concepts in the following way:

Unjust Enrichment is A's receipt of an economic benefit to B's detriment such that A's retaining it without paying B would be unfair.Misappropriation is an improper or dishonest form of unjust enrichment, as distinct from cases where A receives an economic benefit innocently or is unaware of the detriment to B.Restitution is, broadly, a basis for A's liability to B because of unjust enrichment and, narrowly, the payment A should make to B to remove the injustice.[194] Munzer and Raustiala cite the WIPO Composite Study as giving an example of an unjust enrichment argument. The Composite Study describes a 'fourth rationale for IP-related protection of TK' based on the following premise:

> One general argument for international cooperation on IP protection has been that its absence in foreign countries leads to an unfair advantage for local manufacturers, since they do not need to compensate the IP right holder, or to contribute to the cost of research and development. Other factors being equal, foreign IP right owners will be in disadvantage vis-à-vis their local imitators; and therefore such lack of IP protection amounts to non-tariff barriers to trade.

[193] Gibson (n 9) 73.
[194] ibid 75.

The argument then runs that:

> Just as this argument applies to the pharmaceutical, software and entertainment industries, it would apply to IP-related TK and the commercial interests of traditional communities that make use of their TK in their economic life, Similar considerations apply when TK holders see their interests not in direct commercial terms, but in terms of restraining other people's unacceptable commercial practices involving their TK, such as misleading or deceptive behavior.[195]

Munzer and Raustiala refer to this as a 'quasi-utilitarian' argument that is potentially plausible but is not supported by empirical evidence. However, they perceive the argument to be chiefly referring to unjust enrichment of *insiders*, entities within the country in which the traditional knowledge originates. Although this may be correct in part, the key thrust of the argument is actually this: that in the absence of positive protection, traditional knowledge suffers the same disadvantages as befall those subject matters (for which there *are* internationally established intellectual rights) where the machinery for enforcing those rights is not in place or is in practice ineffectual. Essentially the argument is: if you think it is unfair when 'Western' rights are not respected, is it not similarly unfair for traditional knowledge to (perpetually) suffer the same fate? This is certainly a call to fairness and equal treatment, but it is not perhaps entirely the same call to fairness (or is at least a species of that call) upon which an equitable right of restitution would be based.

Munzer and Raustiala simplify the scenario, and argument, to be as follows:

(i) An Indigenous people have a right to their traditional knowledge;
(ii) If not protected, outsiders using that traditional knowledge will obtain unjust enrichment to the detriment of the Indigenous people; and
(iii) It is unfair to retain full benefit from the improper use without making a restitutionary payment to the Indigenous people.[196]

Munzer and Raustiala highlight that determining the quantum of such a royalty is difficult. However, that practical difficulty is not the basis of their opposition to this argument. They state that even if something is *morally* appropriate that is not the same as what is, or should be, *legally* appropriate. This, of course, goes to the very heart of whether there is a rationale for a positive intellectual property right in traditional knowledge. They point to the fact that in some circumstances the balance of other values (such as competition) means that innovators are sometimes not rewarded and point to some examples of situations where this happens. Their examples[197] assume that all traditional knowledge is in the form of broad ideas of the type that would not be protectable per se under copyright law. They

[195] WIPO/GRTKF/IC/5/8, 15, para 38.
[196] Munzer and Raustiala (n 63) 76.
[197] ibid 78.

do not address the question of what should happen when a piece of traditional knowledge is narrower in scope and applicability, such as a specific therapeutic use for a plant extract.

For this author there is another fundamental problem with the argument. It seems to be based on the premise that Western-style IP enforcement is justified and that therefore something similar should exist for traditional knowledge. That Western-style IP enforcement is justified is clearly highly contested by many commentators and at best highly complicated. It seems safer not to rely on this premise and to look directly at the justifications for protection of TKAGR.

IX. Distributive Justice

According to Spinoza, 'Justice consists in the habitual rendering to every man his lawful due.'[198] But as, Comte-Sponville highlights, we are left with the question as to what this lawful due may be – what *is* my own? – what *should* it be?[199] These two approaches highlight the core interaction between distributive and corrective (commutative) justice. The first establishes how property *should* be distributed, the second how that distribution should be properly maintained in the interactions between people. Gordley asserts that within Aristotle's *Nicomachean Ethics* a higher concept of human welfare underlies the requirement for both distributive and corrective justice.[200] For each person to live in a manner in which their human potentialities are realised 'society must distribute resources fairly and, having done so, it must maintain the distribution'. Because of this requirement for the preservation of fair distribution, corrective justice ensures that a person who gains at another's expense must compensate the loser. For Gordley, this Aristotelian account 'underlies the law of property, unjust enrichment and tort' – and it is this account that has informed almost all Western debate on this issues from Aquinas, and the Scholastic rediscovery of the works of Aristotle, onwards.[201]

The interface between these two forms of justice is at the heart of questions of control of property: I should have mechanisms to control property – including compensation for my loss of property – but only to the extent that my right to that property can be supported by a distributive justification, namely a justification as to why I, in particular, should have property in a certain thing rather than

[198] B Spinoza, *A Theologico-Political Treatise*, in *The Chief Works*, vol 1 (New York, Dover, 1951) 208.

[199] A Compte-Sponville, *A Short Treatise on the Great Virtues* (London, Vintage, 2003) 74.

[200] J Gordley, 'Tort Law in the Aristotelian Tradition' in DG Owen (ed), *Philosophical Foundations of Tort Law* (Oxford, Oxford University Press, 1995) 131, 157.

[201] R Tuck, *Natural Rights Theories, Their Origin and Development* (Cambridge, Cambridge University Press, 1979); Richard W Wright, 'Right, Justice and Tort Law' in DG Owen (ed), *Philosophical Foundations of Tort Law* (Oxford, Oxford University Press, 1995) 159, 166.

someone else. In this sense deontological arguments for the existence of intellectual property rights that have been discussed above *are* distributive justice arguments.

As we have seen above, the 'natural rights' justification for ownership of property, and by extension intellectual property, is based on the idea that a person has unalienable rights which cannot be surrendered within the social contract. Both Locke and Hegel's view of property was essentially dependent on an idea of the person – for Locke the inalienable ownership of the self is what allows for ownership of land and goods (subject to his provisos) once a person's labour has been mixed with the material world. For Hegel the self is inalienable, and where intellectual products are created that are the extension of the self, these are similarly inalienable.

However, a core feature of the natural rights argument for the existence of an intellectual property rights is that they should only be owned by the person who is *deserving* of the right. Indeed, in relation to the Lockean labour-desert theory this is a rather circular statement, as it is the desert itself arising from the mixing of labour – essentially the self – with something external to the self which gives rise the right. Accordingly, subject to the provisos, the 'property' acquired is coterminous with the desert. Taking the Lockean analogy further, intellectual property rights should be seen from the perspective of an exception to a general freedom to use of the 'intellectual commons'.[202] Accordingly, asserting ownership over that part of the intellectual commons which you cannot justly claim is improperly removing information from that commons.

In terms of Kantian/Hegelian personality right justifications it is the creation of something which is an extension of the personality that originates the right – the contribution by the personality is key. The corollary of this is that where an individual has not created something/made a contribution, there can be no justifiable ownership and/or moral right to control use.

Both Lockean-desert and personality right justifications meet an immediate *inherent* counter-argument that there can be no natural right to the ownership of information or alternatively takes the form that the information commons cannot ever be enclosed.

What arises is a tension between a natural right to know,[203] and rights to intellectual liberty,[204] on the one hand, and a right to property in that which I have created, on the other. This can either be seen as a limited ownership exception to a broader right to intellectual freedom – a 'fencing off' of a commons – or as a set of limitations upon the conditions in which a natural right can spring into existence

[202] J Trerise, 'Liberty and the Rejection of Strong Intellectual Property Rights' in A Gosseries et al (eds), *Intellectual Property and Theories of Justice* (Palgrave Macmillan, Basingstoke 2010) 122.
[203] Aristotle, *Metaphysics* Book I, 980a 21.
[204] Breakey (n 13) 75.

from a 'vacuum'– though the result is essentially the same. However, wherever one starts the argument, the crucial factor at the centre of the tension is the concept of *contribution*. Whether reflecting the deontological justifications (or not), the idea that the protection afforded by the right can only extend to the contribution made by the potential right holder is the bedrock of formal intellectual property laws.[205] This focus upon contribution is, of course, a core element of the consequentialist incentivisation argument for intellectual property – the putative creators of intellectual products are incentivised to create such products by the provision of a 'reward' for their efforts.

A focus on rewarding contribution is arguably a key element to Gordley's fair distribution of society's resources.[206] However, the ability to 'contribute' is often tied up with the resources that the contributor already possesses – particularly in the field of technological developments. What if that initial distribution of resources is unfair – is it fair to continue to maintain an unfair status quo ante by offering yet further reward? It is here that we need to look to broader questions of distributive justice.

OseiTutu looks at the justification for a positive intellectual property right in traditional knowledge and asks the question whether protecting traditional knowledge through a sui generis intangible right would create a more equitable regime from a distributive justice perspective.[207] She states that for many, the sui generis right is a deontological one based on upon Locke's labour-desert theory. However, she believes that such rights can result in an imbalanced intellectual property system which allows the intellectual property right to take priority over competing interests and fears for the required 'retraction' of the public domain to create an exclusive right. She states: 'If a sui generis traditional knowledge right is to be created, the broader social good served by protecting traditional knowledge as a new form of intellectual property right should be very clearly articulated.'[208] OseiTutu also suggests that an indefinite, monopoly right for traditional knowledge would 'offend the principle of balance between the interests of the right holder and the public'.[209] She concludes that:

> If the goal of access to affordable knowledge and information is a worthy one, then an assessment of traditional knowledge from a distributive justice perspective leads to the conclusion that a sui generis intangible property right in traditional knowledge may not be the most appropriate response to the problems of bio-piracy and misappropriation.

[205] See eg Arts 84, 85, 123(2) and 123(3) of the Convention on the Grant of European Patents (European Patent Convention) of 5 October 1973 as revised by the Act revising Article 63 EPC of 17 December 1991 and the Act revising the EPC of 29 November 2000.

[206] Gordley (n 200) 15.7.

[207] JJ OseiTutu, 'A *Sui Generis* Regime for Traditional Knowledge: The Cultural Divide in Intellectual Property Law' (2011) 15 *Marquette Intellectual Property Law Review* 147.

[208] ibid 190.

[209] ibid 193.

> The corollary to this position is that the international community should be mindful of the need to balance rights and obligations in the development of international intellectual property law and policy.[210]

However, OseiTutu gives no specific guidance as to how to achieve such a balance in relation to the scope of a sui generis traditional knowledge right.

A. The Rawlsian Approach

When approaching distributive justice justifications one cannot ignore the revolutionary influence of John Rawls. For Warburton, Rawls's key contribution is the 'difference principle'.[211] This is about ensuring that society should be arranged in such a way to give more equal wealth and opportunity to the most disadvantaged. In designing a society one should adopt the 'original position' where one is ignorant as to what one's position in the proposed society may be. Rawls expects that in such a position a reasonable individual will try to minimise the negative outcomes of finding themselves in the least-advantaged position in society. This is not the place to discuss whether Rawls's faith in individuals' rationality is misplaced.[212] However, the difference principle remains a useful tool for investigating the distributive justice questions of a putative policy.

Rawls uses a *maximum minimorum* ('maximin') gain and loss analysis as a heuristic tool to demonstrate why it is that a person in her 'original position' would seek a society in which social and economic inequalities are to be to the greatest benefit of the least advantaged members of society. The maximin analysis used by Rawls is set out in Table 2.[213]

Table 2 Rawls's maximin analysis

	Circumstances		
Decisions	C_1	C_2	C_3
d_1	-$700	$800	$1,200
d_2	-$800	$700	$1,400
d_3	$500	$600	$800

As Rawls notes, this table is not a game of strategy – there is no one to play 'against'. Instead, Rawls has the person in the original position facing a number of potential outcomes: circumstances C_1 through to C_3. The person in the

[210] ibid 213.
[211] Warburton (n 89) 231.
[212] ibid 232.
[213] Rawls (n 158) 153.

original position, sitting as she is behind the 'veil of ignorance', cannot know in which of these circumstances she will find herself. She can, however, through her decision (d_x) as to the ordering of society, select a set of outcomes in which the worst outcome is better than the worst outcomes of all the other strategies. In Rawls's table the set of options that provides this 'maximisation of the minimum' is decision d_3. Although d_2 would provide a greater potential upside ($1,400) for some, it also provides the greatest downside (namely a debt of $800) for others.

Rawls uses the maximin analysis as a starting point for arriving at his argument that the social contract should be built on the principle of liberty, namely that each person is to have an equal right to the most extensive total system of equal basis liberties compatible with a similar system of liberty for all, paraphrased as 'people must be allowed the freedom to pursue the kind of life they would wish to lead provided it does not directly or indirectly harm another'.[214]

In addition, in following the maximin approach the person in the original position has to evaluate any institutional framework as if she *was sure* that she would become the most disadvantaged member of a particular society. This is what led Rawls to his 'difference principle'. This asserts that although such inequalities cannot be avoided, social and economic inequalities should be organised such as to give the greatest benefit to the *least advantaged* members of a society. Thus any evaluation of any possible institutional framework must start by identifying with the interests of the worst-off individual in society.[215] It is crucial to note that Rawls is not requiring the sweeping away of all inequalities where such inequalities can be justified on other grounds, provided that such inequalities provide conditions in which the *absolute* (rather than *relative*) condition of the least advantaged in society (C_1 in the table above) is enhanced (the minimum is maximised).

In its purist form, the incentivisation/consequentialist argument for intellectual property could meet this requirement. If the provision of a reward for inventive efforts directly leads to a broader total enrichment of the entirety of society such that the situation of C_1 is improved over the situation without such incentivization, then such a policy is not contrary per se to the principles of Rawlsian distributive justice. Significant questions, of course, remain as to whether such a policy *in fact* enhances the total wealth of society or whether the wealth so created is so unevenly distributed that C_1 sees no benefit or so little benefit as to be essentially unappreciable.

At first blush, one might argue that the creation of sui generis rights in genetic resources and TKAGR is a policy which avoids the 'trickle-down' problems of a broad incentivisation policy, and adheres to the difference principle

[214] P Vardy and P Grosch, *The Puzzle of Ethics* (London, Fount, 1999) 139.

[215] JC Harsanyi, 'Can the Maximin Principle Serve as a Basis for Morality? A Critique of John Rawls's Theory' (1975) 69(2) *American Political Science Review* 594, 596.

by moving directly to enhancing the situation of a group of disadvantaged individuals within global society – namely Indigenous peoples within the Global South. However, we need to immediately note that the difference principle does not, of itself, *create* a deontological or consequentialist right – it is a principle to be adhered to in the *application* of other rights, justifications and policy approaches, if one is seeking to ensure distributive justice. If we are following a Rawlsian approach, we need first to seek fundamental justifications for excluding non-consensual use of TKAGR and *then* seek to ensure that the application of justification serves to maximise the minimum situation for our most disadvantaged person 'C_1'.

X. Restorative/Corrective Justice ('Reparations')

Munzer has proposed a justification for rights in traditional knowledge based upon 'corrective justice'. He proposes six conditions precedent for such a corrective right. The first four he considers 'background' conditions.[216] These are:

> (1) some wrongs must have been committed against an indigenous group, some or all of its members, their successors, or both; (2) the wrongdoers or their successors are identifiable as a group, individual members of a group, some other entity, or some combination of these; (3) the wrongs unjustifiably caused harm to an indigenous people or some of its members, or both; and (4) those harmed are identifiable as an indigenous group or as individual members of an indigenous group, or both.

Once such injustices have been established, one would then need to consider whether:

> (5) no excuse is available such that the wrongdoers or their successors lack a moral duty to rectify their wrongs and undo the harm caused. Finally, (6) recognizing IP rights in TK in principle would be part of an effective and reasonably efficient means of compensating or restoring justice to the indigenous people or its members who have been harmed.

It is important to note that what is envisaged here is that once a sufficient present (or historic) indefensible wrong can be proved, then a right to protect traditional knowledge will be granted where that provides 'effective and reasonably efficient' restorative justice. There is no requirement for any *specific* link between the type of wrong and the remedy, nor, it would seem, a clear link between the magnitude of the wrong and the remedy (other than that the 'reasonable' efficiency does not have to be 'economically optimal' but cannot be 'seriously inefficient').[217]

[216] Munzer (n 28).
[217] ibid 62.

Munzer himself immediately recognises that the corrective justice of which he speaks is not what most would understand as an Aristotelian commutative justice, in which a *specific* wrongdoer directly corrects a *specific* wrong which that wrongdoer has wrought upon a *specific* wronged individual. For Munzer, such an Aristotelian approach is inappropriate as it is 'too rigid to deal with wrongs done by many sorts of wrongdoers to many sorts of victims'.[218] He states further:

> [I]n typical situations involving indigenous groups, harmed over many generations in many different ways by many different individuals, outsiders of various sorts, corporations and nation starts, it would be Procrustean to try to make the remedy due to indigenous groups exactly equal to the gains of wrong doers under an idealized correlatively-structured system of corrective justice. Given the remedial constraints thrown up by these complicated situations, one must make room for some constraints of efficiency. If this is rough corrective justice, so be it.[219]

Of course, what Munzer denigrates as 'Procrustean' logic and an 'idealized correlatively-structured system of corrective justice', namely that legal remedy should match the wrong committed and that one should have certainty in the application of the law against one, is thought by others to be a core principle of the rule of law.[220]

Notwithstanding obvious evidential problems,[221] crucial questions remain as to the *degree* of wrong required to support a claim. A key facet in Munzer's scheme is that there is no requirement for a clear linkage between the precondition for acquiring a right and the right given but we are not told what threshold of wrong needs to be met in the first place. Does a combination of smaller wrongdoings have an additive effect, and if so, how should this effect be determined? Crucially (and closely linked) we are not told upon what basis Munzer's defence of a 'lack a moral duty to rectify their wrongs and undo the harm caused' is to be determined.[222] Is this to be judged against an absolute standard of whether the wrongdoer should have reasonably believed they were acting inequitably? If so, in relation to historic abuses, is that standard to be determined as at the time of commission of the wrongful act or by today's standards?

Assuming that past wrongs of any sort do provide a justification for the creation of a sui generis right in traditional knowledge, what *type* of right is to be considered to be appropriate correction? Munzer divides corrective justice into compensatory justice (equivalent to money damages at law) and restorative justice (equivalent to injunctive relief, restitution and other relief in equity). However, he also sees corrective justice as incorporating 'reparations' for (predominantly

[218] ibid.
[219] ibid.
[220] Bingham (n 17) 37.
[221] For example, the delineation of where one indigenous group ends and another begins and acquiring evidence of historic injustice against a specific indigenous group.
[222] Munzer (n 28) 62.

past) wrongs and sees corrective reparations as either compensatory or restorative, or both. It is this concept of 'reparation' that is at the centre of Munzer's justification for protection of traditional knowledge. Accordingly, there seems no reason why such protection *could not* in principle include the grant of an absolute veto (through injunctive relief) alongside the award of compensation. Crucially, however, Munzer avoids answering the question as to which intellectual property rights in traditional knowledge should be given to Indigenous peoples in a particular circumstance. He also avoids advocating a set of appropriate intellectual property rules. His thrust is that effective compensatory and/or restorative elements in relation to misuse of traditional knowledge should form part of an appropriate suite of reparations for past wrongs (which may also include land grant, healthcare, education and monetary damages) determined on a case-by-case basis.

This type of 'what seems right at the time' *smörgåsbord* of remedies approach has the undoubted benefit of flexibility but fails to address the question of third-party certainty. In addition, the 'past wrongs deserve some type of reparation' justification may benefit from philosophical simplicity but is so loose as to provide little concrete basis determining the correct balance between the compensatory and/or restorative elements of the 'reparation' on a case-by-case basis. Most cases will require determination between competing equities. Under Munzer's reparation justification, a defendant may find themselves essentially burdened with the inequities of entirely unrelated third parties whose actions were unrelated to the case in question and which occurred in distant history.

One might imagine here a defendant party who were entirely happy to pay compensation for a misappropriation, but maintained that their use was so distal to the original information that injunctive relief was inappropriate. Under the reparation justification the (perhaps significant) historic abuses of unrelated others could here go into the balance of equities. Even if this were the case, we have no sense as to how inequities should be weighted as between the current defendant and third-party wrongdoers on one axis, as between current misappropriation and historic wrongs on another axis, and as between gravity of wrongs on yet another axis. Of course, such uncertainties make the translation of Munzer's reparation justification to a set of generally applicable principles for broader application exceptionally difficult.

XI. Human Rights Justifications

The two major heads set out above, Locke/labour-desert and rights based in personality, constitute by far the major deontological justifications for general intellectual property rights, at least in terms of analysis and commentary. However, the question of the justification for intellectual property within the context of developments in international human rights law also needs to be considered.

Dutfield and Suthersanen[223] consider the three main international human rights documents which touch upon intellectual property rights to be:

(a) The Universal Declaration of Human Rights ('UDHR') 1948;
(b) The International Covenant on Economic, Social and Cultural Rights ('ICESCR') 1966; and
(c) The International Covenant on Civil and Political Rights ('ICCPR') 1966.

Article 27 of the UDHR states that:

> (1) Everyone has the right freely to participate in the cultural life of the community, to enjoy the arts and to share in scientific advancement and its benefits.
> (2) Everyone has the right to the protection of the *moral and material interests resulting from any scientific, literary or artistic production of which he is the author.* [emphasis added]

This is supported by rights to property ownership in Article 17:

> (1) Everyone has the right to own property alone as well as in association with others.
> (2) No one shall be arbitrarily deprived of his property.

And rights protecting reputation under Article 12:

> No one shall be subjected to arbitrary interference with his privacy, family, home or correspondence, nor to attacks upon his honour and reputation. Everyone has the right to the protection of the law against such interference or attacks.

The UDHR is not a legally binding document. However, its provisions were put into legally binding form through the ICESCR and ICCPR. As is stated by Dutfield and Suthersanen,[224] the ICCPR fails to provide a positive basis for intellectual property rights although moral rights are indirectly protected through Article 17 ICCPR which essentially repeats the wording of Article 12 UDHR.

Articles 19(2) and (3) ICCPR provide an indirect acknowledgement of intellectual property rights in relation to a proviso to the right to a freedom of expression stating:

> 2. Everyone shall have the right to freedom of expression; this right shall include freedom to seek, receive and impart information and ideas of all kinds, regardless of frontiers, either orally, in writing or in print, in the form of art, or through any other media of his choice.
>
> 3. The exercise of the rights provided for in paragraph 2 of this article carries with it special duties and responsibilities. It may therefore be subject to certain restrictions, but these shall only be such as are provided by law and are necessary:
>
> (a) For *respect of the rights or reputations of others*;
> (b) For the protection of national security or of public order (ordre public), or of public health or morals. [emphasis added].

[223] Dutfield and Suthersanen (n 20) 215.
[224] ibid 217.

Arguably, however, the strongest reference to intellectual property rights comes from Article 15 ICESCR which follows the provisions of Article 27 UDHR. Article 15 states that:

1. The States Parties to the present Covenant recognize the right of everyone:
   (a) to take part in cultural life;
   (b) to enjoy the benefits of scientific progress and its applications;
   (c) to benefit from the protection of the moral and material interests resulting from any *scientific, literary or artistic production of which he is the author.*
2. The steps to be taken by the States Parties to the present Covenant to achieve the full realization of this right shall include those necessary for the conservation, the development and the diffusion of science and culture.
3. The States Parties to the present Covenant undertake to respect the freedom indispensable for scientific research and creative activity.
4. The States Parties to the present Covenant recognize the benefits to be derived from the encouragement and development of international contacts and cooperation in the scientific and cultural fields. [emphasis added]

In the view of Dutfield and Suthersanen, Article 15 identifies a requirement to balance, on the one hand, the right to access scientific and cultural good with, on the other, the right of authors and inventors to be protected without identifying the legal means by which this balance should be achieved.[225] Arguably, then, the right for authors and inventors to have some form of balanced protection is a human right. This would not, however, necessarily seem to be the case.

In November 2005, the UN Committee on Economic, Social and Cultural Right issued its General Comment No 17 (2005) in relation to Article 15, paragraph 1(c), of the ICESCR (the 'General Comment'). This is a somewhat confusing text. It essentially states that whereas human rights are 'timeless expressions of fundamental entitlements of the human person',[226] intellectual property rights should be seen quite differently:[227]

(a) as means by which States seek to provide incentives for inventiveness and creativity;
(b) of a temporary nature, which can be revoked, licensed or assigned to someone else; and
(c) (with the exception of moral rights), capable of being allocated, limited in time and scope, traded, amended and even forfeited.

It concludes that whereas the human right 'to benefit from the protection of the moral and material interests resulting from one's scientific, literary and artistic productions safeguards the personal link between authors and their creations and between peoples, communities, or other groups and their collective cultural heritage', the scope of protection of the moral and material interests of the author

[225] ibid 218.
[226] UN Committee on Economic, Social and Cultural Right General Comment No 17 (2005) para 2.
[227] ibid para 1.

provided for by Article 15, paragraph 1(c) 'does not necessarily coincide with what is referred to as intellectual property rights under national legislation or international agreements'. It concludes that it is 'important not to equate intellectual property rights with the human right recognized in article 15, paragraph 1 (c)'.[228] For Dutfield and Suthersanen it is clear that the concern of the Committee was that intellectual property rights had become too closely associated with large corporate entities, rather than individual authors/creators.[229]

Whilst the General Comment seems to offer support for the moral interests element of the human right (more akin perhaps to a Kantian/Fichtean authorial personality), the treatment of the 'material' interests is far less clear. However, it seems to relate to a right for the author to obtain an adequate standard of living: 'Unlike other human rights, the material interests of authors are not directly linked to the personality of the creator, but contribute to the enjoyment of the right to an adequate standard of living' (Article 11, paragraph 1).

It would be fair to conclude that the position of intellectual property rights as human rights, (with the exception of moral rights for authors to ensure attribution and prevent derogative treatment) is far from clear.

Dutfield and Suthersanen point to the Solemn Declaration adopted at the Centenary Assembly of the Berne Union as the only intellectual property treaty that makes reference to human rights when it states that: 'copyright is based on human rights and justice, as creators of beauty, entertainment and learning, deserve that their rights in their creation be recognized and effectively protected both in their own country and in all other countries of the world'.[230] There are perhaps in this phrase clearer echoes of Hegelian personal 'recognition' and Lockean reward than to human rights per se. In any event, as Dutfield and Suthersanen point out, the status of the Solemn Declaration is legally ambiguous and go on to put forward the counter-argument that classic intellectual property rights (again with the exception of moral rights for authors to ensure attribution and prevent derogative treatment) cannot be human rights as they run counter to the social and ethical aims of human rights law.[231] Whereas human rights laws do advocate some type of 'reasonable' reward, that reward can be delivered in alternative ways than simply giving the author/inventor monopolistic rights to prevent copying/exploitation.

A. Human Rights Justifications and TKAGR

On the basis of the analysis set out above (and given the position of the General Comment) there would appear to be no human right, as such, to what might be described as classic intellectual property rights. Individuals do appear to have

[228] ibid paras 2–3.
[229] Dutfield and Suthersanen (n 20) 219.
[230] ibid 221.
[231] ibid.

a right under Article 15 ICESCR to take part in cultural life, enjoy the benefits of scientific progress and its applications, and to benefit from the protection of the moral and material interests resulting from any scientific, literary or artistic production of which he is the author. However, as stated above, these expressed rights seem to be more closely related to *moral* rights (such as to proper attribution and prevention of derogatory treatment) rather than to monopoly rights to control the product of intellectual endeavour. Can we find support for the protection of traditional knowledge within the ICESCR? The protection to 'benefit from the protection of the moral and material interests resulting from any scientific, literary or artistic production of which [an individual] is the author' seems inherently difficult to apply to the situation of in which a community holds knowledge of which its current members may actually not be the 'author'. However, Article 15 also protects the right to take part in cultural life. The use, and holding, of traditional knowledge clearly could be an important element of the taking part in cultural life of an individual. However, from the ICESCR and General Comment alone, it is difficult to know how far a right to taking part in cultural life would extend to supporting an Indigenous community's right to positive protection of traditional knowledge. However, it is to a deeper discussion of an Indigenous community's inherent right to self-determination (and within that a right to use, hold and protect traditional knowledge) that we will now turn.

XII. Indigenous 'Sovereignty' and 'Indigenous Intellectual Property' in TKAGR

Although this work has so far predominantly taken an approach based on the classic Western high-level philosophical justifications for intellectual property, it is worth noting that alongside these there have been many advocates for a broader concept of 'Indigenous intellectual property' based on alternative claims. Wanjiku Karanja has defined these rights thus:

> Indigenous intellectual property is an umbrella legal term used to identify the special rights of indigenous groups to claim (from within their own laws) all their cultural knowledge and heritage together with their right to maintain, control, protect and develop their intellectual property over such cultural heritage and knowledge.[232]

However, (as we will see) not all advocates agree on the use of the term 'Indigenous intellectual property' or the form that Indigenous intellectual property rights would take or, indeed, the justifications for such rights. Although some of the arguments for such rights have consequentialist elements,[233] by far the most

[232] W Karanja, 'The Legitimacy of Indigenous Intellectual Property Rights' Claims' (2016) 1 *Strathmore Law Review* 165, 168.

[233] For example, that the creation of rights will assist in the preservation of biodiversity or indigenous heritage; those arguments are addressed fully elsewhere in this chapter.

common justification can perhaps best be summed up as deriving from the idea of 'Indigenous sovereignty'.[234] We will see that there is something of an overlap between the concept of Indigenous sovereignty and human rights law (primarily the provisions of UNDRIP). However, there are those (notably Indigenous scholars who reject the entire edifice of Western legal systems) who would not seek to conflate the two.[235] There are also echoes within the Indigenous sovereignty/ Indigenous intellectual property discourse of the restorative/corrective justice arguments mentioned above (in section X). However, for clarity of analysis those justifications will be kept separate from the Indigenous sovereignty basis within this work.

A. Indigenous 'Sovereignty'

So what, then, is Indigenous sovereignty? Barker describes the concept of Indigenous sovereignty as having many (often related) meanings. These range from the formulation of rights to reverse continuing experiences of colonialism, the giving of a basis for local efforts at the redemption of ancestral lands and resources, to ensuring self-governance and the preservation of cultural knowledge and practices.[236] However, it should be stated at the outset that the concept of 'Indigenous sovereignty' is highly contested and its contours are very far from clear.[237] Wiessner has described the concept of 'authentic indigenous sovereignty', which has the power to create a 'safe space' for Indigenous peoples to live a life with difference from settler culture and which should also create a right of free, prior, informed consent, the right to self-governance, the right to enter into treaties and other agreements, and the ability to require a legal duty on the settler state to respect, protect and promote Indigenous languages and culture.[238] For Varese, Indigenous sovereignty means the recognition that 'absolute power over the indigenous community' does not lie in the settler state but 'within the community, in the collective body' of an Indigenous people.[239] However, for Brennan, the concept

[234] Although, as will be discussed, for some this should be framed as an indigenous right to self-determination.

[235] K Engle, 'On Fragile Architecture: The UN Declaration on the Rights of Indigenous Peoples in the Context of Human Rights' (2011) 22(1) *European Journal of International Law* 141.

[236] J Barker, 'For Whom Sovereignty Matters' in J Barker (ed), *Sovereignty Matters: Locations of Contestation and Possibility in Indigenous Struggles for Self-determination* (Lincoln, NE, University of Nebraska Press, 2005).

[237] R Shrinkhal, '"Indigenous Sovereignty" and Right to Self-determination in International Law: A Critical Appraisal' (2021) 17(1) *AlterNative: An International Journal of Indigenous Peoples* 71, 71.

[238] S Wiessner, 'Indigenous Sovereignty: A Reassessment in Light of the UN Declaration on the Rights of Indigenous Peoples' (2008) 41 *Vanderbilt Journal of Transnational Law* 1141; LH Graham and S Wiessner, 'Indigenous Sovereignty, Culture, and International Human Rights Law' (2011) 110(2) *South Atlantic Quarterly* 403.

[239] S Varese, *Witness to Sovereignty: Essays on the Indian Movement in Latin America* (Copenhagen, International Work Group for Indigenous Affairs, 2006) 270.

of Indigenous sovereignty grows out of the idea that sovereignty is valuable only in relation to a nation that has 'its own land base, economic resources and social structure', and since most Indigenous peoples lack that, they should struggle for self-determination by asserting their sovereignty.[240] For Lenzerini, Indigenous sovereignty is inclusive of a right to ownership over traditional land, a right to preserve identity and culture, participatory rights in decision-making processes (especially in matters related to culture and life), and the right to self-governance through customary laws. However, in contrast to some Indigenous rights scholars, he argues that Indigenous sovereignty is only 'parallel' to that of the settler state and should not exceed the supreme territorial sovereignty of the state.[241]

Although the idea of Indigenous sovereignty is often related to the political struggle for Indigenous self-determination, and the return of Indigenous lands, the advocates for Indigenous sovereignty can vary widely in their understanding of the concept depending on their views as to how best to achieve those ends (or indeed whether the aims should be fully achieved). There are those advocates of Indigenous rights who reject the concept of Indigenous sovereignty *within* a state as they entirely reject the underlying concept of the sovereignty of the settler state. For Taiaiake Alfred, 'sovereignty is an exclusionary concept rooted in an adversarial and coercive nation of power' and 'the mythology of [the settler] State is hegemonic, and the struggle for justice would be better served by undermining the myth of the State sovereignty than by carving out a small and dependent space for Indigenous peoples within it'.[242] For Turner, the Western European concepts of rights and sovereignty act as an 'ideological toxin' that has warped the thinking of Indigenous peoples on the Australian continent toward a '[Western] discourse on property, ethics, political sovereignty, and justice'.[243] Notwithstanding these criticisms, there are those who seek to transform the concept of sovereignty and seek to understand an Indigenous sovereignty 'in which the capacity to articulate and defend heterogeneity' is high.[244] For Barker:

> Sovereignty carries the horrible stench of colonialism. It is incomplete, inaccurate, and troubled. But it has also been rearticulated to mean altogether different things by indigenous peoples. In its link to concepts of self-determination and self-government, it insists on the recognition of inherent rights to the respect for political affiliations that

[240] F Brennan, *One Land One Nation* (St Lucia, QLD, *Queensland University Press*, 1995) 127.

[241] F Lenzerini, 'Sovereignty Revisited: International Law and Parallel Sovereignty of Indigenous Peoples' (2006) 42(1) *Texas Journal of International Law* 155.

[242] T Alfred, *Peace, Power, Righteousness: An Indigenous Manifesto* (Oxford, Oxford University Press, 1999) 58.

[243] D Turner, 'Vision: Towards an Understanding of Aboriginal Sovereignty' in R Beiner and WJ Norman (eds), *Canadian Political Philosophy: Contemporary Reflections* (Oxford, Oxford University Press, 2001) 325.

[244] D Kennedy, 'Sovereignty: Responding to Anghie and Aravamudan's Remarks in the Proceedings of the Symposium "Representing Culture: Translating Human Rights"' (2006) 41(3) *Texas International Law Journal* 465, 468; see eg L Whitt, *Science, Colonialism, and Indigenous Peoples. The Cultural Politics of Law and Knowledge* (Cambridge, Cambridge University Press, 2009) 179.

> are historical and located and for the unique cultural identities that continue to find meaning in those histories and relations.[245]

It is arguable to what extent the concept of Indigenous sovereignty is different from the concept of an inherent right to Indigenous self-determination. Perhaps (as is suggested by Barker above) a right to self-determination lies within a broader concept of Indigenous sovereignty. However, the terms are often used interchangeably and 'sovereignty' is certainly a useful shorthand for an inherent right to self-determination. However, given that the term 'sovereignty' is more politically charged (from both sides of the Indigenous rights argument), the inherent right to Indigenous self-determination appears to be the terminology that is used more frequently within diplomatic intergovernmental negotiations. Accordingly, the author will refer in this work to the concept the inherent right of Indigenous peoples to self-determination as opposed to 'sovereignty' (unless the term 'sovereignty' is being deliberately referred to) and has left as moot the question of whether there is any substantive difference between these terms, particularly when applied to Indigenous peoples' rights over genetic resources or TKAGR. In this regard, it is interesting to note that the only mention of 'sovereignty' within the preambles to the CBD and Nagoya Protocol are a reaffirmations of the sovereign rights of states over their natural/biological resources, rather than the rights of Indigenous peoples – although the preamble of the Nagoya Protocol affirms that nothing in the Protocol 'shall be construed as diminishing or extinguishing the existing rights of indigenous and local communities'.[246] The Kunming–Montreal GBF similarly contains no mention of Indigenous sovereignty and the only mention of 'sovereignty' is in relation to respecting *national* sovereignty during implementation of the framework.[247] However, as with the Nagoya Protocol, the GBF states that nothing in the framework 'may be construed as diminishing or extinguishing the rights that indigenous peoples currently have or may acquire in the future'.[248]

Despite its contested and uncertain nature, the idea of a concept of an inherent Indigenous right to self-determination is a recurring theme in arguments for Indigenous intellectual property. As the development of the argument made by academics and activists for Indigenous intellectual property has evolved alongside other political and international developments, it is helpful to present the debate in a narrative form (which is set out in section XII.C below). These argument(s) have been informed by an understanding of how TKAGR is held by Indigenous people and their own (varied) perception of how it is 'owned'. Therefore, before looking at the story of the argument for (and against) Indigenous intellectual property we will look first at how TKAGR is held within Indigenous communities and examine some Indigenous ideas of ownership.

[245] Barker (n 236) 2.
[246] Nagoya Protocol Preamble.
[247] CBD/COP/DEC/15/4, s K, para 19.
[248] CBD/COP/DEC/15/4, s C, para 7(a).

B. How TKAGR Is Held?

Although some Indigenous cultures lack concepts equivalent to 'property',[249] many others will have an idea of ownership or possession in knowledge which falls between that extreme and the Western idea of formalised intellectual property rights. The concept of 'ownership' of traditional knowledge and intangible cultural heritage within Indigenous societies is complex and varied. It reflects the many different ways in which information is managed, controlled and disseminated within an Indigenous society and the different systems of customary law and the relations between Indigenous groups. It also reflects the purpose (or purposes) of information, whether it be instrumental for survival or has a ritual or religious purpose in creating group identity and group cohesion. According to Drahos, some traditional knowledge 'may be open to all (including non-Indigenous people) to use' and 'some knowledge may be open to all clan members to use … while other knowledge may only be available to the initiated … and some individuals may be given temporary appropriation rights over some knowledge'.[250]

Tom Griffiths concludes that access to some traditional knowledge within some Indigenous societies may be 'open', such that all within a group may access it.[251] In these cases possession (or identification with) of a body of knowledge is often the basis of a claim to membership of a particular Indigenous group and such knowledge can be part of the construction of a cultural identity of the broader group.[252] Indeed such inalienable, intangible possessions can, in part, define a people in a historical sense.[253] In contrast to this more open access, in some cases the access to the core traditional knowledge of a society is based on the particular ties that an individual will have to a particular community, and their status within that society. In particular, some exclusive rights in traditional knowledge will be allocated according to gender roles and the relationship of an individual to such knowledge will be shaped by their gender role within that society.[254] For example, the women of the Awajún (an Indigenous people of the Marañón River of Peru) and of the Achuar (an Indigenous people of the Pastaza River and Huasaga Rivers of Peru) both have a perception that the plants in their garden are their 'children' and that in their role as gardener, carer to (and holder of information on) those

[249] C Scott, 'Property, Practice and Aboriginal Rights Among Quebec Cree Hunters' in T Ingold et al (eds), *Hunters and Gatherers 2: Property, Power and Ideology* (Oxford, Oxford University Press, 1988).

[250] P Drahos, 'Indigenous Knowledge and Duties of Intellectual Property Owners' (1997) 11 *Intellectual Property Journal* 179, 186.

[251] T Griffiths *Indigenous Knowledge and Intellactual Property: A Preliminary Review of the Anthropological Literature* (Report prepared for the Foundation for Ethnobiology at the University of Oxford, 1993).

[252] FR Myers, 'Burning the Truck and Holding the Country: Pintupi Forms of Property and Identity' in EN Wilmsen (ed), *We Are Here: Politics of Aboriginal Land Tenure* (Oakland, CA, University of California Press, 1989) 7.

[253] AB Weiner, 'Inalienable Wealth' (1985) 12(2) *American Ethnologist* 210, 210.

[254] D Bell, *Daughters of the Dreaming* (Carlton, Victoria, McPhee Gribble, 1983) 50.

plants, they act as 'mother' to those plants.[255] In other cases, some exclusive rights in traditional knowledge will be allocated to a narrow 'select' band within the society. Within such a select group an individual's exclusive rights to secret 'magical' or 'symbolic' knowledge can confer a special identity and mystical power to the 'owner'.[256] This type of very narrow holding of information can create a species of property 'ownership' which is created through ritual, training and initiation and often obligations of secrecy.[257] In return for the fact that the holder has undergone periods of training and ritual there is often an acknowledgement within the broader society that the holder is deserving of access to (or ownership of) the knowledge.[258]

The holding of knowledge within a narrow 'sect' can be particularly true for select groups of traditional healers. Amongst the Kpelle people of Liberia, knowledge of medicine carries mystical powers amongst the *sâle-naum* ('medicine owners') and to join this select band requires a learning period in which an applicant must provide services for their tutors and the making of ritual oaths of secrecy, the breaching of which would lead to supernatural punishment.[259] Amongst the Giriama people of Kenya, knowledge of herbal remedies and the incantations uttered in their use is secretly held within a tightly integrated, narrow band of practitioners and 'shared only with whom they received and bought it'.[260] Such knowledge may only be 'bought' from a maximum of seven teachers and the pupil forms a father–son relationship with his first teacher and a blood-brother relationship with other members of the group.[261]

In the above cases Indigenous concepts of property or 'ownership' are employed as expressions of interpersonal or political relations and concrete evidence for institutions of ownership are manifested where there exists a social norm that non-owners must ask to use the holder of property for permission before they can use it. For the Pintupi in Australia 'to "own" something is the right to be asked for it'.[262] It is also possible that traditional knowledge has some value in negotiations with neighbouring Indigenous groups, for example in marriage alliances. It can also act as a marker of the identity of a group to external parties which supports

[255] MF Brown, *Tsewa's Gift: Magic and Meaning in an Amazonian Society* (Washington, DC, Smithsonian Institution Press, 1986); P Descola, *La Nature Domestique, Symbolisme et Praxis dans l'écologie des Achuar* (Paris, Editiones del la Maison des Sciences de L'Hommes, 1986).

[256] I Keen, 'Yolngu Religious Property' in T Ingold et al (eds), *Hunters and Gatherers 2: Property, Power and Ideology* (Oxford, Oxford University Press, 1988).

[257] S Harrison, 'Ritual and Intellectual Property' (1992) 27(2) *Man* 225, 230.

[258] ibid 234; K Århem, 'Millennium Among the Makuna: An Anthropological Film Adventure in the Northwest Amazon' (1993) 9(3) *Anthropology Today* 3, 3 and 7.

[259] WP Murphy 'Secret Knowledge as Property and Power in Kpelle Society: Elders versus Youth' (1980) 50(2) *Africa: Journal of the International African Institute* 193, 200.

[260] D Parkin, *Sacred Void: Spatial Images of Work and Ritual Among the Giriama of Kenya* (Cambridge, Cambridge University Press, 1991) 163.

[261] ibid 180.

[262] FR Myers, 'Always Ask: Resource Use and Land Ownership Among the Pintupi Aborigines of the Australian Western Desert' in NM Williams and ES Hunn (eds), *Resource Managers: North American And Australian Hunter-Gatherers* (Routledge, New York, 1982)173; Griffiths (n 251) 25.

other ownership/possession claims to land and environmental resources.[263] In addition, a key part of the autonomy and liberty of an Indigenous group is that the group (and individuals within it) are free to interpret their cultural history and traditional knowledge in their own terms.[264]

It is clear that traditional knowledge can be possessed/owned by Indigenous groups (and individuals within a group) in many different ways and sometimes in ways that the holders themselves would not recognise as conforming to a Western concept of 'property'. However, as Indigenous peoples have been willingly (or unwillingly) drawn into wider market economies they have had to evaluate the value of their knowledge as a potential mechanism for providing the monetary income required in contemporary livelihoods.[265] The discussion between scientists, legal academics, conservationists and anthropologists that income-generating Indigenous knowledge may require a form of structured legal protection to prevent its misappropriation by non-Indigenous enterprises, and that Indigenous peoples have (or should have) some sort of 'Indigenous intellectual property' (broadly conceived) in their traditional knowledge (and intangible cultural heritage), has a relatively recent history. It is to that history that we will now turn.

C. The History of the Argument for (and Against) 'Indigenous Intellectual Property'

As discussed above, the nature of Indigenous traditional knowledge and how it is held and transmitted had long been the subject for anthropological investigation. However, by the mid-1970s there was an increasing fear that the rate of destruction of the environments within which Indigenous peoples were living, and indeed the extinction of Indigenous peoples themselves, would lead to a loss of vital traditional knowledge related to biodiversity, which, in turn, would lead to further environmental loss and Indigenous extinction.[266] In 1975, Goodland and Irwin warned of the existential threats in the Amazonian region to the Indigenous peoples of the Amazon and their invaluable systems:

> Scientists are competing with extinction in their race to inventory what the world contains. Amerindians are the only societies with the necessary knowledge, expertise and tradition to prosper in the Amazon jungle. Amerindians not only profoundly

[263] E Kolig, 'Government Policies and Religious Strategies: Fighting with Myth at Noonkanbah' in R Tonkinson and M Howard (eds), *Going it Alone: Prospects for Aboriginal Autonomy* (Canberra, Aboriginal Studies Press, 1990); K Palmer, '"Owners" and "Managers": Ritual Co-operation and Mutual Dependence in the Maintenance of Rights to Land' (1983) 13(6) *Mankind* 517; L Lindstrom, 'Knowledge and Power in a South Pacific Society' (Washington, DC, Smithsonian Institution Press, 1990).

[264] Griffiths (n 251) 48.

[265] ibid.

[266] DA Posey, 'Indigenous Knowledge and Development in the Amazon' in E Moran (ed), *The Dilemma of Amazonian Development* (Boulder, CO, Westview Press, 1983) 891.

> appreciate what exists, but also understand ecological interrelations of the various components of the Amazonian ecosystem better than do modem ecologists. Indians perceive specific relationships which biologists are only now discovering to be accurate.[267]

In 1980 Brokensha et al highlighted that this Indigenous traditional knowledge performed an important role in enabling Indigenous peoples to protect biodiversity.[268] It should be noted that at this point in history there were no specific international protections for Indigenous peoples' culture other than those set out in the UN International Labour Organisation's Indigenous and Tribal Populations Convention of 1957 (1957 ITPC Convention) which required governments to merely promote the 'social, economic and cultural development' of Indigenous and tribal populations,[269] without setting out any mechanism or positive laws by which that was to happen.[270]

Dutfield highlights the extent to which the relationships between intellectual property, biogenetic resources and TKAGR became increasingly politicised, stating that 'as soon as the disappearance of these resources became apparent and their perceived economic value increased, the uncertain legal situation became a source of conflict between and within nations on matters relating to conservation, commercialisation and ownership'.[271] The absence of positive protection and the ongoing recognition of the vulnerability of biological traditional knowledge stimulated the development of a number of related (and interweaving and cross-fertilising) threads of discussion.

The first thread was a debate around the appropriateness (practically and ethically) of using 'classic' intellectual property rights to protect TKAGR and the second was a debate about the potential use of a sui generis ABS right to achieve protection. Underlying both these threads was a debate about whether the ideas of Indigenous sovereignty/right to self-determination (broadly conceived) support the first two approaches and, also, whether Indigenous sovereignty/right to self-determination supports a yet further right for the protection of the intangible heritage of Indigenous people which sits entirely outwith the structures created by classic intellectual property rights or ABS rights.

Throughout the late 1970s ethnobiologist Darell Posey built a significant body of work examining and documenting the traditional biological knowledge of the

[267] RJA Goodland and HS Irwin, *Amazon Jungle: Green Hell to Red Desert: An Ecological Discussion of the Environmental Impact of the Highway Construction Programme in the Amazon Basin* (Amsterdam, Elsevier, 1975).

[268] D Brokensha et al, *Indigenous Knowledge Systems and Development* (Lanham, MD, University Press of America, 1980).

[269] United Nations International Labour Organisation Indigenous and Tribal Populations Convention, 1957 (No 107) Art 2(2)(b).

[270] See generally S Aga Khan and H bin Talal, *Indigenous Peoples: A Global Quest for Justice: A Report for the Independent Commission on International Humanitarian Issues* (London, Zed Books, 1987).

[271] Dutfield, (n 146) 3.

Kayapó people of the Amazon and Xingu rivers of Brazil.[272] Observing the problems that the Kayapó were encountering from external exploitation of the natural resources of the Amazon (including a proposed hydroelectric damming of the Xingpu), Posey became an activist for Indigenous rights. As part of this drive, in 1988 Posey organised the first International Congress of Ethnobiology in Belém, Brazil, at which was signed the Declaration of Belém. This outlined the importance of scientists and researchers respecting traditional knowledge and Indigenous land.[273] The Declaration of Belém states that all 'inalienable human rights' of Indigenous people 'be recognized and guaranteed' (including rights to 'cultural and linguistic identity') and that 'procedures be developed to compensate native peoples for the utilization of their knowledge and their biological resources'.[274] However, other than this broad call for human rights to cultural and linguistic identity, there is no mention of intellectual property rights, as such, within the Declaration.

By 1989, the relatively nascent political drive to support the protection of Indigenous culture and self-determination had led to a development of the ITPC 1957 Convention into the UNIPO Indigenous and Tribal Peoples Convention, 1989 (No 169) (ITPC 1989). Whilst the ratification of this convention was relatively limited, it did provide (at Article 4) that 'Special measures shall be adopted as appropriate for safeguarding the persons, institutions, property, labour, cultures and environment of the peoples concerned', and that 'Such special measures shall not be contrary to the freely-expressed wishes of the peoples concerned.' It further provided (at Article 13) that 'governments shall respect the special importance for the cultures and spiritual values of the peoples concerned of their relationship with the lands or territories, or both as applicable, which they occupy or otherwise use, and in particular the collective aspects of this relationship'. However, other than this broad protection of 'culture' no specific positive rights were envisioned that would protect traditional cultural heritage or knowledge.

As a Western lawyer (or indeed activist) looking to protect an intangible concept such as traditional cultural heritage or knowledge, one might first find oneself looking at the question of whether 'classic' intellectual property rights could achieve appropriate protection. Indeed, Posey began to introduce the concept of implementing intellectual property rights to protect Indigenous traditional knowledge in the early 1990s. He suggested that economic independence is a way for Indigenous peoples to preserve their knowledge and culture.[275] He further argued that there is an intrinsic link between Indigenous land and Indigenous knowledge, and that both should be protected for Indigenous people

[272] See eg: DA Posey, 'Kayapo Controla Inseto com Uso Adequado do Ambiente' (1979) 14(3) *Revista de Atualidade Indígena* 47; DA Posey, 'Ethnoentomology of the Kayapó Indians of Central Brazil: Wasps, Warriors and Fearless Men' (1981) 1(1) *Journal of Ethnobiology* 165.

[273] Declaration of Belém 1988.

[274] ibid Arts 3 and 4.

[275] DA Posey, 'Intellectual Property Rights: What Is the Position of Ethnobiology?' (1990) 10(1) *Journal of Ethnobiology* 93.

to effectively retain their knowledge.[276] Posey did not suggest a method to implement these rights, nor did he argue for a particular existing intellectual property right to be extended to cover Indigenous traditional knowledge.[277] However, he did advocate for particular steps to be taken to protect Indigenous intellectual property, such as the early steps being discussed within WIPO and UNSECO to protect folklore and 'artistic' aspects of Indigenous knowledge. He also argued for national legislation to be implemented to protect Indigenous intellectual property rights, and the establishment of a Working Committee to investigate issues of intellectual property rights relating to Indigenous rights and to produce guidelines for national and international legislation.[278]

In 1992 the CBD was signed. As has been discussed in chapter two (in section II.C), Article 8(j) contained provisions encouraging the respect, preservation and maintenance of 'knowledge, innovations and practices of Indigenous and local communities embodying traditional lifestyles relevant for the conservation and sustainable use of biological diversity', promoting the wider application of such knowledge with the 'approval and involvement of the holders of such knowledge, innovations and practices' and 'encouraging the equitable sharing of the benefits arising from the utilization of such knowledge, innovations and practices'. Although the Ad Hoc Group of Experts on Biological Diversity who met in Geneva in 1988 and 1990 to develop the draft text of the CBD was asked to take into account 'the need to share costs and benefits between developed and developing countries' as well as 'ways and means to support innovation by local people',[279] its prime focus was to address the threat to biodiversity (and to ameliorate potential conflict between parties from the Global South and North) rather than give effect to Indigenous sovereignty or rights to self-determination as such.[280] It agreed, therefore, that although the 'needs and welfare of indigenous peoples must be given consideration' it would be 'in connection with the conservation of species, habitats and ecosystems'.[281] During the 1990 meeting, the Working Group established that there must be 'recognition for the rights of indigenous peoples to benefit from their highly practical knowledge of local organisms and to incorporate their traditional uses of local ecosystems that often are consistent with conservation goals'.[282] However, there was no expansion

[276] DA Posey, 'Intellectual Property Rights: And Just Compensation for Indigenous Knowledge' (1990) 6(4) *Anthropology Today* 13.

[277] ibid.

[278] ibid.

[279] www.cbd.int/history/.

[280] DM McGraw, 'The Story of the Biodiversity Convention: From Negotiation to Implementation' in PG Le Prestre (ed), *Governing Global Biodiversity: The evolution and implementation of the Convention on Biological Diversity* (Farnham, Ashgate, 2002).

[281] United Nations Environment Programme Ad Hoc Working Group of Experts on Biological Diversity First session Geneva, 16–18 November 1988, para B17, www.cbd.int/doc/meetings/iccbd/bdewg-01/official/bdewg 01 03 en.pdf.

[282] Report of the Ad Hoc Working Group on the Work of its Second Session, United Nations Environment Programme (Geneva, 1990).

past the recognition that Indigenous people should be compensated for the use of their traditional knowledge and that they have the right to benefit from it. Accordingly, the CBD did not create any intellectual property right nor, indeed, address the question of Indigenous intellectual property.

In 1993 the UN Conference on Environment and Development met in Rio de Janeiro, Brazil, and formulated the Rio Declaration on Environment and Development (the Rio Declaration). Principle 22 of the Rio Declaration states that:

> Indigenous people and their communities and other local communities have a vital role in environmental management and development because of their knowledge and traditional practices. States should recognize and duly support their identity, culture and interests and enable their effective participation in the achievement of sustainable development.

Paragraph 26 of the Rio Declaration goes on to urge governments to 'enrol indigenous peoples in full global partnership, beginning with measures to protect their rights and conserve their patrimony' and to 'incorporate their rights and responsibilities into national legislation; recognize and apply elsewhere indigenous values, traditional knowledge and resource management practices'. It is unclear to what extent an encouragement to recognising and applying elsewhere Indigenous 'values' constitutes an acknowledgement of Indigenous sovereignty or Indigenous people's right to self-determination. Certainly no concrete mechanism for protecting an Indigenous right to genetic resources or TKAGR was proposed.

In 1993 Stephen Brush suggested three methods for introducing intellectual property rights for Indigenous traditional knowledge: top-down, middle-ground and bottom-up.[283] The top-down approach advocated for international and national agencies to extend rights to Indigenous people and the middle-ground approach was to apply conventional intellectual property rights to Indigenous knowledge with the aim of balancing the protection between Indigenous groups and the industrial users of the genetic material. The bottom-up approach was to encourage Indigenous groups to declare their knowledge as 'property' and therefore require payment to use it. Brush highlighted the potential barriers to implementing intellectual property rights for Indigenous peoples. He noted that conventional intellectual property rights (such as patents) require the knowledge to be novel and essentially 'discovered'. Although (as discussed above in section VII.B) TKAGR is not static and does evolve, Indigenous knowledge would rarely meet a formal patent novelty requirement. Brush also highlights that it is difficult to establish which Indigenous group should get exclusive control over their knowledge and biological material when much of it is common knowledge between Indigenous groups in similar locations. Furthermore, at the time of writing of Brush's article, many Indigenous groups did not enjoy recognition from states, and the existence

[283] SB Brush, 'Indigenous Knowledge of Biological Resources and Intellectual Property Rights: The Role of Anthropology' (1993) 95(3) *American Anthropologist* 653.

of intellectual property rights would generally assume a positive legal and political relationship between the states and the Indigenous groups. Controversially, Brush also argued that since the market for Indigenous knowledge or biological materials is often poor, he was unsure whether intellectual property protection would even be worth introducing. This recognition of the potential obstacles involved in implementing intellectual property rights for Indigenous traditional knowledge marked a significant advancement in the discourse as academics began to genuinely address the challenges associated with it.[284]

A 1993 US Congressional Research Report addressed many of the same difficulties in implementing 'classic' intellectual property rights in traditional knowledge.[285] In particular, it discussed the issues of obtaining copyright and patents for Indigenous traditional knowledge, before suggesting that the most likely avenue for protection would be to provide sui generis compensation to Indigenous groups for the use of their traditional knowledge whilst trying to promote the preservation of biodiversity.

In 1994, the TRIPS Agreement was signed, which established the minimum standards for the regulation of intellectual property by different states[286] Although the TRIPS Agreement did not have any provision relating to traditional knowledge, it did not prevent the enacting of legislation protecting traditional knowledge past the requirements in the Agreement.[287] For example, Kenya passed an Industrial Property Bill in 1989 which allows for petty patents relating to traditional medicinal knowledge, and this did not violate the Agreement.[288]

In a departure from his previous position, in 1995 Posey began to argue against the implementation of intellectual property rights for traditional knowledge. He stated that the idea that implementation of intellectual property for Indigenous traditional knowledge was the best form of protection was not a sentiment shared by traditional and Indigenous groups, or by environmental and human rights groups.[289] He argued that Indigenous groups had become more well-informed and articulate in understanding the concerns around the loss of local autonomy and biodiversity, and that this had coincided with a wider recognition that 'top-down' development (as discussed by Brush) has serious limitations. Posey

[284] ibid.

[285] JR Axt et al, *Biotechnology, Indigenous Peoples, and Intellectual Property Rights* (Congressional Research Service Report for Congress, 1993).

[286] Agreement on Trade-Related Aspects of International Property Rights (TRIPS) 1994.

[287] G Dutfield, *Intellectual Property Rights, Trade and Biodiversity* (Oxford, Earthscan, 2000).

[288] ibid. It also highlights how some forms of intellectual property can provide effective protection for indigenous traditional knowledge, although these cases are rare.

[289] DA Posey, 'Indigenous Peoples and Traditional Resource Rights: A Basis for Equitable Relationships?' in *Workshop on Indigenous Peoples and Traditional Resource Rights at the Green College Centre for Environmental Policy and Understanding* (University of Oxford, 1995) www.iccaconsortium.org/wp-content/uploads/2015/08/example-ip-and-traditional-resource-rights-addison-posey-1995-en.pdf.

highlighted that there had been a failure of international law (at the time of his writing) to put in place protections for Indigenous traditional knowledge and that the current system of protecting intellectual property could not be adapted to protect Indigenous traditional knowledge. He then went on to suggest the introduction of traditional resource rights (TRRs). TRRs were imagined as a combination of various rights (such as human rights, the right to privacy, and may include intellectual property rights) within national and international law that would essentially act as a 'bundle of rights' to better protect Indigenous traditional knowledge.

Posey, together with Graham Dutfield, began to expand on the idea of TRRs in their seminal 1996 work *Beyond Intellectual Property*.[290] They argued that classic intellectual property rights are inappropriate to protect Indigenous traditional knowledge because they cannot be the solution to the lack of self-determination of Indigenous communities and the inequalities of wealth and power between Indigenous communities and government and corporations. Their principle reasons for proposing TRRs over intellectual property rights were that intellectual property rights are essentially economic, whereas TRRs are more closely linked with the desire for self-determination. They also suggested replacing the term 'community intellectual property rights' with 'community intellectual rights' to address the fact that many Indigenous communities did not accept the concept of ownership of property in the same way as Western societies.[291]

In 1999, Terri Janke, an Indigenous Australian lawyer of Wuthathi/Meriam heritage, stressed the connection between Indigenous traditional knowledge and the land of a people.[292] Janke also highlighted the importance of utilising informed consent in these matters, with parties seeking to use traditional knowledge having to gain consent from Indigenous groups. She went on to suggest adjusting existing Australian law to cover intellectual property rights for Indigenous groups or creating new and specific legislation. Janke also advocated for non-legislative measures to be introduced, such as negotiating rights under agreement, developing new cultural infrastructure, obtaining consent from Indigenous groups to use their knowledge, and using authentication marks on products to encourage purchasing or learning from Indigenous communities.

In 2000, Marilyn Strathern, (a British anthropologist with experience working with the Mbowamb people of Western Highlands Province of Papua New

[290] DA Posey and G Dutfield, *Beyond Intellectual Property: Toward Traditional Resource Rights for Indigenous Peoples and Local Communities* (Ottawa, International Development Research Centre, 1996).

[291] The proportion of indigenous peoples for whom this is the case is a source of contention. Other academics have argued that most indigenous peoples do in fact have a concept of property because they have historically engaged in trading. See T Simpson, 'Indigenous Heritage and Self-determination: The Cultural and Intellectual Property Rights of Indigenous Peoples' (Copenhagen, International Work Group for Indigenous Affairs, 1997).

[292] T Janke, 'Respecting Indigenous Cultural and Intellectual Property Rights' (1999) 22 *University of New South Wales Law Journal* 631.

Guinea) discussed the introduction of intellectual property rights to Indigenous traditional knowledge.[293] Strathern analyses Posey's 'bundle of rights' concept, concluding that the use of such overlapping rights (such as cultural heritage rights and the right to self-determination) would offer more protection than a singular intellectual property right. She highlighted the disadvantages of using existing, classic, intellectual property rights to protect traditional knowledge, notably the problem of allocating copyright to one person when the knowledge belongs to an entire community. She reiterated that the 'Euro-American' attitudes to possession are not necessarily shared by Indigenous peoples. She did, however, argue that there are some advantages to introducing intellectual property rights for Indigenous traditional knowledge, such as asserting claims on valuable knowledge and creating a 'two-way flow of knowledge and recompense'.[294] This latter advantage echoes the sentiment behind the creation of sui generis ABS rights. Strathern highlights a growing argument at this time that classic intellectual property rights would very likely not be effective at protecting traditional knowledge without combining them with another form of sui generis protection, such as ABS. Indeed, Posey continued to advocate against the introduction of classic intellectual property rights for Indigenous traditional knowledge and in favour of introducing sui generis legislation to protect Indigenous communities until his death in 2001.[295]

By 2002 the Bonn Guidelines to the CBD were released.[296] These non-binding guidelines are discussed in chapter two, but it is worth reiterating here that they were designed to aid various parties and governments in developing ABS strategies and policy measures. As clarification of the CBD system it is not surprising that the focus of the Guidelines is in no way on the Indigenous right to self-determination. However, there is a tantalising reference to the protection of customary use of biological resources: there is mention within the Guidelines that where mutually agreed terms are agreed by parties in relation to providing access to genetic resources the granting party should take into account the ethical concerns of 'particular indigenous and local communities concerned'[297] and ensure that 'the knowledge, innovations and practices of indigenous and local communities have been respected, preserved and maintained, and whether the customary use of biological resources in accordance with traditional practices has been protected and encouraged'.[298]

[293] M Strathern, 'Multiple Perspectives on Intellectual Property' in K Whimp and M Busse (eds), *Protection of Intellectual, Biological and Cultural Property in Papua New Guinea* (Canberra, Australian National University Press, 2000).

[294] ibid.

[295] DA Posey, 'Commodification of the Sacred Through Intellectual Property Rights' (2002) 83(1–2) *Journal of Ethnobiology* 3.

[296] Bonn Guidelines on Access to Genetic Resources and Fair and Equitable Sharing of the Benefits Arising out of their Utilization (Secretariat of the Convention on Biological Diversity, 2002).

[297] ibid 43(a).

[298] ibid 44(g).

Writing in 2006, Chidi Oguamanam[299] concedes that there was 'no consensus on the fitness of intellectual property to accomplish the expectation or objectives its advocates have raised for holder of local knowledge'. Oguamanam suggests that the debate had fallen into two arguments:

(i) TKAGR is by its nature not amenable to the 'peculiarities' of Western intellectual property rights (and vice versa) – hence the requirement for a sui generis form of TKAGR capable of accommodating TKAGR forms; and
(ii) Whilst the uniqueness of TKAGR forms is conceded, Western intellectual property rights (as positive policy instruments) are sufficiently 'malleable' to accommodate TKAGR forms.

For Oguamanam, 'both sides of the argument find a meeting point in the notion of a sui generis form of an intellectual property regime, even though its details are open to different configurations and interpretations'.[300] This was notwithstanding the fact that the then likely proposals for a sui generis right were 'cast within the shadow of the Western intellectual property paradigm' and that even with a malleable intellectual property approach 'it is not easy overcome the conceptual and epistemic schism that alienates intellectual property rights from indigenous knowledge'.[301]

Other scholars, such as Peter Drahos, have continued to advocate for the introduction of intellectual property rights for Indigenous traditional knowledge. However, Drahos and Susy Frankel have argued that in order for Indigenous traditional knowledge to be protected effectively, there must be an integrated model of intellectual property rights, real property protection, and acknowledgment of traditional law and customs.[302]

D. United Nations Declaration on the Rights of Indigenous Peoples (UNDRIP)

Although not legally binding on signatory states, a key milestone in the acknowledgment of Indigenous sovereignty (or of an inherent right of Indigenous peoples to self-determination) came with the 2007 adoption by the UN General Assembly of UNDRIP. Indeed, Barelli argues that 'There is no other document more qualified as the starting point for distilling pivotal elements of Indigenous peoples' rights, especially those that will assist in mapping them onto the intersection between [human rights and intellectual property rights].'[303]

[299] Oguamanam (n 121) 156.
[300] ibid.
[301] ibid.
[302] P Drahos and S Frankel, 'Indigenous Peoples' Innovation and Intellectual Property' in P Drahos and S Frankel (eds), *Indigenous Peoples' Innovation: Intellectual Property Pathways to Development* (Canberra, Australian National University Press, 2012).
[303] M Barelli, 'The United Nations Declaration on the Rights of Indigenous Peoples: A Human Rights Framework for Intellectual Property Rights Indigenous Intellectual Property' in M Rimmer (ed),

UNDRIP was the result of over twenty-five years of negotiation following the establishment in 1982 of a Working Group on the Rights of Indigenous Populations with the intention to prepare the draft of a declaration.[304] The idea of Indigenous self-determination was one of the major battlegrounds in the negotiation of the final terms.[305] The final agreed version states (at Article 3) that 'Indigenous peoples have the right to self-determination. By virtue of that right they freely determine their political status and freely pursue their economic, social and cultural development.'

i. The Provisions of UNDRIP

As discussed at chapter two (in section II.A), in addition to the general provision on self-determination, UNDRIP contains three specific provisions relating to the protection of traditional knowledge/cultural heritage: Article 11, Article 24(1) and Article 31(1). As stated above, UNDRIP Article 11 allows for the protection of cultural traditions, cultural property and intellectual property.[306] Article 24(1) provides the right of Indigenous peoples to maintain their traditional medicines and health practices, which includes the conservation of their medicinal plants, animals and minerals.[307] Article 31(1) also allows Indigenous peoples the right 'to maintain, control, protect and develop their cultural heritage, traditional knowledge and traditional cultural expressions, which includes genetic resources'.[308]

Whereas Article 15(1)(c) ICESCR (in the light of the interpretation provided by the General Comment) would seem to exclude intellectual property rights as being a basic human right, Articles 11 and 31 arguably go further in affirming some right to control traditional knowledge per se and intellectual property in that traditional knowledge (in Article 31). However, the nature of that 'control' within Article 31 is unclear: it certainly does not *expressly* extend to an absolute veto over third-party non-consensual use (and with it injunctive relief).

Somewhat more clarity is provided by Article 11, which affirms that there should be 'effective' redress which 'may include restitution'. What does 'restitution' mean in this context? In relation to tangible property (including land) one would imagine that 'restitution' reasonably means the restoration of property misappropriated without free, informed prior consent. However, in relation to *intangible* property such a return cannot be affected. One then has to ask whether in such circumstances compensation in lieu of restitution could constitute

Indigenous Intellectual Property: A Handbook of Contemporary Research (Cheltenham, Edward Elgar 2015) 58.

[304] K Engle, 'On Fragile Architecture: The UN Declaration on the Rights of Indigenous Peoples in the Context of Human Rights' (2011) 22(1) *European Journal of International Law* 141.

[305] ibid.

[306] United Nations Declaration on the Rights of Indigenous Peoples 2007, Art 11.

[307] ibid Art 24(1).

[308] ibid Art 31(1).

'effective redress'. Crucially, UNDRIP itself makes no express mention (anywhere) of whether the right to 'free, informed prior consent' also gives rise to a right to veto future, or ongoing, third-party use.

Working from first principles, if UNDRIP entitles me (as a minimum) to restitution of misappropriated tangible property that restitution would, by virtue of the rivalrous nature of the use of tangible property, of necessity prevent use of that property by the 'misappropriator'. In the light of this, it would seem unfair if the appropriate redress in relation to *intangible* property did not similarly prevent potential use of that property by third parties – ie a veto – merely on the basis of the non-rivalrous nature of intangible property. Indeed, given the import placed upon the preservation and revitalisation of Indigenous culture within UNDRIP, one has to ask why intangible property should be disadvantaged relative to tangible property simply by dint of the non-rivalrous nature of its use. However, this rather simplistic analysis is complicated by the fact that Article 28 of UNDRIP (which relates to the misappropriation without free, prior and informed consent of Indigenous lands, territories and resources) makes specific reference to the award of 'just, fair and equitable compensation' when restitution is not possible. This compensation should 'take the form of lands, territories and resources equal in quality, size and legal status or of monetary compensation or other appropriate redress'.[309] One might ask: if monetary compensation is appropriate address for misappropriation of real property, why should that not be suitable redress for intangible property? We might also ask how much we should read into the absence of compensation wording within Article 11.

Although not specifically focusing on Article 11, Sargent has highlighted the difficulties and uncertainties that have been created by the lack of clear language within UNDRIP with regard to free, prior and informed consent and the affirmation of veto rights.[310] She points to the work of the International Law Association Rights of Indigenous Peoples Committee (2006–2012) which concludes that UNDRIP acknowledges some veto rights in relation to some Articles but not in relation to others.[311] However, in relation to Articles 10, 11, 28 and 29 the ILA committee concludes that

> such a [veto] right seems to exist with respect to measures of relocation of indigenous peoples from their lands or territories, measures resulting in the taking of indigenous peoples' cultural, intellectual, religious and spiritual property or lands, territories and resources, as well as measures of storage or disposal of hazardous materials in the lands or territories of indigenous peoples.[312]

[309] ibid Art 28(1).

[310] S Sargent, 'What's in a Name? The Contested Meaning of Free, Prior and Informed Consent in International Financial Law and Indigenous Rights' in V Vadi and B de Witte (eds), *Culture and International Economic Law* (Oxford, Routledge, 2015) 87, 96.

[311] International Law Association, Rights of Indigenous Peoples Committee (2006–2012) Sofia Conference (2012) Final Report (www.ila-hq.org/en/committees/index.cfm/cid/1024).

[312] ibid 7.

However, no reasoning is given for this position. The view that UNDRIP acknowledges veto rights is not universal. The permanent mission of Canada to the UN has stated that Canada does not interpret free, prior and informed consent as providing Indigenous peoples with a veto.[313] Sargent concludes that the ILA Final Report gives no 'detailed clarity on when FPIC is required to be used, or what it means – consult, consent, or more – in any given situation'.[314]

Broadly speaking, then, we cannot be clear whether UNDRIP envisages a veto right to prevent third-party misappropriation of traditional knowledge or a right to compensation for misuse.

As Savaresi highlights, UNDRIP is not legally binding upon the members of the UN.[315] Of course, many UN members are signatories of the Nagoya Protocol and UNDRIP is expressly 'noted' in the preamble to the Nagoya Protocol, and Article 4(3) of the Nagoya Protocol expressly states that it should 'be implemented in a mutually supportive manner with other international instruments relevant' to the Nagoya Protocol. However, as has been noted by Morgera et al, if the rights acknowledged by UNDRIP are limited to providing compensatory relief this would appear to have been exceeded by the access and benefit sharing requirements of the Nagoya Protocol.[316]

Although UNDRIP is expressly identified at section K paragraph 7(a) of the Kunming–Montreal GBF, which states that the Framework's implementation of ABS provisions must be in accordance with, inter alia, UNDRIP, no explanation of how the provisions of UNDRIP should be understood is provided.

ii. The Status of UNDRIP

How are we to understand the basis for these quite specific rights at Articles 11, 24 and 31? Are they to be understood as specific rights somehow 'created' by these provisions of UNDRIP or are they to be understood as an expression (or clarification) of elements of a pre-existing inherent Indigenous right to self-determination?

Some commentators are broadly of the opinion that Articles 11, 24 and 31 are clarificatory of an underlying right of self-determination which is acknowledged in (and not created by) Article 3.[317] For example, Stamatopoulou is of the opinion that:

> The recognition of the right to self-determination and the breadth of its application, as well as the recognition of the right to lands, territories and natural resources, constitute

[313] www.canadainternational.gc.ca/prmny-mponu/canada_un-canada_onu/statements-declarations/other-autres/2014-09-22_wclpd-padd.aspx?lang=engV.

[314] Sargent (n 310) 98.

[315] A Savaresi, 'The International Human Rights Law Implications of the Protocol' in E Morgera et al (eds), *The 2010 Protocol on Access and Benefit-Sharing in Perspective: Implications for International Law and Implementation Challenges* (Leiden, Martinus Nijhoff, 2012) 53, 66.

[316] E Morgera et al, *Unravelling the Protocol: A Commentary on the Protocol on Access and Benefit Sharing to the Convention on Biological Diversity* (Leiden, Brill/Nijhoff, 2014) 119.

[317] M Barelli, 'The United Nations Declaration on the Rights of Indigenous Peoples: A Human Rights Framework for Intellectual Property Rights Indigenous Intellectual Property' in M Rimmer

> the main pillars of the Declaration that underpin most other rights recognised in the Declaration, including cultural rights.[318]

Chidi Oguamanam is a little more poetic:

> Without discounting the diverse range of rights under UNDRIP, we can identify two of those rights from which all other rights issue. They are the right to [self-determination], and the rights associated with knowledge and culture. The latter are elaborated across the Declaration's text and are associated with its provision on [intellectual property]. In a way, the rights to knowledge and culture are extensions of the right to self-determination. Self-determination is the chart with which to navigate indigenous peoples' rights in their entire detail.[319]

However, Melissa Castan provides a note of caution regarding the provisions of UNDRIP:

> Many outstanding areas of debate about [i]ndigenous peoples' rights are not concluded, and some debates are still evolving, particularly on those issues revolving around the meaning of self-determination, the emerging standard requiring full prior and informed consent and the relationship between collective and individual rights.[320]

Oguamanam agrees:

> The pivotal aspect of indigenous rights, namely the right to self-determination remains a right in a state of continuing negotiation over the detail of its application to indigenous peoples. The pre-eminence of the UNDRIP and its dedication to indigenous-specific [human rights] issues does not necessarily dispense with the need to justify indigenous groups or collective rights claims via a vis the individual thrust of [human rights]).[321]

Whilst not determinative, the preamble to UNDRIP is of interest in this regard as it contains a number of references to the concept of self-determination. It states that Indigenous peoples have 'suffered from historic injustices as a result of, inter alia, their colonization and dispossession of their lands, territories and resources, thus preventing them from exercising, in particular, their right to development in accordance with their own needs and interests', and recognises 'the urgent need to respect and promote the inherent rights of indigenous peoples which derive from

(ed), *Indigenous Intellectual Property: A Handbook of Contemporary Research* (Cheltenham, Edward Elgar, 2015) 57; L Graham and S McJohn, 'Indigenous Peoples and Intellectual Property' (2005) 19 *Washington University Journal of Law and Policy* 313, 323; WR Samaranayake, 'A Critical Evaluation of the Interface Between Intellectual Property Rights and Human Rights with Special Emphasis on Indigenous Intellectual Property' (2022) 25(2) *Journal of World Intellectual Property* 412.

[318] E Stamatopoulou, 'Taking Cultural Rights Seriously: The Vision of the UN Declaration on the Rights of Indigenous Peoples' in S Allen and A Xanthaki (eds), *Reflections on the UN Declaration on the Rights of Indigenous Peoples* (Oxford, Hart, 2011) 392.

[319] C Oguamanam, 'Indigenous Peoples' Rights at the Intersection of Human Rights and Intellectual Property Rights' (2014) 18 *Marquette Intellectual Property Law Journal* 261, 228.

[320] M Castan, 'DRIP Freed: The Slow Reconstruction of Self-determination for Indigenous Peoples' in S Joseph and A McBeth (eds), *Research Handbook on International Human Rights Law* (Cheltenham, Edward Elgar, 2010) 492.

[321] Oguamanam (n 319).

their political, economic and social structures and from their cultures, spiritual traditions, histories and philosophies, especially their rights to their lands, territories and resources'.[322] Further on the preamble goes on to acknowledge that the Charter of the UN, the International Covenant on Economic, Social and Cultural Rights and the International Covenant on Civil and Political Rights,[323] as well as the Vienna Declaration and Programme of Action,[324] affirm the fundamental importance of the right to self-determination of all peoples, by virtue of which they freely determine their political status and freely pursue their economic, social and cultural development.

This would all suggest that the drafters of UNDRIP intended to it act as an acknowledgement of a pre-existing and fundamental right, rather than in some way 'creating' rights afresh. However, things may not be quite that straightforward. There is a problem with UNDRIP with regard to the degree to which the concept of Indigenous sovereignty/self-determination is deemed to be effective outwith the state within which the relevant Indigenous people reside. During the negotiation of UNDRIP many states in the Global South (notably in Africa), fearing for their integrity, were concerned that a strong recognition of Indigenous sovereignty outwith the state would lead to numerous Indigenous declarations of independence and the fractionation of countries. According to Engle,[325] the objections of the African states were addressed by a compromise provision (in Article 46) which states that the Declaration should not be 'construed as authorizing or encouraging any action which would dismember or impair totally or in part, the territorial integrity or political unity of sovereign and independent States'. This limitation on a key form of self-determination would seem deeply at odds with the idea of UNDRIP acting as recognition of inherent and inalienable rights and there is an obvious (and hard to reconcile) tension between Article 46 and the sentiments expressed in the UNDRIP preamble. Engle further states that this compromise language was concerning to many Indigenous peoples involved in the negotiation of the declaration 'but most ultimately decided to support it with the assurance that other key provisions would remain intact, including those on land and resource rights and free and informed consent, which would in some sense protect Indigenous peoples' territorial integrity'.[326] For Engle it appears that Indigenous rights advocates who made claims to strong forms of self-determination never succeeded in having that position fully articulated in UNDRIP.[327]

Where does that leave the source of the rights expressed in Articles 11, 24 and 31? Of themselves, they are very unlikely to 'dismember or impair totally or in part, the territorial integrity or political unity of sovereign and independent

[322] UNDRIP Preamble.
[323] See Resolution 2200 A (XXI), Annex 3.
[324] A/CONF.157/24 (Part I), ch III 6.
[325] Engle (n 304).
[326] ibid.
[327] ibid.

States', so perhaps in relation to those rights UNDRIP can freely serve as a full expression of an inherent right to self-determination even as, in parallel, Article 46 serves to narrow the clarification of the right in other aspects.

For this author, the safest course is to conclude that UNDRIP is a (partially limited) expression of inalienable human rights (within a Western paradigm) which merely serves as an acknowledgement within that paradigm of existing rights to self-determination that do *not* rely on that acknowledgement for their validity. The alternative, to treat UNDRIP the definitive explanation of the right to Indigenous self-determination or even as a justification in itself, would be potentially limiting of Indigenous peoples' claim to inherent rights.

E. A 'Communitarian' Approach

In her monograph *Community Resources*, Gibson[328] proposes a 'communitarian' basis for positive sui generis rights of control over traditional knowledge. The philosophical grounds for the creation of such rights are not grounded in the utilitarianism/consequentialism, individual natural rights (Lockean or Hegelian/Kantian personality right), corrective justice, or Rawlsian distributive justice. A claim to community is the basis of the right – for Gibson the 'freedom to practise tradition and to develop within community in way that are compatible with the values of that particular community are factors that are instrumental to the preservation of culture and community'.[329] Gibson states that:

> Fundamentally, the concept of community resources recognises obligations to cultural diversity and dignity through the acknowledgement of, and respect for, traditional and Indigenous communities. According to the model of community resources, communities are entitled to manage their resources in observance of customary laws, values, and traditional practices.[330]

There are very clear echoes here of the broader concept of an Indigenous right to self-determination (and the rights to control cultural heritage within that right). Indeed, Gibson states that 'the principle of self-identification as a community arguably is implicit in the concept of internal self-determination'.[331] It should be noted that *Community Resources* was published in 2005 (during the negotiation of UNDRIP) but notes the developments within the draft Declaration.[332] However, for this author, what stands out in relation to Gibson's interpretation of the fundamental Indigenous rights to control heritage is that Gibson is highly sensitive to the origination/individuation problems inherent in such claim and

[328] Gibson (n 9).
[329] ibid 39.
[330] ibid 287.
[331] ibid 277 (footnote 2).
[332] ibid.

in the identification of resources under that claim. Accordingly, she carefully sets out the following requirements for such a claim:

1. Assertion of community by community – self-recognition will trigger a presumption in favour of community;
2. Assertion of resources by community – recognition of community and claim by that community to the knowledge in question will trigger a presumption that the knowledge is traditional;
3. Rebuttal of presumption by competing claim – assertion of community and of resources may be rebutted by the parties seeking commercialisation of or access to knowledge (on the grounds set out below); and
4. Proportionality – the application of equitable principles to determine validity of the claim (whether to community or to traditional knowledge).[333]

In applying a principle of proportionality, Gibson states:

> In other words, the process [ie the rebuttable claim to community and rebuttable presumption to traditional knowledge] will involve a balancing of interests according to equitable principles of international law. It is not claimed here that equity is the source of the law, but that equitable principles necessarily inform the decision as to competing interests.[334]

What type of right is envisaged here – a right to compensation or a right to veto non-consensual use, or both? Although she does not expressly outline these options, Gibson considers a requirement for free and prior informed consent before traditional knowledge can be used by others to be 'fundamental' to her model and an essential element of legitimate use or appropriation. This is, of course, consistent with a right to control resources arising out of a claim to community. She states: 'Communities must be entitled to consent to the use of their knowledge as appropriate and under conditions to be determined by the communities and in accordance with their customary laws.'[335]

This absolute right to control would appear to point to a right of veto backed by injunctive relief. However, such a right is not absolute. Gibson highlights the fact that there may be problems identifying those entitled to grant consent in particular circumstances. In such a situation, Gibson's believes that:

> The application of free and prior informed consent within the present model would impose a duty upon those seeking to use what they ought reasonably to believe to be a traditional knowledge or natural/genetic resources, to make reasonable efforts to ascertain and contact the relevant community.[336]

Where such reasonable efforts have been made and an Indigenous community subsequently become aware of a misappropriation and enforce their rights,

[333] ibid 287.
[334] ibid 288.
[335] ibid 290.
[336] ibid.

Gibson sees there being no damages payable to the community, although there may be benefit sharing and return of assets 'where appropriate'.

XIII. Conclusions

We have seen that a number of the philosophical justifications ordinarily used to support the existence of 'classical' intellectual property rights have been raised in support of positive rights in traditional knowledge. However, the translation of those justifications into this area highlights some of the inherent problems with certain of those justifications. In addition, the distinctive nature of traditional knowledge means that many of those justifications are highly stretched. Certainly, none of the justifications are infallible: each approach has problems in its application in certain circumstances. One cannot be purist in applying deontological justifications and neither is the consequentialist account without its difficulties (particularly in relation to assuredly achieving its set goals). There would appear to be significant problems with a Lockean, labour-desert-based justification for a monopolistic intellectual property right in TKAGR. We have seen that Attas strongly argues against the existence of a natural law justification for intellectual property, based on the problems of certainty surrounding the 'origination' and 'individuation' of the subject matter (and the 'squeeze' between the two).

The *origin* of traditional knowledge is, by its very nature, difficult to determine. Even in the (unlikely) presence of concrete evidence surrounding its creation, the trans-generational and iterative (and ongoing) nature of the creation of traditional knowledge may make it particularly sensitive to Attas's criticism. There are also problems as to why such rights should exist *now* whereas the 'inventions'/'disco veries' incorporated within the knowledge may have made by (sometimes very distant) ancestors and also questions as to why any such right should have an indeterminate duration. However, as has been stressed by Dutfield and Suthersanen, even though the labour-desert account has difficulty in giving particular answers to specific questions, it does remind us to examine a right in terms of the balance between the desert of an originator and the liberty of the rest of the world.

From a right based in personality perspective, a key criticism is that it is difficult to imagine a personality right sitting comfortably with a potentially diverse group of Indigenous peoples, particularly within a trans-generational (and potentially multi-site) setting. Chief amongst the problems with this account, however, is that Kantian authorial personality and Fichtean/Hegelian personality rights do not support the control of knowledge per se.

The 'classic' consequentialist justification for intellectual property rights is that through providing a reward to creators they incentivise the creation of new 'products' of intellectual endeavour and further incentivise the commercialisation of such products. The exact application of such a justification to a right in TKAGR is problematic – much of the subject matter of the right will have already been created so, simply put, its creation cannot be incentivised. In contrast, one can potentially see how providing incentives to create commercial value in Indigenous knowledge would accord with the utilitarian aim, not of creating new knowledge, but of preventing the *loss* of existing knowledge (not only from the relevant Indigenous group themselves, but from mankind more broadly). If one can also argue that creating value in such knowledge also provides an incentive to maintain the cultural and ecological environment in which the knowledge resides, then the utilitarian justification will be further strengthened. To this utilitarian account may be added a separate and particular 'utility' that comes from Indigenous peoples controlling their own knowledge in accordance with their customary practices.

In his review with Raustiala, Munzer generally found the usual philosophical justifications for intellectual property rights to be wanting when applied to the protection of traditional knowledge. He has more recently advanced the grant of rights to control traditional knowledge as part of a package of broader 'reparations' for past wrongs committed upon a traditional group. The current work has identified:

(a) The difficulty in translating the 'case-by-case' basis of such a doctrine to broader principles for general applicability; and
(b) The problems associated with determining how inequities should be weighted as between the current defendant and third-party wrongdoers, as between current misappropriation and historic wrongs and as between gravity of wrongs; and any sense of third-party certainty.

To the extent that underlying philosophical justifications for such rights in TKAGR can be determined, the question of whether the allocation of property that arises out of following those justifications gives rise to a fair distribution of property across society still remains.

Although supportive of human creativity and flourishing, and a right to take part in a cultural life, established human rights do not create an express right to intellectual property. However, arguments for positive rights to protect TKAGR have been advanced on the basis of an inherent right to Indigenous self-determination which extends to a right to use, hold and control traditional knowledge. The edges of the rights supported by this argument are not clear. However, certain of the rights of Indigenous peoples to self determination have been acknowledged by UNDRIP, though it has been argued that the rights set out by UNDRIP do not represent the full breadth of those such rights. Article 11 UNDRIP enshrines a right to practise and revitalise Indigenous cultural traditions and custom. However, it does not set a minimum standard in terms of the way in which Indigenous people's cultural, intellectual, religious and spiritual property taken 'without their free, prior and informed consent or in violation of their laws, traditions and customs provides' will be protected other than that there should be 'effective' redress which 'may include restitution'. Clearly, all rights supported by other justifications should at least be compliant with the rights envisaged under UNDRIP. Gibson has advanced a communitarian justification which arises out of a claim to community self-determination and assures that an identified community should be able to control their own information under conditions to be determined by the communities and in accordance with their customary laws. This is, however, a right that may be tempered by concepts of equity where competing interests are to be evaluated.

To conclude then, although there are uncertainties as to the philosophical support for positive rights in TKAGR, the above analysis provides a road map of the approaches (and difficulties) which must be considered in the remainder of this work.

5

The Landscape of Drug Discovery

I. Introduction

It was argued in chapter one above that if we are to gain insight into the limits of a positive right in TKAGR within the field of drug discovery, we need first to understand the process by which drug candidates are discovered, and the ways in which such traditional knowledge has entered (and continues to enter) the discovery process together with the ways in which it has been (and is) used within that process. It is the aim of this chapter, therefore, to explore the topography of the drug discovery process and understand the flow of information within it.

Much of the modern drug discovery process is reliant on an understanding of *why* it is that chemical agents have the biological effect that they do. The first part of this chapter will introduce some of the fundamental concepts that underlie the action of drugs and why plant, fungal, animal and microbially derived active substances (products of genetic expression) have played a major role in drug discovery. The chapter will then look at the non-linear and highly iterative nature of drug discovery (and briefly why it is different from drug *development*) and at the processes that might be involved in taking TKAGR through to a fully characterised drug. Having done this, the chapter will then seek to determine whether there are any points in the described drug discovery process that could be identified as the 'crux points' discussed in chapter one – that is, points in the drug discovery process at which the nature of the movement of information is such as may give rise to break in a causation in law analysis of the scope of positive rights in tradition knowledge associated with genetic resources.

II. The Pharmacological Background

The majority of therapeutic and psychoactive drugs work through the action of a biologically active compound (a 'ligand') at a protein receptor site present on, or within, a cell. The receptor sites are present on/in the cell as part of the body's internal signalling mechanism. Biological signals are often mediated through small endogenous ligands (whether neurotransmitters, hormones, parahormones, trophins or other signals) which interact with their specific target protein receptor to cause a downstream biochemical response. These ligands 'bind' to the receptor, causing a conformational change in the structure of the receptor protein. It is this structural change that elicits the downstream biochemical effect, in many cases mediated through switching an enzyme 'on' or 'off', or opening or closing an ion channel through a membrane.[1] In this way the conformational change induced by the ligand allows for the initiation of signalling cascades that lead to cellular responses.[2]

To minimise the chances that that the individual signalling systems interfere, the receptor sites and ligands in one system often show a high degree of inter-system specificity. This has been (rather simplistically) termed the 'lock and key' hypothesis.[3] Although the analogy serves for present purposes, it is worth noting that the intermolecular interaction between the ligand and receptor is in reality more subtle. In particular, just because a ligand binds to a receptor does not necessarily mean that the receptor will be activated. Different parts of the ligand molecule may be considered as carrying more of a 'binding' functionality, whereas other parts may be considered as carrying more of an 'activation' functionality. Again this is a simplification, and in many cases the functionalities of parts of the ligand molecule are not clear-cut, or are mixed.

It is important to appreciate that the molecular 'key' of the ligand (often termed the 'pharmacophore') has a three-dimensional (3D) structure and will interact with the 3D 'lock' (perhaps better described as a 3D 'pocket') of the receptor. In many cases the 3D structure will 'mirror' the 3D shape of the pocket but other factors are important, particularly the interaction between the electrostatic charge of regions of the pocket and key, or the hydrophilic/hydrophobic interactions between regions of the pocket and key. Relatively small changes in the chemical structure of the ligand can diminish the potency of the ligand at the receptor – analogous to altering the shape of the 'key'. However, some small chemical changes can enhance the potency of the ligand or maintain/enhance its binding capability, but restrict the degree to which the ligand activates the receptor. A compound that activates a receptor is called an *agonist*, and one that prevents agonists from reaching the 'lock' (but without activating the receptor themselves) are called *antagonists*. So-called *inverse* agonists bind to the receptor but elicit an opposite biological effect than would an agonist.[4]

The same endogenous ligand may have different effects in different parts of the body. These differing effects are usually mediated through subtypes within

[1] EM Ross and A Goodman Gilman, 'Pharmacodynamics': Mechanisms of Drug Action and the Relationship between Drug Concentration and Effect Alfred' in Goodman Gilman et al (eds), *Goodman and Gilman's The Pharmacological Basis of Therapeutics* (New York, Macmillan, 1985) 35; R Ng, *Drugs, From Discovery to Approval* (Hoboken, NJ, John Wiley, 2004) 15.

[2] It is also worth noting that some agonists can induce different conformational changes in the same receptor, leading to different downstream effects. This is known as 'biased agonism' or 'functional selectivity' and is an area of active research in pharmacology. See eg JW Wisler et al, 'Recent Developments in Biased Agonism' (2014) 27 *Current Opinion in Cell Biology* 18.

[3] CK Matthews et al, *Biochemistry* (San Francisco, CA, Benjamin Cummings, 1999) 369.

[4] Originally styled 'contragonists'. DJ Nutt et al, 'Unusual Interactions of Benzodiazepine Receptor Antagonists' (1982) 295(5848) *Nature* 436.

the same receptor 'family'. Although these receptors all show affinity for the same endogenous ligand, they can be distinguished by differing affinities for (often biologically derived) exogenous ligands. A classic example is that of the endogenous ligand acetylcholine, the first neurotransmitter to be identified (by Dale and Löwi).[5] Acetylcholine has effects across the body through a variety of signalling systems which are summarised in Table 3.

For brevity, the present description of pharmacologically active agents is limited to those that have actions at 'classic' receptors. Whilst this is true for many such agents, it should be noted that many other drugs act through actions as biochemical precursors (enzyme substrates), enzyme substrates which prevent enzyme activity (sometimes termed 'anti-metabolites'), other enzyme inhibitors, ion-channel blockers or uptake inhibitors, or through a direct action on cell membranes or gene expression. However, for the present purposes many of the points raised about ligand-target specificity and the drug discovery research process remain as true for these agents as for 'classic' receptor ligands.

Table 3 Subtypes of acetylcholine receptors[6]

System	Receptor subtype	Endogenous agonist	Exogenous agonist	Exogenous antagonist
Central nervous system	Nicotinic	Acetylcholine[7]	Nicotine[8] (obtained from tobacco plant *Nicotiana tabacum* and other members of the nightshade family)	Atropine[9] (obtained from deadly nightshade, *Atropa belladonna*)
Motor neurons (neuromuscular junction)	Nicotinic	Acetylcholine	Nicotine	Atropine
Autonomic nervous system	Muscarinic	Acetylcholine	Muscarine[10] (obtained from the mushroom *Amanita muscaria*)	Tubocurarine[11] (obtained from the South American climbing vine *Chondrodendron tomentosum*)

[5] LA Stephens, *Explorers of the Brain* (London, Scientific Book Club, 1973) 152.
[6] HP Rang and MM Dale, *Pharmacology* (Churchill Livingstone, Edinburgh, 1987) 113.
[7] MJ O'Neil (ed), *The Merck Index, An Encyclopedia of Chemicals, Drugs, and Biologicals* (Whitehouse Station, NJ, Merck, 2001) 17.
[8] ibid 1169.
[9] ibid 151.
[10] ibid 1129.
[11] ibid 1746.

A. Therapeutic Agents from Living Organisms

The basis of much modern pharmacology has been the determination of classes of endogenous ligands, and the identification of their receptor sites and downstream actions followed by the development of drugs to mimic the action of the endogenous agonist (or act as antagonists or inverse agonists) at specific target sites.

Throughout the course of evolution of life on Earth, biological organisms have often found an evolutionary advantage in producing compounds that have binding effects at receptors meant for endogenous signalling ligands in other organisms.[12] These compounds are, in most cases, *not* exact copies of the endogenous ligand, but have different structures which allow a remarkable specificity and potency at the receptor sites (better in many cases than the endogenous ligand). Many compounds have evolved as toxins or venoms used in animals for hunting or defence, or used in plants to discourage their being eaten (or to elicit a biological response in the animal which is in some other way advantageous to the plant).[13] Throughout human history the discovery of the biological effects of mostly plant (and some animal) toxins on humans led to the development of the first therapeutic (and psychoactive) drugs. Often these were used in the form of plant or animal extracts.

The ancient Greek word *pharmakon* can mean both 'drug' and 'poison', a mix of meanings that underlies the interplay between the toxic effects of some plant- and animal-derived ligands and their therapeutic benefits.[14] The formal, informal or trial-and-error 'study' of plant and animal 'poisons' often led to the development of folk remedies, or more formalised herbal and traditional medicine systems.

It was the later systematic investigation of the biological effects of many of the biologically derived exogenous ligands that gave the first (Western-scientific) insight into the workings of the body's internal signalling mechanisms. As was the case for the acetylcholine receptor seen in Table 3, many biological receptor sites were discovered (and classified) by using plant-derived drugs. In some cases this was before the existence, or nature of, the endogenous ligand was itself understood.

Although as stated some cases the plant-, or animal-, derived ligands are exquisitely specific for, or potent at, the endogenous target receptor, in other cases the plant/animal-derived ligands are unspecific (causing undesired side effects) and/or lack desired potency. In both cases there may be a therapeutic requirement to modify the performance of the ligand at the receptor.

[12] L Fellows and A Scofield, 'Chemical Diversity in Plants' in T Swanson (ed), *Intellectual Property and Biodiversity Conservation: An Interdisciplinary Analysis of the Values of Medicinal Plants* (Cambridge, Cambridge University Press, 1995) 19.

[13] ibid.

[14] J Derrida with B Johnson (trans), 'Plato's Pharmacy' in *Dissemination* (Chicago, IL, University of Chicago Press, 1981) 70.

It is the task of the medicinal chemist to engineer changes to the plant/animal-derived ligand (or the endogenous ligand) to create the desired specificity/potency profile. In the past this was often done by getting a 'feel' for what changes to the structure of the ligand would cause certain changes. This was often founded upon a database of existing ligands and their known binding at, and downstream effects mediated through, the receptor site. As mentioned, the interaction between the ligand and receptor relies on a complex interplay between the 3D shape, the electrostatic charge and the hydrophobic/hydrophilic character of the ligand molecule. Accordingly, understanding how changes to chemical structure of a ligand impact upon these elements is not trivial. However, increased understanding of the structure of the receptors (through genomic, proteomic and glyconomic studies) gives researchers a better understanding of the structure of the 'lock' and how various aspects of the ligand 'key' interact. This has led to a further rationalisation of the design of modified ligands.[15]

Most endogenous ligands are, in general, relatively small chemical compounds relative to the size of the protein receptor site to which they bind. Many plant-, animal- or microbe-derived ligands or the chemically modified versions of these (or endogenous) ligands developed by medicinal chemists are similarly small and there are relatively few places on the molecule to make chemical changes. In addition, the 'key' part of the ligand molecule which interacts with the 'lock' needs to have a very particular 3D conformation and electrostatic/hydrophobic character, and relatively few departures from this template will retain the desired activity. These limitations have meant that the developers of pharmaceuticals have found little in the way of protectable intellectual property 'space' around the ligands.

In the past four decades, in an attempt to find clear intellectual property space, the pharmaceutical industry initiated lead compound identification based on testing 'random' combinatorial chemistry libraries. In this approach randomly generated compounds were tested in very large numbers against known receptor targets using an automatic testing methodology termed 'fast-throughput screening'. The idea was that by testing a large 'galaxy' of compounds, many unpredicted, and unpredictable (and hopefully therefore patent-protectable), 'hits' would be discovered and form the basis for new pharmaceutical development. To the disappointment of drug companies (and their investors) very few therapeutically useful (and commercially successful) agents have been identified using this methodology.[16] Indeed, Newman and Cragg determined that as of 2016 only two approved NCEs, the antitumour drug sorafenib and ataluren, a treatment for Duchenne muscular dystrophy, had been discovered using the random combinatorial chemistry/fast-throughput

[15] A Schuffenhauer et al, 'Relationships between Molecular Complexity, Biological Activity, and Structural Diversity' (2006) 46 *Journal of Chemical Information and Modelling* 525.

[16] T Kodatek, 'The Rise, Fall and Reinvention of Combinatorial Chemistry' (2011) 47(35) *Chemical Communications* 9757.

screening methodology alone.[17] Part of the explanation for this comparative lack of success is that the vast majority of the compounds randomly produced by combinatorial chemistry lacked the structural complexity that is seen in many biologically active compounds or were not sufficiently 'drug-like'.

Effective pharmaceutical drugs, and biologically derived toxins, are required to be 'bioavailable'. This means that they can be absorbed by the body and distributed within the body to the desired target without being excreted or metabolised before they can reach that target. Broadly speaking, the bioavailability of a compound can be reasonably reliably predicted from a combination of its chemical structure, molecular mass and balance of hydrophobic/hydrophyllic properties (what is now called 'Lipinski's Rule of Five').[18] However, very many of the randomly generated compounds developed by combinatorial chemistry lacked these chemical characteristics, were not bioavailable, and so were essentially useless as a therapeutic drug 'lead' – no matter how effectively they bound, activated or blocked the appropriate receptor.[19]

B. 'Bioprospecting'

The relative failure of random combinatorial chemistry/fast-throughput screening approach has led to something of a renaissance of so-called 'rational' pharmacology. The advances in genomics, proteomics and glyconomics (which allow researchers to better understand biological target structure) mentioned above are now increasingly being allied to the search for biologically active compounds from flora, fauna and microflora (so called 'bioprospecting') to find 'novel' ligands for those sites.

It is possible for a microorganism-, plant- or animal-derived ligand to mimic the 3D 'key' of an endogenous ligand by recreating a similar 3D structure through a different chemical structure than that used by the endogenous ligand. Although that 3D structure may itself be broadly predictable, the way in which the biologically derived ligand reproduces that structure need not be so predictable. Herein lies the potential strength of 'bioprospecting' as a research tool to find 'new' therapeutic approaches – approaches that may also give researchers some intellectual property distance from their competitors.

By far the greatest reservoir of terrestrial biodiversity of the planet (and alongside it a reservoir of biological 'toxins') exists in the tropics, particularly

[17] DJ Newman and GM Cragg, 'Natural Products as Sources of New Drugs from 1981 to 2014' (2016) 79 *Journal of Natural Products* 629, 630.

[18] CA Lipinski et al, 'Experimental and Computational Approaches to Estimate Solubility and Permeability in Drug Discovery and Development Settings' (2001) 46 *Advanced Drug Development Review* 3.

[19] It should be noted that a number of ligands found in natural products have evolved to take advantage of specific active transport systems within the body and they (and their close derivatives) show bioavailbility that is not dependent upon the 'Rule of Five'. See eg Newman and Cragg (n 17).

(but not exclusively) in the equatorial rainforests. However, a tropical rainforest will harbour many thousands of plant species and many of those species may have many separate strains. Random testing of plant species is possible and has had some success. During the early- to mid-1960s random testing of plant samples conducted by the US Cancer Chemotherapy National Service Center resulted in the isolation of the anticancer drug taxol from the Pacific yew *Taxus brevifolia*.[20] However, such random testing tends to give little return on investment.[21]

How, then, could a pharmaceutical researcher looking for new ligands from these environments narrow the search? One approach, *phylogenetic surveying*, is to seek out other species of a genus that is already known to yield bioactive or therapeutic agents, remove samples, purify extracts and test them. A further approach, *ecological surveying*, is to examine plants that occur in similar ecological niches, or have similar phenotypic characteristics, to plants known to yield bioactive or therapeutic agents. However, a further approach (sometimes referred to as *ethnobotanical surveying*) is to rely upon the knowledge of the Indigenous peoples who have lived with and used the biological resource, and who have developed, perhaps over generations, an understanding of the therapeutic or psychoactive effects of the biological resource.[22]

There are a great many examples of the success of the ethnobotanical approach.[23] Cox lists fifty drugs which have been derived from ethnobotanical leads,[24] but suggest that this is an underestimate, and cites Farnsworth's estimate of such drugs numbering closer to eighty-eight.[25] Although impressive, raw numbers do not perhaps give an impression of the importance that these drugs have played in the development of Western medicine (and for that matter in Western recreational drug use). Cox's list of fifty includes the well-used drugs set out in Table 4.[26]

[20] MH Wani et al, 'Plant Antitumor Agents. VI. The Isolation and Structure of Taxol, a Novel Antileukemic and Antitumor Agent from *Taxus brevifolia*' (1971) 93(9) *Journal of the American Chemical Society* 2325.

[21] MJ Balick and PA Cox, *Plants, People, and Culture: The Science of Ethnobotany* (New York, Scientific American Library, 1997) 37.

[22] See by way of example the ethnopharmacological studies on desert teak: M Jaina et al, 'Traditional Uses, Phytochemistry and Pharmacology of *Tecomella undulata* – A Review' (2012) 2(3 Suppl) *Asian Pacific Journal of Tropical Biomedicine* S1918.

[23] L Schiebinger, *Plants and Empire, Colonial Bioprospecting in the Atlantic World* (Cambridge, MA, Harvard University Press, 2004); Bill Laws, *Fifty Plants that Changed the Course of History* (Newton Abbott, David and Charles, 2010).

[24] PA Cox, 'The Ethnobotanical Approach to Drug Discovery: Strengths and Limitations' in DJ Chadwick and J Marsh (eds), *Ethnobotany and the Search for New Drugs* (Ciba Foundation Symposium 185) (Chichester, John Wiley, 1994) 27.

[25] NR Farnsworth, 'The Role of Ethnopharmacology in Drug Development' in *Bioactive Compounds from Plants* (Ciba Foundation Symp 154) (Chichester, John Wiley, 1994).

[26] Not all of the drugs named by Cox and Farnsworth arise from *Indigenous* ethnobotanical leads from the Global South. Some have arisen from Western folk knowledge.

Table 4 Some major ethnobotanically-derived medicines (after Cox)[27]

Drug	Therapeutic use	Plant derived from
Aspirin	Analgesic, anti-inflammatory	Willow, meadowsweet
Atropine	Pupil dilator	Deadly nightshade
Cocaine	Anaesthetic	Coca plant
Codeine	Central nervous system stimulant	Opium poppy
Dicoumarol	Antithrombotic	Rotting sweet clover hay
Digoxin	Cardiotonic	Foxglove
Digitoxin	Cardiotonic	Foxglove
Ephedrine	Bronchodilator	Ma huang (herb)
Hyoscyamine	Antispasmodic	Henbane, mandrake, jimson-weed, angel's trumpets, deadly nightshade
Morphine	Analgesic	Opium poppy
Physostigmine	Glaucoma therapy	Calabar bean
Pseudoephedrine	Decongestant	Ephedra shrub
Quinine	Antimalarial	Chichona tree
Reserpine	Antihypertensive	Sarpagandha root
Scopolamine	Anti-motion sickness	Henbane, mandrake, jimson-weed, angels' trumpets, deadly nightshade
Tubocurarine	Muscle relaxant	*Strychnos toxifera* vine
Tetrahydrocannabinol	Antiemetic	Marijuana
Theophylline	Diuretic	black tea, cocoa bean, dried maté
Vinblastine	Cancer therapy	Madagascar periwinkle
Vincristine	Cancer therapy	Madagascar periwinkle

Within the Western pharmaceutical tradition the science of studying drugs arising from natural (including plant) sources is known as 'pharmacognosy'. This is a science which touches on many other areas of study, most notably phytochemistry (the study of plant-derived chemicals) and 'ethnobotany'. Phytochemistry is, of course, a broader area of study than looking merely at therapeutic ligands. Similarly, 'ethnobotany', a term originating in 1896 with American botanist John W. Harshberger,[28] takes in many areas beyond therapeutic plants but can be broadly defined as the study of the interaction between Indigenous peoples and

[27] Cox (n 24) 27.
[28] JW Harshberger, 'The Purposes of Ethnobotany' (1896) 21 *Botanical Gazette* 146.

plants.[29] Ethnobotany is by its nature an interdisciplinary field. Balick and Cox suggest that the ideal ethnobotanist is a 'combination anthropologist, archaeologist, botanist, chemist, psychologist, ecologist, explorer, folklorist, pharmacologist, and diplomat'.[30]

Notwithstanding the success of the ethnobotanical approach, Balick and Cox suggest that there has been a degree of prejudice in the Western medical community against it. They argue that this may be the result of cultural prejudice during the Western colonial period when Western medicine was 'taken as a prime exemplar of the constructive and beneficial effects of European rule' and 'one of its indisputable claims to legitimacy'.[31]

They suggest, however, that the use of plants as a source of candidate molecules has (re)gained favour due to (a) the awareness of the loss of biodiversity, (b) the use of fast-throughput screening to screen plant-derived candidates, and (c) a growing appreciation of the sophistication of Indigenous knowledge systems. As already mentioned, the relative failure of the random screening of combinatorial chemistry libraries will also have had an influence on the new focus on plant-derived candidates.

Of course, not all research leads provided by Indigenous traditional knowledge will progress in a linear pattern to a marketed drug. In some cases the therapeutically active ligand will be new to science and will be used in a new drug in a purified but unchanged form. In some cases the plant will be found to contain already known ligands. In others the plant may be screened for a therapeutic indication which is different from the indication suggested by the folk use of the plant.[32] Balick and Cox suggest that a plant that is bioactive in one respect may serve as a better candidate for other types of bioactivity than those that show less bioactivity and point to supporting evidence from within the Samoan ethnopharmacopoeia.[33]

C. Potential Drug Discovery Pathways

As set out above, there is a long tradition of Indigenous knowledge and Western folklore providing the starting point for pharmaceutical development. However, in the modern era therapies very rarely take the form of a simple plant extract but are more commonly in the form of pure ligand (or ligands) contained within an inert excipient. This section looks at the potential pathways by which traditional knowledge can be incorporated into a 'modern' pharmaceutical.

The present discussion will assume that a 'new' (to pharmaceutical science) therapeutic use for a 'new' (to pharmaceutical science) genetic resource has been revealed to a pharmaceutical research team. What are the potential ways in which the research

[29] CM Cotton, *Ethnobotany, Principles and Applications* (Chichester, John Wiley, 1996) 1.
[30] Balick and Cox (n 21) 7.
[31] ibid 36.
[32] ibid 33.
[33] ibid 39; PA Cox et al, 'Pharmacological Activity of the Samoan Ethnopharmacopoeia' (1989) 43 *Economic Botany* 487.

lead provided by this information will inform pharmaceutical development? A (by no means comprehensive) overview of the potential pathways by which a piece of genetic material or associated piece of traditional knowledge could find their way through the drug discovery process was summarised in Figure 1 (in chapter one).

It is important to recognise that the progression of steps set out in the figure is not necessarily linear, nor in series. Many steps will be performed in parallel. In addition many steps will require a series of iterative 'feedback loops'. Very often advances in one limb of the research process will inform others, as will previously understanding from the literature or the research team's existing 'know-how'. Initial testing methodologies and extraction techniques may be supplanted by radically different techniques depending on parallel developments.

The 'research team' is described here as one entity. However, it should be noted that the skill sets required for this work are unlikely to be found within a single team. These skills will range from chemical analysis, classic in vitro and in vivo pharmacology, molecular biology, medicinal chemistry, computer (or so-called 'in silico' modelling)[34] and chemical synthesis, to clinical trials. Only within the largest pharmaceutical company would all these skills be found within one organisation. Even if that were the case, it is common for elements of the research effort to be contracted out to other commercial laboratories or to university-based researchers. It is possible for some of the work to be conducted within a public domain environment and here research teams might follow leads set by other groups that have been communicated at conferences and in research publications. Naturally there is a possibility of a mix of these approaches, but where the lead has originated from within a commercial organisation concerns over commercial competitors may limit the degree of disclosure until full patent protection has been achieved. Possible steps in the process are as follows:

(a) Isolation of active constituent(s) from plant material. Extraction techniques may depend on the suspected chemical nature of the active constituent (which may be informed by information on known ligands at receptors suspected of producing the therapeutic effects).
(b) In vitro testing of the active constituent against a known in vitro model. The choice of model may be dependent upon the purported therapeutic benefit of the active constituent.
(c) In vivo testing of the active constituent against known animal models.
(d) Determination of the chemical structure of the active structure (using a variety of chemical analytical tools).[35]
(e) Determination of the receptor site. This may be a known receptor site, a previously unknown subtype of a known receptor family, or a previously unknown receptor family.

[34] N Brown, *In Silico Medicinal Chemistry: Computational Methods to Support Drug Design* (Abingdon, Royal Society of Chemistry, 2015); AGE Wilson (ed), *New Horizons in Predictive Toxicology: Current Status and Application* (Abingdon, Royal Society of Chemistry, 2011).

[35] CSJ Walpole, 'The Role of Chemistry in the Drug Discovery Process' in HP Rang (ed), *Drug Discovery and Development: Technology in Transition* (Edinburgh, Churchill Livingston Elsevier, 2006) 121.

(f) If it is a new subtype (or new family) of receptor, then the active constituent may be used as a tool to determine the distribution of the receptor protein in the body using immuno- or radioligand-histochemistry and similar techniques.[36]
(g) If it is a new subtype or new family of receptor, it is necessary to determine the protein structure of the receptor site. This will include gaining an understanding of shape of the 'pocket' of the receptor and the linkage to a downstream biological process (eg an enzyme or ion channel).
(h) If it is a new subtype or new family of receptor, it is necessary to compare it with genomic libraries to determine the genes coding for the receptor. If the genes coding for the receptor can be identified, this may lead to studies to determine the distribution and control of gene expression for this receptor across the body.[37]
(i) If it is a new subtype or new family of receptor, there will likely be studies of post-translational modification of the protein. There will also likely be studies of the receptor 'life-cycle' and systems for up- and down-regulation of the receptor.
(j) Determination of the endogenous ligand. If it is a previously unknown signalling system, this may lead to an entirely new understanding of a disease process and development of a novel class of therapeutic interventions and the development of new in vivo animal models. This may also lead to an understanding of an entirely new family of receptors, the metabolic processes for producing the endogenous ligand and how the receptors are controlled and how the endogenous ligand is inactivated and/or recycled.
(k) Preparation of simple chemical derivatives of the active component (this will include input from the receptor structure studies).
(l) The 'new' receptor site may also be used as a target in fast-throughput screening against known pharmaceutically active ligands or against a library of ligands produced by combinatorial chemistry to uncover previously unexpected agonist ligands at the site.[38] It is now more common to focus on smaller libraries of compounds which are more closely related to the original biologically derived ligand in a methodology termed 'diversity-orientated synthesis'.[39]
(m) An understanding of the genes coding for the receptor may lead to an understanding of changes to receptor density/expression in disease states and may lead to development of gene therapy to address problems.
(n) Genes coding for the enzyme producing the endogenous active can be spliced into micro-organisms (recombinant DNA) to produce the enzyme/endogenous active.

[36] See generally HP Rang, 'Pharmacology: Its Role in Drug Discovery' in HP Rang (ed), *Drug Discovery and Development: Technology in Transition* (Churchill Livingston Elsevier, Edinburgh, 2006) 163.
[37] See generally H LeVine and HP Rang, 'The Role of Genomics and Bioinformatics' in HP Rang (ed), *Drug Discovery and Development: Technology in Transition* (Edinburgh, Churchill Livingston Elsevier, 2006) 77.
[38] See generally K Stoeckli and H Haag, 'High Throughput Screening' in HP Rang (ed), *Drug Discovery and Development: Technology in Transition* (Churchill Livingston Elsevier, Edinburgh, 2006) 99.
[39] Newman and Cragg (n 17) 630; S Dandapani and LA Marcaurelle, 'Current Strategies for Diversity Oriented Synthesis' (2010) 14 *Current Opinion in Chemical Biology* 362.

(o) An understanding of the gene sequence coding for the receptor, or the enzyme making the endogenous ligand, may allow for the de novo synthetic production of the gene (using DNA synthesis technology) and could eventually be used in the development of artificial organisms.

In some cases the biological effect mediated by the ligand may not be what is therapeutically desired. It may be that the therapeutic effect is mediated through interaction with one subtype of receptor whereas a second effect, a 'side effect', is mediated through interaction with another. It may be that at doses higher than those at which the ligand exerts its beneficial effect there may be other biological effects of the ligand at different receptors or in entirely different biochemical systems. The difference between the dose at which a ligand exerts its beneficial effect and the dose at which it demonstrates deleterious side effects is termed the 'therapeutic window' for the ligand. Some drugs, such as many antibiotics, have a relatively large therapeutic window, whereas anticancer drugs have a very narrow (or essentially no) therapeutic window and were it not for the grave effects of the disease the side effects would not ordinarily be tolerated.

Chemical modification of an exogenous ligand may change the activation/binding characteristics and could also potentially change an agonist into an antagonist (or vice versa) or an inverse agonist (or a 'partial' agonist). Any such change would affect the therapeutic benefit to be derived, the side-effect profile and with it the therapeutic window. The interplay with the receptor itself (termed 'pharmacodynamics') cannot be looked at in isolation. Chemical changes will also impact on the bioavailability (the adsorption, distribution, metabolism and excretion (ADME)[40]) of the ligand. A schematic diagram of the key factors influencing therapeutic efficacy is set out in Figure 3.

Figure 3 Schematic diagram of the factors influencing therapeutic efficacy

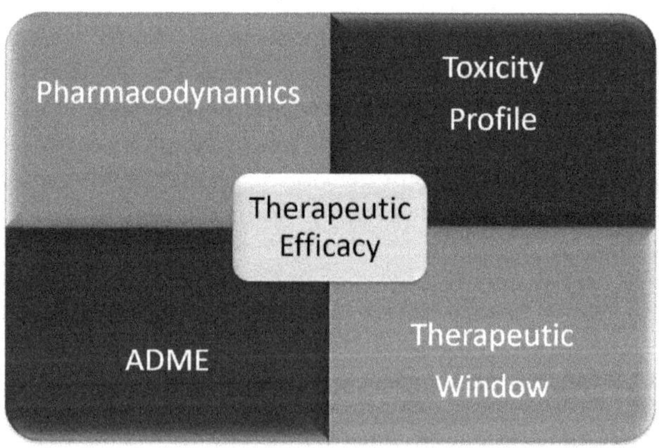

[40] Studies that combine ADME investigations with toxicity studies are termed 'ADMET' trials. The study of the time course and nature of adsorption, distribution, metabolism and excretion of a drug is termed 'pharmacokinetics'.

Knowledge of the structure of the new receptor protein may lead to synthesis of entirely novel agonists or antagonists at that receptor which may find use in the original therapeutic indication, or as will be seen, in second or further indications or in further research into the biological mechanism.[41]

D. 'Biomimetics'

In some circumstances the genetic resource from which the ligand is purified can be difficult to obtain in reliable quantities or the ligand itself may be difficult to extract from the genetic resource. In these cases it may be cost effective to make the ligand through synthesis in the laboratory. However, this may not always be straightforward. Some biologically derived compounds have complex structures that are difficult to replicate using 'non-biological' synthetic pathways. In addition many biologically derived ligands can exist in two (or another multiple of two) 'optical' isomers. This means that the compound can exist either as a 'right-handed' isomer or as a mirror-image 'left-handed' isomer. Although they will share the same atoms their structures are different. In many cases one optical isomer can be biologically active whereas the other isomer is ineffective. For example, all of the amino acids used by all life on Earth are L-isomers; D-isomers of amino acids cannot be used in biological processes. In contrast, all the sugars used by all the life on Earth are D-isomers, the L-form being unused.

Where compounds are made by enzymatic processes the vast majority of the resultant compound will exist as one optical isomer only. Where a compound is made by other (non-enzymatic) chemical pathways the synthetic pathway is ordinarily blind to optical isomerism and a near 50:50 ratio of each isomer (a so-called 'racemic mixture') will be produced. In some cases the racemic mixture will be 'deracemated' (separated out) by researchers (perhaps using affinity chromatography) to leave only the effective isomer.

It is important to note that the desired end product of the synthetic pathway is an exact copy the biologically derived ligand. These compounds are termed 'biomimetics'. A fully deracemated biomimetic would be chemically and biologically indistinguishable from the original ligand of which it was a copy.

However, it should also be noted that where a copy of a *protein* is made by splicing the gene coding for the protein into a cell, the protein produced may *not* be an exact copy of the original. This is because after proteins are synthesised they undergo a process by which sugar groups are attached to the protein. This is called glycosylation (more prevalent in eukaryotic cells). The pattern of glycosylation (and other so-called post-translation modifications) will change depending on the type of host cell. Although the biological effect of the resultant copy may be

[41] See generally DC Blakemore et al (eds), *Synthetic Methods in Drug Discovery* (Abingdon, Royal Society of Chemistry, 2015).

equivalent to that of the original protein, the protein cannot be described as an *exact* copy and therefore the term 'biosimilar' (sometimes 'follow-on biologic') is more appropriate.[42]

Using an entirely synthetic approach to making a ligand may open up new synthetic possibilities for making 'derivatives' which are not reliant upon using the biological -derived ligand as a starting point. Of course, these new ligands may themselves serve as a tool for further investigation of the underlying disease mechanisms.

E. Machine Learning and in Silico 'Prospecting'

As described above, the search for new drugs (or new therapeutic uses for known drugs) has increasingly involved the use of computer-based analyses – so-called 'in silico' studies (to contrast them with in vivo and in vitro studies). Many of these in silico approaches have essentially been used as tools to enhance the types of investigation ordinarily pursued by medicinal chemists for decades – that is, to predict the likely efficacy of making chemical changes to known structures. More recently, however, the in silico approach has moved into using computational power to achieve virtual screening of compounds and this has further developed into the use of artificial intelligence (AI) including deep-learning/machine-learning (ML) neural networks to engage in 'prospecting' for new effects across a very broad libraries of compounds. The use of such networks allows the identification of unexpected new leads both at a much higher speed, and seemingly more effectively, than could be hoped for by using classic high-throughput screening.[43]

i. Target Identification and Network Analysis

AI algorithms can be used to sift through vast amounts of data from genetic and biological databases to identify potential drug targets. This can help researchers to identify novel targets for drug development that may have been missed using traditional methods. AI algorithms can analyse large databases of genomic and proteomic data to identify potential targets for drug development. For example, AI algorithms can be used to analyse genetic mutations that are associated with a particular disease, or to identify proteins that are overexpressed in diseased tissues. AI can also be used to analyse the complex networks of biological interactions that

[42] European Medicines Agency, Committee For Medicinal Products for Human Use, Guideline on Similar Biological Medicinal Products (CHMP/437/04) www.ema.europa.eu/docs/en_GB/document_library/Scientific_guideline/2009/09/WC500003517.pdf.

[43] See generally: S Ekins et al, 'Exploiting Machine Learning for End-to-End Drug Discovery and Development' (2019) 18 (5) *Nature Materials* 435; T Burki, 'A New Paradigm for Drug Development' (2020) 2(5) *The Lancet Digital Health* e226–e227; DL Brata 'Artificial Intelligence and Antibiotic Discovery' (2021) 10(11) *Antibiotics (Basel)* 1376; H Kim et al, 'Artificial Intelligence in Drug Discovery: A Comprehensive Review of Data-Driven and Machine Learning Approaches' (2020) 25 *Biotechnology and Bioprocess Engineering* 895.

occur within cells and between cells. By analysing these networks, AI algorithms can identify potential targets for drug development that are not immediately obvious from individual genes or proteins.[44]

ii. *Machine-Learning-Based Target Prediction*

AI algorithms can be trained to predict potential drug targets based on a variety of factors, such as the chemical properties of drugs and the structure of proteins. These algorithms can analyse large databases of drug–target interactions to identify new targets for drug development.[45]

iii. *Protein Structure Prediction*

Protein structure prediction is the process of predicting the 3D structure of a protein from its amino acid sequence. This allows researchers to determine protein structure once they understand the amino acid sequence produced by a particular gene expression. Being able to predict the structure of a protein is important because (as stated above) the 3D structure of a protein is critical for its function and interactions with other molecules, such as pharmaceutical ligands. By comparing the amino acid sequence of the protein to a database of known protein structures AI can be used to predict the likely structure of a protein (so-called 'homology modelling'). AI can also be used to predict the structure of a protein without relying on known protein structures (de novo structure prediction). Until recently the considerable computing power required for this made the process unfeasible but recent advances in AI algorithms, such as Deepmind's 'AlphaFold', have had very significant successes.[46] Researchers can also use hybrid methods combining homology modelling and de novo prediction, alongside AI improvements to homology modelling, to improve accuracy and reliability.[47]

iv. *Drug Design: Predicting Drug Efficacy and Safety*

By using machine-learning algorithms to analyse data on the structure and properties of known drugs, AI can design and optimize candidate drug molecules by predicting the properties of new drug candidates, such as their binding affinity to a particular target or their potential toxicity. AI algorithms trained on large

[44] See eg Y You et al, 'Artificial Intelligence in Cancer Target Identification and Drug Discovery' (2022) 7(1) *Signal Transduction and Targeted Therapy* 156.

[45] AS Rifaioglu et al, 'MDeePred: Novel Multi-channel Protein Featurization for Deep Learning-Based Binding Affinity Prediction in Drug Discovery' (2021) 37(5) *Bioinformatics* 693.

[46] J Jumper et al, 'Highly Accurate Protein Structure Prediction with AlphaFold' (2021) 596 (7873) *Nature* 583; M Varadi et al, 'AlphaFold Protein Structure Database: Massively Expanding the Structural Coverage of Protein-Sequence Space with High-Accuracy Models' (2022) 50(D1) *Nucleic Acids Research* D439–D444.

[47] T Hameduh et al, 'Homology Modelling in the Time of Collective and Artificial Intelligence' (2020) 18 *Computational and Structural Biotechnology Journal* 3494–3506.

amounts of data from preclinical and clinical trials, such as patient demographics, disease states and drug dosages, can be used to predict the efficacy and safety of a drug candidate. By analysing data on factors such as patient demographics, genetic information and environmental factors, AI can also help researchers to identify patient subgroups that may be more likely to respond to a particular drug or experience certain side effects.[48]

v. Drug Repurposing

AI can be used to identify new uses for existing drugs by analysing data on their molecular structure and pharmacological properties. This can help to accelerate the drug development process by repurposing drugs that have already been approved for use in humans, bypassing the lengthy process of clinical testing and regulatory approval. AI can analyse large amounts of clinical data from electronic health records and other sources to identify patterns and associations between drugs and patient outcomes. This can help identify potential new uses for existing drugs that were not originally intended for a particular disease or patient population. AI can also predict potential drug toxicity by analysing large amounts of data on drug structures, toxicity profiles and clinical trials. This can help identify potential new uses for existing drugs that have been previously abandoned due to toxicity concerns.[49]

F. Machine Learning in Antibacterial Drug Discovery

Bacteria have developed resistance to the majority of current antimicrobial agents used as anti-infectives. This is an area of very deep concern as there is a current paucity in the number of anti-infectives being developed.[50] The WHO suggests that antimicrobial resistance is one of the biggest threats to global health, food security and development today.[51] In silico discovery processes are being used to aid the discovery of new antibacterial drugs.[52] For example, Stokes et al report a revolutionary approach to finding novel antimicrobial compounds.[53] That team 'trained' a deep neural network to become capable of predicting molecules with

[48] See eg D Paul et al, 'Artificial Intelligence in Drug Discovery and Development' (2021) 26(1) *Drug Discovery Today* 80.

[49] CN Choudhury et al, 'Structure-Based Drug Repurposing: Traditional and Advanced AI/ML-Aided Methods' (2022) 27(7) *Drug Discovery Today* 1847; T Aittokallio, 'What Are the Current Challenges for Machine Learning in Drug Discovery and Repurposing?' (2022) 17(5) *Expert Opinion on Drug Discovery* 423.

[50] ED Brown and GD Wright, 'Antibacterial Drug Discovery in the Resistance Era' (2016) 529(7586) *Nature* 336.

[51] www.who.int/news-room/fact-sheets/detail/antibiotic-resistance.

[52] J Marko and B Urban, 'Machine Learning in Antibacterial Drug Design' (2022) 13 *Frontiers in Pharmacology* 864412; MCR Melo et al, 'Accelerating Antibiotic Discovery through Artificial Intelligence' (2021) 4 *Community Biology* 1050.

[53] JM Stokes et al, 'A Deep Learning Approach to Antibiotic Discovery' (2020) 180(4) *Cell* 688.

antibacterial activity. This involved providing the neural network with a teaching library of 2,335 molecules that are known to inhibit the growth of the bacterium *Escherichia coli*. That library included around 300 approved antibiotics, as well as 800 natural products taken from plant, animal and microbial sources. By looking at the chemical structure and growth inhibitory effect of each compound, the network 'taught' itself what types of compound were likely to give antibiotic effects. Importantly for the study, the neural network learns to predict molecular function without any prior 'assumptions' about how the drugs work. The aim of the study was to discover agents which interfere with biological mechanisms within bacteria which are not yet targeted by current therapies – agents that bacteria are unlikely to have developed resistance to. The team hoped that by removing potential assumptions as to functionality, the network could identify previously undiscovered patterns of compound behaviour. Having taught the network (or perhaps, more accurately, allowed the network to teach itself), the team then set it to looking through the 6,000 chemicals within the Drug Repurposing Hub library, asking it to identify compounds with likely anti-*E. coli* action and which did not resemble known antibiotic agents. The neural network came up with a number of predictions (within about four hours) and from these 'hits', the team selected about a hundred candidates for further testing in in vivo animal studies. One of these candidates (halicin) was a compound that has previously been investigated as a potential diabetes treatment. Halicin is structurally divergent from conventional antibiotics and operates through a biological mechanism (inhibition of proton pumps within the bacterial cell membrane) unlike that of any current antimicrobial.

Liu et al have used a combination of more traditional techniques with machine learning to develop an effective agent against the increasingly antibiotic resistant bacterium *Acinetobacter baumannii*.[54] Using high-throughput in vitro techniques the team screened approximately 7,500 molecules for those that inhibited the growth of the bacterium. Using this growth inhibition dataset they trained a neural network to make in silico predictions of new molecules with activity against the bacterium discovering abaucin, an antibacterial compound with narrow-spectrum activity against *A. baumannii*.

G. Drug Development

Much of the discussion set out above deals with what is properly considered drug 'discovery'. We additionally need to briefly consider the related field of drug 'development'. Given the integrated and iterative nature of research the divide between discovery and development can be somewhat unclear. A clearer divide is perhaps between clinical and preclinical work, although again there is substantial

[54] G Liu et al, 'Deep Learning-Guided Discovery of an Antibiotic Targeting *Acinetobacter baumannii*' (2023) 19 *Nature Chemical Biology* 1342.

communication and iterative work between the two areas during the course of the development of a drug.

Much of drug 'discovery' relates to the identification (through preclinical work) of a candidate for clinical trials. Many drugs that form the basis of the modern pharmacopoeia (or their predecessors) were tested on humans or launched onto the market with little (or no) regulatory supervision and many tragic mistakes were made along the way. Accordingly, in the modern era, before a drug can be marketed in a territory it requires 'marketing approval' from the appropriate medicines regulatory authority for that territory.

The process by which that approval is granted is exceptionally highly regulated and a candidate drug is required to pass a number of distinct hurdles before it can pass on to the next stage of the process. Although each regulatory authority will have its own criteria for granting approval, there are substantial commonalities (commonly following US Food and Drug Administration (FDA) and/or European practice) and initiatives towards consistent approaches (particularly harmonisation within the European Union under EU Regulations and the practice of the European Medicines Agency (EMA)).

For the purposes of this work the author will refer to drug 'discovery' as preclinical research which leads to the identification of a potentially useful ligands, and 'development' as both the preclinical and clinical research process required to obtain medicines regulatory agency marketing approval.

A brief description of the phases of drug development is set out in Table 5. As will be seen the preclinical phase of drug development deals predominantly with assessment of the toxicology profile of the candidate molecule. It is worth noting that AI/ML can be used to optimise the design and execution of clinical trials. By analysing data from previous trials, AI algorithms can help researchers to identify patient subgroups that are most likely to benefit from a particular treatment, as well as predict the likelihood of success for a trial and optimise the trial design to minimise costs and maximise efficiency.[55]

In most pharmaceutical markets the 'originator' drug companies that are involved in the development of new drugs are in constant competition with companies who will seek to sell a reduced-priced 'generic' copy of a particular drug once intellectual property protection over that drug has expired. In the same way as is the case for the original drug, such a 'generic' copy will require regulatory approval before it can be launched. However, requiring 'generic' competitors to engage in a full reproduction of the drug development process before they can sell an identical product is perceived to be both wasteful of animal and human testing, and to present a very high barrier to entry for competitor products with a resultant elevated price payable by health systems. Accordingly, in a number of jurisdictions the manufacturer of a generic copy is permitted to obtain a marketing

[55] A Zhavoronkov et al, 'Will Artificial Intelligence for Drug Discovery Impact Clinical Pharmacology?' (2020) 107(4) *Clinical Pharmacology and Therapeutics* 780–85.

authorisation for the copy drug by reference to the original regulatory data set provided by the originator company, provided that the maker of the copy can demonstrate that the copy drug intended to be marketed is the exactly the same as the drug for which authorisation has already been granted (a so-called 'abridged' procedure). However, given the very considerable cost of assembling an original regulatory dataset, and to provide an incentive to innovate, originator companies are commonly provided with a time-limited period of data and marketing 'exclusivity' during which only the originator (or their licensees), but not the makers of generic copies, can rely on that dataset. Such data exclusivity is an important, and valuable, quasi-intellectual property right.

Although the grant of a marketing authorisation will allow a drug to be marketed for a particular therapeutic indication, there is in many territories a further hurdle to the widespread use of the drug. This is a requirement to pass a 'health technology assessment' to determine whether, in a particular territory, the public authority funding healthcare can justify funding the use of the drug or other therapy (on usually a cost-effectiveness basis).

Table 5 Phases of drug development[56]

Development phase	Nature
Preclinical testing	Data gathered on genotoxicity, toxicity, oncogenicity, reproductive toxicology
Phase I	First study in humans: assessment of tolerability, pharmacokinetics and pharmacodynamics in (usually) healthy volunteers
Phase II	First study in patients with the disease to be treated: assessment of tolerability, pharmacokinetics and pharmacodynamics in patients; assessment of optimum dose and side-effect profile
Phase III	Assessment of outcomes in patients approximating to the 'real-life' population of patients – forms a significant part of the data portfolio used to gain regulatory approval
Phase IIIB	Phase III-style studies that are not intended to form part of the regulatory dossier but will provide further evidence to persuade practitioners to use the drug – including evidence of cost–benefit and quality-of-life advantages
Phase IV	Post-marketing surveillance. Phase III studies cannot hope to cover all real-life situations and Phase IV surveillance allows for an ongoing assessment of safety and efficacy.

[56] J Hall, 'The Drug Development Process' in I Di Giovanna and G Hayes (eds), *Principles of Clinical Research* (Petersfield, Wrightson Biomedical Publishing, 2001) 1; I Hägglöf and Å Holmgreen, 'Regulatory Affairs' in HP Rang (ed), *Drug Discovery and Development: Technology in Transition* (Edinburgh, Churchill Livingston Elsevier, 2006) 281.

H. Drug Discovery: A Linear Path?

As has been described in the earlier parts of this chapter, there are many paths that can be taken by a pharmaceutical research team involved in drug discovery.

The external perception of drug research is often of a linear process by which a solution is inevitably arrived at. This is, however, rarely the case – the drug discovery process is often iterative and there are many parallel steams. Often there are dead ends where the hoped-for result, whatever it may be, is not arrived at. Often important discoveries are made but are not taken up. This may be the result of the researcher being outwith the scientific 'mainstream', publishing in a less-well-read language or in an inappropriate, or obscure, journal. The process can be influenced by personalities, scientific fashion and by commercial concerns. As will be seen, serendipitous discoveries, particularly observations of side effects of existing drugs, can play an important role. Any sense of linearity may be the result of 'hindsight', an inherent 'outcome reporting bias' amongst research teams themselves (and the editors of scientific journals) against the publication of negative rather than positive results, or the desire by the media (and drug marketers) to present a coherent and easily accessible story of development.[57] Such reporting, both in scientific journals and the media, may give the impression of a certain *inevitability* to the research outcome that is not apparent to those working in the field at the time. However, as a compound enters the drug development stages the process, driven by medicines regulatory requirements, becomes (as is seen above) somewhat more linear and proscribed (though still beset by uncertainty).

Kubinyi's diagrammatic representation of the 'drug design cycle'[58] divides into two parts. Part 1 (reproduced in Figure 4) deals with lead *structure* identification; this is a chemical whose structure shows promise as the basis for further examination. As can be seen, this process may take its 'inspirations' from a wide variety of sources including the existing literature and patent searching, reviews of endogenous and exogenous natural ligands (including from bioprospecting), reviews of synthetically produced ligands, in silico screening and modelling, and the understanding of biological processes underlying the pathological condition. Key to the process is screening of the candidate molecule against an in vivo animal model or an in vitro molecular target (and very likely both). Once a lead structure is identified it is entered into a process of 'lead structure optimisation' (part 2 of Kubinyi's design cycle; reproduced here in Figure 5) in the hope of finding a compound that is a drug 'candidate'.

[57] K Dwan et al, 'Systematic Review of the Empirical Evidence of Study Publication Bias and Outcome Reporting Bias' (2008) 3(8) *PLoS ONE* e3081; B Goldacre, *Bad Science* (London, Harper Perennial, 2009) 224.

[58] H Kubinyi in E Raviña *The Evolution of Drug Discovery: From Traditional Medicines to Modern Drugs* (Weinheim, Wiley-VCH, 2011) 463.

Figure 4 Drug design cycle: lead structure identification (after Kubinyi)[59]

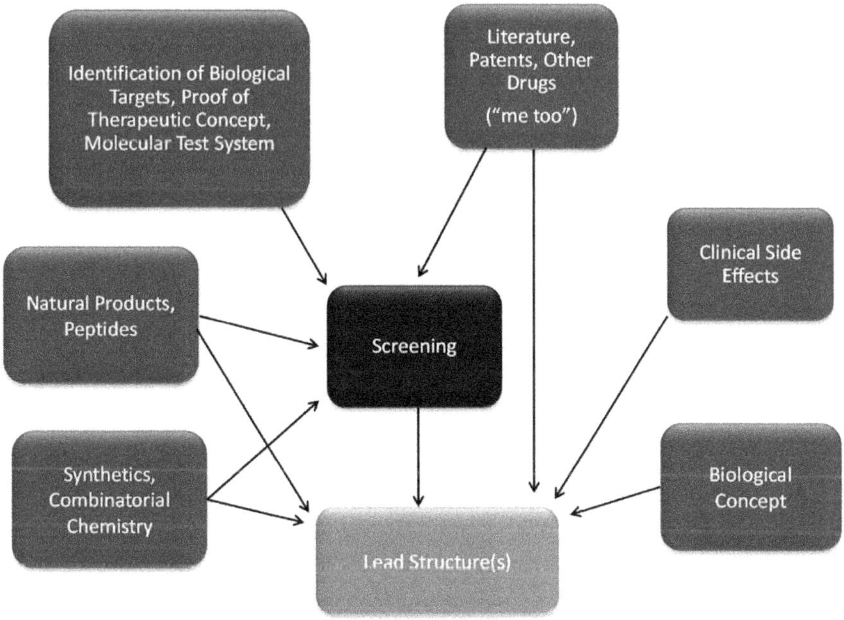

As can be seen, this lead structure optimisation is again a highly iterative process involving a large number of feedback loops between design of a new derivative, design of a new synthetic pathway to produce that derivative, actual chemical synthesis and the biological testing of the new derivatives. A drug candidate is required to be a good deal more than a biologically active substance that has the desired effect at a particular receptor site – it must have the desired clinical efficacy and additionally meet appropriate absorption, distribution, metabolism, excretion and toxicology (side-effect profile) requirements in both in vitro tests and animal/human in vivo testing. Much of the final work on taking a candidate to final marketed drug is done within clinical trials work (the somewhat more linear process shown at the bottom of Figure 5). Although separation into these two phases in the diagrams is helpful to our understanding of the overall processes, lead structure identification and optimisation are in fact closely linked together with feedback loops between the two, particularly in the development of biological testing mechanisms.

[59] ibid.

Figure 5 Drug design cycle: lead structure optimisation (after Kubinyi)[60]

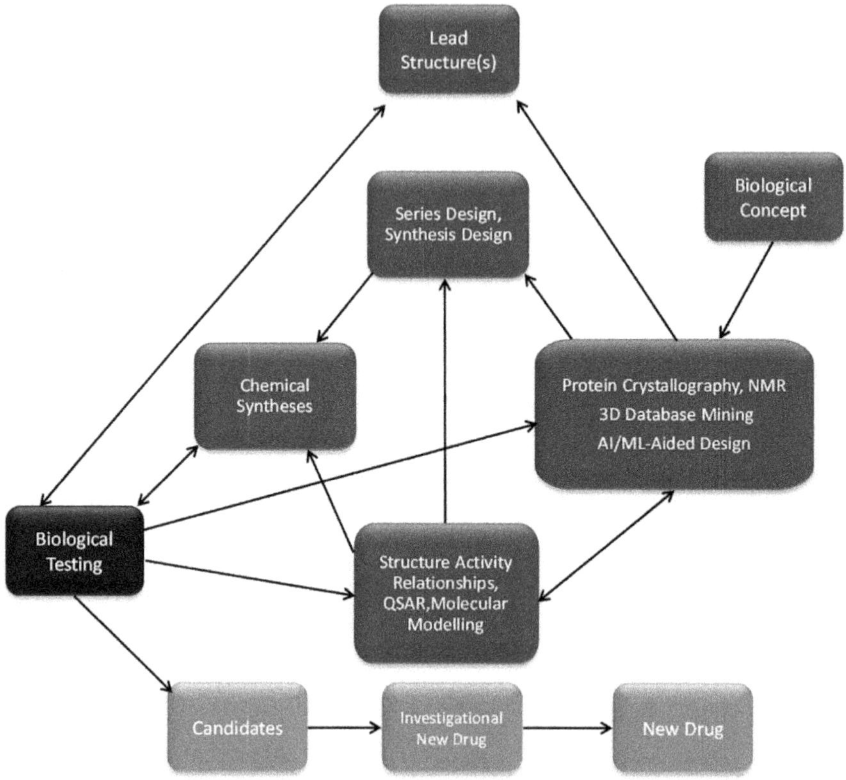

Key: QSAR, quantitative structure–activity relationship models[61]

III. Looking for Crux Points – The Flow of Information and the 'Dilution' of Contribution

The description given above (including the schematics in Figures 4 and 5) highlights the extreme degree of mixing of ideas and concepts in the drug discovery process. Very many separate inspirations will be mixed together stimulating the collection of data which will itself be fed back into the cycle. As has

[60] ibid.

[61] C Nantasenamat et al, 'A Practical Overview of Quantitative Structure–Activity Relationship' (2009) 8 *Experimental and Clinical Sciences Journal* 74; M Cronin and J Madden (eds), *In Silico Toxicology: Principles and Applications* (Abingdon, Royal Society of Chemistry, 2010).

been stressed, the overall process of moving from a piece of TKAGR to a lead compound or new marketed drug (or indeed any downstream point on the way to these outcomes) involves significant mixing of information such as to cause a 'dilution' of the original inspiration into a body of other information. The use of AI and ML trained on large datasets is only adding to the depth of this admixture.

Notwithstanding this dilution effect, it is clear that if we apply a pure sine qua non causation test, *all* such downstream use flowing from the original inspiration will be caused in fact by the information within the original inspiration. However, as has been discussed above in chapter one, the appropriate test for any situation in which one is seeking to determine a legal liability is not one of causation *in fact*, but one of causation *in law*.

Although we can seek to 'describe' dilution of information in that we can (in a particular circumstance) seek to locate the disparate sources of information, determine how those pieces of information have come together and have created an outcome, it is harder to measure what we might term the degree or 'amount' of dilution of a piece of information. To do so requires an understanding of what one means by 'amount' – the test cannot be merely quantitative: some pieces of information are clearly more 'important' than other pieces of information and retain their importance, even where they have been quantitatively 'swamped' by other data. However, deciding what is meant by 'important' is an evaluative judgement based on one's frame of reference (which may, in part, relate to what one is seeking to achieve with the information).

If we now imagine that alongside the mixing and dilution of information we see a mixing and dilution of 'contribution', we see a parallel problem. If we imagine that contribution is connected with information, then, as we follow the passage of information through the system, we can see concomitant flows of 'contribution'. As with information per se we can describe the sources of contribution, how they have come together and the eventual outcome. However, as with the concept of importance, measuring the 'dilution' of contribution cannot be a quantitative exercise but is based upon an evaluative determination of what one means by contribution. One might simplistically say that contribution should be 'based upon' or 'linked to' importance, but this merely takes us back to what one means by importance and indeed it may be difficult to divorce one's definition of 'important' from that of contribution.

One might argue, then, that what we see when we look at the passage of a piece of TKAGR through the drug discovery process is a 'morass' of competing contributions sitting on the back of an entanglement of information. There clearly is some form of epistemic dilution going on, but how can we hope to measure it or categorise it?

When one examines the topography of drug development, we see that much of drug discovery efforts could be described as sequential and accumulative – where each successive development builds in an essential way on its predecessor.[62] Here the work performed by pharmaceutical researchers follows on from (or merely adds to) the core epistemic elements provided by the TKAGR. There is a substantial increase in the volume of additional knowledge, but no matter how much the original traditional knowledge is diluted in terms of volume, the underlying nature of the contribution made by the traditional knowledge to the downstream product remains unchanged.

Perhaps if we are to find a putative 'crux point' we need to determine a third-party downstream contribution which affects a 'step change' in the *nature* of the downstream product when compared to the original contribution. On examination we find there appear to be few obvious such points.

It is here that we need to turn to the long interface between patent law and the drug discovery process for inspiration. As has been stated in chapter one, any parallels between patent law and putative positive rights in traditional knowledge need to be treated very carefully, and it must be stressed that direct analogies with patent law are to be avoided. However, patent law has (as will be discussed further in the analysis in chapter seven) particularly had to wrestle with the question of whether newly discovered uses for an 'old' thing should be awarded separate patent protection.[63] This has come to a notable head in addressing the question of whether a second therapeutic use of a known substance which is already known to have a therapeutic benefit should be patentable.[64]

This is an area where there is a distinct clash of conflicting contributions (and an arguable 'step change' in the *nature* of the downstream product when compared to the original contribution). Accordingly, the current work has taken that problem as an inspiration in the identification of the following putative 'crux point' in the drug development process, namely where an unexpected ('serendipitous') discovery of a new use for a particular genetic resource (or the compounds found in a particular genetic resource or their chemical derivatives) is made on the back of the original piece of TKAGR.

Having identified such discoveries as a putative crux point, the determination of whether that point can be justified as a point at which the chain of causation *in law* is broken can only (as is discussed in chapter one) be determined by the application of high-level philosophical principles which take into account the reasons for the existence of the right in the first place. That analysis is taken forward in the next chapter. However, before moving on to that analysis, this chapter will conclude by looking more closely at the nature and history of serendipitous discoveries within the drug discovery process.

[62] See generally J Bessen and E Maskin 'Sequential Innovation, Patents, and Imitation' (2009) 40(4) *RAND Journal of Economics* 611.

[63] See eg *Mobil Friction Reducing Additive G 2/88* (OJEPO 4/90); *Bayer G 6/88* (OJEPO 4/90).

[64] See eg 'Legal Advice from the Swiss Federal Intellectual Property Office (FIPO), dated 30 May 1984' [1984] OJ EPO 581; Eisai (Second medical indication) G 5/83 [1984] OJEPO 64.

IV. The Nature of 'Serendipitous' Discoveries of New Uses

Let us assume that our plant-derived ligand has been isolated, purified and chemically characterised. As has been stated, such ligands may have effects on more than one area of the body, so leading to undesirable side effects. However, sometimes the 'side effects' are in some way desirable and here the ligand may become a candidate for providing a second therapeutic benefit to an apparently unrelated set of symptoms. This is often referred to as a 'second medical use' of the compound. However, such second uses need not be limited to medicine or, indeed, even to biology. The distinctive element in such a step from one part of the research process to the next is that there has been an entirely non-obvious, or unexpected, revelation of a new feature (use) of the 'thing' (for example, ligand) obtained from the genetic resource.

It is crucial to point out immediately that not all steps to a new use will be appear quite so momentous. The more one understands about the underlying biological target of a ligand, the more that the second use may seem obvious. Figure 6 shows this in schematic form. By way of example, when one combines our current knowledge of the inhibitory effect of acetylsalicylic acid (aspirin) on the activity of cyclooxygenase enzymes with our current understanding that the prostaglandins and thromboxanes synthesised by cyclooxygenase enzymes have a role both in the mediation of in the inflammatory response in injured tissue *and* in the regulation of blood platelet adherence, the 'discovery' that aspirin not only serves as an anti-inflammatory but also as a cardio- and stroke-protective agent may seem trite. However, this understanding of the underlying biochemical connection was not at all the situation when the anticoagulant benefits of aspirin were originally uncovered by Craven (see the case study in section V.C below).

Of course, what happens in practice (and what happened in the case of aspirin) is that the discovery of an unexpected second therapeutic benefit will initiate research into the biological processes which may underlie the two apparently different benefits.

Figure 6 Schematic of the nature of serendipitous discoveries in biology

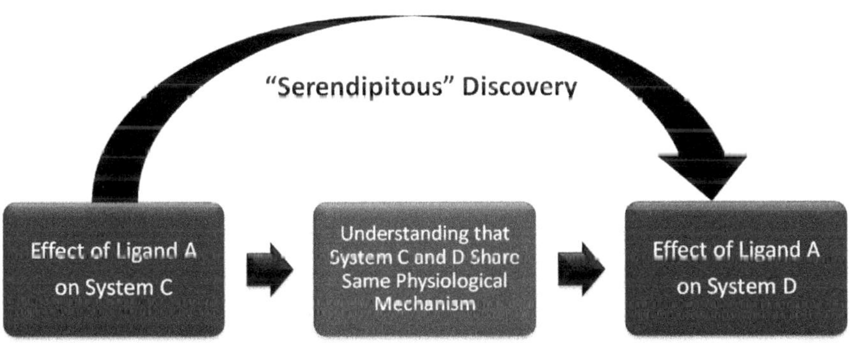

For the purposes of the current work, a 'serendipitous discovery' of a second use will be taken to mean one in which the second use is truly unexpected in the light of the current understanding of the underlying biology when the discovery of the second use is made. It is accepted that with our increasing understanding of the ways in which ligands mediate their effects, such serendipitous discoveries are likely to be far less common than was the case in the past. However, we cannot assume that we have reached an 'end of history' with regard to our understanding of biological processes, and new genetic resource-derived ligands are still leading us to as yet unknown biological targets.[65] By way of example we may look to the discovery of the mechanistic target of rapamycin (mTOR).[66] This is a protein involved in mammalian intracellular regulation which was only uncovered through research on the immunosuppressant effect of the macrocyclic antibiotic rapamycin. Rapamycin was itself found in the *Streptomyces hygroscopicus* bacterium which was in turn found in prospected soil samples found on the Pacific island of Rapa Nui (Easter Island).[67] There surely yet remain many unknown biological mechanisms that may reveal unexpected routes to clinical therapy. For example (and as was mentioned in chapter three), relatively recent developments in epigenetics have overturned scientific dogma in relation to the control of expression of the genome.[68]

V. Case Studies of Serendipitous Discoveries within Drug Discovery

A. Introduction

The question posed in relation to serendipitous discoveries of second uses is far from theoretical. Such serendipitously discovered uses have been major contributors to the development of medical (and other) science. Table 6 summarises some examples of compounds arising out of research performed on plant-derived drugs and some serendipitously discovered second uses of plant-derived drugs (or their derivatives) derived from research on those compounds.

Sometimes such discoveries have been in relation to the initial plant-derived compound – the discovery of the anaesthetic effect of cocaine represents an

[65] F Fukuyama, 'The End of History?' *The National Interest* (Summer 1989) ps321.community.uaf.edu/files/2012/10/Fukuyama-End-of-history-article.pdf.

[66] EJ Brown et al, 'A Mammalian Protein Targeted by G1-arresting Rapamycin–Receptor Complex' (1994) 369 *Nature* 756.

[67] C Vézina et al, 'Rapamycin (AY-22, 989), A New Antifungal Antibiotic: (I) Taxonomy of the Producing Streptomycete and Isolation of the Active Principle' (1975) 28(10) *Journal of Antibiotics* 721.

[68] A Bird, 'Perceptions of Epigenetics' (2007) 447 *Nature* 396; see also: K Kampourakis, *Making Sense of Genes* (Cambridge, Cambridge University Press, 2017) 215.

example of this. Occasionally the serendipitously discovered second use relates to a chemical derivative of the initial plant-derived compound, such as the cardioprotective effect of acetyl salicylic acid (aspirin).

Table 6 Examples of serendipitously discovered second uses of plant-derived drugs[69]

Compound initiating trail	Plant	Compounds arising from research trails	Original therapeutic benefit	Serendipitously discovered second use or new compound
Salicin	*Salix alba* (willow) *Spirea ulmaria* (meadowsweet)	Aspirin Mefanamic acid Flufenamic acid Diclofenac Celecoxib Refecoxib	Antipyretic	Reduced blood clotting (aspirin)
Cocaine	*Erythoxylum coca* (coca)	β-Eucaine Orthocaine Benzocaine Bupivicaine Lignocaine Procaine	Mild central nervous system stimulant	Local anaesthetic (cocaine)
Morphine	*Papaver somniforum* (opium poppy)	Codeine Diacetylmorphine ('heroin') Oxycodone Hydrocodone Metopon Dextromethorphan Etorphine Buprenorphine Pethidine Methadone Dextromoramide Piritamide Fentanyl Remifentanil	Pain relief	Haloperidol (antipsychotic)

(continued)

[69] Table compiled from a review of case studies provided in W Sneader, *Drug Discovery: The Evolution of Modern Medicines* (Chichester, John Wiley, 1985); W Sneader, *Drug Discovery: A History* (Chichester, John Wiley, 2005); and E Raviña, *The Evolution of Drug Discovery: From Traditional Medicines to Modern Drugs* (Weinheim, Wiley-VCH, 2011).

Table 6 ***(Continued)***

Compound initiating trail	Plant	Compounds arising from research trails	Original therapeutic benefit	Serendipitously discovered second use or new compound
Quinine	*Cinchona* spp. (*Quina quina*)	Pamaquin Mepacrine Sontoquine Chloroquine Primaquine Antipyrine	Antimalarial	Mauveine dye Antipyrine
Vinblastine Vincristine	*Catharanthus roseus* (Madagascar or rosy periwinkle)	Vindesine Vinorelbine	Antidiabetic	Antitumour effect

In the case of the Madagascar (or rosy) periwinkle an unsuspected (antitumour) effect of compounds found in the plant (vincristine and vinblastine) was discovered even though the antidiabetes research trail stimulated by traditional knowledge relating to the plant was unsuccessful.

Chemical work related to a plant-derived compound can sometimes uncover previously unthought-of compounds with unthought-of uses. Perkin's discovery of mauveine dye whilst trying to synthesise quinine is a truly startling (and world-changing) example of this. Although it is not itself the discovery of a second medical use of the same compound, it is an example of a different type of serendipitous discovery which serves as a useful contrast to second medical use discoveries in our later analysis.

The remainder of this chapter is devoted to abbreviated case studies of four of these examples, both by way of illustration and as examples for further analysis within chapters six and seven below.

B. Salicin – Fever and Cardiovascular Effects

The development of naturally derived salicin into aspirin has been called 'the beginning of medicinal chemistry as a science, the optimization of a drug through alternating biological testing and chemical modification'.[70] The discovery of aspirin is also interesting as it was essentially discovered through two parallel research streams, each looking at different, and unrelated, plants.

[70] G Albers-Schönberg, 'The Pharmaceutical Discovery Process' in T Swanson (ed), *Intellectual Property Rights and Biodiversity Conservation: An Interdisciplinary Analysis of the Values of Medicinal Plants* (Cambridge, Cambridge University Press, 1995) 68.

An eighteenth-century Oxfordshire clergyman, the Reverend Edward Stone, identified the antirheumatism and antifever effects of the bark of the white willow or *Salix alba*. He was led to study this tree by the bitter taste of its bark (similar to that of the antifebrile bark of the South American cinchona tree) and by that fact that the tree grew in damp conditions which were thought to give rise to fevers. This latter 'lead' came out of Stone's application of the so-called 'Doctrine of Signatures', a long-standing concept in which physical or habitat characteristics of a plant which were considered to be 'similar' to a particular disease or symptom were thought to be 'pointing the way' to a cure for that disease or symptom. Although he recorded the effects of willow bark extract in a letter to the Royal Society of 1763,[71] Stone did not personally take his discovery any further.[72] Although Stone appears to have been unaware of the fact, infusions of willow bark had in fact long been used against fever in European herbal folklore. Willow brew was used by Hippocrates for pain in childbirth, and Pliny and Galen both suggested it be use against inflammation.[73]

Following Stone's communication to the Royal Society, willow bark extract was used as a cheaper substitute for cinchona bark. In 1826 Brugnatelli and Fontana determined the active substance in willow bark to be salicin, a compound that was isolated by Leroux in 1829.

In 1838, Italian chemist Raffaele Piria working in Italy developed an acid derivative of salicin which showed enhanced antifever efficacy. He named this derivative salicylic acid. The pharmacological effect of willow bark is mediated through salicylic acid, the metabolite of the compound salicin found in the bark. In 1830 Johann Pagenstecher, working in Switzerland (independently of the work of Stone), determined that an extract of the meadowsweet flower (*Spirea ulmaria*) would have antifever effects.[74] Again meadowsweet was known within European herbal medicine for its pain-reducing properties. In 1835 Karl Jakob Löwig (working in Berlin) read of the work of Pagenstecher and determined that the active constituent was an acid, which he named *spirsäure* from the Linnean name for the meadowsweet plant. This was the same salicylic acid that had been produced by Pirea.[75]

Salicylic acid was found to be effective against pain and inflammation. However, due (in part) to its acidity, salicylic acid can cause severe irritation to the gastric mucosa, causing extreme gastric pain. This was a great limitation to its use and eventually German chemists Felix Hoffmann and Arthur Eichengrün, working for Bayer AG, developed an acetyl derivative of salicylic acid, sodium acetylsalicylate, which avoided many of the gastric complications of the original substance.[76]

[71] E Stone, 'An Account of the Success of the Bark of the Willow in the Cure of Agues' (1763) 53 *Philosophical Transactions* 195.

[72] P Fairley, *The Conquest of Pain* (London, Michael Joseph, 1978) 125.

[73] Raviña (n 69) 24.

[74] ibid 24.

[75] Sneader, *Drug Discovery: The Evolution of Modern Medicines* (n 69) 82; Sneader, *Drug Discovery: A History* (n 69) 359.

[76] Sneader, *Drug Discovery: The Evolution of Modern Medicines* (n 69) 82; Sneader, *Drug Discovery: A History* (n 69) 359.

Looking for a name for the new drug, Bayer developed the trade name 'Aspirin' from its German name *Acetylspirsäure*. When the history of the development of Aspirin was written in 1933, Eichengrün's significant role was excluded due to his Jewish background. His role in testing sodium acetylsalicylate on himself and then arranging for clinical trials after Bayer's pharmacologists had initially rejected the compound was replaced by a story that Hoffmann had tested the new drug on his poorly father.[77] Aspirin became for many years (until the advent of other non-steroidal anti-inflammatory drugs, notably paracetamol and ibuprofen, in the late 1950s and early 1960s) one of the first lines of treatment of inflammation.

Based upon anecdotal observations of bleeding in patients taking aspirin, cardiologist Paul Gibson proposed (in a 1948 letter to *The Lancet*) that salicylates may have a role in treating coronary heart disease,[78] and followed this up in 1949 with publication of a small-scale study demonstrating a benefit in angina patients.[79] This lead was not taken up.

In the late 1940s California family physician Lawrence Craven made an observation that during tonsillectomies and tooth extractions patients who had been used aspirin for gum pain relief required longer for their bleeding to stop. Without any understanding of the underlying biochemical mechanism, Craven hypothesized aspirin was prolonging clotting time and that this effect may be beneficial in preventing coronary heart disease. In an uncontrolled study of 400 patients over two years Craven gave 'preventative' aspirin to patients aged between 40 and 65. He published his results in a one-page letter to a local medical journal.[80] This work was followed up with a further uncontrolled study in 8,000 patients published in the *Mississippi Valley Medical Journal*.[81] Craven's work received little immediate recognition, perhaps due to the uncontrolled nature of his trial and the relative obscurity of its publication. However, the concept of using aspirin to prevent cardiovascular disease gained more credibility when Weiss and Aledort, working in New York, demonstrated that aspirin had an effect of platelet aggregation.[82] This stimulated a series of randomized controlled trials in patients that successfully demonstrated the cardioprotective effects of aspirin.[83] The effect of low-dose aspirin as a prophylaxis against stroke and heart attacks is perhaps one of the classic examples of a serendipitous 'second medical use'.

[77] W Sneader, 'The Discovery of Aspirin: A Reappraisal' (2000) 321 *British Medical Journal* 1591.

[78] PC Gibson, 'Salicylic Acid for Coronary Thrombosis?' (1948) 1 *Lancet* 965.

[79] PC Gibson, 'Aspirin in the Treatment of Vascular Diseases' (1949) 2 *Lancet* 1172.

[80] LL Craven, 'Acetylsalicylic Acid, Possible Preventive of Coronary Thrombosis' (1950) 4(2) *Annals of Western Medicine and Surgery* 95.

[81] LL Craven, 'Experiences with Aspirin (Acetylsalicylic Acid) in the Nonspecific Prophylaxis of Coronary Thrombosis' (1953) 75 *Mississippi Valley Medical Journal* 38; LL Craven 'Prevention of Coronary and Cerebral Thrombosis' (1956) 78 *Mississippi Valley Medical Journal* 213.

[82] HJ Weiss and LM Aledort, 'Impaired Platelet/Connective-Tissue Reaction in Man after Aspirin Ingestion' (1967) 290 *The Lancet* 495.

[83] PC Elwood et al, 'A Randomized Controlled Trial of Acetyl Salicylic Acid in the Secondary Prevention of Mortality from Myocardial Infarction' (1974) 1 *British Medical Journal* 436; PM Ridker et al, 'Inflammation, Aspirin, and the Risk of Cardiovascular Disease in Apparently Healthy Men' (1979) 336 *New England Journal of Medicine* 973.

Following the Nobel Prize-winning work of a team led by John Vane at the Wellcome Foundation, London, it is now understood that aspirin exerts its anti-inflammatory effect through the irreversible inhibition of one of the enzymes (cyclooxygenase) responsible for the synthesis of prostaglandins and thromboxanes (inflammatory mediators that are in part responsible for the body's inflammation response).[84] It is now also understood that as well as being inflammatory mediators, prostaglandins and thromboxanes both play a role in the platelet aggregation seen in blood clotting which explains aspirin's previously surprising effects on the two systems.[85]

C. Cocaine – Psychoactivity and Anaesthetic Effect

Erythoxylum coca and *Erythoxylum novogranatense* are shrubs which grow on the Amazonian slopes of the Andes of Peru, Ecuador and Bolivia. The chewing of coca leaves has long been practised by the Indigenous peoples and is an integral part of Indigenous culture which continues to the present day – the practice was reported in Pedro Cieza de Leon's *Crónica del Perú* of 1565,[86] and by Nicholas Monardes in his *Historia medicinal de Indias occidentales* in 1569.[87] Archaeological evidence suggests that *E. coca* was brought under cultivation in the eastern Andes by 5000 BCE.[88] Pre-Columbian Andean ceramic figurines have been found which look to have a plug in their cheek, and small ceramic containers which may be associated with coca chewing and dating from 3000 BCE have been found in coastal Ecuador.[89] The chewing of coca leaves was well established under the Inca empire, but was limited to nobles, priests and the *chasquis* couriers.[90] The chewing of coca leaves has a mild euphoric effect, which in the Andes is used to counteract the effects of altitude.[91]

After the Spanish conquest of the Andes, Spanish missionaries attempted to restrict the use of coca, but Spanish slave-owners (and later slave-owners in the United States) encouraged its use amongst slaves as a way of enhancing productivity.[92] In the 1880s coca leaf became a major component of various

[84] JR Vane 'Inhibition of Prostaglandin Synthesis as a Mechanism of Action of Aspirin-Like Drugs' (1971) 231(25) *Nature: New Biology* 232; SH Ferreira et al, 'Indomethacin and Aspirin Abolish Prostaglandin Release from the Spleen' (1971) 231(25) *Nature: New Biology* 237.

[85] H Tohgi et al, 'Effects of Low-to-High Doses of Aspirin on Platelet Aggregability and Metabolites of Thromboxane A2 and Prostacyclin' (1992) 23(10) *Stroke* 1400.

[86] Raviña (n 69) 29.

[87] Sneader, *Drug Discovery: The Evolution of Modern Medicines* (n 69) 49.

[88] Balick and Cox (n 21) 169.

[89] ibid.

[90] Laws (n 23) 72.

[91] JM Watt, 'Magic and Witchcraft in Relation to Plants and Folk Medicine' in T Swain (ed), *Plants in the Development of Modern Medicine* (Cambridge, MA, Harvard University Press, 1972) 68, 85; WJ Bishop, 'Some Early Literature on Addiction with Special Reference to Tobacco' (1949) 46 *British Journal on Addiction* 49.

[92] Laws (n 23) 72.

'tonics' (famously including Coca-Cola) and untested medicines.[93] In 1855, Friedrich Gaedchke extracted an active alkaloid from coca leaves, and in 1860 Albert Niemann (at the University of Gottingen) isolated pure crystals of this alkaloid from the coca leaf which he named 'cocaine'. During this work Niemann had tasted his crystal and found that it made his tongue insensitive to pain but did not act on this finding.[94]

In the mid to late nineteenth century cocaine and coca leaf extract were seen as being nothing more than a mild stimulant, much like caffeine found in tea and coffee, and the risk of addiction was unsuspected. In the 1880s, Sigmund Freud began investigating how the Indigenous peoples of the Andes used coca leaves to stave off exhaustion. According to DuQuesne and Reeves,[95] Freud initially saw cocaine as something of a panacea – describing it as a 'magical substance' – that might be used as an antidepressant and potential treatment for morphine addicts, and invited many of his friends to try it.[96] However, whilst using cocaine as part of a treatment for morphine addiction in a friend, the development of cocaine addiction in that friend led to Freud's rejection of drug therapy for psychiatric disorders.[97]

In 1882 Carl Koller, an ophthalmologist working in Vienna, began searching for a way in which to conduct eye surgery on patients whilst they were awake. In 1884 Koller's friend Sigmund Freud invited Koller to work on the stimulant effects of the cocaine alkaloid. During this work Freud told Koller that he (and others) had found that cocaine produced a numbing effect on the tongue when taken orally. Koller was still working in parallel on his search for an ophthalmic anaesthetic, and on hearing of cocaine's numbing effects immediately began to test a cocaine solution in the eye of a frog. He moved on to testing it on his own eye and that of his colleague with great success. Within months of Koller's paper on the anaesthetic effects of cocaine being delivered at a conference in Heidelberg, cocaine was being used as a local anaesthetic for eye surgery and ear, nose and throat surgery.[98] From 1885 cocaine was synthesised and marketed as a local anaesthetic by the Merck company.[99] This local anaesthetic effect of cocaine acted as the stimulant for a broad range of derivatives which have created very effective local anaesthetic agents including benzocaine,[100] procaine,[101] Novocaine (an injected local anaesthetic for dental surgery),[102] lignocaine (or

[93] ibid 73.

[94] Sneader, *Drug Discovery: The Evolution of Modern Medicines* (n 69) 49.

[95] T DuQuesne and J Reeves, *A Handbook of Psychoactive Medicines* (London, Quartet Books, 1982) 65.

[96] R Porter, *The Greatest Benefit to Mankind, A Medical History of Humanity from Antiquity to Present* (London, HarperCollins, 1997) 368.

[97] Sneader, *Drug Discovery: The Evolution of Modern Medicines* (n 69) 49.

[98] Raviña (n 69) 30; Sneader, *Drug Discovery: A History* (n 69) 98; MG Seelig, 'History of Cocaine as a Local Anaesthetic' (1941) 117(15) *Journal of the American Medical Association* 1284.

[99] Porter (n 97) 368.

[100] Sneader, *Drug Discovery: The Evolution of Modern Medicines* (n 69) 53; Raviña (n 69) 31.

[101] Raviña (n 69) 31.

[102] Sneader, *Drug Discovery: The Evolution of Modern Medicines* (n 69) 55; Raviña (n 69) 31.

lidocaine),[103] mepivacaine, ropivacaine and bupivacaine (used for continuous epidural anaesthesia in childbirth).[104]

These compounds are now understood to exert their effect through preventing the conduction of a nerve impulse in the nerve cell membrane. The seminal (and Nobel Prize-winning) work on the conduction of the nerve impulse was done by Alan Hodgkin and Andrew Huxley at the Physiological Laboratory at Cambridge University in 1952,[105] and the understanding of the effect of local anaesthetics on the nerve action potential was only understood in the 1970s and early 1980s.[106] However, since this work came later than the discovery of most local anaesthetics, that knowledge was unknown to the majority of those involved in the history of the development of local anaesthesia using cocaine derivatives. Those workers were reliant only on structure–function correlations gained through the amassed data from trial-and-error studies (some of these correlations were not widely disseminated as much of the work was undertaken within the commercial laboratories of pharmaceutical companies).

The central nervous system stimulant effects of cocaine – the effects that cause euphoria and arousal – are now understood to be mediated through a blocking effect on the neuronal dopamine transporter within the presynaptic axon terminal. This inhibits reuptake of dopamine reuptake from the synaptic cleft, causing higher dopamine levels in the cleft and dopamine receptor activation in the postsynaptic neuron.[107] Although this is, of course, an effect on a nerve cell, it is by a different physiological mechanism than the local anaesthetic effect of cocaine on peripheral nerve transmission, which is mediated through a blockade of (predominantly) voltage-sensitive sodium channels.[108]

The case study has some interesting features. Although the central and peripheral effects of cocaine are not mediated through a common pathway, it was in fact long known by the Indigenous people of the Andes that the chewing of a plug of coca leaves not only provides a central stimulant effect, but results in a tingling and numbness in the mouth.[109] It could convincingly be argued that a mild anaesthetic

[103] Sneader, *Drug Discovery: The Evolution of Modern Medicines* (n 69) 56; Raviña (n 69) 32.

[104] Sneader, *Drug Discovery: The Evolution of Modern Medicines* (n 69) 57.

[105] AL Hodgkin and AF Huxley, 'A Quantitative Description of Membrane Current and its Application to Conduction and Excitation in Nerve' (1952) 117(4) *Journal of Physiology* 500; CJ Schwiening, 'A Brief Historical Perspective: Hodgkin and Huxley' (2012) 590(11) *Journal of Physiology* 2571.

[106] B Hille, 'Local Anaesthetics: Hydrophilic and Hydrophobic Pathways for the Drug Receptor Interaction' (1977) 69 *Journal of General Physiology* 497; A Goodman Gilman et al, *Goodman and Gilman's The Pharmacological Basis of Therapeutics* (London, Macmillan, 1985) 303.

[107] L Proebstl et al, 'Effects of Stimulant Drug Use on the Dopaminergic System: A Systematic Review and Meta-analysis of In Vivo Neuroimaging Studies' (2019) 59 *European Psychiatry* 15.

[108] ME O'Leary and JC Hancox, 'Role of Voltage-Gated Sodium, Potassium and Calcium Channels in the Development of Cocaine Associated Cardiac Arrhythmias' (2010) 69(5) *British Journal of Clinical Pharmacology* 427.

[109] G Mendoza-Azpur et al, 'Clinical and Histological Manifestations of Chronic Coca Leaf Chewing in a Peruvian Population: A Cross-sectional Study' (2021) 23(1) *Journal of the International Acadamy of Periodontology* 11.

effect of coca leaves is a part of the TKAGR of the Andean peoples. However, in this case it did not, of itself, appear to serve as a stimulus for the work of Koller in producing a local anaesthetic within the Western medical context.

D. Quinine and Mauveine

Malaria has historically been, and still is, one of the most lethal and debilitating diseases. It is now known to be caused by a microorganisms of the genus *Plasmodium* (particularly in humans, *P. falciparum* and *P. vivax*) which are transmitted by mosquitoes of the genus *Anopheles*. These microorganisms mature and reproduce in the liver and blood cells (at different stages of their life cycle), causing cell damage and fever.[110] Before any understanding of the cause of the disease, or of its mode of transmission, it was called (in English) the ague fever and believed to be transmitted by the 'bad air' (*mal aria* in Italian) often found near stagnant water (which is of course also the breeding ground of the *Anopheles* mosquito).[111]

The beginnings of the Western understanding of the bark from which quinine is obtained is surrounded by uncertainty. On one account, it begins with the treatment in 1638 (in Lima) of the Countess of Chinchón (the wife of the then Viceroy of Peru) who was critically ill with malaria. The Viceroy's physician suggested that they use the bark of the *quinaquina* tree as a treatment, as there was a long history of its use by the Indigenous peoples of Andes for relieving fever.[112] After Chinchón's wife recovered from the fever it is reported that she brought the bark of the *quinaquina* tree back to Spain. Although these reports have since been put into doubt,[113] Carl Linnaeus, believing the story, named the genus of *quinaquina* tree, *Cinchona*, after the Countess (though in the process misspelling her name).[114]

However, previous to these events, in 1633, an Augustinian monk, Antonio de la Calancha, had recorded the properties of the *quinaquina* tree in his *The Chronicle of St Augustine*. It appears that the Spanish missionaries had been informed of the properties of the bark of the *quinaquina* by the Indigenous peoples of the 'Land of Loxa' (now Ecuador). The Jesuits began to use the *quinaquina* bark for the prophylaxis and treatment of malaria. Cardinal Johannes de Lugo, Superior General of the Jesuit Order in Rome, asked for the so-called 'Peruvian Bark' to be sent to the (malaria-troubled) Vatican in 1645. In 1655 it was used during the Papal convocation and successfully prevented deaths from malaria amongst the cardinals. In protestant Europe the *quinaquina* bark powder became known as 'Jesuit Powder'

[110] WHO Word Malaria Report 2023, www.who.int/teams/global-malaria-programme/reports/world-malaria-report-2023.

[111] Laws (n 23) 42.

[112] ibid; J Achan et al, 'Quinine, An Old Anti-malarial Drug in a Modern World: Role in the Treatment of Malaria' (2011) 10 *Malaria Journal* 144.

[113] Raviña (n 69) 126.

[114] Balick and Cox (n 21) 28; see generally: M Honigsbaum, *The Fever Trail: The Hunt for the Cure of Malaria* (London, Macmillan, 2001).

and (although the powder had already reached England by 1654) Oliver Cromwell died of malaria in 1658 having refused to be 'Jesuited' by its administration.[115]

European science in the late eighteenth century was generally looking to isolate specific chemical substances from plant extracts. With its clear advantages as an antimalarial, the *quinaquina* bark was a key focus of this effort. In 1820 Joseph Pelletier and Joseph Caventou isolated an alkaloid compound, which they called quinine, from the bark of the yellow *quinaquina* tree.[116] Since an infusion of *quinaquina* bark was unpleasant to taste and varied widely in concentration of active constituent, purified quinine had great advantages in terms of patient compliance and control of side effects over the natural bark. However, quinine itself could not be synthesised and its only source remained purification of *quinaquina* bark. The high demand for the bark led to substantial supply problems and denudation of *Cinchona* species across its natural range in the Andes. In what might be considered as an early attempt to control genetic resources, the governments of Bolivia, Ecuador, Peru and Colombia prohibited the export of *Cinchona* seeds and plants. However, many of the European imperial powers succeeded in smuggling seeds out of the Andean nations and developed their own *Cinchona* plantations within their own tropical imperial holdings. The most successful were alkaloid-rich strains of *Cinchona* planted in the Dutch East Indies.[117] Balick and Cox state that: 'By 1930 the Dutch plantations in Java produced 22 million pounds of bark, yielding 97 percent of the world's quinine.'[118] The difficulties in obtaining the *quinaquina* bark in sufficient quantities led to a drive to make artificial quinine and the effort to produce quinine through a synthetic route had begun in earnest by the mid-nineteenth century.

In early 1856, eighteen-year-old William Henry Perkin was working as a student and assistant of August Wilhelm von Hofmann at the Royal College of Chemistry in London (what is now Imperial College, London) on a project to synthesize quinine. Hofmann was trying to make the quinine alkaloid by the oxidisation of aniline with potassium dichromate. Whilst Hofmann was away in Germany during the Royal College's Easter vacation, Perkin performed one such experiment at the laboratory he had set up in his home in Stepney, London. Reacting toluidine (4-methylphenylamine) with chromic acid, Perkin was left with a dark sludge which suggested to him that the reaction had been a failure – probably due to contaminants in the reagents. He repeated the experiment using aniline (phenylamine) and again produced a dark residue.[119] On washing the sludge from the glassware with ethanol he noticed a vibrant purple colour. With perhaps something of an eye to industrial ethics, and considering this finding not to be a part of the quinine project he had been set by Hofmann, Perkin began independent work on investigating the purple compound. Working with Pullars dye works in Perth, Scotland, to find a suitable

[115] Sneader, *Drug Discovery: The Evolution of Modern Medicines* (n 69) 9; Balick and Cox (n 21) 27.
[116] Sneader, *Drug Discovery: The Evolution of Modern Medicines* (n 69) 9 and 13; Raviña (n 69) 128.
[117] Balick and Cox (n 21) 28; Raviña (n 69) 129.
[118] Balick and Cox (n 21) 29.
[119] R Porter (ed), *The Hutchinson Dictionary of Scientific Biography* (Abingdon, Helicon, 1994) 545.

mordant, Perkin found his purple compound (which he named aniline purple, but which eventually became known as mauveine) to be an effective colour-fast dye of silk and applied for a patent for it (UK Patent AD 1856 No 1984) in mid-1856.[120] Before this discovery, a strong, colour-fast purple dye, Tyrian purple, could only be obtained from sea snails of the family *Muricidae*, but this was very expensive and difficult to obtain (a reason why purple had come to be controlled by, and became symbolic of, Roman emperors).[121] Despite Hofmann's contrary advice, Perkin and his father built a factory in Greenford, Middlesex (opened in 1859) to commercially (and very successfully) exploit the aniline purple dye.[122] Interestingly (and perhaps not surprisingly), Hofmann was at this time embarking on his own development of violet dyes (which he patented in 1863).[123]

Silk dyed with Perkin's mauveine dye became popularised by Queen Victoria and the Empress Eugénie of France. The structure of Perkin's mauve dye was only elucidated in 1994.[124] However, the use of aniline as a starting point for the manufacture of vibrant, colour-fast dyes initiated by Perkin was very rapidly taken up from the mid-nineteenth century onwards.[125] Atkins states: 'Thus [Perkin] laid the foundation of all his and much of Britain's national wealth.'[126] Sneader describes Perkin's discovery as 'the single greatest stimulus for the development of organic chemistry'.[127] The discovery led to the development, particularly in Germany, of major dye manufacturers such as BASF (originally the Badische Anilin- und Soda-Fabrik company),[128] Bayer, and Höchst.[129]

The first antibiotic drug to be used systemically, the sulfonamide Prontosil, was developed within the laboratories of Bayer AG from an analine dye.[130] This stimulated the further exploration of dyes as the starting point for the development of antibiotic drugs, and many dye companies became, in turn, significant actors in drug discovery.[131] In the light of all this, Perkin's mauve has been called (perhaps without undue hyperbole) 'the colour which changed the world'.[132]

[120] S Garfield, *Mauve: How One Man Invented a Colour which Changed the World* (London, Faber & Faber, 2000).

[121] CJ Cooksey, 'Tyrian Purple: 6,6'-Dibromoindigo and Related Compounds' (2001) 6 *Molecules* 736.

[122] Porter (n 119).

[123] ibid 340.

[124] O Meth-Cohn and M Smith, 'What Did WH Perkin Actually Make when he Oxidised Aniline to Obtain Mauveine?' (1994) 1 *Journal of the Chemical Society Perkin Transactions* 5.

[125] R Brightman, 'Perkin and the Dyestuffs Industry in Britain' (1956) 177 *Nature* 80.

[126] Atkins (n 390) 88.

[127] Sneader, *Drug Discovery: A History* (n 69) 125.

[128] W Abelshauser et al, *German Industry and Global Enterprise. BASF: The History of a Company* (Cambridge, Cambridge University Press, 2004).

[129] AS Travis, 'Perkin's Mauve: Ancestor of the Organic Chemical Industry' (1990) 31(1) *Technology and Culture* 51.

[130] H Otten, 'Domagk and the Development of the Sulphonamides' (1986) 17(6) *Journal of Antimicrobial Chemotherapy* 689.

[131] E Bäumler *In Search of the Magic Bullet: Great Adventures in Modern Drug Research* (London, Thames & Hudson, 1965) 15.

[132] S Garfield, *Mauve: How One Man Invented a Colour which Changed the World* (London, Faber & Faber, 2000).

In 1918 German chemist Paul Rabe eventually determined the structure of quinine.[133] In 1944 details of a de novo route for quinine synthesis were published by the American chemists Robert Woodward and William Doering.[134] Although since then there have been many improvements in the method for the synthesis of quinine, extraction from *Cinchona* bark remains more economically viable.[135] The quinolone ring structure seen within the core of the quinine molecule has also served as a starting point for the development of chloroquine and mefloquine, which are used as antiparisitic drugs.[136] Quinine also served to stimulate another research trail when in 1887 German chemist Ludwig Knorr (whilst again seeking to make a quinoline derivative) made a chemical called phenazon (also referred to as antipyrine) which had antipyretic and analgesic effects. Phenazon became the basis of a family of pyrazole drugs which were very widely used in pain relief.[137]

E. The Vinca Alkaloids – Antitumour Effects

The Madagascar or rosy periwinkle (*Catharanthus roseus* previously categorised as *Vinca rosea*) is a plant originally indigenous to Madagascar but which has long been cultivated for ornamental purposes across the tropics and subtropics.[138] In 1949, inspired by stories of folk use in the Caribbean of the rosy periwinkle in the treatment of diabetes, endocrinologist Robert Noble examined the effect of rosy periwinkle extract on rat blood glucose.[139] Working as he was at the (decidedly non-tropical) University of Western Ontario, Noble sourced leaves from the rosy periwinkle plant from Jamaica and prepared an extract from those. Neither oral nor injected administration of that extract affected blood glucose levels. However, after injecting the animals with extract, Noble found that the rats seemed to suffer from an enhanced level of infection. Investigating this further, Noble found that, after an initial enhancement, treated rats showed greatly reduced leucocyte levels which seemed to be the result of damage to the bone marrow of the animals. These effects were similar to those seen with then current antitumour drugs and Noble wondered whether the extract might contain an agent which might work to treat leukaemia (which is caused by excessive levels of abnormal leucocytes). Together with an organic chemist, Charles Beer, Noble isolated the alkaloid, vincristine

[133] P Rabe and K Kindler, 'Uber die partielle Synthese des Chinins. Zur Kenntnis der China-Alkaloide XIX' (1918) 51 *Berichte der Deutschen Chemischen Gesellschaft* 466.

[134] RB Woodward and WE Doering, 'The Total Synthesis of Quinine' (1944) 66(5) *Journal of the American Chemical Society* 849.

[135] Raviña (n 69) 129.

[136] S Sharma and N Anand, 'Approaches to Design and Synthesis of Antiparasitic Drugs' (1997) 24 *Pharmacochemistry Library* 393; SK Bardal et al, *Applied Pharmacology* (Amsterdam, Elsevier, 2011) 233.

[137] Raviña (n 69) 26.

[138] M van Bergen and W Snoeijer, '*Catharanthus* G.Don. The Madagascar Periwinkle and Related Species' (1996) 96(3) *Wageningen Agricultural University Papers* 1.

[139] J Duffin, 'Poisoning the Spindle: Serendipity and Discovery of the Anti-tumor Properties of the Vinca Alkaloids' (2000) 17(1–2) *Canadian Bulletin of Medical History* 155.

(originally named vincaleukoblastine), from the periwinkle extract and this was found to have an inhibitory effect on transplanted tumours. In 1958, this work was reported at the New York Academy of Sciences.[140]

In parallel to the work undertaken by Noble and Beer, the American pharmaceutical company Eli Lilly and Co, having been similarly stimulated by reports of the folk use of rosy periwinkle against diabetes – although this time in the Philippines – had (entirely separately from the work of Nobel and Beer), examined the effect of extracts of the plant (obtained from the southern United States) for antidiabetic efficacy. Although no such efficacy had been found, Eli Lilly put the extract through their general pharmacological screening programme and a beneficial effect was observed when it used against transplanted acute lymphocyte leukaemia in mice.[141] This work eventually led to the use of a further alkaloid found in rosy periwinkle extract, vinblastine, against lung and breast cancer.[142] Further pharmacological screening studies at the Institut de Chimie des Substances Naturelles at Gif-sur-Yvette, Paris, have since led to the development of two semi-synthetic analogues of the naturally occurring vinca alkaloids –vindesine and vinorelbine – both of which have antitumour activity.[143]

The vinca alkaloids are believed to exert their antitumour effects by having an effect on disruption of cell division through an effect on the tubulin microtubules within the mitotic spindles which are used to separate eukaryotic chromosomes during cell mitosis.[144]

[140] RL Noble et al, 'Role of Chance Observations in Chemotherapy' (1958) 76 *Annals of the New York Academy of Science* 882.

[141] Sneader, *Drug Discovery: The Evolution of Modern Medicines* (n 69) 356; Sneader, *Drug Discovery: A History* (n 69) 102; G Dutfield, 'Protecting the Rights of Indigenous Peoples: Can Prior Informed Consent Help?' in R Wynberg et al (eds), *Indigenous Peoples, Consent and Benefit Sharing: Lessons from the San-Hoodia Case* (Dordrecht, Springer, 2009) 53, 63; Raviña (n 69) 157.

[142] N Neuss et al, 'Vinca Alkaloids. III.1. Characterisation of Leurosine and Vincaleukoblastine, New Alkaloids from *Vinca rosea* Linn' (1959) 81 *Journal of the American Chemical Society* 4754.

[143] Sneader, *Drug Discovery: A History* (n 69) 103; Raviña (n 69) 158.

[144] L Wilson et al, 'On the Mechanism of Action of Vinblastine' (1974) 63 *Journal of Cell Biology* 373a; RH Himes et al, 'Action of the Vinca Alkaloids Vincristine, Vinblastine, and Desacetyl Vinblastine Amide on Microtubules in Vitro' (1976) 36 *Cancer Research* 3798; MA Jordan and L Wilson, 'Microtubules as a Target for Anticancer Drugs' (2004) 4 *Nature Reviews Cancer* 253.

6

The Application of Philosophical Justifications for Positive Rights in TKAGR to the Serendipitous Discovery of Second Uses

I. Introduction

The analysis of the topography of drug discovery set out in chapter one supported the claim that (notwithstanding significant admixture with other information), there always remains a causation *in fact* thread by which even the most remote downstream uses of a piece of TKAGR can be said to have taken some advantage of the original 'inspiration'. The analysis also showed that the majority of the causal chains which run from the 'inspiration' provided by a piece of traditional knowledge to a marketed drug appear to show no special features that might give rise to a break in the chain of causation *in law*; the progression commonly resembles a smooth continuum involving many sequential and accumulative contributions. That analysis did, however (with inspiration from problems encountered in patent law), identify 'serendipitous' discoveries of second uses of the resource as a point at which the third-party downstream contribution may, arguably, change the nature of the downstream product relative the original Indigenous contribution and that such serendipitous discoveries may act as a putative 'crux point' at which the key high-level justifications for an ABS right in traditional knowledge may be brought to bear. It is the aim of this chapter to perform that analysis.

II. Policy Options

To assist with a consistent analysis across each philosophical justification (and in coming to a synthesis of the approaches in chapter seven) this work will examine to what extent (if at all) the findings from each analysis comply with five potential policy options in relation to the legal treatment of a serendipitous discovery of a second use based on a piece of TKAGR.

In the Rawlsian *maximin* analysis set out later in this chapter, the person in Rawls's 'original position' is asked to choose between these five policy options or (as they are termed there) 'decisions'. For consistency, this 'decision' terminology (and their numbering) is used throughout the entire study. These decisions are as follows:

- in decision d_1 it is decided there should be no veto right to TKAGR *at all*;
- in decision d_2 it is decided that there should be a veto right to TKAGR which extends to all and anything which is derived *in fact* from the original piece of TKAGR, without limitation;
- in decision d_3 it is decided that although there should be an access right to TKAGR it is also decided that any such access right should not extend to preventing the use of a product arising out of a truly serendipitous discovery (even where such discovery would not *in fact* have been made without the lead provided by the traditional knowledge associated with the genetic resource);
- in decision d_4 it is decided that although there should be an access right to TKAGR it is also decided that any such access right should not extend to preventing the use of a product arising out of a truly serendipitous discovery (even where such discovery would not in fact have been made without the lead provided by the traditional knowledge associated with the genetic resource). However, any such use is subject to a *compensatory mechanism* based on an apportionment determined by an assessment of relative contributions; and
- In decision d_5 it is decided that, although there should be an access right to TKAGR, it is also decided that any such access right should not extend to preventing any downstream use of a product. However, any such use is subject to a compensatory mechanism based on an apportionment determined by an assessment of relative contributions.

III. Deontological Justifications

A. The Application of Lockean Labour-Desert Theory

i. Initial Considerations: Ownership and Temporal Scope

As was stated in chapter four (in section III.A), there are some difficult questions to be addressed in relation to the application of either labour-desert or personality-right approaches to ownership of TKAGR, not least due to the lack of certainty of subject matter for the right. The question of ownership is especially acute in light of the transgenerational evolution of TKAGR over a long course of time, with potentially multiple authors and influences.

Similarly, the forward-looking individuation and backward-looking origination and in-imitativeness boundaries of any right cannot help but touch on questions of *temporal* scope. Backward-looking boundaries need to be examined at the time the protected innovation is made or (more likely for a right in traditional knowledge) when the claim to the 'innovation' is made. Forward-looking boundaries need to be assessed at the time the claim is asserted against another or when a third party is seeking to individuate a follow-on concept from an inspiration.

Under Articles 7 and 5(5) of the Nagoya Protocol the rights in TKAGR are not time limited (and neither is the restriction on use of genetic resources under Articles 6 and 5). Current WIPO proposals for positive rights in traditional knowledge similarly do not envisage a time limitation.[1] This may appear on the face of it highly unusual – the majority of intellectual property rights are time limited,[2] and this time limitation is considered by Hughes to be part of the 'social bargain' between the grant of rights to innovators and the preservation of the right of others to innovate.[3]

It is interesting to note that when one examines those time-limited rights one realises that there is often, and of necessity often has to be, a close link between a temporal limitation and *certainty* of the originator. For example, Article 7(1) of the Berne Convention requires that signatory states should have a minimum term of copyright protection of the life of the author and fifty years after his death.[4] Similarly, Article 7*bis* of that Convention requires that an identical minimum term of protection shall also apply in the case of a work of joint authorship, provided that the terms measured from the death of the author shall be calculated from the death of the last surviving author.

As was stated above, the question of 'authorship' is acute in light of the transgenerational evolution of TKAGR. There is likely to be no single or identifiable 'author' upon which to hang a start point for the time limitation of the right. This lack of an identifiable author is problematic from a pure natural rights perspective. As we have seen much of the classical natural rights account, whether Lockean desert or based on personality rights, relies on the extension of the inalienable freedom of the individual, and in our present case that 'individual' is either lost to history or (more likely) consists of a number of separate individuals (all similarly lost to history) who have developed the knowledge over time. However, if we are to accept that there is a natural rights justification for a positive right in TKAGR, we may have to similarly accept that there can be no temporal limitation on the positive right. It is, in fact, difficult to see how such a right could function with such a limitation. Such a lack of temporal limitation is entirely consistent with looking at the positive right as a right of the *entire* Indigenous community. As Gibson argues: 'Indigenous and traditional interests in medicinal and agricultural knowledge, cultural expressions, stories, dance, and so on, are integral to

[1] See eg WIPO/GRTKF/IC/28.

[2] Those which are not time limited include registered trade marks, rights in passing off and unfair competition (all of which are fundamentally orientated toward the protection of trading goodwill) and the right to prevent the inequitable disclosure of confidential information.

[3] J Hughes, 'The Philosophy of Intellectual Property' (1988) 77 *Georgetown Law Journal* 287, 296.

[4] Berne Convention for the Protection of Literary and Artistic Works of 1886 (as last amended on 28 September 1979), www.wipo.int/treaties/en/text.jsp?file_id=283698#P127_22000.

continuing Indigenous and traditional cultures. That significance and relationship to the community exists in perpetuity.'[5]

As a heuristic tool, the current work will seek to limit the number of variables in the overall problem and assume in the Lockean and personality right analyses undertaken below that the *inherent* problems of ownership are resolved. Similarly, with regard to the analyses set out below, it has been assumed, again as a heuristic tool, that all positive rights to control the use of TKAGR are *without* temporal limitation.

ii. The Importance of 'Contribution'

Let us assume that an Indigenous group tells a bioprospector that 'plant A is good for treating ailment X'. From a Lockean perspective there is an argument that the group has a justifiable claim over that which they have contributed, namely that plant A is good for treating ailment X. However, does that *specific* basis allow the Indigenous group to *also* have a justifiable claim to general 'therapeutic usefulness' which would cover not only the treatment of ailment 'X' or creation of effect 'B' (which was their specific 'contribution') but also to the treatment of ailment 'Y' (or even ailment 'Z'), or is their supportable claim limited only to that which was their *original* contribution? The difference is potentially crucial.

There is a unifying factor which is entirely central to a Lockean/labour-desert-based account of the propertisation of intangibles. That is that the right to control the use of information is inextricably linked to the *contribution* being made by the individual seeking to claim a right over the information. Contribution here is akin to the 'mixing of labour' with the commons in Locke's original account; it is the conception of an idea which pulls that idea out of the commons of 'yet to be had ideas' and into the ownership of the author of the idea. Without contribution it is impossible to see why there should be any 'reward' or indeed to whom one would give it. However, although there can be no reward without contribution, we are left asking what *degree* of contribution is required for there to be a reward? Here, then, we see the term 'contribution' needing to encompass elements of Gibson's 'in-imitativeness', a sense that desert is based on achieving a 'worthy' level of originality and non-obviousness from what has gone before. We must also examine the contribution of others who are using the first idea as an inspiration: at what point does their contribution outweigh the contribution of the originators and achieve a sufficient level of in-imitativeness such that their development is 'worthy':

(a) of its own protection; and
(b) to break free of the original idea?

Within a consequentialist account, where one is seeking to affect a particular outcome through imposition of a particular positive law, one can envisage how

[5] J Gibson, *Community Resources: Intellectual Property, International Trade and Protection of Traditional Knowledge* (Farnham, Ashgate, 2005) 121.

one might look to set appropriate thresholds of in-imitativeness. Although it would undoubtedly be extremely difficult in practice, within this approach there is, in theory, a way of 'titrating' your threshold such as to give the effect (or balance of effects) you wish to achieve. One might think here of ongoing debates and case law surrounding the setting of an inventive step requirement within patent law, but there are, of course, very many more examples.

In contrast, the setting of a threshold for in-imitativeness within a Lockean account is harder, perhaps even impossible. How does one know what *degree* of contribution should deserve reward? This, of course, echoes Attas's 'uncertainty of origination/individuation' attack on the entire natural rights justification for intellectual property.[6] Although we can immediately acknowledge these potential difficulties, is there anything that a Lockean analysis can bring to the current problem?

As stated above, within the natural rights account we can, at the very least, say that without *any* contribution *at all* there can be no reward. To what extent can we take this very basic proposition to investigate competing claims to contribution? We need to know what 'claims' are being asserted before we can make judgement upon them. To do so we would have to identify, and deconstruct, the 'building blocks' of the concepts in play – what will be referred to here as the epistemological 'elements' of a putative contribution. In the present case, the crucial question is to ask: what epistemological elements have been contributed by the Indigenous holders of the information that could give rise to a right to control? What type of 'claim' is being made by the Indigenous group? How would this claim compare with that made by a third-party discoverer of a serendipitous discovery of a second use? Once the epistemological elements have been identified, we will then need to determine from whom they have originated. Given the potential complexity of meaning of the term 'contribution' within the Lockean account, within the analysis set out below 'contribution' will be used in what is its most basic way – the test applied will be the mere *independence* of contribution of an epistemological element from third party contributions of other elements. Let us consider the following two scenarios:

(a) The 'North versus South Scenario' in which, with respect to the same plant A, we find that a group of Indigenous peoples (the 'North' group) have identified only that it can treat ailment X, whereas another group of Indigenous people (the 'South' group) have identified that it can treat ailment Y (but do not know of the effect on X); and
(b) The 'North versus West Scenario' in which Western pharmaceutical company West knows, on the basis of the traditional knowledge divulged by Group North that plant A is useful for the treatment of ailment X and begins working on plant A and extracts the previously unknown pharmaceutically active

[6] D Attas, 'Lockean Justifications of Intellectual Property' in A Gosseries et al (eds), *Intellectual Property and Theories of Justice* (London, Palgrave Macmillan 2008) 29, 53.

compound, Red, from it. Red is found to have an even more potent effect on ailment X than plant A. However, during the testing of Red in animals an *entirely unexpected* biological response is noted which leads to the investigation of Red as a treatment for ailment Y. Red becomes a successful (and profitable) drug for the treatment of Y.

The knowledge of North and South can arguably be divided into two epistemological elements:

(a) Knowledge of very existence of plant A; and
(b) Knowledge therapeutic effect of plant A:
    (i) in the case of North that it treats ailment X; and
    (ii) in the case of South that it treats ailment'.

The knowledge of West arguably consists of three epistemological elements:

(a) Knowledge of existence of plant A (knowledge obtained from North);
(b) Knowledge that plant A treats ailment X (knowledge obtained from North); and
(c) Knowledge that plant A treats ailment Y (knowledge discovered by West).

Assuming, as a heuristic tool, that a right to control information is dependent upon the *independent* contribution of the putative right holder, what would that give us in relation to each epistemological element?

In the North versus South scenario, *both* North *and* South have found that plant A is therapeutically valuable. North understands that A can treat X (but not Y) whereas South understands that A can treat Y (but not X). In each case, their understanding is contingent upon understanding that plant A exists and is therapeutically valuable (which has been independently determined by both North and South). However, in both cases the scope of their understanding of the *whole* range of therapeutic effect is partially compromised. If their rights are *exactly* coterminous with their independent contribution, then arguably North can control the use of A for treatment of X (but not Y) and South can control the use of A for treatment of Y (but not X).

In the West versus North scenario, *only* North has independently found that plant A is therapeutically valuable (what will be described as the broad 'claim'). North understands that A can treat X (but not Y), whereas West understands that A can treat Y (and X). For both North and West, their narrow understanding is contingent upon the understanding that plant A exists *and* is therapeutically valuable (the broad 'claim'). However, in marked contrast to the North versus South scenario, West's broader understanding has not been *independently* determined by West, but by North. If North's rights are coterminous with their *independent* contribution, then North should control West's use of A for treatment of X.

If West's rights are coterminous with their *independent* contribution, then West has in fact made no *entirely* independent contribution – its understanding of the effect of A on Y is contingent upon the broad knowledge (the existence and therapeutic usefulness of A) determined by North. However, North has not *independently* contributed the understanding that A can treat Y – the understanding of the effect of A on Y has been determined by West (even though West's understanding is contingent upon knowledge determined by North).

The concept of rights being coterminous with independent contributions would seem to reasonably solve the North versus South conundrum. However, applied to West versus North it leaves us in a state of limbo – although it obviously supports North's control over the use of plant A to treat X, in relation to plant A treating disease Y, West has not independently arrived at an understanding that A treats Y. However, importantly, *neither has North*. They have at most made only a *part contribution*. So, on an 'independently arrived at' test, North cannot assert control ownership over the use of A for Y as it has not contributed the 'beneficial effect on Y' element.

Clearly, using this test gives a very limited outcome: one would only have a right to control over *all* those epistemological elements you have *independently* conceived (or discovered). No broader claims that encompass other narrower epistemological elements would be permitted, but neither would any new narrow claims be awarded. So, if we are going to allow any future claims such a strict test cannot apply. However, going back to Attas's criticism above, although one can perhaps make such a system work, the doing of this (for example, by setting thresholds for in-imitativeness) is a question of the imposition of positive law, not of *natural* law.

iii. Types of Claim

If we are to permit North to have a claim over West's later use of plant A for treatment of Y, we need to consider how such a claim would be structured. Such a broader claim might be considered to operate in two ways:

(a) as an 'inchoate' claim; or
(b) as an 'inherent' claim

iv. An 'Inchoate' Claim

Here we are saying that within North's original discovery there are in fact *two* claims. One is the narrow claim to the use of plant A for treatment of X. The other is an inchoate claim to 'use of plant A for other therapeutic purposes which will incorporate use of plant A for other therapeutic indications'. The validity of this inchoate claim is dependent upon North's narrower discovery of 'the use of plant A for treatment of X' – this has to be the case because without the support of the narrower claim there can be no claim at all. This inchoate claim is in some way 'made whole' at some future date when a further discovery is made in relation to plant A.

Is such an inchoate claim which catches later developments 'as and when' they arise consistent with a Lockean account of propertisation of ideas? Looking at the problem by way of analogy to Locke's 'inclosure' of common land, one could imagine that the claimant is inclosing one small area (based upon the narrow contribution) from the commons. The claimant is also inclosing a larger area which corresponds to the larger (though partial) claim. This area may not be so developed as the narrower one – perhaps only services and drainage have been put in – but nothing has yet been built. The question remains, however, if I come to build a house on the serviced and drained land, does the original claimant have an *absolute* right to bar me from building, or only a right to charge me for the provision of services and drainage. If so, how much can he charge? One might argue that the charge should be in line with their part contribution, but how is *that* to be determined? Again, the Lockean natural rights approach per se desperately struggles to address questions of degree. However, although a justification for an absolute bar to downstream use cannot be ruled out, we can see that the idea of a partial inchoate claim, justified by a partial contribution and warranting a partial degree of compensation, is not inherently *inconsistent* with the Lockean account for rights in intellectual property.

v. An 'Inherent' Claim

Within an Indigenous context, when a plant (or an extract from it) is administered to a patient it is possible that the active compound (or compounds) found within the plant will (dependent on dose) have *all* their pharmacological effects to a greater or lesser degree. However, only *some* of these effects, the more obvious ones, may be recognised by the Indigenous users of the plant. Let us suppose that West's 'serendipitously discovered' second medical effect was *in fact* present throughout the use by North, but remained unrecognised. Can, North, the Indigenous originators of the 'first' medical use say that any serendipitously discovered second medical effect was *inherently* disclosed within the first administration, and that this was part of its 'contribution'. If so, might that, of itself, support a claim to broad ownership that the plant was simply 'therapeutically' or (still more broadly) 'biologically' useful?

Questions relating to inherency have exercised patent law for decades.[7] The crucial question has been whether the discovery of a new technical effect in relation to a previously known compound should form the basis for a patent to that new technical effect, even where that technical effect was *inherently* present in the previous use of the compound, but not recognised.

Generally speaking, case law in EPC signatory states and the EPO (notably the approach of the Enlarged Board of Appeal of the European Patent Office in *Mobil Friction Reducing Additive G 2/88* and *Bayer G 6/88*) and in the United States[8]

[7] JM Mueller and DS Chisum, 'Enabling Patent Law's Inherent Anticipation Doctrine' (2008) 45 *Houston Law Review* 1101.

[8] DL Burk and MA Lemley, 'Inherency' (2005) 47(2) *William and Mary Law Review* 371.

supports the proposition that disclosure of a product for a narrower use does not prevent a patent for a later-discovered use, even if the later-discovered effect was inherently present in the first use. The crucial factor to be considered is whether previous disclosures, or patents relating to the compound, have made the 'hidden' effect available to the public. If so, a patent for the second effect will be invalid for lack of novelty. Mere prior use (in which the hidden effect is not recognised) is insufficient to invalidate such a second patent.

The case of *Merrell Dow Pharmaceuticals*[9] before the UK House of Lords, examined the related question of whether a previously unknown mechanism for achieving a known effect was patentable. Here Merrell Dow had discovered that its antihistamine drug, terfenadine, actually mediated its effect through a carboxylic acid metabolite of terfenadine (fexofenadine, produced in the liver of humans), not through terfenadine itself as had been previously believed. Merrell Dow sought to patent the acid metabolite. The court held that the original terfenadine patent disclosed how to use terfenadine, notwithstanding that the mechanism by which this was achieved was unknown.

This approach is consistent with the approach taken in *Mobil*; the crucial difference between this situation in *Merrell Dow* and that in *Mobil* is that in *Merrell Dow* the claims in both patents were directed to the same end – the antihistamine effect – rather than to a hidden second effect. In *Mobil* the claims in the patent in suit were directed to an entirely different use (friction reduction) as opposed to antirust effects.

Within EPC signatory states, the patentability of products for therapeutic use can appear somewhat byzantine. Article 54(4) EPC ensures that one can have a patent to a therapeutic or diagnostic use of a known substance or composition provided that such use of the known substance is not already known. In practice this means that the first discoverer of the 'first medical use' of a compound is entitled to a broad protection for the compound.[10]

So-called 'second medical use' claims under EPC patent law are also permitted, but have received special legislative treatment. This treatment has been driven in very large part by the impact of the exclusion (for public policy reasons) of methods of medical treatment, surgery and diagnosis from patentability.[11] The potential problem was that where a second therapeutic effect was identified for a known chemical compound (all else in the invention being the same as that which went before) any novelty would reside only in a method of treatment, which is specifically excluded under EPC Article 53(c). This problem exercised many patent offices, and courts (and led to some interesting legal fictions).[12] However,

[9] *Merrell Dow Pharmaceuticals Inc v HN Norton and Co Ltd and Penn Pharmaceuticals Ltd* [1996] RPC 76; See generally H Cline, 'The House of Lords Decision in Merrell Dow Pharmaceuticals -v- Norton Limited and Penn Pharmaceuticals' (1995) 14 *Biotechnology Law Report* 956.

[10] See eg S4A(3) UK Patents Act 1977 and UKIPO Manual of Patent Practice on s 4A(3).

[11] EPC Art 53(c); see also s 4A(1) UK Patents Act 1977.

[12] See eg Legal Advice from the Swiss Federal Intellectual Property Office (FIPO), dated 30 May 1984 [1984] OJEPO 581; Eisai (Second medical indication) G 5/83 [1984] OJEPO 64.

the problem was eventually dealt with by way of a specific legislative allowance[13] (although the effect of claims permitted by such allowance has been the subject of litigation).[14] Any second (or subsequent) medical use patent (narrowed by 'use') serves its commercial purpose either by extending patent protection for the first patentee or by allowing a second patentee to have rights (although those rights will be subject to the first, broader, patent during its monopoly period).

vi. Inchoate Claims versus Inherent Claims

Whilst the 'inchoate' claim envisaged above may seem to be achieving a similar end to the inherent claim by increasing the scope of protection, when we look closely, we see that both claims are achieving that end in distinctly different ways.

Returning to our Lockean commons analogy, rather than the inchoate claim based on the part contribution (services and drains) situation seen above, in the inherent claim situation our Lockean builder is essentially saying: 'I have built some houses over here (which I am claiming) but in doing so I have inadvertently built some other (invisible) houses over there, of which you (and I) were until now unaware, but which will stop you from building your identical (to the invisible houses) houses on that land.'

If such an approach *was* acceptable within a Lockean model, one might envisage that it would be less amenable to a 'payment for services provided solution' and more consistent with creating an absolute bar. However, it seems this approach has significantly greater problems than mere questions of degree. It is hard to see that an invisible house of which no one (not even the builder) knows can be a contribution deserving of reward.

There are, as is stressed elsewhere, significant problems in reading across from posited patent law to a natural rights account. However, looking at European patent law's approach to inherency, we can perhaps say that the approach taken in *Mobil* and *Bayer* is broadly consistent with the natural rights account for property rights set out above. In *Mobil* the friction-reducing effect of the compound (which had originally been used as a rust inhibitor) had been unknown, and the 'discovery' of this new effect was deemed to provide adequate novelty to warrant a new patent. The new understanding was a 'contribution' and was rewarded with *separate* protection.

In marked contrast, the provisions of European patent law which allow broad claims to therapeutic use in relation to *first medical use claims* appear to be inconsistent with Lockean natural rights account in that the allowable claim seems broader than underlying contribution.

[13] s 4A(4) UK Patents Act 1977; UKIPO Practice Notice: Patents Act 1977 – Second Medical Use Claims (www.ipo.gov.uk/pro-types/pro-patent/p-law/p-pn/p-pn-medical.htm); see also ED Ventose, 'Patent Protection for Second and Further Medical Uses Under the European Patent Convention' (2009) 6(1) *SCRIPTed* 57 (www.law.ed.ac.uk/ahrc/script-ed/vol6-1/ventose.asp).

[14] See eg *Warner-Lambert Company LLC v Generics (UK) Ltd and Oths* [2018] UKSC 56.

vii. 'Fundamental' Elements

We have established above that if North *is* to have control over the use of A to treat disease Y it needs to have a justifiable claim to the 'broader' understanding of the general 'therapeutic usefulness' of A. Might it argue that the understanding that A exists, and is therapeutically valuable, is in some way a *fundamental* piece of information in the calculation which 'trumps' other (newly determined) epistemological elements? What would such a 'fundamental' epistemological element look like? One approach might be to argue that:

(a) an epistemological element is *fundamental* to the drug discovery process if further developments would not have happened (or not happened in the way they did) without that element; and
(b) all developments dependent on that *fundamental* epistemological element are subject to control. Applying this definition of fundamental to the North versus West scenario, the knowledge of the existence and therapeutic usefulness of plant A was undeniably fundamental to West's discovery (in that it would not have been arrived at but for North's knowledge) and accordingly the new use should be subject to control by North.

This is, of course, an entirely circular argument – the definition of 'fundamental' is defined here by what arises out of it – if the distal discovery does not arise out of the initial information, then the original information is not fundamental in relation to the discovery. It is also, merely, a causation *in fact* test: all distal use would be subject to control – notwithstanding that the originator(s) of the original information could never have ever anticipated that distal use.

The advocate of a total veto over all downstream use (our decision d_2) might argue that this definition of 'fundamental' is correct. However, what we are missing in the Lockean account is a reason to say why should be so – an answer to the question: why is the fundamental element *so* fundamental that the contribution of others, no matter how significant, cannot be recognised? Again, a natural rights account runs into difficult problems with determining degree.

Setting any definition of *fundamental* can clearly be done through positive law. It is, however, in reality, the same as setting thresholds for individuation and in-imitativeness of a follow-on right and this brings us directly back to the problem of setting the limits on the 'inchoate' partial claim discussed above.

viii. 'Too-Broad' Claims and 'Insufficient' Epistemological Elements

An alternative approach to our problem may be to analyse what would constitute 'too broad' a claim. Let us consider the two following scenarios:

(a) North, thinking to make claims to various plants in its environment, and knowing that plant A is without effect, fraudulently claims that plant A treats X (when it does not). Whilst investigating the claim, pharmaceutical company East uncovers the fact that plant A treats Y.

(b) North, thinking to make claims to various plants in its environment, merely makes a broad claim that plant A is therapeutically beneficial, but refuses to disclose in what way. In fact, it does not know whether it is effective; it merely makes the assertion as part of a 'land grab' for rights in knowledge. Following up this broad 'lead', pharmaceutical company Down uncovers that plant A does, in fact, successfully treat disease Y.

In both cases East's and Down's discoveries have only been arrived at following North's assertion of a therapeutic benefit of plant A. Although it seems intuitively wrong for North to be able properly assert a right to control over East's and Down's use of Plant A, why is this so?

North's claims in North versus East and North versus Down are fraudulent. Can such fraudulent behaviour give rise to a Lockean natural right? Aquinas's *Secunda Secundæ* of his *Summa Theologiæ* examines certain virtues and vices in detail.[15] At Question 77 of *Secunda Secundæ* Aquinas turns his attention to the concept of fraud committed in the course of buying and selling.[16] He concludes that:

> Ambrose says (De Offic. iii, 11): 'It is manifestly a rule of justice that a good man should not depart from the truth, nor inflict an unjust injury on anyone, nor have any connection with fraud. … A threefold fault may be found pertaining to the thing which is sold. One, in respect of the thing's substance: and if the seller be aware of a fault in the thing he is selling, he is guilty of a fraudulent sale, so that the sale is rendered unlawful.'[17]

Although North's fraudulent claim is not based upon fraud within trading per se, we can perhaps extrapolate from Aquinas's thinking that taking fraudulent advantage is not permitted within a natural rights account for property. Indeed, Locke himself is keen to stress that an initial acquisition of property in the natural state can occur only where such acquisition does not disadvantage the wider community – acquisition can happen only where there remains 'enough and as good' in the commons for others. It is hard to see how a fraudulent acquisition could sit within this community framework.

There is, however, a further reason why such claims lack a Lockean basis. As discussed above the key to the Lockean/labour-desert thesis is that a man may properly acquire that which is his desert and no more. Taking a pure desert approach to rights in the claimed traditional knowledge in both scenarios, North has not actually made any genuine contribution *at the time the claim is made*. The claim to therapeutic usefulness is not supported by any specific example – it is essentially insufficient to be worthy of 'reward'. As far as North actually knows, plant A has no therapeutic benefit. Taking a parallel from patent law, the claim

[15] F Copleston, *Thomas Aquinas* (London, Search Press, 1976) 12; Brian Davies, *Aquinas* (London, Continuum, 2002) 4.

[16] M Lefébure, *St Thomas Aquinas: Summa Theologiæ*, vol 38: *Injustice* (Blackfriars, London 1975) 213.

[17] Fathers of the English Dominican Province, *Summa Theologiæ of St Thomas Aquinas* (2nd and rev edn, 1920) (2a 2æ, Q77) (www.newadvent.org/summa/3077.htm).

to therapeutic usefulness might be said to extend beyond the scope of the actual invention.[18] Although, in each case a genuine contribution is eventually arrived at (by East, and Down respectively), this could not have been known, or even suspected, before those discoveries were made.

However, let us look at one further scenario: North mistakenly (but honestly) believes that plant A treats X when in fact it does not. The effect that North has observed is in fact caused by a mould growing on the plant although this is unknown. Following up this mistaken 'lead', pharmaceutical company Up uncovers that plant A successfully treats disease Y, an effect that was unknown by North.

Here, there has been no fraud committed – the error is genuine. When we apply a desert basis to justify a right to control of downstream use, we find ourselves in a position where the Lockean analogy becomes somewhat stretched. Although North has not *actually* made the contribution it thinks it has, it has arguably made *a* contribution – we know that, in North's hands at least, plant A is effective against X. Is this mistaken contribution sufficient to justify protection? Arguably it (and other permutations of mistaken contribution) are no different from a true understanding that 'A treats X', so perhaps should be treated no differently. Such an analysis does not, however, assist us any further in answering the question as to whether the broader claim to 'therapeutic usefulness' is justifiable.

ix. Conclusions from a Lockean Perspective

The underlying principle of the Lockean justification for intellectual property can be distilled into the statement that the justifiable scope of protection given by a right has to be coterminous with the contribution of the person claiming that right. However, that account struggles to tell us what that *contribution* actually means, both the contribution of the right holder and the competing contribution of a third party who has developed a follow-on concept from (or made a discovery from) the original idea.

The analysis conducted above would seem to suggest both that:

(a) the idea of an 'inherent claim', in which the unrecognised presence of the second use within the first Indigenous use provides the basis for a claim over the second use once it is made, seems more difficult to support from a Lockean perspective; and
(b) there is no inherent conflict with the Lockean justification where one envisages a partial inchoate claim based upon a partial contribution and giving rise to a partial degree of control.

However, what this entire analysis *really* demonstrates is the inherent difficulties the Lockean account faces in relation to origination and individuation. We see

[18] See, for example, the enablement requirement under Title 35 USC 112; the requirement for disclosure of the invention under EPC Art 83; and the requirement for claims to be supported by the specification under EPC Art 84.

that setting levels of in-imitativeness (particularly in relation to follow-on works) are absolutely crucial in terms of establishing scope, but can realistically only be done through the imposition of *positive* law and not in some way 'divined' from natural rights.

No matter how we attempt to analyse things in terms of 'inchoate' and 'inherent' claims, the complete uncertainty surrounding both the meaning of 'contribution' and ways to compare competing contributions under the Lockean justification means we cannot entirely exclude that a *partial* contribution will warrant an *absolute* right to veto the downstream use arising out of the serendipitous discovery. One might suspect that for this to happen the initial partial contribution would need to be considered so 'fundamental' as to trump all other subsequent third-party contributions. However, under this account we simply have no certainty that an understanding as to the existence of a plant with a particular therapeutic effect is appropriately *fundamental* so as to supersede all other subsequent contributions such that they are deemed unworthy of reward, or indeed otherwise. We are in the dark.

However, where we have conflicting partial contributions what we can say is that it is not inconsistent with a Lockean account to dispense with an *absolute* veto and in its place provide permission for the user of the serendipitous (or indeed lesser) discovery to use their discovery subject to an acknowledgement of the partial contribution made by the holder of the traditional knowledge (perhaps based on compulsory licensing, apportionment of reward/compensatory damages).

So applying the analysis set out above to our policy options d_1 to d_5 we find that the Lockean justification does not appear to support decision d_1 (no veto/compensation at all).

We find that neither d_4 (limited veto with compensation) nor d_5 (no veto but compensation) are inconsistent with the Lockean account. However, given the problem of defining contribution, the account can give us no concrete guidance as to which of those approaches is more justified. With regard to decision d_2, again all we can really say with any confidence is that the total veto of *all* downstream uses is not inconsistent with the Lockean model.

Looking at the question of which approach is more justifiable as between d_3 and d_4, we might intuitively say that the provision of compensation commensurate with degree of contribution would appear more fundamentally consistent with a Lockean account than not providing any compensation at all. We should note, however, that since the Lockean approach cannot give us any absolute guidance as to the definition of contribution, it might be difficult to say that a situation in which the degree of contribution was so minimal as not to warrant compensation was inconsistent with a Lockean justification. Perhaps all we can realistically say is that d_4 (limited veto with compensation) seems to be closer 'in spirit' to Locke's account of propertisation than does d_3 (limited veto without compensation). These outcomes are summarised in Table 7.

Table 7 Application of Lockean justification to potential policy options (up arrows signify support for the decision; down arrows signify lack of support for the decision)

Decision	**Lockean labour-desert**
d_1 (no veto, no compensation)	↓↓↓
d_2 (total veto)	↑ (Not inconsistent)
d_3 (limited veto)	↑ (Not inconsistent)
d_4 (limited veto + compensation)	↑ (Not inconsistent)
d_5 (no veto, but compensation)	↑ (Not inconsistent)

B. Rights Based on Personality

Although their justifications of rights differed somewhat, Fichte and Hegel argued that a right that protects how ideas are *expressed* should exist. Kant developed a concept that authorial personality should be respected. Crucially, however, none of these thinkers proposed that ideas per se should attract such protection. Indeed, Kant *expressly* excluded such protection, and the exclusion is inherent in Hegel's and Fichte's justifications for protection.

In chapter four, we saw the difficulty that arose in applying rights based upon personality to a situation in which the subject matter for protection had likely been created by multiple, unknown and undocumented 'authors' across an inter-generational time frame. Even assuming a sufficient degree of closeness such that a relevant Indigenous group can be considered an 'author' for these purposes, the TKAGR held by that group is most likely properly defined as information per se rather than as an 'expression' of information. Accordingly, Hegel's, Kant's and Fichte's justification of protection of *expression* alone militates against *any* right of veto of the non-consensual use of TKAGR. However, if sufficient authorial 'closeness' can be imputed, then there is an argument that such a group would be at least be entitled to a right of attribution.

Looking at our potential policy options, these justifications support decision d_1 (no veto). The strength of the prohibition against protection of ideas applies equally to all decisions (d_2, d_3, d_4 and d_5) in which some type of veto or compensation is permitted. These outcomes are summarised in Table 8. The weighting of support shown is to be considered *within* a justification, there is no attempt to represent weighting as between justifications.

Table 8 Application of personality rights theories to potential policy options (up arrows signify support for the decision; down arrows signify lack of support for the decision)

Decision	Kantian	Fichtean	Hegelian
d_1 (no veto)	↑↑↑	↑↑↑	↑↑↑
d_2 (total veto)	↓↓↓	↓↓↓	↓↓↓
d_3 (limited veto)	↓↓↓	↓↓↓	↓↓↓
d_4 (limited veto + compensation)	↓↓↓	↓↓↓	↓↓↓
d_5 (no veto, but compensation)	↓↓↓	↓↓↓	↓↓↓

IV. Utilitarian Goals and the Scope of the Positive Right in TKAGR

Chapter four of this work (in section VII) outlined a number of utilitarian goals that might potentially be served by the existence of positive right in TKAGR. These were broadly:

(a) preservation of a biodiverse environment;
(b) preservation of traditional knowledge for its own sake (broader patrimony of mankind); and
(c) 'utility through control' – a specific utility for an Indigenous group derived through the knowledge that they are controlling their own patrimony according to traditional laws and cultural norms.

A. The Valorisation Model

It was posited in chapter four that the first two identified utilitarian goals outlined above would be achieved, in the main, by influencing the behaviour of relevant actors through the creation of 'value' in the information contained within TKAGR. This value would, in turn, be created through an artificial scarcity in the information achieved through the imposition of positive law limiting use of the information. Here control over information would allow for the results of commercial exploitation to be directed to the rights holders (or indeed also to licensees under those rights, eg a pharmaceutical company, who would derive a commercial advantage over their competitors). However, it was acknowledged that:

(a) a 'valorisation' model only works where there is some actual or potential use for the information – control over the use of something inherently useless is highly unlikely to create any value;
(b) value is a more complex concept than merely creating artificial scarcity in something;
(c) subjective perception is crucial in creating value;
(d) the terms of exclusivity established by positive law – such as certainty of definition and ease of enforcement – become paramount in determining the subjective value of the right.

Given this final point, in particular, it seems reasonable (at first examination) to suggest that the scope of a positive right in TKAGR cannot help but be an important element in determining the degree of perception of value of such a right and thereafter the effect on the chosen utilitarian goals. However, we need to recognise that in this valorisation mechanism we are presented with a potentially tenuous causal link between the imposition of rights of control over TKAGR and the achievement of utilitarian goals. That overall link relies on certain actors perceiving sufficient value in TKAGR such that it drives their behaviour towards actions which will promote (or at least support) the utilitarian ends. Any stimulus for preservation of the environment also faced significant challenges in the light of massive financial drives to 'utilise' the environment in destructive ways. So going from positive right to environmental/traditional knowledge preservation involves many major causation leaps, each leap not without difficulty. This creates a number of problems in examining the desirable scope of the positive right.

Firstly, we cannot be certain that the relevant actors' behaviour will in every case actually serve to save a biodiverse environment and/or traditional knowledge per se (or indeed conflation of the two within the concept of 'biocultural diversity').

Secondly, given such causal complexity, it is surely unlikely that we could deduce any sort of clear linear correlation between perceived value and utilitarian benefit along the lines that 'increase in value *x* gives enhancement in utilitarian effect *y*' and 'reduction in *z* value gives reduction in utilitarian effect *w*'. Still further, it is difficult with any certainty to determine the minimal scope of protection that would give rise to the requisite increase in value required to affect the desired utilitarian benefits or confirm:

(a) that the perceived value of TKAGR is maximally optimised by giving it the broadest possible scope to a positive right; or
(b) that the broadest possible scope to a positive right in TKAGR is required to give effect to the utilitarian goals of the positive right.

However, notwithstanding these uncertainties, it seems broadly reasonable to suggest that the utilitarian goals are probably best served by ensuring that the highest possible number, and type, of actors perceive *genuine* value in genetic resources and traditional knowledge.

The factors feeding into a person's perception of value are numerous. Such perception is, by definition, subjective and will vary from one individual to another, and from one cultural group to another. Notwithstanding this, it seems difficult to argue other than that the perception of value will be weakened if it becomes clear that the rights can easily be bypassed. However, would a right holder realistically expect that the right in traditional knowledge would extend to extremely remote downstream uses and to what degree would excluding such extremely remote uses diminish the perception of value?

We might intuitively surmise that permitting *proximate* uses to escape would have a more significant effect on perceived value than permitting *remote* uses to escape. However, as we are dealing with perception, there is a substantial subjective element at work here and much could be based upon the existing hopes, and prior expectations, of the right holder. If I am told (erroneously) that my right will cover everything and I subsequently find this not to be the case, the faith and value I place on my right may be more impacted than if I am initially given a realistic view of the power of my right. Similarly, one might expect that the right holder's consideration of what she considers to be a 'fair' scope of protection will similarly impact on perception of value – although it is perhaps difficult to divorce a sense of what an individual will consider to be 'fair' from her initial expectations.

In other fields of activity significant perceived value is given to rights that do not cover 'everything'. Newcomers to the field of intellectual property – especially those who believe they have some or other 'rights' – are often initially disappointed to realise just how curtailed those rights are – whether it be due to the inherent limitations of the appropriate rights themselves, their statutory exclusions or, especially, by the competing rights of others. Many people will, however, readily accept that there has to be a balance between the rights allocated to the right holder and the rights which remain with the 'intellectual commons'. Acknowledgement of this balance does not necessarily diminish the perceived value in that which they own.

At this point the staunch (and single-minded) advocate of consequentialist justifications might simply ask: why are we worried about minimum scope in any event? Why do we not simply give the policy its best chances of success by creating a positive right with the broadest possible scope? The first point to note here is that we should not immediately assume that the above uncertainties are inherently fatal to the underlying utilitarian justification(s) for positive protection. Rule utilitarian justifications for legal policy do not ordinarily rely on a clear linear correlation between policy 'cause' and desired 'effect'; their aim is toward creating a social and/or economic environment which will *generally* serve to encourage the achievement of the goal of the policy. Why then, is more scope of protection not automatically better?

The critics of rule utilitarianism are many. Hart[19] (among others, including Rawls[20]) attacks utilitarianism on the basis that it treats humans as a means to an end rather than as ends in themselves, highlighting that utilitarianism:

(a) treats humans as having no value as persons in themselves but merely as experiencers of pleasure;
(b) treats the pleasure of one individual as being replaceable by the greater happiness of the community; and
(c) looks to the enhancement of the overall happiness of society without concern for the distribution of that wealth.

Comte-Sponville supports the second criticism by putting forward a Kantian view that it can never be right to condemn an innocent individual for the maximisation of the collective well-being.[21] To all these criticisms can be added the difficulty of calculating *total* happiness (or well-being) of society, the difficulty of assessing what is meant by happiness/well-being, how 'true' happiness can be separated from 'conditioned' happiness, and the difficulty in determining that future 'pleasures' are indeed result of present policies.[22] If we assume that rule utilitarianism is a broadly valid philosophy, might the criticism that individuals are disadvantaged for the maximisation of the collective well-being be met in part by implementing an approach that only the minimum positive laws required to achieve the utilitarian aim be put in place, but no more? If we seek to adopt this 'balanced' approach in the current problem we would indeed look to find the minimal scope of protection that would give us our desired utilitarian outcomes. However, as we have seen, the uncertainty of a causal connection between value and effect in this case militates against our easily determining such a minimal scope.

How, then, does one then go about 'squaring the circle'? Perhaps one approach is to look to achieve a balance between a utilitarian 'push' in the direction of ever-broader scope and a deontological push in the other direction. At this point the advocate of natural rights might argue that that the logical train set out in the valorisation model is overly complex and we might find that the application of Ockham's *lex parsimoniae*[23] pushes us further toward a direct examination of a (much more direct) deontological account for positive rights in TKAGR than a (tortuous) utilitarian one. However, as we have seen, the natural rights account fails to give us much clear guidance in terms of justifiable limits to scope.

[19] HLA Hart, 'Between Utility and Rights' in *Essays in Jurisprudence and Philosophy* (Oxford, Clarendon Press, 1983) 198, 200.

[20] J Rawls, *A Theory of Justice* [1971] (rev edn Cambridge MA, Belknap Press, 1999) 160.

[21] A Compte-Sponville, *A Short Treatise on the Great Virtues* (London, Vintage, 2003) 62.

[22] JJC Smart and Bernard Williams, *Utilitarianism For and Against* (Cambridge, Cambridge University Press, 1973) 82.

[23] William of Ockham's *Numquam ponenda est pluralitas sine necessitate* [Plurality must never be posited without necessity], 'Sentences of Peter Lombard' (*Quaestiones et decisiones in quattuor libros Sententiarum Petri Lombardi* (ed Lugd. 1495), i, dist 27, qu 2, K).

The validity of synthesised analyses will be discussed in the next chapter, but it might be noted here that if the deontological argument for rights in TKAGR can be found to be at least *not inconsistent* with achieving utilitarian aims, then this will assist in our reaching a synthesised approach which may (partially) satisfy advocates for both rule utilitarianism *and* deontological approaches.

B. 'Utility Through Control'

As was identified in chapter four (in section VII) there is arguably a separate utilitarian goal – a utility gained through the control of information feeding into the spiritual life of an Indigenous group – that is *directly* served by giving control over access to TKAGR. Such a goal does not rely on a process of valorisation and accordingly does not rely upon a potentially tortuous and/or causally tenuous route between positive law and utilitarian goal. The creation of control inherently delivers the narrow utility.

In this situation the greater degree of control is broadly likely to deliver a greater degree of 'utility', but again the degree to which it does so will depend on the cultural norms of the relevant Indigenous peoples. To what extent would those Indigenous groups believe that their traditional knowledge is being improperly exploited by truly distal uses? Again, this will depend on the group in question and the use. It is, however, difficult to immediately accommodate the idea of monetary compensation for downstream use (as in option d_4) within this account. It seems likely that true control envisaged within this account means the ability to definitively bring non-consensual use to a stop, rather than a right to an award of compensation.

C. Conflict between Utilitarian Goals – The Global Health 'Counter-utility'

We have seen in the discussion above that the inherent uncertainties seen in the valorisation model create significant problems in reliably achieving the stated utilitarian goal of preservation of the biodiverse environment and/or traditional knowledge per se (or a 'biocultural diversity' conflation of the two). That discussion assumed, however, that the attempt to achieve such ends was consistent with a *broader* utilitarian account.

There is, however, a potential problem with such an assumption and it is this. If we are seeking to enhance the greatest social utility in the greatest number, might not that broad utility be better served by allowing those with the better skill and financial resources untrammelled access to a piece of TKAGR? Let us imagine that a pharmaceutical company (which we will assume will have those skills and resources) can take a piece of TKAGR and develop it into a product which successfully removes a disease state (or alleviates its symptoms) in a broad population of people that would otherwise not have access to that drug. Does that not create a greater utility for the greater number of persons than where the use of that TKAGR is restricted to a small band of Indigenous people – notwithstanding that the pharmaceutical company will be (perhaps handsomely) compensated for its own investment? In contrast, providing a *total* veto on all downstream use would mean that the development of a therapy which could benefit all of humanity (or a significant part of it) could potentially be prevented by the decision of a small group of Indigenous people. The existence of the veto right, which is supposed to bring about one set of utilitarian goals (preservation of the environment and traditional knowledge per se) through the creation of value in the TKAGR, would here arguably directly counter another type of utility (that of wider human life and health).

In addition, as we have seen the causal link between the imposition of veto rights, the valorisation of TKAGR and the preservation of the environment and Indigenous lifestyles is reliant on an uncertain idea of 'perception of value' in traditional knowledge. In marked contrast, the causal link between a piece of traditional knowledge serving as the inspiration for a drug discovery and development of a final therapeutic product is arguably more concrete. One might therefore argue that the potential, but definite, 'negative' impact of the veto rights on the felicific calculus of humanity (through inhibiting drug development) is likely to outweigh any 'positive' utilitarian impact the veto rights may elicit.

When we look to creating 'utility through control' we see what is, perhaps, the most *direct* link between the creation of a positive right and a utilitarian goal. However, such a goal is still subject to the same overall criticism of utilitarianism and the problems raised with regard to competing utilities: Is the happiness of a small group of Indigenous peoples more important than wider human health? Milius touches upon the question thus (but takes the discussion no further):

> Should one give consideration to the value of utility, it might be more instrumentally productive that, for instance, [traditional knowledge] about medicinal properties of a specific plant held by its custodians be 'shared' with a powerful pharmaceutical company that intends to develop a drug out of that knowledge. This is of course assuming that the principle of utility favours doing good for, or reaching, the greatest number possible. Alternatively, it is true that holding this knowledge secret within the community might also be useful to its members, or other groups (or perhaps also particular individuals) judged to qualify by the community. In terms of numbers however, the principle of utility might suggest the [traditional knowledge] be readily and most efficiently transferred to the company.[24]

This crucial balance will be returned to below at chapter eight.

[24] D Milius, 'Justifying Intellectual Property in Traditional Knowledge' [2009] *Intellectual Property Quarterly* 184, 198.

D. The Global Health 'Counter-utility' – Exemptions and Flexibilities

In considering the global health 'counter-utility' we need to remind ourselves of the limitations of the special provisions of the Nagoya Protocol at Article 8(a) and Article 8(b).

Article 8(a) ensures that parties should create conditions to 'promote and encourage research' which 'contributes to the conservation and sustainable use of biological diversity' including through 'simplified measures on access for non-commercial research' (and relates to both genetic resources and TKAGR). However, as was discussed at chapter three (in section XVII.A), even if drug discovery could fall within the definition of 'sustainable use of biological diversity', the great majority of drug discovery work is done within a *commercial* environment. Even if work is initially done within a non-commercial research institute or university (and without commercially related funding), the later stages of drug discovery and development will invariably switch to a commercial environment to produce a drug that can prescribed to patients. It is unlikely that the putting into effect of Article 8(a) would in any way ameliorate the impact of a veto on the use of TKAGR on the global health 'counter-utility'.

Article 8(b) directs parties to pay 'due regard to cases of present or imminent emergencies that threaten or damage human, animal or plant health, as determined nationally or internationally'. That, of course, points to an attempt by the negotiators of the Nagoya Protocol to ameliorate the utilitarian conflict between ABS protection and global health particularly in the event of a global pandemic.[25] However, as was discussed at chapter three (in section XVII.A), Article 8(b) only requires that parties may take into consideration the need for *expeditious* access to genetic resources and *expeditious* fair and equitable sharing of benefits arising out of the use of such genetic resources. It does not apply to TKAGR.

In itself, the non-inclusion of TKAGR is interesting. One might imagine that such non-inclusion reflects a sentiment that the justification for control over genetic resources is utilitarian/consequentialist in nature (and rightly susceptible to amelioration in the face of a global health counter-utility) whereas the right to control TKAGR is more fundamentally grounded in a right of Indigenous people to self-determination (and less properly susceptible to amelioration). However, we cannot be sure that that was the sentiment behind the exclusion of TKAGR. What is certain is that a putting into effect of Article 8(b) will not ameliorate the potentially 'freezing' effect of a veto over the use of TKAGR on drug discovery.

It should be noted that the provisions of Article 8(b) are something of an echo of language of the 'Declaration on the TRIPS Agreement and Public Health'

[25] T Dedeurwaerdere et al, 'Governing Global Scientific Research Commons Under the Nagoya Protocol' in *The 2010 Nagoya Protocol on Access and Benefit-Sharing in Perspective*, 389 (Leiden, Brill Nijhoff, 2013).

adopted at Doha on 14 November 2001 (the Doha Declaration).[26] This reaffirms the right of WTO members to use to the full the existing 'flexibilities' within the TRIPS Agreement to prevent intellectual property rights (notably pharmaceutical patents) from restricting access to medicines in the Global South, particularly during public health emergencies.

The full story of the need for (and negotiations behind) the Doha Declaration, and of the difficulties created by the adoption of TRIPs on access to medicines in the Global South, is beyond the scope of this work.[27] However, the first point to note is the problems that have been seen in the application of the TRIPs flexibilities.[28] The second point to note is that as a right to control TKAGR under the Nagoya Protocol is not a part of the TRIPs/WTO mechanism (see discussion at chapter two, in sections III and IV) the TRIPs flexibilities do not apply to TKAGR.

E. Conclusion and Policy Proposals

How do these arguments apply to our policy proposals d_1, d_2, d_3, d_4 and d_5? The outcomes of the utilitarian analysis above are summarised in Table 9.

Table 9 Comparison of utilitarian arguments versus potential policy options

	Utilitarianism		
Decision	**Valorisation model**	**'Utility through control'**	**Global health for all**
d_1 (no veto, no compensation)	↓↓↓↓	↓↓↓	↑↑↑↑
d_2 (total veto)	↑↑↑↑	↑↑↑	↓↓↓
d_3 (limited veto)	↑↑	↑↓	↑↑
d_4 (limited veto + compensation)	↑↑↑	↑↓	↑†
d_5 (no veto, but compensation)	↑	↓	↑↑↑†

† Subject to levels of compensation.

[26] WT/MIN(01)/DEC/2.

[27] See generally D Matthews, *Intellectual Property, Human Rights and Development: The Role of NGOs and Social Movements* (Cheltenham, Edward Elgar, 2011) 15.

[28] D Matthews, 'TRIPS Flexibilities and Access to Medicines in Developing Countries: the Problem with Technical Assistance and Free Trade Agreements' (2005) 27 *European Intellectual Property Review* 421; EM Solovy and PS Krishnamurthy, 'TRIPS Agreement Flexibilities and their Limitations: A Response to the UN Secretary-General's High Level Panel Report on Access to Medicines' (2017) 50 *George Washington International Law Review* 69; B Tenni et al, 'What Is the Impact of Intellectual Property Rules on Access to Medicines? A Systematic Review' (2022) 18(1) *Globalization and Health* 10.

Again, up arrows signify support for the decision. Down arrows signify lack of support for the decision. The weighting of support shown is to be considered *within* a justification, there is no attempt to represent weighting as between justifications.

Clearly decision d_1 (no veto, no compensation) does not support the valorisation model of achieving the utilitarian aim of preservation of biodiverse environments and/or traditional knowledge, whereas decisions d_2, d_3 d_4 and d_5 do (to varying degrees) support it.

Our first question is to ask to what extent is it important to have a veto over downstream use *at all*. Is option d_5 alone enough to create a perception of value sufficient in the minds of the relevant actors to achieve the utilitarian ends of preservation of the environment/TKAGR per se or do we need a true, independently exercised, veto of some sort?

Let us assume that we can determine a reasonable mechanism for determining 'respective contribution' as between the Indigenous group and a downstream user. The Indigenous holders of the right would receive some compensation and downstream users who had made a contribution would gain some recognition in terms of paying less. Would that create a sufficient perception of value to affect the behaviour of the relevant actors?

The first impact is likely to be upon the perception of value within an Indigenous group. Realistically no mechanism for determining 'respective contribution' is foolproof – even within the most ostensibly transparent determinative mechanism, mistakes are made – there is always an element of what we might call 'litigation risk'. However, within systems where there may be an imbalance of resources and of legal representation, potential bias within the determinative mechanism and/or corruption, there will likely be a greater perception that such a system cannot be relied upon to deliver a just reward. Where a veto is in place there is likely to be a clearer and more certain path to achieving value than with a separate determination of contribution. With an enforceable veto a third party will need to negotiate compensation through licence payments or be unable to use the subject matter of the veto rights. Provided that royalty rates are broadly equivalent to that which would be paid under our imaginary compensation regime, then a veto regime will likely create more (and more easily accessed) value.

Third-party users (potential licensees) will also likely perceive more value in veto rights than in a right that gives the right holder a right to compensation (again assuming the rates of both to be broadly similar). One advantage of being a licensee (especially an exclusive licensee) is that the licensee obtains an advantage over competitors that are not licensees. Under option d_5, where there is a determination of compensation relative to contribution, it would likely be open to a number of downstream users to seek 'permission' to use in return for payment. As well as this situation being likely to be exceptionally difficult to administer, it would also probably deny the opportunity for the degree of exclusivity (and with it value) that potential licensees could see under mechanisms that granted a veto of some form.

We need to look now between those options (d_2, d_3 and d_4) that deliver an element of veto. Although the causal complexity between imposition of rights and utilitarian effect in the valorisation model cannot convincingly predict the extent to which valorisation will actually achieve the utilitarian goals (if at all), taking a simplistic rule-utilitarian 'more scope is likely to provides more effect' view, then d_2 is likely to provide a greater utilitarian effect than either d_3 or d_4. Certainly, the point about the likely perceived value of a veto over a compensatory mechanism set out above will apply when comparing option d_4 (limited veto + compensation) to d_2 (total veto). However, as this element is in respect of a second use (which may never arise) the difference in perceived value (although likely to be there) may not be significant.

When looking as between the utilitarian efficacy of d_3 or d_4, we need to ask whether the imposition of a requirement for compensation to be paid (d_4) enhances the perceived value of the subject matter of the rights relative to a situation in which such compensation is not required (d_3). Of course, the difference in scarcity as between the subject matter in the rights in d_3 or d_4 is marginal and such small differences may have little true effect on a perception of value (especially when arraigned against the greater economic forces of logging, mining and ranching). However, the requirement to pay compensation is likely to have some impact on perception of value *within* the Indigenous group holding the rights. As such there would seem to be an argument to prefer d_4 over d_3.

Turning now to the global health utility discussed above, we find that d_2 (a total right to veto) exacerbates the Indigenous rights versus global health conflict, whereas decision d_1 (no veto) arguably removes this conflict entirely. Decision d_5 essentially provides total freedom to pharmaceutical companies to exploit TKAGR in return for a payment of compensation.

Both d_3 and d_4 might be said to strike something of a balance between valorisation and the Indigenous rights versus global health conflict, with decision d_4 (no total veto but a right to compensation commensurate with contribution) perhaps providing the best balance. With this option (d_4), pharmaceutical companies remain free (in part) to serve the needs of global health (subject to paying compensation), whilst value as perceived by the Indigenous rights holders is perhaps marginally enhanced relative to decision d_3.

Of course, the true availability of the traditional knowledge to the furtherance of global health goals under options d_4 and d_5 would, in practice, rely on the level of compensation not being such as to render as unworthwhile the commercial risk of engaging in drug discovery and development.[29]

When comparing the five policy decisions against the achievement of 'utility through control' we of course find that decision d_1 (no veto, no compensation) cannot create that utility and decision d_5 (no veto but compensation) is unlikely to, whereas d_2 (total veto) clearly would.

[29] In this regard, the overall compensation load would need to be considered in the event that numbers of indigenous groups were able to make valid claims.

What we cannot easily determine is whether a *partial* veto as in d_3 or d_4 would fail to meet that 'utility through control' goal. To what extent would conceding some control of downstream activity affect this utility? This determination will depend on the cultural norms and customary practice of the Indigenous group in question. It seems likely, however, that if absolute control is important, this will be a commodity that cannot be easily partitioned without destroying the total utility.

In deciding between d_3 or d_4, it is, as discussed above, unlikely that the presence, or absence, of compensation would have much of an effect on this utilitarian goal if the desire for control is key. Again, however, this is a question that is reliant upon very specific cultural norms and the customary practice of the Indigenous group in question.

As was the case with the valorisation model, we find that pursuing the 'utility through control' goal through provision of a total veto on all downstream use (decision d_1) is potentially completely at odds with the achievement of a global health utility. Perhaps more so even than with the valorisation model (where the number of beneficiaries could be large), we may here find ourselves 'weighing' a utility for a potentially small group of people (an Indigenous group) against the utility of potentially millions of people who would have benefited from the new treatment but who are denied by a veto right. However, we cannot always assume that the Indigenous group will be small and the class of 'deprived' patients large. One can certainly envisage a situation in which the Indigenous group (or even collection of Indigenous groups) entitled to control is large and the number of deprived patients is small – for example, sufferers from a rare 'orphan' disease. Even if we were able to predict the number of persons impacted by a policy, weighing competing utilities on the basis of numbers of individuals is inherently flawed. How does one compare the upset caused to the member of an Indigenous group who has lost control of a piece of traditional knowledge concerning a genetic resource with the suffering of parents denied a treatment for their child's cancer? Even if we look to a Derclaye and Taylor-style assessment of broader well-being,[30] versus 'mere' Benthamite or Millian 'happiness' (which one might imagine would place greater weight upon those denied treatment), we still find we are attempting to compare 'biscuits and hyacinths'.[31]

This brings us back again to the fundamental difficulty with any utilitarian account – one cannot realistically measure a societal hedonic calculus, and even to attempt to do so would require a delineation of *which* particular society you are measuring – a delineation that could be fraught with problems of arbitrary definition and partiality. Notwithstanding this inherent difficulty in weighing directly competing utilities, one can still seek to assess which policy options *tend* to the advantage of all utilities. Therefore whilst decision d_1 (no veto) cannot aid the 'utility through control' utility and d_2 cannot aid the global health utility,

[30] E Derclaye and T Taylor, 'Happy IP: Replacing the Law and Economics Justification for Intellectual Property Rights with a Well-being Approach' (2015) 37(4) *European Intellectual Property Review* 197; E Derclaye and T Taylor, 'Happy IP: Aligning Intellectual Property Rights with Well-being' (2015) 2015(1) *Intellectual Property Quarterly* 1.

[31] C Sandburg, *Good Morning, America* (New York, Harcourt Brace, 1928).

and vice versa, the 'partial' veto options (d_3 and d_4) both aid, in part, the global health utility. However, as discussed above, whether a partial degree of control is sufficient to meet an Indigenous group's desire to control information in accordance with customary norms is unclear but perhaps unlikely. When looking as between option d_3 and d_4, as previously discussed, the presence or absence of a requirement for compensation is unlikely to impact upon the 'utility through control' utility but may impact the global health utility depending on levels of compensation.

It is worth noting at this point that the ways in which a veto on healthcare research may be exercised in practice could potentially become quite complex. If an Indigenous group is in possession of a veto right over a piece of TKAGR which is exclusively theirs, it is entirely conceivable that an Indigenous group could choose a variety of licensing strategies to maximise their revenue or, indeed, maintain a degree of control over use. Obviously, the range of options available to such licensors is wide and susceptible to all manner of conditions, including field of use restrictions on licensor use. In this way it is entirely plausible that an Indigenous group may decide to grant permission for the use of their TKAGR on an exclusive basis to one single pharmaceutical company.[32] From a global health utility perspective this could lead to a situation in which some global health utility is achieved in a limited way through the exclusive exploitation of the permission to use TKAGR but where broader, more free research by excluded third parties would be potentially stifled. One might even envisage that the exclusivity could be further enhanced where the licensed pharmaceutical company looks to build a web of patents on the developments coming out of their research exploration of the original TKAGR. Such a pharmaceutical company would also have a strong motive to enforce its TKAGR exclusivity through litigation either on its own behalf or by supporting actions brought by the original rights holders (or both). Although this is not perhaps how one might immediately envisage the effect of creating a positive right to control TKAGR, it would be a logical consequence of the existence of a veto to prevent use and arguably not unlikely.

Of course, one can also envisage here a situation where an Indigenous group's claim to exclusivity over the TKAGR is contested by other Indigenous groups (or other pharmaceutical companies on behalf of other Indigenous groups). Article 11(2) of the Nagoya Protocol seeks to deal (up to a point) with this situation, stating that:

> Where the same traditional knowledge associated with genetic resources is shared by one or more indigenous and local communities in several Parties, those Parties shall endeavour to cooperate, as appropriate, with the involvement of the indigenous and local communities concerned, with a view to implementing the objective of this Protocol.

Those with experience of (say) patent validity and inventorship disputes (especially where there is a significant amount of money at stake) will recognise that

[32] Thanks go to Professor Phillip Johnson, University of Cardiff, for outlining this possibility.

achieving resolution through 'endeavours to cooperate', whilst not impossible, is perhaps somewhat optimistic.

It is also worth noting that where genetic resources (and TK associated with those genetic resources) occur in transboundary situations (or for which it is not possible to grant or obtain prior informed consent), Article 10 of the Nagoya Protocol acts as a back-stop provision that requires that parties shall consider the need for and modalities of a 'global multilateral benefit-sharing mechanism' to address the fair and equitable sharing of benefits derived from the of such utilization of genetic resources and TKAGR. Whilst such circumstances are likely to reasonably common, by their very nature they are unlikely to generate a situation in which there is a negative impact on the global health utility. Whilst the presence of Article10 helped in the final negotiation stages of the agreement of the Nagoya Protocol by deferring the definition of controversial (but fundamental) topics such as the temporal and geographical scope,[33] there has, to date, been no achievement of such a 'global multilateral benefit-sharing mechanism' and progress to that end has been slow.[34]

V. A Rawlsian Distributive Justice Analysis

As discussed in chapter three (in section IX), to the extent that underlying philosophical justifications for such rights in TKAGR can be determined, the question of whether the allocation of property which arises out of following those justifications gives rise to a fair distribution of property across society still remains. The role of a distributive justice approach in the current analysis is to determine how, if there is to be such a right, it might best be arranged to maximise the least negative outcome for affected individuals.

A. Application of 'Maximin' Analysis to the Scope of Positive Right Problem

Could a Rawlsian original position 'maximin' analysis be applied to the current question of whether a positive right in TKAGR should extend to cover serendipitous discoveries of second uses? How might it work?

Such a maximin analysis requires determination between certain decisions. The decisions (d_1 to d_5) that will be used for this analysis have, of course, been outlined at the start of this chapter. In terms of possible circumstances, we will assume two separate situations. In Rawls's original maximin analysis the person in the 'original position' has to imagine herself as an individual.[35] In this current

[33] T Greiber et al, 'IUCN Explanatory Guide to the Protocol on Access and Benefit-sharing' (IUCN Environmental Policy and Law Paper No 8326, 2012).

[34] CBD/SBI/REC/3/17 of 28 March 2022.

[35] Rawls (n 20) 153.

analysis she imagines herself as two distinct groups. In circumstance C_1 the person in the original position finds herself as an Indigenous group in possession of the TKAGR. In circumstance C_2 the person in the original position finds herself a drug company that is seeking to utilise downstream uses inspired by C_1's TKAGR. Of course, being in the original position behind the veil of ignorance, our person cannot tell whether she will be fall into circumstance C_1 (Indigenous group) or C_2 (drug company). How, then, would our person in the original position seek to maximise the potential minimum?

The immediate problem in our analysis is that we cannot easily allocate definite monetary values to each circumstance. However, although we cannot put monetary figures to the outcomes, we might attempt to crudely represent gain and loss on a table as set out in Table 10.

Table 10 Indigenous group versus drug company maximin analysis

	Circumstances	
Decisions	C_1	C_2
d_1 (no veto, no compensation)	–	↑↑↑↑
d_2 (total veto)	↑↑↑↑	–
d_3 (limited veto)	↑↑	↑↑
d_4 (limited veto + compensation)	↑↑↑	↑
d_5 (no veto, but compensation)	↑	↑↑↑

The relative outcomes of decisions d_1 and d_2 are easy to approximate (occupying as they do the extreme positions of the five options). However, in the light of such raw approximation, discriminating between the outcomes of decisions d_3, d_4 and d_5 is more difficult.

Taking decision d_5 first, here pharmaceutical company C_2 is free to use any downstream use inspired by C_1's knowledge, provided it pays appropriate compensation to C_1. It is hard to evaluate the relative gain between C_1 and C_2 as this will depend on the contribution to be paid by C_2. However, C_2 has freedom to exploit any downstream use without being subject to any absolute veto and this is likely a better option for C_2 than would be options d_3 and d_4.

Although under decision d_5, C_1 is entitled to a compensation stream, determination of that stream may in practice be subject to uncertainty (as outlined above) and d_5 would not offer the strength of negotiating position to arrive at royalty payments (in relation to uses up to a serendipitous discovery) as would options d_3 and d_4.

Under decision d_4, Indigenous group C_1 is entitled to *both* absolute control of downstream use 'up to' the serendipitous discovery *and* receive compensation for use arising out the serendipitous discovery. This is arguably a better outcome for C_1 than would be decision d_3 where C_1 is denied any degree of control of use arising out the serendipitous discovery.

In reality (subject to the level of compensation payable to Indigenous group C_1) the difference in loss for C_2 as between decisions d_3 and d_4 may be small relative to the C_2's total wealth. However, d_3 clearly ranks as a better decision for C_2 than would d_4.

However, what we find in this exercise is that although we might come to a realistic assessment of how to rank the various options for each party, it is much harder in an abstract situation to assess the relative gains and losses *as between* C_1 and C_2. In truth, *much* hangs on how one measures advantage. Without knowing how a determination of compensation based on contribution would work in practice, we find ourselves essentially unable to say whether that process would provide a better outcome for C_1 than would negotiation of royalties for permissions to use. Accordingly, we cannot realistically determine as between the 'middle' options (d_3, d_4 and d_5) but would likely seek to avoid options d_1 and d_2.

B. Criticisms of an Original Position Maximin Analysis

Before we place too much reliance upon any maximin analysis we need to appreciate the problems inherent in such analyses. Since the publication of *A Theory of Justice* many reasons have been advanced for the inappropriateness of persons in the original position entering into a maximin analysis.[36] One of the chief criticisms is put forward by pharmacologist, philosopher and game theorist, John Harsanyi.[37] Harsanyi argued that, although it was right to reason from an original position, the use of the maximin test was inappropriate as it takes no account of the probabilities of the various circumstances arising. Rawls objects to using any probabilities in the original position – in the absence of *empirical* probabilities (which are impossible to determine) he rejects the use of *subjective* or *logical* probabilities. Harsanyi believes this to be wrong. In taking no account of the *probabilities* of the various circumstances occurring, the maximin approach forces the person in the original position to take account of extreme, but unlikely, events. Harsanyi uses the example of a person in New York who is offered two jobs – one dull and badly paid in New York, one fulfilling and well paid in Chicago. Although the choice might seem easy, Harsanyi notes that for those engaging

[36] OA Oyeshile, 'A Critique of the Maximin Principle in Rawls's Theory of Justice' (2008) 3(1) *Humanity and Social Sciences Journal* 65.

[37] JC Harsanyi, 'Can the Maximin Principle Serve as a Basis for Morality? A Critique of John Rawls's Theory' (1975) 69(2) *American Political Science Review* 594.

in a maximin analysis they must consider the possibility (no matter how slim) that the New Yorker will die in travelling to the job in Chicago. As death is the worst of the possible outcomes available in the gain/loss table, maximising the minimum results in the New Yorker taking the dull post in New York. Having no regard for real-world probabilities, the 'maximinimiser' will always take the most risk-adverse position.

Harsanyi notes that as a result of Rawls's maximin approach, and the difference principle arising out of it, the person in the original position has to evaluate any institutional framework as if she *was sure* that she would become the poorest member of a particular society. Of course, this approach has appeal in its very simplicity. However, Harsanyi notes that this can have strange effects when applied to extreme situations and can result in an excessive focus on the situation of one extremely disadvantaged individual to the disadvantage of a greater number of members of society. Harsanyi notes in a postscript to his paper that Rawls challenged Harsanyi's extreme counter-examples on the basis of scale, stating that 'maximin is a macro not a micro principle'.[38] Harsanyi describes this as a 'singularly inept defense' on the basis that although his extreme counter-examples refer to small-scale situations, they are readily scaled-up and also, on the more fundamental basis, that the basic principles of morality cannot be in some way scale-dependent.[39] He asks at what point on the scale should maximin apply and at what point should it not?

Harsanyi is a self-confessed and unapologetic utilitarian. Having stressed the flaws in a maximin analysis, he argues that a more appropriate test to apply when making a decision under uncertainty is the *expected-utility maximisation test* in which a decision-maker cannot help but act as if she tried to maximise her expected utility computed on the basis of some set of *subjective* probabilities (what she perceives is the likelihood of a particular circumstance coming to pass).[40] Harsanyi argues that if the person in the original position applies the expected-utility maximisation test in which she will weigh up all the possibilities and their probabilities, she will arrive at an outcome that not only enhances her chances of personally being in a better position when the veil of ignorance is removed, but also leads to an overall improvement in wealth of society – essentially a rule utilitarian approach. In addition, such an approach avoids the extreme positions seen with the maximin approach. For Harsanyi, the maximin approaches are most successful when dealing with differences in circumstance with similar probabilities of occurrence.[41] This is because here the analysis actually begins to resemble

[38] J Rawls, 'Some Reasons for the Maximin Criterion' (1974) 63 *American Economic Review* 141, 142.

[39] Harsanyi (n 37) 605.

[40] Determined by calculating the weighted average of all possible outcomes within a set of circumstances, with the weights being assigned by the probability that any particular circumstance will occur.

[41] Harsanyi (n 37) 605.

that seen using expected-utility maximisation test. Accordingly, the outcomes of maximin analysis of such circumstances are usually consistent with a utilitarian approach.

In the light of Harsanyi's criticisms, what criticisms might we level at the maximin analysis performed in Table 10? Could we perform an expected-utility maximisation test on the circumstances set out in that table? How would that compare to the maximin analysis performed? As mentioned above, we cannot apportion accurate figures to the gains and losses attributable to each decision in each circumstance, but we have an understanding of the relative extremes (and that decisions d_3 d_4 and d_5 create outcomes that are positioned between two extremes arising in decisions d_1 and d_2). However, this tells us little in itself as to the similarity of this maximin test to an expected-utility maximisation test on the same facts.

What can we say about probability of outcomes? We can have no way to determine *empirical* probabilities for the two posited circumstances – we cannot realistically know our chance of becoming a pharmaceutical company or an Indigenous group. However, although there are a large number of pharmaceutical companies, there are also a very large number of Indigenous groups, so perhaps the best we can say is that the probabilities are not too divergent. If that is correct, this does not represent one of Harsanyi's situations of *extremely* divergent probabilities.

C. Problems with Determination of Advantage

In the maximin analysis set out in Table 10, it was stated that much hangs on how one measures advantage and whether it is absolute or relative. This is correct. However, it will likely be immediately apparent that the greatest difficulty facing the analysis in Table 10 is that it is attempting to examine *relative* advantage in a very narrow way indeed. It looks merely at advantage derived from having a positive right over downstream use of TKAGR and does not consider the larger picture.

Whether one would want (on the removal of the veil of ignorance) to 'be' Glaxo SmithKline plc or the Mentawai peoples of Indonesia is no doubt a matter of personal taste, but there is no doubt that from a purely monetary position you would be better off being Glaxo SmithKline (or even a small trading subsidiary thereof) than the alternative. Herein lies the problem of a 'narrow' maximin analysis – considering only the immediate rights in question it produces a solution that on the face of it appears strange. Indeed, one of the extreme 'negative' outcomes to be avoided is 'being' in the pharmaceutical company C_2 under decision d_2! From a monetary perspective you would more likely in the vast majority of cases want to 'be' C_2 and avoid 'being' C_1. We might represent this by a great (and constant) preponderance of 'up' arrows on a revised analysis (see Table 11).

Table 11 Indigenous group versus drug company 'broader situation' maximin analysis

	Circumstances	
Decisions	**C_1**	**C_2**
d_1 **(no veto, no compensation)**	–	↑↑↑↑↑↑↑↑↑↑↑↑↑↑
d_2 (total veto)	↑↑↑↑	↑↑↑↑↑↑↑↑↑↑↑↑↑↑
d_3 (limited veto)	↑↑	↑↑↑↑↑↑↑↑↑↑↑↑↑↑
d_4 (limited veto + compensation)	↑↑↑	↑↑↑↑↑↑↑↑↑↑↑↑↑↑
d_5 (no veto, but compensation)	↑	↑↑↑↑↑↑↑↑↑↑↑↑↑↑

In this case the worst-case scenario (the one you would most want to avoid) is now being C_1 under d_1 (an Indigenous group with no positive rights in TKAGR *at all*), whereas the situation that 'maximises the minimum' is now d_2 (where any right to veto use extends to preventing *all* uses including those arising out of a truly serendipitous discovery). In the Table 10 analysis we had great trouble differentiating between the relative gains and losses made by either side in decisions d_3 and d_4 and d_5. By holding the gain on the C_2 side of the equation as constant (and overwhelming) the relative ranking of the different decisions on the C_1 side of the equation becomes the important factor.

Of course, the exercise of holding the advantage to C_2 as constant *in all cases* does not necessarily reflect the true situation – C_2 will of course be disadvantaged *to a degree* in that it will have to make royalty or compensation payments or indeed decline from pursuing a research strategy if consent is not granted. In respect of smaller drug companies such payments may well make a significant difference. Even for a large company, being unable to pursue a research lead could have a major effect. However, provided we accept the limitations of our assumptions (predominantly that the company is permitted to make royalty payments in return for consent to use), this approach does allow us to perform a maximin analysis which would otherwise be denied to us. Accordingly, (with this proviso) the ranking order of policy choices established in this analysis (namely d_2, d_4, d_3, d_5, d_1) will be taken forward into the analysis in chapter seven.

VI. Restorative/Corrective Justice ('Reparations')

As discussed in chapter four (in section X), Munzer has proposed the grant of rights to control traditional knowledge as part of a package of broader 'reparations' for past wrongs committed upon a traditional group.[42] Munzer essentially sets out a simple philosophy that as wrongs have been committed they should be repaired, and that a grant of rights to control traditional knowledge could form part of a suite of appropriate reparations. Munzer establishes a set of conditions precedent to be met before a claim for reparations can be made. However, it is crucial to note that determination of damage (wrong) and requirements for repair are to be determined on a case-by-case basis. Also, there is no requirement, whatsoever, for any *specific* link between the type of wrong and the remedy, or necessarily a clear link between the magnitude of the wrong and the remedy.[43] We cannot determine what right is appropriate in the light of the wrong. Of course, if the 'wrong' happens to be a particular example of misappropriation of genetic resource and associated traditional knowledge the broad remedy may be more easily determined, if not its detail.

Given this *smörgåsbord* approach, there seems to be no reason in principle why the protection to be granted cannot include the grant of an absolute veto (through injunctive relief) alongside the award of compensation. However, Munzer deliberately avoids advocating a specific set of intellectual property rules. Munzer anticipates that a defence may be available where the potential defendant 'lacks a moral duty to rectify the wrongs and undo the harm caused'.[44] This seems entirely at odds with the concept of a broad award of reparations for past acts unconnected with current activities, or parties. We are not given a sense of what equitable conduct might give rise to this 'defence'. Might extremely distal downstream use of TKAGR fall within this sphere of equity? We simply cannot say.

Overall, such uncertainties, and inherent case-by-case specificity, make the translation of Munzer's reparation justification to a set of generally applicable principles for broader application exceptionally difficult. One might imagine that Munzer's broad desire of reparation for past wrongs may weigh into other assessments of equitable considerations between putative Indigenous right holders in TKAGR and those looking to develop follow-on concepts. However, even if philosophically valid, the uncertainty in Munzer's proposal (teamed with its inherent case-by-case specificity of application) makes it impossible to know how much 'weight' should be allocated.

VII. Human Rights Justifications – The Indigenous Right to Self-determination

We saw at chapter four (in section XII.A) that many advocates for Indigenous peoples' rights to control genetic resources and TKAGR have pointed to the

[42] SR Munzer, 'Corrective Justice and Intellectual Property Rights in Traditional Knowledge' in A Lever (ed) *New Frontiers in the Philosophy of Intellectual Property* (Cambridge, Cambridge University Press, 2012) 58.

[43] ibid, 62.

[44] ibid.

concept of Indigenous 'sovereignty' (or the inherent right of Indigenous peoples to self-determination) as the key justification for such rights. We also saw that the term 'sovereignty' was, of itself, contentious as certain Indigenous advocates perceived the concept as having been derived from Western philosophical principles and/or confirming settler-state legitimacy. For some nation states, (jealous of their own sovereignty) the concept of Indigenous sovereignty was unsettling, as it could erode their territorial integrity. We also saw that, on that basis, the author has decided to refer in this work to the concept the inherent right of Indigenous peoples to self-determination as opposed to 'sovereignty' as such (and has left as moot the question of whether there is any substantive difference between these terms, particularly when applied to Indigenous peoples' rights over genetic resources or TKAGR).

We also saw in chapter 4 (also in section XII.A) that the nature of the inherent right of Indigenous peoples to self-determination and, in particular, how such a right should be expressed in the form of rights over intangibles or 'Indigenous intellectual property' is subject to significant discussion. How, then, should we seek to apply the concept of the inherent right of Indigenous peoples to self-determination to our selection of policy options, d_1, d_2, d_3, d_4 and d_5?

If the key to a right of self-determination is simply the right to have control over those elements of Indigenous culture which are held by an Indigenous group *and* we assume that the control of TKAGR is such an element, then, almost by definition, the inherent right of Indigenous peoples to self-determination is broadly supportive of those policy decisions which involve a veto. Accordingly, this ground would not support decision d_1 (no veto, no compensation) and would also not seem to support option d_5 (no veto but with compensation). However, as between the three 'veto' decision options (d_2, d_3 and d_4) and the question of whether the veto right should extend to preventing the use of a product arising out of a truly serendipitous discovery (even where such discovery would not *in fact* have been made without the lead provided by the TKAGR), the uncertainty as to the scope of the right is such that, for this author at least, we have little basis upon which to address the question. Let us look, then, at two attempts to give more clarity as to the scope of the right to self-determination over elements of Indigenous culture.

A. UNDRIP

In chapter four (in section XII.D) we also saw that the UN had sought to acknowledge the rights of Indigenous peoples through UNDRIP (although we should note the rights acknowledged in UNDRIP do not represent the totality of the inherent right of Indigenous peoples to self-determination). We saw that UNDRIP Article 11 embodies a right to practise and revitalise Indigenous cultural traditions and customs and provides that Indigenous people's cultural, intellectual, religious and spiritual property should not be taken 'without their free, prior and informed consent or in violation of their laws, traditions and customs provides'. However, it does not do more than establish that there should be 'effective' redress which 'may include restitution'. We also saw that Article 31 provides that Indigenous peoples specifically have the right to maintain, control, protect and develop their knowledge of the properties of fauna and flora. Neither Articles give any indication as to the proper scope of those rights in relation to downstream use.

As previously stated, although UNDRIP does not establish a binding set of laws, it would appear appropriate that we determine whether rights in TKAGR supported by other justifications are at least compliant with the rights envisaged under UNDRIP. This is not easy. As has been discussed in chapter four, UNDRIP provides no guidance as to what 'effective redress' (which 'may include restitution') and 'control' mean in this context and particularly whether a veto is envisaged. On the analysis provided in chapter four we can, however, say that howsoever the wording of Article 11 is interpreted, compensation for misappropriation is likely to be the *minimum* redress envisaged. However, the minimum redress available under Article 31 remains entirely unclear.

Examining the four policy options, d_1, d_2, d_3 d_4 and d_5, we see that option d_1 (no right whatsoever) is not compliant with UNDRIP which envisages *some* control. However, as to distinguishing between options d_2, d_3 d_4 and d_5 we have little guidance – d_2, d_3 d_4 are all remedies greater than compensation for misappropriation, whereas d_5 could be argued to reflect the *minimum* compensation envisaged within UNDRIP.

B. A Communitarian Justification

As was discussed in chapter four (in section XII.E), Gibson has advanced a 'communitarian' justification which arises out of a claim to community and assures that an identified community should be able to control their own information under conditions to be determined by the communities and in accordance with their customary laws, values, and traditional practices. As was mentioned in chapter 4, there are very clear echoes here of the broader concept of the Indigenous right to self-determination (and the rights to control cultural heritage within that right), but Gibson is highly sensitive to the origination/individuation problems inherent in such claim and in the identification of resources under that claim. Gibson's communitarian right also has some echoes with a right required to achieve a 'utility through control' goal in which utility for an Indigenous group is created (or perhaps more accurately preserved) though the control of information in accordance with their customary practice. This is, though, a right that may be tempered by concepts of equity where competing interests are to be evaluated. Gibson does not explicitly address the question of the proximal-distal scope of the right. However, she does refer to 'extinguishment' of rights, stating:

> Community custodianship over resources cannot be extinguished by subsequent creation of intellectual property rights, according to the concept of community resources set

> out here. Therefore, where a community consents to traditional resources being used, the model may require that this in no way extinguishes their rights to that knowledge. Therefore, consent in one instance will not justify subsequent open access, or delivery into the 'public domain' and the model may require fresh consent for every use of a particular aspect of traditional knowledge. While blanket consent may be easier in its practical application, the argument for fresh consent acknowledges the importance of the use of knowledge to the decision to grant consent by the community. Blanket consent cannot anticipate the many uses to which knowledge may be put once it is appropriated in this way.
>
> Nevertheless, this ideal does not preclude the granting of blanket consent where appropriate. For instance the conditions and terms of the appropriation and use may be qualified in agreements to allow for blanket consent.[45]

According to Gibson's account:

(i) The creation of subsequent intellectual property does not extinguish the right to knowledge; and
(ii) The granting of consent in relation to one use does not extinguish the requirement for users to obtain prior informed consent in relation to a second use.

In relation to point (i), it is not clear what 'subsequent' means in this respect. Within the context of the rest of the paragraph it suggests that where consent has been granted to use, and that use has led to the creation *by others* of intellectual property, that does not lead to a wholesale waiver of the rights of the Indigenous peoples to control of the knowledge. What it is not saying, in itself, is that all downstream uses are controllable.

In relation to point (ii), depending on the terms of consent granted in relation to the first use, it seems unlikely that a use arising out of a serendipitous discovery would be considered to fall within the ambit of the first use – almost by definition it could not be envisaged as part of the first use. If it is not so envisaged then it would not be a part of the *informed* consent granted by the holders of the knowledge. Although that might seemingly suggest that use of a serendipitous discovery is non-consensual we cannot be sure. In her comment about 'blanket consent' Gibson certainly envisages that there may be many downstream uses. However, we cannot determine whether *use* of a serendipitous discovery (or other distal downstream activity) constitutes *use* (or should constitute *use*) of the original information.

We saw in chapter four that Gibson considers a requirement for free and prior informed consent before traditional knowledge can be used by others to be 'fundamental' to her model and an essential element of legitimate use or appropriation. This suggests that Gibson has a preference for a right to veto non-consensual use over a mere right to compensation.

Gibson, of course, highlights the role of the relevant Indigenous group in consenting to the use of their knowledge under conditions to be determined by the

[45] Gibson (n 5) 292.

communities and in accordance with their customary laws. To an extent, then, the decision over what would constitute a downstream activity is to be decided under customary laws. It is unlikely that the specific question of control second uses will have been addressed under such law, other than a general notion of a desire for absolute control (as was discussed in relation to the 'utility through control' goal). Again, the question of the appropriateness of compensation in lieu of control is unlikely to have been addressed under such law. We may imagine that a desire for absolute control would be deemed more appropriate, but we cannot be sure of that, and such determinations (if any) will of course vary from situation to situation.

Gibson envisages a duty upon those seeking to use what they ought reasonably to believe to be a traditional knowledge or natural/genetic resources to make reasonable efforts to ascertain and contact the relevant community to obtain consent to use of the knowledge. We again have to ask whether *use* of a serendipitous discovery constitutes *use* (or should constitute *use*) of the original information which triggers such duty. This account gives us no clear guidance in this respect.

Turning to the policy options, d_1, d_2, d_3, d_4 and d_5, we see that Gibson's communitarian justification strongly opposes d_1 (no veto, no compensation). It would also seem to oppose option d_5 (no veto but with compensation). However, as between the three veto options d_2, d_3 and d_4, in the end the communitarian claim offers us little concrete guidance.

Table 12 provides a summary of the application of the broader Indigenous right to self-determination, UNDRIP and the communitarian claim to potential policy options d_1, d_2, d_3, d_4 and d_5.

Table 12 Summary of the application of the Indigenous right to self-determination, UNDRIP and the communitarian claim to potential policy options. Queries denote where no clear conclusion can be arrived at.

Decision	Self-determination claim	UNDRIP	Communitarian claim (Gibson)
d_1 (no veto, no compensation)	↓↓↓	↓↓↓	↓↓↓
d_2 (total veto)	?	↑	?
d_3 (limited veto)	?	↑	?
d_4 (limited veto + compensation)	?	↑	?
d_5 (no veto, but compensation)	↓↓	↑	↓↓

VIII. Conclusions

The key outcomes from the above analysis are set out below. As can be seen, different philosophical justifications have generated differing outcomes (see Table 13 in chapter seven). The discussion of how (if at all) those outcomes can be synthesised is addressed in the following chapter.

A. Utilitarianism

There are significant problems in linking valorisation of TKAGR with the identified utilitarian aims of enhancement of biodiversity and preservation of traditional culture (or a conflation of both). Within the utilitarian account there is also a serious conflict between granting Indigenous peoples an *absolute* veto over all third-party use of TKAGR and the enhancement of global health for all. The 'utility through control' utility has the possible advantage of a short causal link between the creation of the right and the creation of utility, but suffers from uncertainty due to variation in the type of control required under customary law from Indigenous group to group. If giving rise to a total veto, it also is likely to conflict with the global health for all utility.

B. Natural Rights

A Lockean labour-desert natural right to ownership of knowledge broadly supports a right based upon contribution rather than no right at all (decision d_1).

Neither d_2 (total veto) nor d_3 (limit veto) nor d_4 (limited veto with compensation) nor d_5 (no veto but compensation) are inconsistent with the Lockean account. However, given the problem of defining contribution, the account can give us no concrete guidance as to which of those four approaches is more justified.

Looking at the question of which approach is more justifiable as between d_3 and d_4, we might intuitively say that, as between the two, provision of compensation commensurate with degree of contribution would appear more fundamentally consistent with a Lockean account than not providing any compensation at all. We should note, however, that since the Lockean approach cannot give us any absolute guidance as to the definition of contribution, it might be difficult to say that a situation where the degree of contribution was so minimal as not to warrant compensation was inconsistent with a Lockean justification. Realistically all we can conclude is that all options other than d_1 are consistent with a labour-desert account.

Rights based upon personality such as those proposed by Kant, Fichte and Hegel are not supportive of any positive right to control ideas.

C. Rawlsian Maximin Analysis

Provided one looks at the *proportionate* advantage to each side of each of the proposed decisions (essentially applying the difference principle), decision d_2 (an absolute veto on all downstream use) is the situation the person in the original position would choose as maximising the minimum. The order of 'least-worst' options seen on that maximin analysis is d_2, d_4, d_3, d_5, d_1.

D. Restorative/Corrective Justice ('Reparations')

The uncertainties, and inherent case-by-case specificity, make the translation of Munzer's reparation justification to a set of generally applicable principles for broader application exceptionally difficult.

E. Inherent Right of Indigenous Peoples to Self-determination

The right to control TKAGR based on an inherent right of Indigenous peoples to self-determination would appear to exclude decisions d_1 and d_5. However, there is little explicit guidance from this doctrine as to whether very distal uses, including uses arising out of serendipitous discoveries, should be considered as use of the traditional knowledge.

F. UNDRIP

Compensation for misappropriation is likely to be the *minimum* redress envisaged under UNDRIP. Option d_1 (no right whatsoever) is not compliant with UNDRIP which envisages some degree of control. However, in distinguishing between options d_2, d_3, d_4 and d_5, UNDRIP gives us little guidance as all are remedies greater than (or in the case of d_5 equivalent to) compensation for misappropriation.

G. Communitarian Justification

The communitarian account suggests that Indigenous peoples should have a significant degree of control over information that is their community resource. Such doctrine would appear to exclude decision d_1 and d_5. However, there is little explicit guidance from this doctrine as to whether very distal uses, including uses arising out of serendipitous discoveries, should be considered as use of the traditional knowledge.

7

Synthesis of Findings and Further Analysis

I. Introduction

As we have seen from chapter six, the results of the application of the various philosophical justifications to our question of whether a right to prevent third-party use of TKAGR should extend to coverage of serendipitous discoveries of second uses are wide ranging and, in some cases, directly contradictory.

Table 13 is an attempt to present the answers derived from each approach within a single matrix. As with the other results tables seen in chapter six, up arrows signify support for the decision; down arrows signify lack of support for the decision. Queries denote where no clear answer can be drawn. Again, the weighting of support shown is to be considered *within* a justification; there is no attempt in this matrix to represent weighting as between justifications.

II. How Might We Achieve Synthesis?

Looking at these findings we are immediately presented with a problem: how are we to come to any synthesis of these results? One approach may be simply to read across Table 13 to find which decision finds the least contradiction across the application of justifications. Arriving at such a 'least contradictory' outcome has clear strengths; it sets the framework for further examination and helps us to focus on key points of conflict. However, such an approach treats all justifications as being of equal validity and all of equal applicability. We need an approach that, though maintaining simplicity, is more nuanced and takes into account an assessment of applicability of justification.

We also have a deeper problem. Many of the underlying justifications outlined here are philosophically incompatible. However, as was previously stated, it is not the aim of this study to reconcile widely differing philosophical justifications – for example, to demonstrate the inherent primacy of utilitarianism over natural rights theories, or indeed vice versa. How, then, might we go about a synthesis whilst avoiding this high-level conflict? Naturally, such a question is not unique to our current problem and approaches to examining such potentially conflicting inputs have long exercised legal theorists. The key approaches can be summarised as 'overlapping consensus' and 'incompletely theorised agreements'.

Table 13 Summary matrix of results from various approaches

Decision	Utilitarianism			'Natural rights'				Maximin (Rawls)	Inherent right to self-determination/ communitarian claim (Gibson)	Reparation (Munzer)	UNDRIP
					'Right based on Personality'						
	Valorisation model	Utility through control	Global health	Lockean 'labour-desert'	Kantian	Fichtean	Hegelian				
d_1 (no veto, no compensation)	↓↓↓↓	↓↓↓	↑↑↑	↓↓	↑↑↑	↑↑↑	↑↑↑	↓	↓↓↓	↓↓↓	↓↓↓
d_2 (total veto)	↑↑↑↑	↑↑↑	↓↓↓	↑	↓↓↓	↓↓↓	↓↓↓	↑↑↑↑	?	?	↑
d_3 (limited veto)	↑↑	↑↓	↑↑	↑	↓↓↓	↓↓↓	↓↓↓	↑↑	?	?	↑
d_4 (limited veto + compensation)	↑↑↑	↑↓	↑*	↑	↓↓↓	↓↓↓	↓↓↓	↑↑↑	?	?	↑
d_5 (no veto but compensation)	↑	↓	↑↑↑*	↑	↓↓↓	↓↓↓	↓↓↓	↑	↓↓	?	↑

* Subject to levels of compensation.

In *A Theory of Justice*, Rawls suggests that within a nearly just society there is no need for strict consensus of views on a political conception of justice, merely a sufficient 'overlapping consensus'.[1] For Rawls, the overlapping need not be perfect: 'Both sides must believe that (however much their conceptions of justice differ) their views support the same judgment in the situation at hand, and would do so even if even if their respective positions be interchanged.'[2] Rawls subsequently developed this 'overlapping consensus' concept.[3] He highlighted that within a stable society the adherents of different views did not merely a get along together in a 'modus vivendi' founded upon each group primarily pursuing their own interest (which was itself served by not disturbing the 'treaty' with the other side) but by having sufficient genuine 'shared ground' or 'public reason' notwithstanding their differing philosophical starting points. It is this possession of shared ground that gives the overlapping consensus its stability and security.[4] It does not unravel as might a merely pragmatic treaty arrangement between opposing groups within society.

Rawls's overlapping consensus is a means by which individuals can find true agreement at higher levels of theoretical abstraction when agreements about certain particulars are untenable.[5] It has been described as depending 'in effect, on there being a morally significant core of commitments common to the "reasonable" fragment of each of the main comprehensive doctrines in the community'.[6] Crucially the existence of disagreement about some lower-level particulars does not of necessity destroy the higher level consensus.

Together with Posner,[7] Sunstein argues for a different approach to legal reasoning which minimises the reliance upon philosophical theory. He describes three classes of 'incompletely theorized agreements':

(i) incompletely theorized agreements on a *general principle*. Such agreements are incompletely theorized in the sense that people who accept the principle need not agree on what it entails in particular cases. The agreement is incompletely theorized in the sense that it is *incompletely specified*;
(ii) agreement on a mid-level principle, but disagreement about the more general theory that accounts for it *and* about outcomes in particular cases; and
(iii) incompletely theorized agreements on particular outcomes (who wins and who loses a case), accompanied by agreements on the low-level principles

[1] J Rawls, *A Theory of Justice* (Oxford, Oxford University Press, 1972) 340.
[2] ibid.
[3] J Rawls, 'The Idea of an Overlapping Consensus' (1987) 7(1) *Oxford Journal of Legal Studies* 1; John Rawls, *Political Liberalism* (New York, Columbia University Press, 1993) 134.
[4] Rawls, *The Idea of an Overlapping Consensus* (n 3) 12.
[5] Y Bathaee, 'Incompletely Theorized Agreements: An Unworkable Theory of Judicial Modesty' (2006) 34(5) *Fordham Urban Law Journal* 7.
[6] F D'Agostino, 'Original Position' in EN Zalta (ed), *The Stanford Encyclopedia of Philosophy* (Summer 2003 edn) (plato.stanford.edu/archives/sum2003/entries/original-position/).
[7] RA Posner, *Overcoming Law* (Cambridge MA, Harvard University Press, 1995); RA Posner, *Law, Pragmatism and Democracy* (Cambridge MA, Harvard University Press, 2005) 24.

> that account for them. Such low-level principles include the 'ordinary material of legal doctrine' that have ambiguous relations to high-level theories, and that are compatible with more than one such high-level theory.[8]

Sunstein suggests that where people diverge on some (relatively) high-level proposition they may be able to agree if they lower the level of abstraction.[9] Common agreement on legal problems can be arrived at by seeking an 'incompletely theorized agreement' by looking to a level of theory (low- to mid- to high-level) on which you can find convergence/common ground and incompletely theorising (essentially 'agreeing to disagree') about those higher-level areas on which you disagree. This approach is arguably the 'inverse' of Rawls's 'overlapping consensus' approach.[10]

The approach means that instead of creating a broad theory concerning the law ahead of its application, Sunstein's incompletely theorised agreements allow resolutions to evolve by way of 'casuistical judgments at the point of application'.[11] It is essentially a bottom-up, as opposed to Rawls's 'top down', approach. One way of achieving such casuistical judgments is through the use of analogical reasoning in which the case in hand is compared to those cases with an equivalent fact pattern and equivalent decisions made.[12] This approach has been greatly criticised.[13] Chief amongst these critics is Dworkin, whose concern is essentially that legal decision-makers should not be shy of using theory as guidance.[14] For Dworkin, Sunstein and Posner's reliance on 'pragmatism' and Sunstein's 'theoretically modest' approach to problem solving, encourage (and allow) an avoidance of theory. In truth Sunstein's position may not be entirely contrary to that of Dworkin; indeed, as highlighted by Dworkin,[15] Sunstein has stated that

> some cases cannot be decided *at all* without introducing a fair amount of theory. Moreover, some cases cannot be decided *well* without theory. If a good theory is available and if judges can be persuaded that the theory is good, there should be no taboo on its judicial acceptance.[16]

Of course, that relies on there being a sole, obvious and incontrovertible 'good' theory and not a contradiction of a number of difficult-to-reconcile theories.

In relation to our current question, it is hard to see how one might apply Sunstein's 'theoretically modest' approach. As was discussed in chapter three, where

[8] CR Sunstein, 'Incompletely Theorized Agreements' (1995) 108(7) *Harvard Law Review* 1733; CR Sunstein, 'On Legal Theory and Legal Practice' in I Shapiro and J Wagner DeCew (eds), *Theory and Practice NOMOS XXXVII* (New York, New York University Press, 1995); CR Sunstein, *Legal Reasoning and Political Conflict* (Oxford, Oxford University Press, 1996) 35.
[9] Sunstein 'Incompletely Theorized Agreements' (n 8) 1740.
[10] Bathaee (n 5).
[11] Sunstein, *Legal Reasoning and Political Conflict* (n 8).
[12] See generally CR Sunstein, 'On Analogical Reasoning' (1992) 106 *Harvard Law Review* 741, 744.
[13] Bathaee (n 5).
[14] R Dworkin, *Justice in Robes* (Cambridge, MA, The Belnap Press of Harvard University Press, 2006) 66.
[15] ibid 71.
[16] Sunstein, *Legal Reasoning and Political Conflict* (n 8) 54.

one is seeking to limit third-party use of an idea the *only* guide we can find as to the extent of such control can be the theoretical justification(s) for creating (or not creating) such control. If we avoid such theoretical guidance we might arrive at the imposition of essentially arbitrary limits, or the misapplication of precedent from other laws (such as patent law) which although they might appear superficially similar, are different both in terms of history, subject matter of protection and underlying theoretical justification.

Rawls was describing a 'shared ground' approach in terms of the broader governance of society, rather than in relation to the determination of a particular (low-level) legal problem. However, he does allow us not to be inhibited by inherent high-level philosophical conflicts. If we can find agreement in the low-level application of conflicting higher-level theories, we need not be concerned that the justifications originate from different philosophical places. The reconciliation of conflicting low-level applications is altogether more difficult, even if those may not, of necessity, destroy a higher-level consensus in other respects.

Taking his inspiration from Rawls's overlapping consensus approach, Merges accepts a theoretical pluralism of high-level (what he refers to as 'foundational') principles.[17] He sees utilitarian, deontological and other accounts as giving rise to a shared body of 'mid-level' principles that are equally valid whichever high-level justification you consider the more supportable. As he puts it:

> Midlevel principles provide our common space, our place of engagement. They are like a musical score, allowing us all to play together, even if we disagree about the deep wellsprings or ultimate significance of our shared performance, our common musical practice. The midlevel principles allow us to be tolerant about questions of ultimate importance. In my theory, the conceptual hierarchy includes a ground floor that is airy and capacious. There is room at the bottom.[18]

Merges proposes four such mid-level principles:

(i) efficiency – enhancement of the efficiency of an economy;
(ii) non-removal – information and ideas in the public domain must not be taken away or privatised;
(iii) proportionality – the scope of an IP right ought be commensurate with the magnitude of the contribution underlying the right; and
(iv) dignity – the dignity interest can be thought of as an invisible string that connects individual creators with their works, and that survives even a formal act of legal alienation.

In further support of a mid-level approach, Merges states:

> The more systemic view supplied by Rawls's way of thinking can get us out of the unproductive and often divisive trap of thinking that each individual rule of IP must

[17] RP Merges, *Justifying Intellectual Property* (Cambridge MA, Harvard University Press, 2011) 10.
[18] ibid.

> balance out perfectly. Rawls's approach frees us from this excessively internalist perspective and ought to be embraced for that reason alone.[19]

Merges has separately stated that he believes that in the intellectual property field utilitarian foundations are 'inadequate' as the data required by a comprehensive utilitarian perspective are not in evidence. He believes, however, that deontic conceptions growing out of the ideas of Locke, Kant and Rawls provide a 'better' set of foundational commitment.[20] He is aware that others disagree, stating this 'is why the midlevel principles are so important as a shared policy language for those with divergent foundational commitments'.[21] However, as might be anticipated, Merges's approach has put the mid-level 'cat' amongst the theoretical 'pigeons'. Blankfein-Tabachnick has recently criticised Merges's mid-level approach as 'untenable'.[22] Blankfein-Tabachnick contends that:

> [Merges's] midlevel principles conflict with important liberal 'foundational' accounts of property, thereby calling into question the justificatory force such principles might hold. Moreover, contrary to Professor Robert P. Merges' view, different foundational principles, whether maximizing wealth, net aggregate value, or the position of the least well-off, will yield different substantive outcomes in IP cases. Accordingly ... any project conjoining this set of midlevel principles with maximizing distributive principles cannot be sustained. A sophisticated understanding of IP, its theory, and crucially its legal doctrine and practice, does not, and should not, include midlevel principles understood to be consistent with such variously competing foundations.[23]

Whilst, broadly speaking, concepts of non-removal, proportionality and dignity (the former two demonstrating a distinctly Lockean 'flavour' and the latter obvious echoes coming from Kantian/Fichtean rights based in personhood) would seem relatively uncontroversial, Merges's continued adherence to elements of a utilitarian model (in his efficiency mid-level principle) remains counter to those for whom such a utilitarian approach is fundamentally flawed.[24] Citing Merges's attempt at this reconciliation of these deontological and utilitarian approaches, Fromer has recently highlighted that the utilitarian economic incentive to invent provided by patent law also provides 'expressive incentives' to inventors to develop their personality through invention (although she ignores the fact Kant, Fichte and Hegel were not supportive of control over ideas per se).[25]

[19] ibid 21.

[20] RP Merges, 'Book Club: Justifying IP – Midlevel Principles: Response to Jonathan Masur' (2013) prawfsblawg.blogs.com/prawfsblawg/2013/01/book-club-justifying-ip-midlevel-principles-response-to-jonathan-masur.html.

[21] ibid.

[22] DH Blankfein-Tabachnick 'Intellectual Property Doctrine and Midlevel Principles' (2013) 101(5) *California Law Review Art* 1315; see also: DH Blankfein-Tabachnick, 'Book Review: Does Intellectual Property Law Have Foundations? A Review of Robert Merges's *Justifying Intellectual Property*' (2013) 45 *Connecticut Law Review* 995.

[23] Blankfein-Tabachnick, 'Intellectual Property Doctrine and Midlevel Principles' (n 22) 2.

[24] Merges (n 17) 10.

[25] JC Fromer, 'Expressive Incentives in Intellectual Property' (2012) 98 *Virginia Law Review* 1745.

The validity (or otherwise) of Merges's mid-level principles (particularly the presence of a utilitarian account within those principles) remains to be determined by the academic community and no doubt the finding of a Rawlsian 'shared ground' will continue to stimulate a vigorous ongoing debate.

Accordingly, the present study adopts a conservative analytical approach which might be described as seeking a 'least contradiction', but with giving due concern for theoretical conflict. Closer to the approach of Rawls than Sunstein, it seeks to find what common consensus there is between the outcomes suggested by different philosophical justifications. However, if these clash, it seeks to give appropriate weight to the appropriateness and suitability to the justifications in conflict to the situation under examination. This approach is in line with the pluralistic account advocated by Resnik (mentioned above) which acknowledges that the analysis of different intellectual property rights requires differing assessments of competing moral values in the light of the particular facts and circumstances which affect that right.[26]

III. A Synthesis

Our first step in this examination is to look at the relevance of the traditional natural rights justifications. The rights based upon personality (following the philosophies of Kant, Fichte and Hegel) all fail to support a veto/compensation right on the basis that ideas per se (as opposed to the protection of expression or of a right to attribution) cannot be the proper subject matter of such a right. We also saw that significant arguments have been raised as to whether the problems of origination/individuation are so severe within a natural rights account as to entirely undermine application of a Lockean labour-desert justification. Even if a Lockean account *does* give us an underlying foundation for the existence of a right (and reminds us of the important of balancing the rights of claimants to intellectual property with those of 'commoners') its application *in particulars* is greatly limited by the origination/individuation problems, notably in questions of degree.

If, as a heuristic tool, we exclude the natural law justifications based on the ideas of Locke, Kant, Fichte and Hegel, then we are left looking at rights based on the justifications set out in Table 14.

Looking across these remaining justifications, we find that *none* of the approaches (save for the utilitarian global health justification in respect of vetoes alone) favour a complete absence of veto/right to compensation. So a maximum consistency approach suggests that we are looking toward *some* type of veto/right to compensation.

Examining the four types of veto/right to compensation in play – that is, decision d_2 (total veto), decision d_3 (limited veto), decision d_4 (limited veto with

[26] DB Resnik, 'A Pluralistic Account of Intellectual Property' (2003) 46(4) *Journal of Business Ethics* 319, 319.

Table 14 Summary matrix of results (without justifications based on Locke, Kant, Fichte and Hegel)

	Utilitarianism						
Decision	**Valorisation model**	**'Utility through control'**	**Global health**	**Maximin (Rawls)**	**Reparation (Munzer)**	**Self-determination/ communit-arianism (Gibson)**	**UNDRIP**
d_1 (no veto)	↓↓↓↓	↓↓↓	↑↑↑	↓	↓↓↓	↓↓↓	↓↓↓
d_2 (total veto)	↑↑↑↑	↑↑↑	↓↓↓	↑↑↑↑	?	?	↑
d_3 (limited veto)	↑↑	↑↓	↑↑	↑↑	?	?	↑
d_4 (limited veto + compensation)	↑↑↑	↑↓	↑*	↑↑↑	?	?	↑
d_5 (limited veto but compensation)	↑	↓	↑↑↑*	↑	?	↓↓	↑

* Subject to levels of compensation.

compensation) and decision d_5 (no veto but compensation) – we saw that our Rawlsian *maximin* analysis most favoured a total veto (d_2), followed by d_4 (limited veto + compensation), followed by decision d_3 (limited veto), followed by d_5 (no veto but compensation).

We also saw that none of these decisions are entirely inconsistent with the achievement of utilitarian goals through valorisation of traditional knowledge, or Indigenous peoples' right to self-determination, communitarian justification, or UNDRIP

Broadly speaking, Munzer's reparations approach favours control. However, as discussed in chapter five, the uncertainties surrounding the reparation justification are so great as to really be of no assistance in the current analysis.

Although it was more consistent with a global health utility than any of the veto options, it was argued that option d_5 (no veto but compensation) was unlikely to create the same perception of value amongst relevant actors as would a veto (provided that the compensation provided under the determinant mechanism was broadly equivalent to royalties that would be paid under a licence) as the absence of a veto mechanism would preclude the creation of exclusive licensees who could rely upon their competitors being excluded from the market.

Of all the *veto* options, d_4 (limited veto + compensation) and decision d_3 (limited veto) would appear on first examination to be more consistent with the preservation of global health utilitarian justification. Both approaches allow pharmaceutical companies to use a serendipitous discovery without *absolute* hindrance. If we consider the global health utilitarian justification to be an important determinant, this leaves us with a choice between d_4 (limited veto with compensation) and decision d_3 (limited veto without compensation). Of these two choices decision d_4 (limited veto with compensation) is more strongly supported by the Rawlsian maximin analysis.

The question of whether d_4 is more likely to provide value to traditional knowledge than d_3 (limited veto without compensation) is somewhat more moot. As was discussed in chapter four, the mechanism by which the creation of value in traditional knowledge achieves the utilitarian goals of preservation of the environment/traditional knowledge (or a conflation of the two) is most likely to be through the subjective perception of some economic value in the knowledge amongst all the actors (both Indigenous and third party) involved in a situation in which the preservation of the environment and/or traditional knowledge is pitted against development that might lead to the destruction or diminution of the environment/traditional knowledge.

As was also stated in chapter four, notwithstanding a scepticism in relation to the overall efficacy of a valorisation model, the perception amongst all the concerned actors of *some* value in genetic resources and in traditional knowledge associated with those resources (created through the existence of a right to control use) must be better than *no* perceived value whatsoever (created through the absence of a right to control use). As between option d_1 and d_3, then, the requirement to pay compensation is likely to have little effect on value as perceived by third parties, but is likely to have an impact on perception of value within the Indigenous group holding the rights. As such there would seem to be an argument here to prefer d_4 over d_3.

In relation to achieving a 'utility through control' utilitarian goal, it was argued in chapter six that this goal was most likely to be achieved through a total veto (option d_2), whereas options d_4 (limited veto + compensation) and decision d_3 (limited veto only) may or may not achieve this utility depending on the Indigenous group concerned. This utility was unlikely to be achieved (or achieved only minimally) through option d_5.

As was also discussed in chapter six, seeking a resolution of the conflict between the 'utility through control' and 'global health' utilities is exceptionally difficult. Those options, which are likely to fulfil the goal of 'utility through control', will work against the global health utility and vice versa. This conflict certainly highlights the difficulties (and perhaps the potential futility) in attempting to compare and rank such differing utilities.

Earlier in this analysis we excluded the Lockean labour-desert justification due to inherent uncertainties of origination and individuation. However, in formulating a *positive* law we may at least seek some consistency with *natural* law principles where we can. This may be particularly true where we are looking at rights based on *contribution* – as we have seen, the concept of contribution is fundamental to all positive intellectual property laws and it seems not unreasonable to apply a contribution requirement to a positive law relating to the protection of TKAGR. That said, however, perhaps all we can safely say from our labour-desert analysis is that all options, other than d_1 (no veto/compensation), are consistent with a labour-desert account. Not a contribution which takes us particularly far.

So, overall, in applying a 'least contradiction' analysis we find that decision d_4 (limited veto with compensation) would seem to give us the least contradictions across most analyses. However, if we re-examine the justifications in Table 14, we find that this is arguably a strange result. In fact all the justifications favour (or are least consistent with) option d_2 – a total veto – *save alone* for the 'global health' utility. We must therefore ask ourselves to what extent the global health utility would truly be undermined by the existence of an *absolute* veto on all downstream use.

The veto envisaged in d_2 does give an absolute right for an Indigenous group to prevent *any* downstream use of TKAGR, notwithstanding that the use may considered by many to be very distal to the original understanding. There is no doubt that in this case (d_2) one cannot entirely rule out a situation in which a new (perhaps serendipitously discovered) treatment may be denied to the world by an Indigenous group choosing to exercise their right of veto absolutely (or seeking to licence the right at a royalty level which was not viable for licensees).

However, although this is entirely *possible*, we might ask whether it is *likely*. The exercise of an absolute veto without the grant of a licence would likely mean that the Indigenous group would be unlikely to enjoy any economic benefit sharing of the fruits of the downstream exploitation of the information. One might imagine that the drive to partake in benefits of being a licensor would be strong. However, such a drive is likely to be based upon a Western-economic perspective. It is entirely possible to imagine a situation in which absolute control is deemed by a group to be more important than such benefits. Simply put, without further work, we cannot say what would be the actual likelihood of a new drug being denied to the global population. However, if one were to pursue the total veto policy proposal this *always* has to remain a possibility.

We must also note that it is significantly in the broader interest of the global pharmaceutical industry that the great reserve of biologically active compounds which are to be found in the flora, fauna, fungi and bacteria of biodiverse environments are preserved and can be located. If it is more likely that a total veto will more strongly serve the protection of our ways of accessing such compounds, then the risk of an occasional absolute veto might be outweighed by the overall instrumental utility of the preservation of such knowledge and the relevant environment/genetic resources. At this point we simply do not know. This is point which will be returned to in the Conclusions of this work at chapter eight.

That brings us back again to the question of whether a total veto serves to create a greater perception of value in the appropriate traditional knowledge than would option d_4 (limited veto plus compensation). Here one might argue that the majority of the perceived value in the knowledge is created by the control of the first use rather than any downstream second (or subsequent) use which may, or may not, arise. However, as was highlighted in the valorisation model analysis, where one is seeking to create an optimum perception of value there is significant merit in a system that is simple to understand and simple to administer. Again, this is a point to which we will be returning in chapter eight.

IV. The Workability of a Limited Veto – Introduction

As mentioned, looking over the entire picture, option d_4 would appear to meet many of the requirements for a justifiable 'consensus' position. In practice, however, whether it represents such a 'consensus' (or indeed is at all workable) might depend upon the details of how the normative concept was brought into positive law. There are two crucial questions which need to be addressed in this regard:

(a) If the compensatory mechanism is based on an apportionment determined by an assessment of relative contributions, how do we assess those relative contributions?
(b) What *is* a truly serendipitous discovery?

As we will see, both questions are (very) closely related.

V. The Workability of a Limited Veto – Assessment of 'Contribution'

Questions of 'contribution' in intellectual property law have most commonly focused on the determination of the degree to which an infringer's use of an infringing concept or product has contributed to the infringer's overall profits and the extent therefore to which the infringer need account for those profits to the intellectual property right holder.[27] In this respect, much of the work of the courts has been to assess contributory causes to profits made.[28] Attention has similarly been paid to assessment of royalty rates within non-voluntary patent licensing. Mechanisms for determining such rates exist[29] and similar principles as exist in the apportionment of an account of profits are applied in a non-voluntary patent licensing context where the patent in question covers part of a complex object.[30]

All these approaches are essentially based on apportionment of *commercial* value and do not (it is argued here) assist in our present investigation. We need to recognise that the assessment of contribution which is important in relation to options d_4 and d_5 does not relate to the splitting of profits between infringing and non-infringing activities, but to an assessment, in a particular situation, of the various epistemic elements of the 'discovery' which have been brought by the contributing parties. This question is, arguably, much closer to the question of determination of the in-imitativeness of a follow-on concept in the light of the concepts that have gone before, than it is to the splitting of profits or commercial value.

In relation to patents, the question of in-imitativeness is structured as whether the new right is novel or inventive and is (in relation to both tests) set as a binary 'yes or no' in the light of prior art and (sometimes) the common general knowledge. What patent offices do not do (and indeed are not required to do) is determine whether a new patent application is made up of, say, 95 per cent 'old' contribution and 5 per cent 'new' contribution. Indeed, in much patent practice and case law, great efforts are made to simplify the process by the use of formulaic tests which seek to narrow down those things against which the claimed invention will be tested

[27] See generally L Bentley, 'Accounting for Profits Gained by Infringement of Copyright: When Does it End?' (1991) 13(1) *European Intellectual Property Review* 5; see also AJ Stack et al, 'Accounting of Profits Calculations in Intellectual Property Cases in Canada' (2001) 17(2) *Canadian Intellectual Property Review* 405.

[28] See eg *Redwood Music Ltd v Chappell and Co Ltd* [1982] RPC 109; see also *Beloit Canada Ltée v Valmet OY* (1994) 55 (3d) CPR 385 (FCTD Canada); *The Wellcome Foundation Ltd et al v Apotex* (1999) 82 3d CPR 359 (FCTD Canada); *Celanese International Corp v BP Chemicals Ltd* [1999] RPC 203.

[29] E Välimäki, 'Calculation of Royalties in Compulsory Licensing of Pharmaceutical Patents in Europe – How Much Is Justified?' (2011) *Nordic Journal of Commercial Law Special Edition*; JH Reichman, 'Non-voluntary Licensing of Patented Inventions Historical Perspective, Legal Framework under TRIPS, and an Overview of the Practice in Canada and the USA' (UNCTAD-ICTSD Project on IPRs and Sustainable Development, 2003); World Health Organization Health Economics and Drugs TCM, 'Remuneration Guidelines for Non-voluntary Use of a Patent on Medical Technologies', WHO/TCM/2005.1.

[30] World Health Organization (n 29) 61.

against.[31] For an extreme example, in the European Patent Office an inventive step is assessed using a highly formulaic 'problem-solution' test based upon selection of a single closest piece of prior art and determination of an 'objective technical problem' posed by that prior art which the claimed invention successfully solves.[32]

We saw in our analysis of the Lockean labour-desert justification in chapter six (in section III.A) that the crucial question was what constituted a 'contribution'. That thorny question remains where one is looking to create an apportionment based on contribution. Of course, if our grounds for creating the right are based on *positive* (rather than natural) law it is always open to lawmakers to arrive at positive law solution. However, in reality, the formulation of a mechanism to fairly balance contribution to a discovery is fraught with difficulty. On what basis might we determine that one part of a discovery is more important than another? Do we (and how do we) factor in the effluxion of time? Are newer contributions to be given weighting over older contributions? In addition, we have assumed that the determination would be between two parties, the Indigenous group and the serendipitous 'discoverer', but there may be many partial contributions by others which could greatly complicate our (already difficult) bipartite determination.

What is common to these questions is that they refer to relative contribution made in relation to a serendipitous discovery. Therefore, in many ways we actually find that these questions bring us back round to the core question of what constitutes a 'true' serendipitous discovery?

VI. The Workability of a Limited Veto – Serendipity and 'Retrospective Obviousness'

In chapter five, it was highlighted that where a serendipitous discovery has been made, the crucial element is that there has been an entirely non-obvious, or unexpected, revelation of a new feature (use) of the 'thing' (eg ligand) obtained from the genetic resource to which the traditional knowledge relates. Accordingly, when examining the policy options (d_1 to d_5) earlier in this work we defined a 'serendipitous discovery' of a second use to mean a discovery in which the second use is truly unexpected in the light of the *current* understanding of the underlying biology when the discovery of the second use is made. However, it was also highlighted in chapter five that not all steps to a new use will appear so momentous; some second uses may be reached (without a serendipitous leap) through a steady step-wise process in which researchers progressively understand more about the underlying biological target of a ligand. It was also stated that, even though a serendipitous discovery will *appear* unexpected at the time that it is made, as soon

[31] See eg *Graham et al v John Deere Co of Kansas City et al* (1966) 383 US 1 (USSC); see also *Pozzoli Spa v BDMO SA and Anor* [2007] EWCA Civ 588.

[32] EPO Guidelines G-VII 5; see also Case Law of the EPO Boards of Appeal I.D.2; EPO Guidelines G-VII 5; Case Law of the EPO Boards of Appeal I.D.3.1; EPO Guidelines G-VII 5.2; Case Law of the EPO Boards of Appeal I.D.4.1.

as the discovery of an unexpected second therapeutic benefit has been made, it will initiate research into the biological processes underlying the two apparently different (but in fact physiologically linked) therapeutic effects. This further work might be said to eventually render the discovery *retrospectively* obvious (just as such work performed ahead of the discovery could render it *prospectively* obvious).

Of course, *retrospective* obviousness would seem to be oxymoronic. When we ask whether something is obvious we are inherently asking whether it is obvious *at the time* the question is being asked of us. We may debate what materials and other understandings we might compare a discovery with, but all the materials and understandings to hand can have only been created *in the past*.

This focus on the date upon which a question is asked is a fundamental element within existing intellectual property laws. Notably, the priority date of a patent application (and what knowledge can be considered to form the state of the art at that date) is critical to determining the novelty and inventiveness of a patent.[33] The requirement that patent novelty and obviousness be determined at a certain date stems from the fact that patents are registered rights which have to be applied for and which have a fixed monopoly period – in one sense they have to have a start date otherwise they would not have an end date.

As previously mentioned, most intellectual property rights have an end date. This 'self-defined expiration, a built-in sunset' is for Hughes what enhances the social neutrality of intellectual property rights.[34] Limiting the term of protection balances the negative of denying others an opportunity to use the subject matter of the right and in the long-term allows for an expansion of the common weal. The start date within patent law is central to the determination of the 'contribution' made by the invention and of whether it is deserving of patent protection at the date it is applied for. The requirement of a start date also 'cements' what is claimed. Most patent laws contain strict rules as to post-application amendment and the addition during prosecution of 'added-matter' which does not form a part of the original application.[35]

The UK Court of Appeal's invalidation of Pfizer's patent surrounding the effect of cyclic-guanosine monophosphate (cGMP)-specific phosphodiesterase (PDE) Type 5 inhibitors (including sildenafil citrate (Viagra)) on erectile dysfunction presents an excellent example of a 'surprising' second therapeutic use rendered obvious by prior publication of the understanding of the underlying biological mechanism.[36] During a study examining the effect of sildenafil on angina pectoris (affected through a dilatation effect on cardiac blood vessels), it was observed that the drug had a 'second' effect on penile erectile tissue. Such a discovery could have been seen as a non-obvious serendipitous discovery. Indeed Pfizer, the sponsors of the study, certainly felt so and, after further work, filed a patent for the effect of the drug on erectile dysfunction. However, ahead of this filing a group led by Snyder at Johns Hopkins University had been examining the effect of nitric oxide

[33] See eg Arts 56 and 54 EPC.

[34] J Hughes, 'The Philosophy of Intellectual Property' (1988) 77 *Georgetown Law Journal* 287, 296.

[35] See eg Arts 123(3) and 123(2) EPC.

[36] See generally Y Liu, 'The Tale of Viagra Patents: Comparative Studies of the Global Challenges in China and Other Countries' (2013) 18 *Japanese Intellectual Property Review* 523.

(NO) on the relaxation of blood vessels. The group suspected that NO was (unusually for a gas) a neurotransmitter responsible for the regulation of smooth muscle tone in the wall of blood vessels. During their studies they discovered that nitric oxide synthase (NOS, the enzyme that catalyses the production of NO) is found in localised concentrations in the erectile material of the penis. Given that the inhibition of NOS also inhibited penile erections, Snyder's group suggested that the release of NO in penile erectile tissue is responsible for causing penile erections.[37] As it was separately understood that NO mediated its effect on vascular smooth through stimulating the production of the intracellular messenger cGMP, it was a short step to understand that an inhibitor of cGMP inactivation (such as sildenafil) would have a stimulatory impact on blood flow in erectile tissue.[38] The *Pfizer* case demonstrates that timing is crucial. A schematic representation of the biochemical mechanism of action of sildenafil citrate is given in Figure 7.

Figure 7 Schematic representation of the biochemical mechanism of action of sildenafil citrate

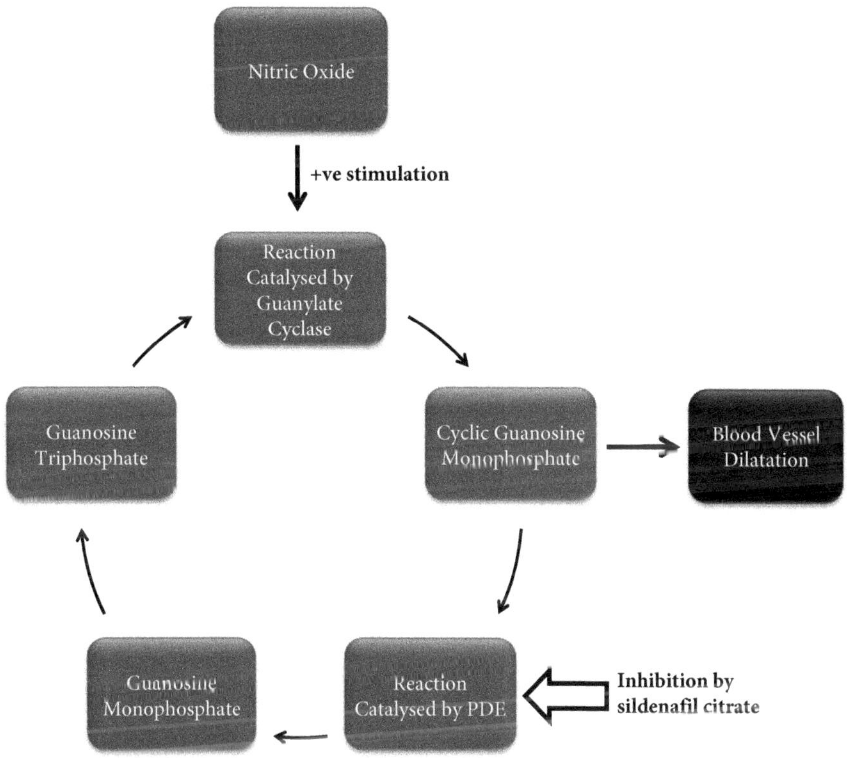

[37] AL Burnett et al, 'Nitric Oxide: A Physiologic Mediator of Penile Erection' (1992) 257(5068) *Science* 401.

[38] SH Snyder, 'Forty Years of Neurotransmitters' in TA Ban, D Healy and E Shorter (eds), *From Psychopharmacology to Neuropsychopharmacology in the 1980s and the Story of CINP as Told in Autobiography* (Budapest, Animula, 2002) 36; TA Ban, 'The Role of Serendipity in Drug Discovery' (2006) 8(3) *Dialogues in Clinical Neuroscience* 335.

A similar story is, of course, seen with discovery of the 'unexpected' cardiovascular protective 'second use' of aspirin (described in chapter five, in section V.B) but which is actually caused by a shared biochemical pathway with the anti-inflammatory 'first use'. At the time of the discovery of the anticoagulant effect of aspirin (when used to treat gums during dentistry) the effect was wholly unexpected. However, once one fully understands the shared biochemical pathway for both therapeutic effects, the second use would hardly be surprising

Let us consider, then, the situation in which we have a subsisting right to control downstream use of an idea which has an *infinite* temporal duration. We are immediately forced to ask at what point in time we should determine that any new downstream development of that idea is 'non-obvious' in the light of that right?

When the new discovery of a second use is made (say the effect of plant A on disease Y in our North versus West scenario) at time α, it may appear to be unexpected (or serendipitous). Now let us imagine that research work is being done in parallel which uncovers that A has its effect of disease X through physiological mechanism P. This work also reveals that disease Y is also caused through mechanism P. We are now at time β. Had the finding of the effect of A on Y been made after time β, then it is unlikely that the finding would be considered as a non-obvious discovery – indeed it would most likely be considered the natural consequence of the effect of A on joint physiological process P (just as was the case for Pfizer with sildenafil as discussed above).

If we assume that the discovery of the joint effect through mechanism P is inevitable, we might ask ourselves this: is the appearance of 'serendipity' merely an artefact of the time at which we have chosen to test it? Although we cannot know with certainty when it will be determined, we do know that with enough time the *entire* biological benefit of A will be uncovered – all of which can trace its causal 'inspiration' from the awareness that A can treat disease X.

So, with a right with a duration in perpetuity, could not the Indigenous group holding that right at a date well beyond that upon which the serendipitous discovery was made say 'now we understand that your discovery and ours are linked through common biology and accordingly we now seek to claim absolute control over your new downstream use'? To stop such a claim being successful one would have to envisage that the making of a third-party serendipitous discovery of a second use would in some way 'cement' the claim of the Indigenous group such that, even were the serendipitous discovery to subsequently become obvious, the Indigenous group's claim against the serendipitous discoverer (or perhaps other third parties using that discovery) would be barred.

In truth the workings of such a bar could be complex. We would also still be left asking what degree of discovery would be required to 'cement' the Indigenous people's claim. Would the bar work in favour of the serendipitous discover alone, or also in favour of other third parties using that discovery? How would the bar work in relation to subsequent serendipitous discoveries? Would that subsequent serendipitous discoverer benefit from a new bar to the Indigenous claim? What would constitute such a subsequent serendipitous discovery in the light both of the original traditional knowledge and the first serendipitous discovery, and the work on biological mechanism triggered by that discovery?

However, as was discussed above, such complexities *can* be solved through the formulation of positive law, but we need to consider what philosophical justification can be made for such a bar to/cementation of the Indigenous claim in the first place – essentially, why is serendipity *special*?

Although it is framed in a different way, this question is essentially just the same as that addressed earlier in this work and analysed in relation to policy options d_1 to d_5 above. Restricting the scope of the Indigenous claim beyond a serendipitous discovery is arguably the same as seeking a bar to cementation of the claim upon the making of a serendipitous discovery. Accordingly, the conflicting justifications that we have seen in relation to policy options d_1 to d_5 remain the same. We are essentially left again with the fundamental conflict we have seen between (on the one hand) a promotion of global health utility and (on the other hand) the other analysed justifications.

Looking at the overall utilitarian considerations, one might perhaps suggest that the creation of a bar on the Indigenous claim could create an incentive for researchers to search for serendipitous discoveries (perhaps through the testing of newly discovered ligands against a range of biological targets). However, one might consider that pharmaceutical companies are provided with more than sufficient incentive to investigate the effects of ligands through existing patent systems, without requiring enhancement of such incentive through a limitation of Indigenous rights.

Paradoxically, such a bar might (in theory at least) encourage a certain ignorance as to the underlying physiology of a ligand which was subject to an Indigenous right to control. The less you know about the underlying biology, the more likely a discovery will be 'serendipitous'. However, whether a drive to avoid an ongoing Indigenous right would seriously influence such investigation (which would be crucial to the development of the first use of the ligand as a therapeutic agent) is highly questionable. Indeed the 'search' for serendipitous discoveries would be likely to unavoidably throw 'unwelcome' light upon underlying biological mechanisms in any event.

So, as regard our non-Locke-, Kant-, Fichte- and Hegel-based justifications we would appear to be in much the same place as we were with our initial consideration of policy options d_1 to d_5.

We might, however, ask whether giving the positive right (of whatever type) an infinite temporal duration has a complicating impact on the labour-desert justification for the right. In chapter six (in section III A) we discussed the different treatments of 'inchoate' and 'inherent' claims, concluding that a labour-desert analysis was broadly supportive of an inchoate claim and with it a partial veto (even if the exact details of degree of contribution were difficult, perhaps impossible, to pin down) and perhaps less supportive of an inherent claim. However, overall it was concluded that the uncertainties of the labour-desert account were such as to provide us with little concrete guidance other than that a positive right of some sort was supported.

In looking at a right of control with infinite duration we do have one factor which is likely to be constant throughout and that is the *initial* contribution made by the Indigenous group – the discovery of an effect of the genetic resource which was deserving of a right to control. It is that contribution which should be compared to the chain of new third-party discoveries which are made during the (infinite) duration of the right. Each new discovery, in effect, creates a new contribution which is to be tested against the original. If we are seeking to determine whether there should be a bar to an ongoing claim, we need to ask whether there is a degree of third-party contribution which is of sufficient merit to warrant that bar.

That contribution would need to be significant enough to somehow 'stand above' the mass of smaller steps, such that even though the same place was reached (the understanding of a second use) the step was itself great enough to break the chain. Here, of course, the labour desert account fails us – we are looking again at questions of *degree*. Of course, determining such differential contribution (practically, and theoretically, difficult to determine in any event) would continually change with time as incremental developments were made rendering an ongoing assessment essentially impossible in any event.

However, stepping back from such difficulties one might ask oneself, if the same 'total' of third-party contribution is reached (the understanding of a second use) should it really matter whether it is reached by way of a series of small steps, or by one larger one? From this point we might ask is it the nature of the second use which provides grounds for a break in causation, rather than how that second use is arrived at?

VII. The Workability of a Limited Veto – 'Coincidental' Second Uses

Looking at the question of scope from the perspective of a right of 'infinite' duration also gives us a further insight that was not quite so apparent in our previous analysis. We envisaged above that, with sufficient time, it would inevitably become obvious that the fact that A's effect of X and on Y was mediated through joint physiological mechanism P and that accordingly in the long life of the right to control downstream use what might have initially appeared to be 'serendipity' would actually be an artefact of the time at which the discovery was considered. However, the appearance of 'retrospective obviousness' in that analysis is entirely reliant upon a shared underlying *physiological* mechanism.

How, though, might we consider the position where a serendipitously discovered downstream use is *unrelated* to a shared underlying physiological mechanism (or indeed any physiological mechanism)? Perkin's serendipitous discovery of mauveine whilst attempting to synthesise quinine provides (a perhaps extreme, but instructive) starting point for analysis. Although Perkin would not have attempted the oxidisation of aniline with potassium dichromate *but for* an attempt to synthesise quinine, his discovery of mauveine was clearly an accident. It could have as easily happened in a different context by someone looking for an entirely different end result. Perkin's finding was in no way reliant upon the biological properties of quinine. In addition, mauveine[39] has a very different chemical structure from (and indeed is not a chemical derivative of) quinine.[40]

As has been discussed, the discovery of mauveine was the stimulus for the growth of the synthetic dye industry, which in due course led to the development of antibiotics (such as the sulfonamide Prontosil) based on synthetic dyes. However, the biochemical mechanism by which those compounds have their antibiotic effect (as an antimetabolite which competes within the bacterial cell with *para*-aminobenzoic acid for incorporation into folic acid)[41] is entirely unrelated to the way in which it is likely that quinine has its pharmacological effect (through a plasmodium-selective inhibition of haematin biocrystallization).[42] Further, the biological target of quinine (the eukaryotic malaria-causing plasmodium) is taxonomically entirely unrelated to the prokaryotic bacterial target of antibiotics.[43] So, although there is a true causation *in fact* link between the understanding of the Indigenous peoples of the Andes that the bark of the *quinaquina* (or Cinchona) tree has fever-controlling properties, the use of mauveine dye, and the use of the sulfonamides to treat bacterial infection, one cannot say that either of those downstream uses is *inevitably* derived from the use of quinine as an antimalarial. Nor, indeed, were such uses inherently present within the original Indigenous understanding of the use of *quinaquina* bark.

It was mentioned above that the question of whether the 'cementation' of the Indigenous claim is appropriate will come down to a determination of the issues discussed in relation to policy options d_1 to d_5 – notably the question of a preservation of global health utility versus other justifications. However, whatever may be the outcome of that analysis, we need to ask whether the imposition of a bar (or not) should apply *only* where the first and second use arising out of the traditional knowledge inspiration are *biologically* linked.

Realistically, it seems impossible to argue that a 'mauveine-like' downstream use (which is neither inevitably derived from the original knowledge nor was

[39] O Meth-Cohn and M Smith, 'What Did WH Perkin Actually Make when He Oxidised Aniline to Obtain Mauveine?' (1994) 1 *Journal of the Chemical Society Perkin Transactions* 5.

[40] MJ O'Neil (ed), *The Merck Index, An Encyclopedia of Chemicals, Drugs, and Biologicals* (Whitehouse Station, NJ, Merck, 2001) 1444.

[41] WB Wood, 'Studies on the Antibacterial Action of the Sulfonamide Drugs. I. The Relation of *p*-Aminobenzoic Acid to the Mechanism of Bacteriostasis' (1942) 75(4) *Journal of Experimental Medicine* 369.

[42] DJ Sullivan, 'Theories on Malarial Pigment Formation and Quinoline Action' (2002) 32 (13) *International Journal of Parasitology* 1645.

[43] SM Rich et al, 'The Origin of Malignant Malaria' (2009) 106 (35) *Proceedings of the National Academy of Sciences of the USA* 14902.

inherently present within the original Indigenous understanding), though linked *in fact* to the use of quinine, should *ever* be subject to downstream control based on a right to TKAGR. It is hard to see that any of the justifications for a positive protection in Indigenous knowledge could justify control over this type of non-inevitable downstream uses. Crucially, looking to the utilitarian account, it seems difficult to argue that their exclusion would lead to a diminution in the perceived value of traditional knowledge associated with traditional knowledge. However, as we have established, mauveine is an entirely different compound to quinine. What might the situation be where we have a non-biologically linked second use of quinine *itself*? Let us imagine that quinine is found to have a rust-inhibiting effect in diesel fuel. Let us also imagine that this effect is unrelated to quinine's biological action. Again, there would be a causal linkage *in fact* back to the Indigenous knowledge of the properties of the *quinaquina* tree. However, it is difficult to argue that the rust-inhibiting effect of quinine was in any way 'inherent' in the original Indigenous use of the bark.

Could the discovery of the rust-inhibiting effect be said to be an inevitable consequence of the original understanding? Unlike Perkin's discovery of mauveine, this is not a situation that could have as equally happened without a knowledge of quinine. However, notwithstanding the duration of the positive right, it seems difficult to see a point at which the rust-inhibiting effect would ever be *retrospectively obvious* in relation to an underlying mechanism, or that the effect would inevitably be reached.

Again, from a utilitarian perspective it would seem difficult to argue that the exclusion of this type of non-inevitable downstream use from coverage of a positive right would realistically lead to a diminution in the perceived value of traditional knowledge associated with traditional knowledge. However, even if we accept that such uses should be excluded from a right of veto/compensation, we are left with a difficult question of how to determine whether a second use is coincidental or is, in fact, related to an underlying shared physiological mechanism. We could confidently determine at the time that the discovery was made that the discovery of mauveine was in no way an *inevitable* result of understanding that the *quinaquina* tree had fever-reducing properties. As stated, one could have come to an understanding of the structure of quinine, or of its biological effect, without ever having reacted aniline with potassium dichromate, and indeed one could have thought to react aniline with potassium dichromate without seeking to synthesise quinine. Their connection is *entirely* coincidental. This obviousness of coincidental connection is arguably true for our imagined rust-inhibiting effect of quinine – it would, one imagines, be relatively easy to demonstrate that the effect had no biological basis (unless the effect was on organisms living within the diesel fuel!).

However, at the time the discovery of a second use is made it is not always immediately apparent that there is no ground for assuming *physiological* linkage. In the early 1990s it was discovered that quinine serves as a way of increasing the sensitivity of certain cancer cells to cytotoxic therapy.[44] It might be that this effect is mediated through a common physiological pathway as the inhibition of haematin biocrystallization seen in the effect of quinine on plasmodium, or not. It appears that ATP-dependent transporters may have a role in multi-drug resistance in cancer,[45] and that antimalarial drugs have an effect on such transporters,[46] but the linkage is far from proven. Quinine provides a yet further example of this type of complexity. There is some evidence for a mild effect of quinine on muscle cramps, which could potentially be caused by a direct effect of the compound on membrane excitability in neurons and muscle cells.[47] Again, the linkage to an underlying mechanism for haematin biocrystallization (the antimalarial mechanism), or an effect on ATP-dependent transporters, is currently unclear.

As was highlighted in chapters one and five, many biologically active ligands have been honed by millions of years of evolution to be exquisitely specific for biological mechanisms. It might seem unlikely, then, that a biologically active ligand would evolve specificity for two entirely separate biological systems. Indeed, the more complex the structure of the ligand and the more specific its interaction with its target receptor, the more likely it might seem for this to be true. One might then argue that, on balance, one might be safe in most situations to assume that two apparently separate *biological* uses are actually mediated through the same mechanism – even when one does not yet know what that mechanism actually is. However, there can be absolutely no certainty that such an assumption is correct in all situations.

How do we resolve this problem of determination? In relation to use of a ligand (or a derivative of a ligand) which is the subject matter of the traditional knowledge, then arguably the onus should be upon the discoverer of the second use to demonstrate that the mechanism of action was different from the biological mechanism underlying the use originally uncovered by the Indigenous rights holders. That the onus should reasonably lie with the third-party discoverer is based upon the time, difficulty, skill-set and background knowledge required to demonstrate a shared biological mechanism. That said, we should recognise that such determination may be difficult, or even impossible, given the then existing understanding of biological mechanisms.

[44] B Chauffert et al, 'Potential Usefulness of Quinine to Circumvent the Anthracycline Resistance in Clinical Practice' (1990) 62(3) *British Journal of Cancer* 395.

[45] MM Gottesman et al, 'Multidrug Resistance in Cancer: Role of ATP-Dependent Transporters' (2002) 2 *Nature Reviews Cancer* 48.

[46] SR Rijpma et al, 'Atovaquone and Quinine Anti-malarials Inhibit ATP Binding Cassette Transporter Activity' (2014) 13 *Malaria Journal* 359.

[47] S El-Tawil et al, 'Quinine for Muscle Cramps' [2015] *Cochrane Report* (www.cochrane.org/CD005044/NEUROMUSC_quinine-for-muscle-cramps); X Lin et al, 'Effects of Quinine on the Excitability and Voltage-Dependent Currents of Isolated Spiral Ganglion Neurons in Culture' (1998) 79(5) *Journal of Neurophysiology* 2503.

This brings us to a further, perhaps more difficult, question. How should we treat the rosy periwinkle case? In the rosy periwinkle case study (described in chapter five, section V.E), the original stimulus to explore the extract of the plant was a folk understanding that an infusion of the plant would treat diabetes. However, the clinical effects of the vinca alkaloid drugs used in therapy today, vincristine and vinblastine (and their derivatives), are as anticancer drugs (an effect mediated through an inhibition of cell division in rapidly dividing cells), not as antidiabetes agents. If rosy periwinkle extract *does* have an effect on diabetes (and given our current knowledge) it is hard to imagine how there is a shared underlying the physiological mechanism which links an antidiabetes effect with the effects that vincristine and vinblastine have on cell division. Indeed, it would seem far more likely that the plant would mediate its antidiabetic effect through one or more of the other 130 or so alkaloids now understood to be present in the plant.[48]

Putting to one side the difficulties and appropriateness of obtaining consent to use in this particular case,[49] if we could assume that an Indigenous group could have made a valid claim to a diabetes efficacy, it would have by no means been apparent at the time when vincristine and vinblastine were discovered that the effects were unrelated. Indeed, what would Eli Lilly and Co have needed to demonstrate to avoid such a claim in respect of vinblastine? Perhaps once the effects of vincristine and vinblastine on tubulin and mitotic spindles were recognised (in the 1970s) it may have become apparent that the antitumour and antidiabetic effects were probably unrelated. However, Eli Lilly would surely have had to entirely exclude the biochemical effect on tubulin and mitotic spindles from the benefits provided in relation to diabetes. That would likely prove to be an arduous task. It is hard to prove a negative in any event, and exceptionally difficult in an environment such as drug discovery – the absence of evidence is not evidence of absence.

To conclude this analysis it is worth looking at the unusual (and challenging) case of the 'serendipitous' discovery of the local anaesthetic effect of cocaine by Carl Koller (see chapter five, in section V.C). As stated above, it could convincingly be argued that a mild anaesthetic effect of coca leaves is a part of the TKAGR of the Andean peoples. So too, is the understanding that chewing coca leaves (or making coca tea/maté) has a mild stimulant effect causing euphoria and assisting with fatigue and altitude sickness. However, (as was discussed in chapter five in V.C) the two effects are not mediated through an identical

[48] R van der Heijden et al, 'The Catharanthus Alkaloids: Pharmacognosy and Biotechnology' (2004) 11(5) *Current Medicinal Chemistry* 607.

[49] G Dutfield, 'Protecting the Rights of Indigenous Peoples: Can Prior Informed Consent Help?' in R Wynberg et al (eds) *Indigenous Peoples, Consent and Benefit Sharing: Lessons from the San-Hoodia Case* (Dordrecht, Springer, 2009) 53, 64.

physiological mechanism – one would not *inevitably* arrive at the anaesthetic effect of cocaine if you were investigating the biology of the dopamine uptake blockade which mediates the central nervous system effect of cocaine. In that sense it is not a question here of serendipity being an 'artefact' of the timing of discovery (as it was with aspirin or with sildenafil citrate).

In this case, the 'causal chain' from the Andes to Koller's serendipitous discovery in Vienna was not based on the Indigenous understanding of the local anaesthetic effect of chewing coca leaves. If it had been it could hardly have been called 'serendipitous'. Instead, if there was an understanding by Koller of a biological effect of a constituent of coca leaves, it came to Koller via the Indigenous understanding of the (physiologically unrelated) central stimulant effect of chewing coca (and indeed through the effect of the purified active ingredient within coca leaves – namely cocaine – rather than the leaf itself).

Assuming Koller knew nothing about the mild anaesthetic effect of coca leaves (and assuming a TKAGR ABS right with no temporal limitation), would it have been open to an Indigenous group to claim control over Koller's anaesthetic use of cocaine once he had discovered it? Would it matter that his discovery had not, in fact, *used* the Indigenous understanding of the mild anaesthetic effect of coca leaves? Would it be sufficient for a valid claim that there was a more convoluted causal link to his discovery through a 'second' Indigenous understanding of the plant – the central stimulant effect – even though there was, in fact, no shared physiological mechanism between the 'first' and 'second' effects? Is it sufficient for a valid claim merely for the Indigenous people to know that coca leaves have a broad 'biological effect' on humans? For this author there is no easy answer. However, asking these questions acutely highlights that there are indeed some hard cases which are not easily addressed without a broader understanding of the intention of, and justifications for, ABS rights in TKAGR.

VIII. Conclusions

This chapter has covered a significant amount of, often difficult, ground. Details of the conclusions reached in this chapter are set out in chapter eight, and to avoid repetition they will not be reiterated here. However, there are some points that are worth highlighting. As is discussed at the beginning of this chapter, achieving a synthesis of competing justifications is inherently difficult. However, the performance of the exercise does help shape a structured appreciation all the aspects that need to be brought to mind when looking to shape policy decisions. Notably, here the exercise brings us to a focus upon competing utilities as a key area for further theoretical and practical consideration. This synthetic approach has also, in the current case, taken us to consider a deeper analysis of the workability of the 'least conflicting' policy decision, which, in itself, brings us back to a deeper analysis of the meaning of second uses, and of serendipity.

Perhaps the most surprising outcome of that further analysis is the complicating impact of the nature of a right to control knowledge which is of unlimited *temporal* duration. As has been discussed above, one can make out arguments for why a right to control traditional knowledge has to be of unlimited duration. However, it may yet be that it is that unlimited temporal scope (within a right to control information) which is one of the more theoretically radical, and difficult, elements of the new rights.

The next chapter seeks to bring together the conclusions of each section of this work and determine what overall conclusions can (and cannot) be arrived at.

8

Conclusions

I. Introduction – Aims of the Work

Highlighting the origins of the concept of prior informed consent within the field of medical ethics, Dutfield has suggested that the 'stretching' of that concept from medical ethics into the area of misappropriation of genetic resources and traditional knowledge has been done 'without sufficiently thinking through the practicalities, without much theoretical reflection and without necessary consideration of political economy'.[1] He goes on to cite Burns's warning on the probability of unintended outcomes: 'The best-laid schemes o' mice an' men, Gang aft agley.'[2]

It has been the aim of the current work to investigate one such underexplored (and crucial) practicality (the justifiable downstream scope of a sui generis positive right to control downstream use of TKAGR within the context of drug discovery) and to redress the relative paucity of theoretical reflection in relation to that area.

We saw in chapter three that what seems to be missing from the 'positive' rights in relation to TKAGR under the Nagoya Protocol is any principle or guidance for determining a balance which combines fair protection for the traditional knowledge/genetic resources rights holders with a reasonable degree of legal certainty for third parties. Where such knowledge serves as a research 'lead' for subsequent development, the Nagoya Protocol gives no guidance as to how far that knowledge has any 'reach-through effect' into new scientific discoveries or at what point a downstream researcher could consider themselves 'free' of the traditional knowledge ABS right.

Chapter three also concludes that although TKAGR is a species of information, it is of an unrelated type to the informational component of a genetic resource. Traditional knowledge *associated with* a genetic resource (though it may serve as a gateway to their study) is not related to, and stands separate from,

[1] G Dutfield, 'Protecting the Rights of Indigenous Peoples: Can Prior Informed Consent Help?' in R Wynberg et al (eds), *Indigenous Peoples, Consent and Benefit Sharing: Lessons from the San-Hoodia Case* (Dordrecht, Springer, 2009) 53, 66.

[2] Robert Burns from 'To a Moose, On turning her up in her nest with the Plough November, 1785' in *The Poems of Robert Burns, Introduction by James MacKenna* (Collins, London and Glasgow 1945) 116. To which we may well reply with the next stanza: 'An' lea'e us nought but grief an' pain, For promis'd joy!'.

DNA or epigenetics (or indeed biochemicals produced through the expression of the genome of a resource). Accordingly, arguments that are applied to extend the definition of a genetic resource (for example, through the development of the concept of protection of DSI) cannot properly be used to extend the definition of TKAGR. Equally, however, the definition of a genetic resource does not delimit the meaning or scope of TKAGR and, in principle, the downstream scope of a right to control such traditional knowledge cannot be curtailed by considerations that would apply in relation to genetic 'information'. In this respect the TKAGR is a broader, and less proscribed, concept than the genetic information held *within* the resource.

Although the uncertainty of the Nagoya Protocol acted as a stimulus for the current work, the question of what is a *justifiable* scope for such a right is broader than can be answered by an examination of the Nagoya Protocol itself (or indeed of any other extant or proposed positive right). As was discussed in chapter four, the inherent non-rivalrous and non-excludable nature of knowledge is such that its use can only be controlled through the imposition of positive law. However, for the limits of the scope of that positive law to be justifiable they must be supported by the philosophical reasons for the existence of that right.

In chapter five, this work went on to empirically examine the processes by which new drugs (or new uses for old drugs) are discovered. A key finding of that empirical study is the many ways by which an original piece of traditional knowledge can be admixed to a greater body of existing information regarding a clinical problem, and that there may be further admixture to the original information of discoveries derived from it and subsequent admixture to other, 'parallel', information which is not derived from it. The study also found that these processes may themselves go through several feedback iterations and that, overall, the original information within the traditional knowledge may become significantly 'diluted' by other information before a useful drug is arrived at. This process of dilution is potentially accelerated by the use of in silico prospecting using AI/ML, particularly where the ML tool has been trained on a vast body of existing data. It was also noted that any such downstream discovery based on the inspiration of a piece of traditional knowledge will *always* be causally linked *in fact* to the original inspiration. However, (as was further discussed in chapter five), although one can correctly envisage the drug discovery process as chains of causation with flows of information, one can also envisage it as a field of inputs of competing contributions which are concomitant with those flows of information. Here, with increasing admixture of information, the information arising from the contributions of the Indigenous originators is progressively diluted within a morass of competing contributions sitting on the back of an entanglement of information.

The examination of the topography of drug development in this work also revealed that many drug discovery efforts could be described as sequential and accumulative. Here (although there is a substantial increase in the volume of additional knowledge) the underlying nature of the contribution made by the traditional knowledge to the downstream product arguably remains unchanged.

Taking inspiration from the long interface between patent law and the drug discovery process, this work identified the unexpected ('serendipitous') discovery of a new use for a particular genetic resource (or the compounds found in a particular genetic resource or their chemical derivatives) as a putative 'crux point' at which a third-party downstream contribution affects a 'step change' in the *nature* of the downstream product, when compared to the original contribution. Some case studies highlighting the types of serendipitous discoveries which have been made in drug discovery processes (inspired by or derived from genetic resources) were described. These were:

(a) The discovery by Paul Gibson and Lawrence Craven of the blood thinning (and with it cardio- and cerebroprotective) effects of aspirin;
(b) The discovery by Carl Koller of the local anaesthetic effects of cocaine;
(c) The discovery by William Perkin of the aniline dye, mauveine, whilst attempting to synthesise quinine (its stimulus of the aniline dye business and its in turn leading to the discovery of sulfonamide antibiotics); and
(d) The discovery by Ralph Noble (and others) of the antitumour effects of vinca alkaloids extracted from the rosy periwinkle.

Taking a serendipitous discovery to mean one where the second use is non-obvious *at the time* the discovery is made, in chapter six a number of potential policy decisions in respect of the scope of a veto surrounding such discoveries were tested against the philosophical justifications for the existence of a positive right in TKAGR.

II. Application of Philosophical Justifications

In applying the philosophical justifications, significant difficulties were encountered in relation to the application of natural rights justifications. It was argued that rights based in personality do not support a positive right to control knowledge per se.

Although application of a Lockean labour-desert right supported *some* form of positive right (as opposed to no right at all), inherent problems with determination of origination and individuation arising out of the uncertainty of the meaning of 'contribution' meant that, in the end, little concrete guidance could be determined in terms of justifiable downstream scope.

Within the consequentialist account, three key utilitarian goals were identified:

(a) the preservation of traditional knowledge and culture within its Indigenous setting;
(b) the preservation of the environment within which the genetic resources associated with the relevant knowledge are found; and
(c) an inherent utility in directly controlling the knowledge (termed 'utility through control').

It was posited that these first two goals (or a biocultural conflation of both) might be achieved through creating a perceived value in the minds of relevant actors (although it was acknowledged that there may be causal uncertainties in this regard). It was argued that the greatest likelihood of perceived value was through granting a veto right which extended to *all* downstream use. It was also argued that the 'utility through control' goal would be achieved without the need for creating value, and again the likelihood of achieving that utility was enhanced by providing a veto which covered *all* downstream use.

However, it was noted that, within the broader utilitarian account, the granting of veto rights over TKAGR could conflict with the potential enhancement of 'global health' which would be provided by allowing pharmaceutical companies freedom to use their resources and expertise to develop drugs without hindrance.

Looking at the application of a right from the perspective of distributive justice, it was found that provided one looks at the *proportionate* advantage to each side of each of the proposed decisions (essentially applying the difference principle), the granting of an absolute veto on *all* downstream use is the situation the person in the original position would choose as maximising the minimum – that is, avoiding the worst outcome.

In respect of the restorative/corrective justice account proposed by Munzer,[3] it was found that the uncertainties (and inherent case-by-case specificity) make the translation of this reparation justification to a set of generally applicable principles for broader application exceptionally difficult.

It was noted that the argument for positive rights over traditional knowledge which is based upon an inherent right of Indigenous peoples to self-determination also suggests that Indigenous peoples should have a significant degree of control over information which is their community resource. However, it was found that there is little explicit guidance from this doctrine as to whether very distal uses, including uses arising out of serendipitous discoveries, should be considered as use of the traditional knowledge. A similar conclusion was reached in respect of the communitarian claim proposed by Gibson[4] (which has strong echoes with the right of Indigenous peoples to self-determination).

Whilst it was noted that UNDRIP does not represent a full acknowledgement of the inherent right of Indigenous peoples to self-determination, in relation to the application of the provisions of UNDRIP alone, it was found that compensation for misappropriation is likely to be the *minimum* redress envisaged under that Declaration. Accordingly, any positive right that delivers this or more will be compliant with UNDRIP. However, UNDRIP itself gives no guidance in terms of determining the downstream scope of such a right.

[3] SR Munzer, 'Corrective Justice and Intellectual Property Rights in Traditional Knowledge' in A Lever (ed), *New Frontiers in the Philosophy of Intellectual Property* (Cambridge, Cambridge University Press, 2012) 58.

[4] J Gibson, *Community Resources: Intellectual Property, International Trade and Protection of Traditional Knowledge* (Farnham, Ashgate, 2005).

III. Synthesis

Chapter seven examined the potential options for using 'mid-level' techniques to achieve synthesis of our potentially conflicting philosophical justifications. It was concluded that Sunstein's 'theoretically modest' approaches were inappropriate when all we could realistically use to determine a justifiable scope was *theory*.[5] Although Merges's application of Rawls's overlapping consensus approach was examined, since this approach is untried a somewhat more conservative 'least contradiction' (teamed with a ready appreciation of the applicability and relevance of a particular theory) analysis was undertaken.

It was found that the policy option tested which demonstrated the least contradiction across all justifications was a veto on downstream use that did not extend beyond the making of a serendipitous discovery but which involved a mechanism under which the Indigenous holders were compensated for third-party use of the serendipitous discovery on the basis of comparative contribution (termed in this work option d_4). Although option d_4 does represent a least contradiction approach, when one re-examines the justifications employed in this work (outwith those based on the philosophies of Locke, Kant, Fichte and Hegel)[6] it was found that all those justifications favoured (or are least consistent with) a total veto on downstream use – *save alone* for what was identified as the 'global health' utility. This particular conflict will be addressed further below.

IV. What is Serendipity?

In chapter seven, having identified the 'limited veto plus compensation' policy option as that being least conflicting across the justifications employed, the workability of that option was analysed. The key question arrived upon was how we should determine what a 'serendipitous discovery' actually is.

In examining this point it was identified that the way in which TKAGR is created, and held, is such that it is difficult to see how a right to control its use can have a *fixed* duration. It was also identified that this lack of fixed duration may pose a distinct (and unique) challenge in relation to the assessment of in-imitativeness of follow-on developments. The situation was considered in which we have a subsisting right to control downstream use of an idea that has an *infinite* temporal duration. We are here immediately forced to ask at what point in time should we

[5] CR Sunstein, 'Incompletely Theorized Agreements' (1995) 108(7) *Harvard Law Review* 1733; CR Sunstein, 'On Legal Theory and Legal Practice' in I Shapiro and JW DeCew (eds), *Theory and Practice NOMOS XXXVII* (New York, New York University Press, 1995); CR Sunstein, *Legal Reasoning and Political Conflict* (Oxford, Oxford University Press, 1996) 35.

[6] Which were excluded, as Kant, Fichte and Hegel do not support the protection of ideas as such and the Lockean approach has difficulties in its specific application.

determine that any new downstream development of that idea is 'non-obvious' in the light of that right.

Chapter seven went on to establish that given this *infinite* temporal duration, if an Indigenous claim to a positive right *was* to be limited to a serendipitous discovery, then a bar to an ongoing claim would have to be put into place on the making of a serendipitous discovery. However, it was argued that the philosophical grounds for establishing a bar were, in fact, the same as those analysed in respect of scope. However, we are left here a logical lacuna (or perhaps more correctly a 'whirlpool'). These grounds cannot realistically tell us *how* to define a serendipitous discovery. Each new third-party discovery creates a new contribution which is to be tested against the original contribution of the Indigenous people claiming the right. If we are seeking to determine whether there should be a bar to an ongoing claim, we need to ask whether there is a degree of third-party contribution of sufficient merit to warrant that bar. That contribution would need to be significant enough to stand above the mass of smaller steps such that even though the same final epistemological 'place' was reached (the understanding of a second use), the step was itself great enough to break the chain. It was argued that here the labour-desert account (again) fails us – we are looking at questions of degree.

However, perhaps the hardest observation to reconcile in determining a meaning of serendipitous second use is this. If the same 'total' amount of third-party contribution is reached (the understanding of a second use), should it (where one has a right of control of unlimited duration) really matter whether it is reached by way of a series of small steps or by one larger one? In addition, determining differential contributions (theoretically difficult to determine in any event) would continually change with time as incremental developments were made, rendering an ongoing assessment essentially impossible in any event.

Perhaps the most surprising outcome of the analysis of the meaning of serendipity is the complicating impact of the nature of a right to control knowledge that is of unlimited *temporal* duration. As has been discussed above, it may yet be that it is that unlimited temporal scope within a right to control information which is one of the more radical elements of the new rights. Clearly this is an area that may reward further theoretical investigation.

V. Coincidental Discoveries

If we assume that determining what is meant by a 'serendipitous' discovery is essentially impossible, we need to ask whether the *nature* of the second use gives us grounds for a break in causation, rather than how that second use is arrived at?

Chapter seven went on to examine this question. Of course, the key to this question is determining what a second use *is* in this context. It was argued that coincidental discoveries (such as the discovery of mauveine by William Perkin whilst seeking to synthesise quinine where the finding could have as easily happened without a connection to quinine and could not have been inevitably arrived at) should not be considered covered by an ABS right to control downstream use. It was also argued that uses unrelated to any 'claimed' biological effect of the genetic resource (such as an unrelated physical effect) should be excluded as these would not be inevitably arrived at when examining the biological effect. Of course, if the original knowledge related to a *physical* property the analysis would be different.

However, it was argued that the question of whether different biological effects should be considered to be different uses is difficult. It was pointed out that what appear initially to be second uses can turn out to be linked through a common physiological mechanism. It might be argued that such second uses are essentially the same as the first as (in the fullness of time) they would inevitably be arrived at. However, at the time such a second use was uncovered this would not be apparent and indeed one would require a significant amount of scientific research to disprove the linkages.

Chapter seven then went on to examine how one might deal with the rosy periwinkle/vinca alkaloid case. Here it was suggested that the originally disclosed antidiabetic effect (if present) was probably mediated through a different alkaloid present in the plant rather than vincristine and vinblastine which mediated the plant's antitumour effects. It was also pointed out that such an assumption could only be made in the light of significant study into the alkaloids of the plant and their biological effects.

Chapter seven concluded with an analysis of the 'serendipitous' discovery of the local anaesthetic effect of cocaine. This was (arguably) a genuinely serendipitous discovery in which the first and second effects are not mediated through an identical physiological mechanism. Although, the 'first' and 'second' effects were in fact known to the Indigenous peoples, the causal chain from the Andes to Koller's serendipitous discovery in Vienna was not based on the Indigenous understanding of the anaesthetic effect of coca leaves but, instead, the information about a biological effect of coca leaves came to Koller via a 'second' Indigenous understanding of the (physiologically unrelated) central stimulant effect of chewing coca. Asking whether an Indigenous ABS claim could be based on a causal link through such an unrelated 'second' Indigenous understanding of the plant (even though there was no shared physiological mechanism) acutely highlights the potential complexities in unpacking an Indigenous ABS claim. It further highlights that there are hard cases which are not easily addressed without a broader understanding of the intention of, and justifications for, ABS rights in TKAGR.

VI. Overall Conclusions

The *leitmotif* of this work is the complexity of the drug discovery process. A significant part of this work has been an attempt to bring that complexity within the bounds of analysis. Indeed, the key driver of this work has been to investigate the interface between the complexity of the drug discovery process and a right to control TKAGR, and to identify and analyse a number of further theoretical, and practical, complexities which arise from the creation of workable and philosophically justifiable policy options at that interface.

Envisaging the drug discovery process as one of epistemic dilution with a concomitant conflict of contribution does appear to provide us with a lens to see (at least on a larger scale) potential points where we might further analyse the justifiable downstream scope of a positive right in TKAGR. However, when we come to analyse the question on a smaller scale we find that the inherent uncertainties (in both origination and individuation) of the contribution-based natural rights model for the existence of rights to control intangible intellectual products leaves us with significant inherent uncertainties.

The synthesis exercise performed in chapter six arrives at a preferred putative policy optioned where the right of veto extends as far as the making of a serendipitous discovery of a second use for a product of a genetic resource. In respect of the second use under this policy option, the right holder has no veto but has a right to be compensated according to their 'contribution'. However, as was discussed in the latter parts of chapter six, this solution (option d_4) leads us to face a number of significant practical and/or theoretical difficulties. These will include:

(a) determining a definition of 'serendipitous discovery';
(b) determining a definition of a 'second use';
(c) determining how one would go about compensating a party on the basis of their 'contribution';
(d) determining what 'contribution' means;
(e) assuring a contributing party that the determinant mechanism for compensating contribution was fair, transparent and followed due process;
(f) assuring a contributing party that the determinant mechanism for compensating contribution would provide as reliable compensation as a negotiated royalty for granting permission to use;
(g) ensuring that a compensatory mechanism in some way mitigated the negative effects on potential licensees denied an opportunity for an exclusivity advantage over competitors;
(h) determining whether a second use is (or is not) actually linked to the first use through a shared physiological mechanism; and
(i) determining whether a second use is mediated (or is not mediated) through a second ligand present in the genetic resource.

Some of these problems can, of course, be addressed through the imposition of positive law. However, some solutions are likely to be arbitrary as the application of natural rights contribution-based approaches are (as has been seen) very difficult. Even if such solutions can be arrived at to the operation of the d_4 option, the evidential and administrative burden in determining questions of contribution and such points as whether a second use is (or is not) actually linked to the first use through a shared physiological mechanism or determining whether a second use is mediated (or is not mediated) through a second ligand present in the genetic resource is likely to be extremely onerous.

The analysis throughout this work suggests that simplicity both in the operation of a positive right (and in the message received by relevant actors) enhances perceived value which has greater likely efficacy (though no certainty) in achieving the utilitarian goals of the right of preservation of the traditional knowledge and the environment in which the genetic resource is found. Complexity in operation (notably in the examination of whether or not the 'new' biological effects seen on a serendipitous discovery are physiologically related to the original Indigenous 'claim' or otherwise) is likely to work counter to the consequentialist justification for this option.

From a Rawlsian 'difference principle' perspective, it is highly likely that a pharmaceutical company will possess greater legal and scientific expertise to argue its position relative to an Indigenous group. Complexity of operation of the right (again particularly is the assessment of evidential questions) will likely advantage the pharmaceutical researchers relative to the Indigenous actors.

A. A Simpler Solution?

In the light of the problems seen with the partial veto option and the 'failure' of a contribution-desert model when looking at smaller-scale problems, we might ask again: is there justification for a broad, simpler, right to control *any* downstream use that uses a non-coincidental (effectively biologically mediated) use?

Given the inherent problems we have seen with the classic natural rights accounts (notably with the ideas of Locke, Kant, Fichte and Hegel), the question of whether such a broad scope is justifiable falls back on the utilitarian account and (arguably) its compliance at least with other non-natural rights accounts and with the principle of the inherent right of Indigenous people to self determination.

From a utilitarian perspective we noted in chapter six that (but for the question of a global health utility, to which we will return) there existed a justification for a total veto over downstream use. It is worth noting that coverage of *all* biological effects arising out of genetic resource gives us a simplicity in operation which works in support of the valorisation model. It seems unlikely in this regard that the exclusion of 'coincidental effects' – essentially those that were unrelated to the biological effects of the genetic resource – would have an impact on perceived value. In any event, such coincidental effects are likely to be rare. Outwith the valorisation model, a veto right to control all downstream biological uses of a genetic resource (based upon traditional knowledge associated with that genetic resource) also directly meets the goal of 'utility through control'.

In relation to the other non-consequentialist accounts ('Munzerian' reparations, Indigenous peoples' right to self-determination, UNDRIP, or 'Gibsonian' communitarianism), there seems to be no reason why such a broader right would be excluded. Using the Rawlsian maximin analysis used above, the broader a right given to the Indigenous group, the better the right complies with the difference principle. As mentioned above, simplicity of operation and reduced evidential burdens also supports the difference principle.

If one does want to look to a contribution-reward justification for such a right, the argument here may be that the Indigenous people's contribution which warrants a positive right is simply opening the 'gateway' into the biology of the genetic resource. However, as we have seen the application of such a model outwith broad sweeping statements (whilst acting as a useful reminder to consider conflicting parties) is difficult to apply.

B. Indigenous Culture, the Environment and Spiritual Happiness vs Global Healthcare – A Squeeze?

The performance of the synthetic analysis in chapter seven brings us to a focus upon competing utilities as a key area for further theoretical and practical consideration. Overall we appear to be 'squeezed' on that analysis between the great complexities of operating a veto option which does not cover serendipitously discovered second uses (but which, in part, ameliorates the global healthcare utility concerns identified) and a total veto which avoids complexity and looks to meet the utilitarian justification of preservation of traditional knowledge, genetic resources and the environment in which they are found, but which runs counter to allowing pharmaceutical companies to freely develop pharmaceuticals for the benefit of global health without the risk of imposition of a veto on their activity.

In considering this squeeze, we firstly need to note (as was discussed at chapter six, section IV.E, and chapter seven) that not all rights to a total veto would be exercised *absolutely*. It is possible that many vetoes would be used as the foundation upon which to demand the receipt of royalties for permission to use, so (subject to royalty rates) not significantly limiting the activities of pharmaceutical companies. However, we simply do not know to what extent this would happen. What we certainly can say is that if a total right to veto *all* downstream biological use does exist, we will also have to accept the possibility that an Indigenous group will at some point choose to veto a potentially important therapeutic product.

Given we have here conflicting consequentialist goals, we may arguably arrive at a better understanding of the justificatory balance between our competing policy options if we had a better sense of the degree to which the conflicting policy options might actually achieve their aims, or interfere with the achievement of the aims of the conflicting policy. The empirical assessment of these competing risks and probabilities is outwith the scope of the current work, but further work in that respect may aid our determination of whether such a broad veto over downstream use would be justifiable. Crucial here might be an empirical understanding of the likelihood that Indigenous groups would seek to apply an absolute veto rather than follow a licensing route, which may, in turn, reflect the degree to which they value an absolute restriction over the use of their knowledge over its commercialisation. However, such a decision would likely be a function of a wide variety of factors, notably the customary law of the Indigenous group, and be highly case-specific.

One further approach to investigating this dilemma might be to examine potential exemptions, suspension of rights and compulsory licensing mechanisms to support public access to medicines in major global health emergencies, and such examination would again form the basis for further research. However, the problems encountered in the application of TRIPs 'flexibilities' (discussed at chapter two) are noted. It should also be noted that the types of healthcare emergencies for which one might classically activate 'flexibilities' in the application of rights are more often the result of a spillover of a zoonotic pathogen (such as Ebola, MERS-CoV, SARS-CoV-1, SARS-CoV-2 and H5N1 avian influenza) into the human population.[7] These are not, usually, the types of medical problem for which TKAGR might usually be expected to provide a solution. Similarly, many important chronic healthcare problems, for which TKAGR might provide a stimulus for a solution, do not, usually, fall within the understood definition of an 'emergency'. However, when looking any such questions we always need to recall that the argument essentially boils down to this: is Indigenous traditional knowledge sufficiently at risk of extinction that it is worth the risk of potential restriction over drug discovery and development activity?

Perhaps we should conclude this work with this observation: millions of years of evolution have honed compounds within all forms of life on Earth which have astoundingly exquisite selectivity and potency in biological systems. They are remarkably useful tools. As highlighted by Atkins, the extinction of species potentially extinguishes our sources of new molecular tools.[8] Similarly, the extinction of Indigenous knowledge potentially extinguishes our ability to locate such new molecular tools. If such tools disappear, they are unlikely ever to be regained.

[7] JH Ellwanger and JAB Chies, 'Zoonotic Spillover: Understanding Basic Aspects for Better Prevention' (2021) 44(1) (Suppl 1) *Genetics and Molecular Biology* e20200355.

[8] P Atkins, *What Is Chemistry?* (Oxford, Oxford University Press, 2013) 13.

BIBLIOGRAPHY

Abelshauser, W, et al, *German Industry and Global Enterprise. BASF: The History of a Company* (Cambridge, Cambridge University Press, 2004).

Achan, J, et al, 'Quinine, An Old Anti-malarial Drug in a Modern World: Role in the Treatment of Malaria' (2011) 10 *Malaria Journal* 144.

Adkins, NL, and Georgel, PT, 'MeCP2: Structure and Function' (2011) 89 *Biochemical Cell Biology* 1.

Aga Khan, S, and Hassan bin Talal, H, *Indigenous Peoples: A Global Quest for Justice: A Report for the Independent Commission on International Humanitarian Issues* (London, Zed Books, 1987).

Aittokallio, T, 'What Are the Current Challenges for Machine Learning in Drug Discovery and Repurposing?' (2022) 17(5) *Expert Opinion on Drug Discovery* 423.

Albers-Schönberg, G, 'The Pharmaceutical Discovery Process' in T Swanson (ed), *Intellectual Property Rights and Biodiversity Conservation: An Interdisciplinary Analysis of the Values of Medicinal Plants* (Cambridge, Cambridge University Press, 1995) 68.

Alfred, T, *Peace, Power, Righteousness: An Indigenous Manifesto* (Oxford, Oxford University Press, 1999).

Allen, B, *Last of the Medicine Men* (London, BBC Worldwide, 2000).

Allis, CD, et al (eds), *Epigenetics* (Cold Spring Harbor, NY, Cold Spring Harbor Laboratory Press, 2009) 36.

Aoki, K, 'Distributive Justice and Intellectual Property: Distributive and Syncretic Motives in Intellectual Property Law (with Special Reference to Coercion, Agency, and Development)' (2007) 40 *UC Davis Law Review* 717.

Aquinas, T, Fathers of the English Dominican Province (trans), *Summa Theologiæ of St Thomas Aquinas* (2a 2æ, Q77) (Canton, OH, Pinnacle Press, 2017).

Aristotle, *Metaphysics* Book I, 980a 21.

Århem, K, 'Millennium Among the Makuna: An Anthropological Film Adventure in the Northwest Amazon' (1993) 9(3) *Anthropology Today* 3.

Arnon, SS, et al, 'Working Group on Civilian Biodefense "Botulinum Toxin as a Biological Weapon: Medical and Public Health Management"' (2001) 285(8) *Journal of the American Medical Association* 1059.

Richard Ashcraft, *Revolutionary Politics and Locke's Two Treatises of Government* (Princeton, NJ, Princeton University Press, 1986).

Atkins, P, *What Is Chemistry?* (Oxford, Oxford University Press, 2013).

Attas, D, 'Lockean Justifications of Intellectual Property' in A Gosseries et al (eds), *Intellectual Property and Theories of Justice* (London, Palgrave Macmillan 2008) 29.

Aubertin, C, and Filoche, G, 'The Nagoya Protocol on the Use of Genetic Resources: One Embodiment of an Endless Discussion' (2011) 2(1) *Sustentabilidade em Debate - Brasília* 51.

Axt, JR, et al, *Biotechnology, Indigenous Peoples, and Intellectual Property Rights* (Congressional Research Service Report for US Congress, 1993).

Balick, MJ, and Cox, PA, *Plants, People, and Culture: The Science of Ethnobotany* (Washington, DC, Scientific American Library 1997).

Ban, TA, 'The Role of Serendipity in Drug Discovery' (2006) 8(3) *Dialogues in Clinical Neuroscience* 335.

Barker, J, 'For Whom Sovereignty Matters' in J Barker (ed), *Sovereignty Matters: Locations of Contestation and Possibility in Indigenous Struggles for Self-determination* (Lincoln, NE, University of Nebraska Press, 2005).

Barelli, M, 'The United Nations Declaration on the Rights of Indigenous Peoples: A Human Rights Framework for Intellectual Property Rights' in M Rimmer (ed), *Indigenous Intellectual Property: A Handbook of Contemporary Research* (Cheltenham, Edward Elgar, 2015) 57.

Bathaee, Y, 'Incompletely Theorized Agreements: An Unworkable Theory of Judicial Modesty' (2006) 34(5) *Fordham Urban Law Journal* Article 2.

Bäumler, E, *In Search of the Magic Bullet: Great Adventures in Modern Drug Research* (London, Thames & Hudson, 1965).

Bavikatte, K, and Robinson, DF, 'Towards a People's History of the Law: Biocultural Jurisprudence and the Nagoya Protocol on Access and Benefit Sharing' (2011) 7 *Law, Environment and Development Journal* 35.

Bell, D, *Daughters of the Dreaming* (Carlton, Victoria, McPhee Gribble, 1983) 50.

Bentham, J, *The Principles of Morals and Legislation* [1789] (London, Legare Street Press, 2022).

Bentham, J, *Manual of Political Economy* [1839] reprinted in Stark, W. (ed) *Jeremy Bentham's Economic Writings* (London, George Allen and Unwin, 1952).

Bentley, L, 'Accounting for Profits Gained by Infringement of Copyright: When Does it End?' (1991) 13(1) *European Intellectual Property Review* 5.

Bessen, J, and Maskin, E, 'Sequential Innovation, Patents, and Imitation' (2009) 40(4) *RAND Journal of Economics* 611.

Bird, A, 'Perceptions of Epigenetics' (2007) 447 *Nature* 396.

Bingham, T, *The Rule of Law* (London, Penguin Law, 2011).

Bishop, WJ, 'Some Early Literature on Addiction with Special Reference to Tobacco' (1949) 46 *British Journal on Addiction* 49.

Blackburn, S, *Oxford Dictionary of Philosophy* (Oxford, Oxford University Press, 1996).

Blackmore, S, *The Meme Machine* (Oxford, Oxford University Press, 1999).

Blakemore, DC, et al (eds), *Synthetic Methods in Drug Discovery* (Abingdon, Royal Society of Chemistry, 2015).

Blasiak, R, et al, 'The Ocean Genome and Future Prospects for Conservation and Equity' (2020) 3(8) *Nature Sustainability* 588.

Burki, T, 'A New Paradigm for Drug Development' (2020) 2(5) *The Lancet Digital Health* e226.

Burns, R, *The Poems of Robert Burns, Introduction by James MacKenna* (Glasgow, Collins, 1945).

Brata, DL, 'Artificial Intelligence and Antibiotic Discovery' (2021) 10(11) *Antibiotics (Basel)* 1376.

Brandt, RB, *Ethical Theory* (Englewood Cliffs, NJ, Prentice-Hall, 1959).

Brandt, RB, 'Toward a Credible Form of Utilitarianism' in H-N Castañeda and G Nakhnikian (eds), *Morality and the Language of Conduct* (Detroit, MI, Wayne State University Press, 1963).

Breakey, H, *Intellectual Liberty – Natural Rights and Intellectual Property* (Farnham, Ashgate, 2012).

Brennan, F, *One Land One Nation* (St Lucia, QLD, Queensland University Press, 1995).

Brightman, R, 'Perkin and the Dyestuffs Industry in Britain' (1956) 177 *Nature* 80.

Brokensha, D, et al, *Indigenous Knowledge Systems and Development* (Lanham, MD, University Press of America, 1980).

Bronowski, J, *The Ascent of Man* (London, Book Club Associates, 1977).

Brown, ED, and Wright, GD, 'Antibacterial Drug Discovery in the Resistance Era' (2016) 529(7586) *Nature* 336.

Brown, EJ, et al, 'A Mammalian Protein Targeted by G1-arresting Rapamycin–Receptor Complex' (1994) 369 *Nature* 756.

Brown, MF, *Tsewa's Gift: Magic and Meaning in an Amazonian Society* (Washington, DC, Smithsonian Institution Press, 1986).

Brown, N, *In Silico Medicinal Chemistry: Computational Methods to Support Drug Design* (Abingdon, Royal Society of Chemistry, 2015).

Brüggemeier, G, et al, (eds) *Personality Rights in European Tort Law* (Cambridge, Cambridge University Press, 2010).

Brush, SB, 'Indigenous Knowledge of Biological Resources and Intellectual Property Rights: The Role of Anthropology' (1993) 95(3) *American Anthropologist* 653.

Buck, M, and Hamilton, C, 'The Nagoya Protocol on Access to Genetic Resources and Benefit-sharing Arising from their Utilisation to the Convention on Biological Diversity' [2011] *Review of European Community and International Environmental Law* 47.

Burk, DL, and Lemley, MA, 'Policy Levers in Patent Law' (2003) 89 *Virginia Law Review* 1575.

Burk, DL, and Lemley, MA, 'Inherency' (2005) 47(2) *William and Mary Law Review* 371.

Burnett, AL, et al, 'Nitric Oxide: A Physiologic Mediator of Penile Erection' (1992) 257(5068) *Science* 401.

Camargo, BA, and Vázquez-Maguirre, M, 'Humanism, Dignity and Indigenous Justice: The Mayan Train Megaproject, Mexico' (2021) 29(2–3) *Journal of Sustainable Tourism* 372.

Campos, DJ, *Shaman and Ayahuasca – Journeys to Sacred Realms* (San Francisco, CA, Divine Arts, 2011).

Castan, M, 'DRIP Freed: The Slow Reconstruction of Self-determination for Indigenous Peoples' in S Joseph and A McBeth (eds), *Research Handbook on International Human Rights Law* (Cheltenham, Edward Elgar Publishing, 2010) 492.

Chander, A, and Sunder, M, 'Is Nozick Kicking Rawls's Ass? Intellectual Property and Social Justice' (2007) 40 *UC Davis Law Review* 563.

Chauffert, B, et al, 'Potential Usefulness of Quinine to Circumvent the Anthracycline Resistance in Clinical Practice' (1990) 62(3) *British Journal of Cancer* 395.

Chon, M, 'Intellectual Property from Below: Copyright and Capability for Education' (2007) 40 *UC Davis Law Review* 803.

Choudhury, CN, et al, 'Structure-based Drug Repurposing: Traditional and Advanced AI/ML-aided Methods' (2022) 27(7) *Drug Discovery Today* 1847.

Cline, H, 'The House of Lords Decision in Merrell Dow Pharmaceuticals -v- Norton Limited and Penn Pharmaceuticals' (1995) 14 *Biotechnology Law Report* 956.

Compact Oxford English Dictionary (Oxford, Oxford University Press, 1979).

Compte-Sponville, A, *A Short Treatise on the Great Virtues* (London, Vintage, 2003).

Cooksey, CJ, 'Tyrian Purple: 6,6′-Dibromoindigo and Related Compounds' (2001) 6 *Molecules* 736.

Coombe, RJ, 'The Recognition of Indigenous Peoples' and Community Traditional Knowledge in International Law' (2002) 14 *St Thomas Law Review* 275.

Copleston, F, *Thomas Aquinas* (London, Search Press, 1976).

Correa, CM, 'Implications for BioTrade of the Nagoya Protocol on Access to Genetic Resources and the Fair and Equitable Sharing of Benefits Arising from their Utilization' (2012) paper prepared for the BioTrade Initiative on UNCTAD (UNCTAD/DITC/TED/2011/9).

Cotton, CM, *Ethnobotany, Principles and Applications* (Chichester, John Wiley, 1996).

Cox, PA, 'The Ethnobotanical Approach to Drug Discovery: Strengths and Limitations' in DJ Chadwick and J Marsh (eds), *Ethnobotany and the Search for New Drugs* (Ciba Foundation Symp 185) (Chichester, John Wiley, 1994) 25.

Cox, PA, et al, 'Pharmacological Activity of the Samoan Ethnopharmacopoeia' (1989) 43 *Economic Botany* 487.

Craven, LL, 'Acetylsalicylic Acid, Possible Preventive of Coronary Thrombosis' (1950) 4(2) *Annals of Western Medicine and Surgery* 95.

Craven, LL, 'Experiences with Aspirin (Acetylsalicylic Acid) in the Nonspecific Prophylaxis of Coronary Thrombosis' (1953) 75 *Mississippi Valley Medical Journal* 38.

Craven, LL, 'Prevention of Coronary and Cerebral Thrombosis' (1956) *Mississippi Valley Medical Journal* 213.

Cronin, M, and Madden, J (eds), *In Silico Toxicology: Principles and Applications* (Abingdon, Royal Society of Chemistry, 2010).

D'Agostino, F, 'Original Position' in EN Zalta (ed), *The Stanford Encyclopedia of Philosophy* (Summer 2003 edn). plato.stanford.edu/archives/sum2003/entries/original-position/.

Dandapani, S, and Marcaurelle, LA, 'Current Strategies for Diversity-Oriented Synthesis' (2010) 14 *Current Opinion in Chemical Biology* 362.

Davies, B, *Aquinas* (London, Continuum, 2002).

Davies, H, *Introductory Immunobiology* (London, Chapman & Hall, 1997).

Dedeurwaerdere, T, et al. 'Governing Global Scientific Research Commons Under the Nagoya Protocol' in E Morgera et al (eds), *The 2010 Nagoya Protocol on Access and Benefit-Sharing in Perspective* (Leiden, Brill Nijhoff, 2013) 389.

Denicolo, V, and Franzoni, LA, 'The Contract Theory of Patents' (2003) 23 *International Review of Law and Economics* 365.

Derclaye, E, 'Patent Law's Role in the Protection of the Environment – Re-assessing Patent Law and its Justifications in the 21st Century' (2009) 40(3) *International Review of Intellectual Property and Competition Law* 249.

Derclaye, E, and Taylor, T, 'Happy IP: Replacing the Law and Economics Justification for Intellectual Property Rights with a Well-being Approach' (2015) 37(4) *European Intellectual Property Review* 197.

Derclaye, E, and Taylor, T, 'Happy IP: Aligning Intellectual Property Rights With Well-being' (2015) 2015(1) *Intellectual Property Quarterly* 1.

Derrida, J, 'Plato's Pharmacy' in *Dissemination*, trans B Johnson (Chicago, IL, University of Chicago Press, 1981) 70.

Descola, P, *La Nature Domestique, Symbolisme et Praxis dans l'écologie des Achuar* (Paris, Editiones del la Maison des Sciences de L'Hommes, 1986).

Devall, W, and Sessions, G, *Deep Ecology: Living as if Nature Mattered* (Salt Lake City, UT, Gibbs M Smith, 1985).

Drahos, P, *A Philosophy of Intellectual Property* (Aldershot, Dartmouth, 1996).

Drahos, P, 'Indigenous Knowledge and Duties of Intellectual Property Owners' (1997) 11 *Intellectual Property Journal* 179.

Duffy, JF, 'Intellectual Property as Natural Monopoly: Toward a General Theory of Partial Property Rights' (2004) http://www.utexas.edu/law/magazine/wp/wp-content/uploads/centers/clbe/duffy intellectual_property_natural_monopoly.pdf"http://www.utexas.edu/law/magazine/wp/wp-content/uploads/centers/clbe/duffy_intellectual_property_natural_monopoly.pdf.

Dunham, I, et al, 'An Integrated Encyclopedia of DNA Elements in the Human Genome' (2012) 489(7414) *Nature* 57.

Du Plessis, P, 'Disclosure of Origin of Biological Resources and Potential Effects of the Protocol' (2011) 40(5) *Chartered Institute of Patent Attorneys Journal* 331.

Du Plessis, P, 'CBD and Nagoya' (2011) 40(7) *Chartered Institute of Patent Attorneys Journal* 466.

DuQuesne, T, and Reeves, J, *A Handbook of Psychoactive Medicines* (London, Quartet Books,1982).

Dutfield, D, *Intellectual Property Rights, Biogenetic Resources and Traditional Knowledge* (London, Earthscan, 2004).

Dutfield, G, 'Protecting the Rights of Indigenous Peoples: Can Prior Informed Consent Help?' in R Wynberg et al (eds), *Indigenous Peoples, Consent and Benefit Sharing: Lessons from the San Hoodia Case* (Dordrecht, Springer, 2009) 53.

Dutfield, G, 'A Critical Analysis of the Debate on Traditional Knowledge, Drug Discovery and Patent-Based Biopiracy' (2011) 33(4) *European Intellectual Property Review* 238.

Dutfield, G, and Suthersanen, U, *Global Intellectual Property Law* (Cheltenham, Edward Elgar, 2008).

Dutfield, G, 'Traditional Knowledge, Intellectual Property and Pharmaceutical Innovation: What's Left to Discuss?' in M David and Halbert (eds), *The Sage Handbook of Intellectual Property* (Thousand Oaks, CA, Sage, 2014).

Dwan, K, et al, 'Systematic Review of the Empirical Evidence of Study Publication Bias and Outcome Reporting Bias' (2008) 3(8) PLoS ONE e3081.

Dworkin, R, *Justice in Robes* (Cambridge MA, The Belknap Press of Harvard University Press, 2006).

Ellwanger, JH, and Chies, JAC, 'Zoonotic Spillover: Understanding Basic Aspects for Better Prevention' (2021) 44(1) (Suppl 1) *Genetics and Molecular Biology* e20200355.

El-Tawil, S, et al, 'Quinine for Muscle Cramps' [2015] *Cochrane Report* www.cochrane.org/CD005044/NEUROMUSC_quinine-for-muscle-cramps.

Ekins, S, et al, 'Exploiting Machine Learning for End-to-End Drug Discovery and Development' (2019) 18 (5) *Nature Materials* 435.

Elwood, PC, et al, 'A Randomized Controlled Trial of Acetyl Salicylic Acid in the Secondary Prevention of Mortality from Myocardial Infarction' (1974) 1 *British Medical Journal* 436.

Engle, K, 'On Fragile Architecture: The UN Declaration on the Rights of Indigenous Peoples in the Context of Human Rights' (2011) 22(1) *European Journal of International Law* 141.

Fairley, P, *The Conquest of Pain* (London, Michael Joseph, 1978).

Farnsworth, NR, 'The Role of Ethnopharmacology in Drug Development' in *Bioactive Compounds From Plants* (Ciba Foundation Symposium 154) (Chichester, John Wiley 1994) 2.

Fellows, L, and Scofield, A, 'Chemical Diversity in Plants' in T Swanson (ed), *Intellectual Property and Biodiversity Conservation: an Interdisciplinary Analysis of the Values of Medicinal Plants* (Cambridge, Cambridge University Press, 1995) 19.

Felsenfeld, G, 'A Brief History of Epigenetics' in CD Allis et al (eds), *Epigenetics* (Cold Spring Harbor, NY, Cold Spring Harbor Laboratory Press, 2009) 15.

Ferguson, N, *Empire* (London, Penguin, 2003).

Ferguson, N, *The Ascent of Money: A Financial History of the World* (London, Allen Lane, 2008).

Ferguson, N, *Civilization, The West and the Rest* (London, Allen Lane, 2011).

Ferreira, SH, 'Indomethacin and Aspirin Abolish Prostaglandin Release from the Spleen' (1971) 231(25) *Nature: New Biology* 237.

Fromer, JC, 'Expressive Incentives in Intellectual Property' (2012) 98 *Virginia Law Review* 1745.

Ferguson, GK, *The Human Genome: Poems of the Book of Life.* http://www.thehumangenome.co.uk/THE_HUMAN_GENOME/Primer.html.

Fisher, M, 'Classical Economics and Philosophy of the Patent System' (2005) 1 *Intellectual Property* 5.

Garfield, S, *Mauve: How One Man Invented a Colour which Changed the World* (London, Faber & Faber, 2000).

Garvey, J, and Stangroom, J, *The Story of Philosophy: A History of Western Thought* (London, Quercus, 2012).

Gibson, DG, et al, 'Creation of a Bacterial Cell Controlled by a Chemically Synthesized Genome' (2010) 329(5987) *Science* 52.

Gibson, J, *Community Resources: Intellectual Property, International Trade and Protection of Traditional Knowledge* (Farnham, Ashgate, 2005).

Gibson, J, 'Community and the Exhaustion of Culture, Creative Territories in Creative Cultural Expressions' in F Macmillan and K Bowrey (eds), *New Directions in Copyright Law*, vol 3 (Cheltenham, Edward Elgar, 2006) 21.

Gibson, PC, 'Salicylic Acid for Coronary Thrombosis?' (1948) 1 *Lancet* 965.

Gibson, PC, 'Aspirin in the Treatment of Vascular Diseases' (1949) 2 *Lancet* 1172.

Gillmor, D, and Turgeon, P, *Canada, A People's History*, vol 1 (Toronto, McClelland & Stewart, 2000).

Githaiga, J, 'Intellectual Property Law and the Protection of Indigenous Folklore and Knowledge' (1998) 5(2) *E Law: Murdoch University Electronic Journal of Law* para 18, http://www.murdoch.edu.au/elaw/issues/v5n2/githaiga52.html"http://www.murdoch.edu.au/elaw/issues/v5n2/githaiga52.html.

Gerwick, WH, and Moore, BS, 'Lessons from the Past and Charting the Future of Marine Natural Products Drug Discovery and Chemical Biology' (2012) 19(1) *Chemistry and Biology* 85.

Goldacre, B, *Bad Science* (London, Harper Perennial, 2009).

Goldberg, R, *Perspectives on Causation* (Oxford, Hart, 2011).

Goldring, P, 'Historians and Inuit: Learning from the Qikiqtani Truth Commission, 2007–2010' (2015) 50(3) *Canadian Journal of History* 492.

Goodman Gilman, A, et al, *Goodman and Gilman's The Pharmacological Basis of Therapeutics* (New York, Macmillan, 1985).

Goodland, RJA, and Irwin, HS, *Amazon Jungle: Green Hell to Red Desert: An Ecological Discussion of the Environmental Impact of the Highway Construction Programme in the Amazon Basin* (Amsterdam, Elsevier, 1975).

Gordley, G, 'Tort Law in the Aristotelian Tradition' in DG Owen (ed), *Philosophical Foundations of Tort Law* (Oxford, Oxford University Press, 1995) 131.

Gottesman, MM, et al, 'Multidrug Resistance in Cancer: Role of ATP-Dependent Transporters' (2002) 2 *Nature Reviews Cancer* 48.
Graham, L, and McJohn, S, 'Indigenous Peoples and Intellectual Property' (2005) 19 *Washington University Journal of Law and Policy* 313.
Graham, LH, and S Wiessner, S, 'Indigenous Sovereignty, Culture, and International Human Rights Law' (2011) 110(2) *South Atlantic Quarterly* 403.
Grahame-Smith, DG, and Aronson, JK, *Oxford Textbook of Clinical Pharmacology and Drug Therapy* (Oxford, Oxford University Press, 1992).
Grayling, AC, *Towards the Light, The Story of the Struggles for Liberty and Rights that Made the Modern West* (London, Bloomsbury, 2007).
Greiber, T, et al, *IUCN Explanatory Guide to the Nagoya Protocol on Access and Benefit-Sharing* (IUCN Environmental Policy and Law Paper No 83, 2012).
Griffiths, T, *Indigenous Knowledge and Intellectual Property: A Preliminary Review of the Anthropological Literature.* A Report Prepared for the Foundation for Ethnobiology at the University of Oxford (1993).
Gupta, A, 'Getting Creative People, Individuals and Communities Their Due: Framework for Operationalizing Articles 8(j) and 10(c)' (paper submitted to the Secretariat of the Convention on Biological Diversity, 1996).
Guyer, P, *Kant on Freedom, Law and Happiness* (Cambridge, Cambridge University Press, 2000).
Hägglöf, I, and Holmgreen, Å, 'Regulatory Affairs' in HP Rang (ed), *Drug Discovery and Development: Technology in Transition* (Edinburgh, Churchill Livingston/Elsevier, 2006) 281.
Hall, J, 'The Drug Development Process' in I Di Giovanna and G Hayes (eds), *Principles of Clinical Research* (Petersfield, Wrightson Biomedical, 2001) 1.
Hameduh, T, et al, 'Homology Modelling in the Time of Collective and Artificial Intelligence' (2020) 18 *Computational and Structural Biotechnology Journal* 3494.
Hanson, NR, *Patterns of Discovery, An Inquiry into the Conceptual Foundations of Science* (Cambridge, Cambridge University Press, 1965).
Hardin, G, 'Meaninglessness of the Word Protoplasm' (1956) 82(3) *Scientific Monthly* 112.
Hardin, G, 'The Tragedy of the Commons' (1968) 166 *Science* 1103.
Harrington, R, (Carpenter, E (ed)) *Padlei Diary, 1950: An Account of the Padleimiut Eskimo in the Keewatin District West of Hudson Bay during the Early Months of 1950* (New York, Rock Foundation, 2000).
Harris, JW, *Property and Justice* (Oxford, Oxford University Press, 1996).
Harris, S, *The Moral Landscape: How Science Can Determine Human Values* (London, Black Swan, 2010).
Harrison, PS, 'Grasping Frankenstein's Monster: Uncertainty in the Downstream Scope of the Nagoya Protocol' (2019) 1 *Intellectual Property Quarterly* 61.
Harrison, PS, 'A Good Idea Gone Bad. Can We Still Justify Patent Monopolies?' in A Johnston and L Talbot (eds), *Great Debates in Commercial and Corporate Law* (London, Red Globe Press, 2020) 62.
Harrison, S, 'Ritual and Intellectual Property' (1992) 27(2) *Man* 225.
Hart, HLA, 'Between Utility and Rights' in *Essays in Jurisprudence and Philosophy* (Oxford, Clarendon Press, 1983) 198.
Hart, HLA, and Honoré, T, *Causation in the Law* (Oxford, Oxford University Press, 1985).
Harsanyi, JC, 'Can the Maximin Principle Serve as a Basis for Morality? A Critique of John Rawls's Theory' (1975) 69(2) *American Political Science Review* 594.
Harshberger, JW, 'The Purposes of Ethnobotany' (1896) 21 *Botanical Gazette* 146.
Heller, MA, 'The Tragedy of the Anticommons: Property in the Transition from Marx to Markets' (1998) 111 *Harvard Law Review* 621.
Heller, MA and Eisenberg, R, 'Can Patents Deter Innovation? The Anticommons in Biomedical Research' (1998) 280 *Science* 698.
Hess, C, and Ostrom, E, 'Introduction' in C Hess and E Ostrom (eds), *Understanding Knowledge as a Commons: From Theory to Practice* (Cambridge, MA, MIT Press, 2007) 3.

Hettinger, EC, 'Justifying Intellectual Property' (1989) 18 *Philosophy and Public Affairs* 30.
Hille, B, 'Local Anaesthetics: Hydrophilic and Hydrophobic Pathways for the Drug Receptor Interaction' (1977) 69 *Journal of General Physiology* 497.
Himes, RH, et al, 'Action of the Vinca Alkaloids Vincristine, Vinblastine, and Desacetyl Vinblastine Amide on Microtubules in Vitro' (1976) 36 *Cancer Research* 3798.
Hobbes, T, *Leviathan* [1651] (London, JM Dent, 1940).
Hodgkin, AL, and Huxley, AF, 'A Quantitative Description of Membrane Current and its Application to Conduction and Excitation in Nerve' (1952) 117(4) *Journal of Physiology* 500.
Hohfeld, WN, 'Some Fundamental Legal Conceptions as Applied in Judicial Reasoning' (1913) 23 *Yale Law Journal* 16.
Hohfeld, WN, 'Fundamental Legal Conceptions as Applied in Judicial Reasoning' (1917) *Faculty Scholarship Series*, Paper 4378.
Hollis, A, 'Me-too Drugs: Is there a problem?' (2004) www.who.int/intellectualproperty/topics/ip/Me-tooDrugs_Hollis1.pdf.
Honderich, T, 'The Question of Well-being and the Principle of Equality' (1981) xc *Mind* 481.
Houssen, W, et al, 'Digital Sequence Information on Genetic Resources: Concept, Scope and Current Use' (2020) Annex to CBD/DSI/AHTEG/2020/1/3.
Houston, J, 'Fifty Years of Thinking it Over' in M von Finckenstein (ed), *Celebrating Inuit Art 1948–1970* (Toronto, Key Porter Books, 1999) 36.
Hsu, PD, et al, 'Development and Applications of CRISPR for Gene Engineering (2014) 157(6) *Cell* 1262.
Hughes, J, 'The Philosophy of Intellectual Property' (1988) 77 *Georgetown Law Review* 287.
Hussain, M, 'Patenting of Life Forms: Reflections on Some Legal and Ethical Issues' (2014) 4(2) *IUP Law Review* 7.
Hutchinson, HR, *How Drugs are Developed: A Practical Guide to Clinical Research* (Wilmslow, Brook Medical, 1997).
Hyde, L, *Common as Air: Revolution, Art and Ownership* (London, Union Books, 2010).
Iborra, FJ, et al, 'The Functional Organization of Mitochondrial Genomes in Human Cells' (2004) 2 *BMC Biology* 9.
Ince, OU, *Colonial Capitalism and the Dilemmas of Liberalism* (Oxford, Oxford University Press, 2018).
Irwandi, A, and Rifki Taufik, R, 'Cultural Identity in the Shackles of Modernization: The Case of Mentawai Indigenous Peoples' (2023) 9(2) *Jurnal Sosiologi Andalas* 211.
Jaina, M, et al, 'Traditional Uses, Phytochemistry and Pharmacology of *Tecomella Undulate* – A Review' (2012) 2(3) *Asian Pacific Journal of Tropical Biomedicine* S1918.
James, L, *The Rise and Fall of the British Empire* (London, Abacus,1995).
Jamieson, D, *Ethics and the Environment* (Cambridge, Cambridge University Press, 2008).
Janke, T, 'Respecting Indigenous Cultural and Intellectual Property Rights' (1999) 22 *University of New South Wales Law Journal* 631.
Jefferson,T, 'Letter to Isaac McPherson, 13 August 1813' 13 *Writings* 333.
Jenuwein, T, and Allis, CD, 'Translating the Histone Code' (2001) 293 *Science* 1074.
Johnson, IS, et al, 'The Vinca Alkaloids: A New Class of Oncolytic Agents' (1963) 23(8) *Cancer Research* 1390.
Jordan, MA, and Leslie Wilson, L, 'Microtubules as a Target for Anticancer Drugs' (2004) 4 *Nature Reviews Cancer* 253.
Jumper, J, et al, 'Highly Accurate Protein Structure Prediction with AlphaFold' (2021) 596(7873) *Nature* 583.
Kamau, EC, et al, 'The Nagoya Protocol on Access to Genetic Resources and Benefit Sharing: What Is New and What Are the Implications for Provider and User Countries and the Scientific Community?' (2010) 6(3) *Law, Environment and Development Journal* 246.
Kampourakis, K, *Making Sense of Genes* (Cambridge, Cambridge University Press, 2017).
Kant, I, 'Of the Injustice of Counterfeiting Books' [1785] www.staffweb.hkbu.edu.hk/ppp/fne/essay3.html.

Kant, I, 'The Metaphysics of Morals' [1797] in MJ Gregor (trans and ed) *Immanuel Kant, Practical Philosophy* (Cambridge, Cambridge University Press, 1996).

Karanja, W, 'The Legitimacy of Indigenous Intellectual Property Rights' Claims' (2016) 1 *Strathmore Law Review* 165.

Keen, I, 'Yolngu Religious Property' in T Ingold et al (eds), *Hunters and Gatherers 2: Property, Power and Ideology* (Oxford, Oxford University Press, 1988).

Kennedy, D, 'Sovereignty: Responding to Anghie and Aravamudan's Remarks in the Proceedings of the Symposium "Representing Culture: Translating Human Rights"' (2006) 41(3) *Texas International Law Journal* 465.

Khorana, HG, et al, 'Studies on Polynucleotides. 103. Total Synthesis of the Structural Gene for an Alanine Transfer Ribonucleic Acid from Yeast' (1972) 72(2) *Journal of Molecular Biology* 209.

Kiene, T, *The Legal Protection of Traditional Knowledge in the Pharmaceutical Field: An Intercultural Problem on the International Agenda* (Münster, Waxmann, 2012).

Kim, H, et al, 'Artificial Intelligence in Drug Discovery: A Comprehensive Review of Data-Driven and Machine Learning Approaches' (2020) 25 *Biotechnology and Bioprocess Engineering* 895.

King, GF, (ed), *Venoms to Drugs: Venom as a Source for the Development of Human Therapeutics* (Abingdon, Royal Society of Chemistry, 2014).

Kodatek, T, 'The Rise, Fall and Reinvention of Combinatorial Chemistry' (2011) 47(35) *Chemical Communications* 9757.

Koller, C, 'History of Cocaine as a Local Anaesthetic' (1941) 117 *Journal of the American Medical Association* 1284.

Kolig, E, 'Government Policies and Religious Strategies: Fighting with Myth at Noonkanbah' in R Tonkinson and M Howard (eds), *Going it Alone: Prospects for Aboriginal Autonomy* (Canberra, Aboriginal Studies Press, 1990).

Kosaka, R, *The Negotiating History of the Nagoya Protocol on ABS: Japanese Perspective* (2012) www.ipaj.org/english_journal/pdf/9-1_Kohsaka.pdf"www.ipaj.org/english_journal/pdf/9-1_Kohsaka.pdf.

Kouzarides, T, 'Chromatin Modifications and their Function' (2007) 128 *Cell* 693.

Kubinyi, H, 'The Drug Design Cycle' in E Raviña, *The Evolution of Drug Discovery: From Traditional Medicines to Modern Drugs* (Weinheim, Wiley-VCH, 2011) 463.

Laiolo, E, et al, 'Metagenomic Probing Toward an Atlas of the Taxonomic and Metabolic Foundations of the Global Ocean Genome' (2024) 1 *Frontiers in Science* 1038696.

Laslett, P, *Locke, Two Treatise of Government* (Cambridge, Cambridge University Press, 1988).

Latha, SS, 'Biopiracy and Protection of Traditional Medicine in India' (2009) 31(9) *European Intellectual Property Review* 465.

Laws, B, *Fifty Plants that Changed the Course of History* (Newton Abbott, David & Charles, 2010).

Lawson, C, et al, 'The Future of Information Under the CBD, Nagoya Protocol, Plant Treaty, and PIP Framework' (2019) 22 *Journal of World Intellectual Property* 1.

Lee, CH and PC Ruben, PC, 'Interaction Between Voltage-Gated Sodium Channels and the Neurotoxin, Tetrodotoxin' (2008) 2(6) *Channels* 407.

Lefébure, M, *St Thomas Aquinas: Summa Theologiæ*, vol 38: *Injustice* (2a 2æ, 63–79) (London, Blackfriars, 1975).

Lewis, J D, et al, 'Purification, Sequence, and Cellular Localization of a Novel Chromosomal Protein that Binds to Methylated DNA' (1992) 69 *Cell* 905.

Lesk, AM, *Introduction to Genomics* (Oxford, Oxford University Press, 2012).

Lin, X, et al, 'Effects of Quinine on the Excitability and Voltage-Dependent Currents of Isolated Spiral Ganglion Neurons in Culture' (1998) 79(5) *Journal of Neurophysiology* 2503.

Lemley, MA, 'Ex Ante versus Ex Post Justifications for Intellectual Property' (2004) 71(1) *University of Chicago Law Review* 129.

Lemley, MA, 'Property, Intellectual Property, and Free Riding' (2005) 83 *Texas Law Review* 1031.

Lenzerini, F, 'Sovereignty Revisited: International Law and Parallel Sovereignty of Indigenous Peoples' (2006) 42(1) *Texas Journal of International Law* 155.

Leopold, A, *A Sand County Almanac* (New York, Oxford University Press, 1949).
LeVine, H, and Rang, HP, 'The Role of Genomics and Bioinformatics' in HP Rang (ed) *Drug Discovery and Development: Technology in Transition* (Edinburgh, Churchill Livingston/Elsevier, 2006) 77.
Leung, S, 'The Commons and Anticommons in Intellectual Property' (2010) 16 *UCL Jurisprudence Review* 16.
Lindstrom, L,'Knowledge and Power in a South Pacific Society' (Washington, DC, Smithsonian Institution Press, 1990).
Lipinski, CA, et al, 'Experimental and Computational Approaches to Estimate Solubility and Permeability in Drug Discovery and Development Settings' (2001) 46 *Advances in Drug Delivery Review* 3.
Liu, G, et al, 'Deep Learning-Guided Discovery of an Antibiotic Targeting *Acinetobacter baumannii*' (2023) 19 *Nature Chemical Biology* 1342.
Liu, Y, 'The Tale of Viagra Patents: Comparative Studies of the Global Challenges in China and Other Countries' (2013) 18 *Japanese Intellectual Property Review* 523.
Lührmann, S, 'Arctic' in CF Feest (ed), *The Cultures of Native North Americans* (Cologne, Könemann, 2000) 30.
MacIntyre, A, *A Short History of Ethics: A History of Moral Philosophy from the Homeric Age to the Twentieth Century* (Oxford, Routledge Classics, 2002).
Machlup, F, and Penrose, E, 'The Patent Controversy in the Nineteenth Century' (1950) 10(1) *Journal of Economic History* 1.
Maffi, L, 'Biocultural Diversity for Sustainability' in J Pretty et al (eds), *The Sage Handbook of Environment and Society* (Los Angeles, Sage, 2007).
Maffi, L, and Woodley, E, *Biocultural Diversity Conservation: A Global Sourcebook* (Abingdon, Earthscan, 2010).
Marguerat, SH, *Private Property Rights and the Environment: Our Responsibilities to Global Natural Resources – Palgrave Studies in Environmental Policy and Regulation* (London, Palgrave Macmillan, 2019) 311.
Marko, J, and Urban, B, 'Machine Learning in Antibacterial Drug Design' (2022) 13 *Frontiers in Pharmacology* 864412.
Matthews, CK, et al, *Biochemistry* (San Francisco, Benjamin Cummings, 1999).
Matthews, D, 'TRIPS Flexibilities and Access to Medicines in Developing Countries: The Problem with Technical Assistance and Free Trade Agreements' [2005] 27 *European Intellectual Property Review* 421.
Matthews, D, *Intellectual Property, Human Rights and Development: The Role of NGOs and Social Movements* (Cheltenham, Edward Elgar, 2011).
May, C, *The Political Economy of Intellectual Property Rights*, vol 1 (Cheltenham, Edward Elgar, 2010).
Mayeda, G, 'Commentary of Fichte's "The Illegality of the Unauthorised Reprinting of Books": An Essay on Intellectual Property During the Age of the Enlightenment (2008) *University of Ottawa Law and Technology Journal* 141.
Mazzocchi, F, 'Western Science and Traditional Knowledge: Despite their Variations, Different Forms of Knowledge Can Learn from Each Other' (2006) 7(5) *EMBO Reports* 463.
McGraw, DM, 'The Story of the Biodiversity Convention: From Negotiation to Implementation' in PG Le Prestre (ed), *Governing Global Biodiversity: The Evolution and Implementation of the Convention on Biological Diversity* (Farnham, Ashgate, 2002).
Medaglia, JC, 'Study on the Relationship Between the ABS International Regimen and Other International Instruments Which Govern the Use of Genetic Resources: The World Trade Organization (WTO); the World Intellectual Property Rights Organization (WIPO); and the International Union for the Protection of New Varieties of Plants (UPOV)' (2009) *Comments of UPOV for the Secretariat of the Convention on Biological Diversity*, 7 (www.upov.int/export/sites/upov/about/en/pdf/upov_comments_medaglia_study_final.pdf).
Medaglia, JC, 'Digital Sequence Information (DSI) and Benefit-Sharing Arising from its Use: An Unfinished Discussion.' (2020) 69(6) *GRUR International* 565.

Meiners, RE, and Staaf, RJ, 'Patents, Copyrights, and Trademarks: Property or Monopoly?'(1990) 13 *Harvard Journal of Law and Public Policy* 911.

Melo, MCR, et al, 'Accelerating Antibiotic Discovery Through Artificial Intelligence' (2021) 4 *Community Biology* 1050.

Mendoza-Azpur, G, et al, 'Clinical and Histological Manifestations of Chronic Coca Leaf Chewing in a Peruvian Population: A Cross-Sectional Study' (2021) 23(1) *Journal of the International Academy of Periodontology* 11.

Merges, RP, *Justifying Intellectual Property* (Cambridge MA, Harvard University Press, 2011).

Meth-Cohn, O, and Smith, M, 'What Did W H Perkin Actually Make when He Oxidised Aniline to Obtain Mauveine?' (1994) 1 *Journal of the Chemical Society Perkin* 5.

Milius, D, 'Justifying Intellectual Property in Traditional Knowledge' [2009] *Intellectual Property Quarterly* 184.

Mill, JS, *Utilitarianism, Liberty and Representative Government* (London, JM Dent, 1910).

Milstein, C, 'The Hybridoma Revolution: An Offshoot of Basic Research' (1999) 21 (11) *BioEssays* 966.

Moore, A, *Stanford Encyclopedia of Philosophy* (2011) http://plato.staford.edu/enties/intellectual-property.

Moore, MS, *Causation and Responsibility: An Essay in Law, Morals and Metaphysics* (Oxford, Oxford University Press, 2009).

Morgera, E, et al, *Unravelling the Nagoya Protocol: A Commentary on the Nagoya Protocol on Access and Benefit Sharing to the Convention on Biological Diversity* (Leiden, Brill/Nijhoff, 2014).

Morgera, E, and Geelhoed, M, 'Consultancy on the Notion of "Utilisation" in the Nagoya Protocol and the EU ABS Regulation for the Upstream Actors' (European Commission, 2015) www.ec.europa.eu/environment/nature/biodiversity/international/abs/pdf/ABS%20Final%20Report%20upstream%20users.pdf.

Mt Pleasant, J, 'The Science Behind the Three Sisters Mound System: An Agronomic Assessment of an Indigenous Agricultural System in the Northeast' in JE Staller et al (eds), *Histories of Maize: Multidisciplinary Approaches to the Prehistory, Linguistics, Biogeography, Domestication, and Evolution of Maize.* (London, Academic Press, 2006).

Munzer, SR, and Raustiala, K, 'The Uneasy Case for Intellectual Property Rights in Traditional Knowledge' (2009) 29 *Cardozo Arts and Entertainment Law Journal* 39.

Munzer, SR 'Corrective Justice and Intellectual Property Rights in Traditional Knowledge' in A Lever (ed), *New Frontiers in the Philosophy of Intellectual Property* (Cambridge University Press, Cambridge, 2012) 58.

Murphy, WP, 'Secret Knowledge as Property and Power in Kpelle Society: Elders versus Youth' (1980) 50(2) *Africa: Journal of the International African Institute* 193.

Myers, FR, 'Always Ask: Resource Use and Land Ownership Among the Pintupi Aborigines of the Australian Western Desert' in NM Williams and ES Hunn (eds), *Resource Managers: North American and Australian Hunter-Gatherers* (Routledge, New York, 1982) 173.

Myers, FR, 'Burning the Truck and Holding the Country: Pintupi Forms of Property and Identity' in EN Wilmsen (ed), *We Are Here: Politics of Aboriginal Land Tenure* (Oakland, CA, University of California Press, 1989).

Naess, A, 'The Shallow and the Deep, Long Range Ecology Movements: A Summary' (1973) 16 *Inquiry* 95.

Nan, X, et al, 'Transcriptional Repression by the Methyl-CpG-Binding Protein MeCP2 Involves a Histone Deacetylase Complex' (1998) 393 *Nature* 386;.

Nantasenamat, C, et al, 'A Practical Overview of Quantitative Structure–Activity Relationship' (2009) 8 *Experimental and Clinical Sciences Journal* 74.

Neuss, N, 'Vinca Alkaloids. III. 1. Characterisation of Leurosine and Vincaleukoblastine, New Alkaloids from *Vinca Rosea* Linn' (1959) 81 *Journal of the American Chemical Society* 4754.

Ng, R, *Drugs, From Discovery to Approval* (New Jersey, John Wiley and Sons, 2004).

Nijar, GS, *The Nagoya Protocol on ABS: An Analysis* (Kuala Lumpar, Centre of Excellence for Biodiversity Law, 2011).

Noble, RL, et al, 'Role of Chance Observations in Chemotherapy' (1958) 76 *Annals of the New York Academy of Sciences* 882.

Nozick, R, *Anarchy, State and Utopia* (New York, Basic Books, 1974).

Nutt, DJ, et al, 'Unusual Interactions of Benzodiazepine Receptor Antagonists' (1982) 295(5848) *Nature* 436.

Oldham, P, et al, 'Digital Sequence Information in the UN High Seas Treaty: Insights from the Global Biodiversity Framework-Related Decisions' 53 (*LSE Law-Policy Briefing* Paper, 2023) papers.ssrn.com/sol3/papers.cfm?abstract_id=4343130).

O'Leary, ME, and Hancox, JC, 'Role of Voltage-Gated Sodium, Potassium and Calcium Channels in the Development of Cocaine-Associated Cardiac Arrhythmias' (2010) 69(5) *British Journal of Clinical Pharmacology* 427.

O'Neil, MJ (ed), *The Merck Index, An Encyclopedia of Chemicals Drugs, and Biologicals* (Whitehouse Station, NJ, Merck and Co Inc, 2001).

Ostrom, V, and Ostrom, E, 'Public Goods and Public Choices' in ES Saras (ed), *Alternatives for Delivering Public Services: Toward Improved Performance* (Boulder CO, Westview Press, 1977).

Otten, H, 'Domagk and the Development of the Sulphonamides' (1986) 17(6) *Journal of Antimicrobial Chemotherapy* 689.

Oguamanam, C, *International Law and Indigenous Knowledge: Intellectual Property, Plant Biodiversity, and Traditional Medicine* (Toronto, University of Toronto Press 2006).

Oguamanam, C, 'Indigenous Peoples' Rights at the Intersection of Human Rights and Intellectual Property Rights' (2014) 18 *Marquette Intellectual Property Law Journal* 261.

OseiTutu, JJ, 'A *Sui Generis* Regime for Traditional Knowledge: The Cultural Divide in Intellectual Property Law' (2011) 15 *Marquette Intellectual Property Law Review* 147.

Oyeshile, OA, 'A Critique of the Maximin Principle in Rawls's Theory of Justice' (2008) 3(1) *Humanity and Social Sciences Journal* 65.

Palmer, K, '"Owners" and "managers": Ritual Co-operation and Mutual Dependence in the Maintenance of Rights to Land' (1983) 13(6) *Mankind* 517.

Papadopoulou, F, *The Protection of Traditional Knowledge on Genetic Resources* (Cheltenham, Edward Elgar, 2018).

Parkin, D, *Sacred Void: Spatial Images of Work and Ritual Among the Giriama of Kenya* (Cambridge, Cambridge University Press, 1991) 163.

Paul, D, et al, 'Artificial Intelligence in Drug Discovery and Development' (2021) 26(1) *Drug Discovery Today* 80.

Pelletier, JF, et al, 'Genetic Requirements for Cell Division in a Genomically Minimal Cell' (2021) 184(9) *Cell* 2430.

Pennisi, E, 'Genomics. ENCODE Project Writes Eulogy for Junk DNA' (2012) 337 (6099) *Science* 1159.

Peters, P, *Biotechnology A Guide to Genetic Engineering* (Dubuque, IA, Wm C Brown, 1995).

Pievatolo, MC, 'Freedom, Ownership and Copyright: Why Does Kant Reject the Concept of Intellectual Property?' (2010) http://ssrn.com/abstract=1540095.

Porter, R (ed), *The Hutchinson Dictionary of Scientific Biography* (Oxford, Helicon, 1994).

Porter, R, *The Greatest Benefit to Mankind: A Medical History of Humanity from Antiquity to Present* (London, HarperCollins, 1997).

Posey, DA, 'Kayapo Controla Inseto com Uso Adequado do Ambiente' (1979) 14(3) *Revista de Atualidade Indígena* 47.

Posey, DA, 'Ethnoentomology of the Kayapó Indians of Central Brazil: Wasps, Warriors and Fearless Men' (1981) 1(1) *Journal of Ethnobiology* 165.

Posey, DA, 'Indigenous Knowledge and Development in the Amazon' in E Moran (ed), *The Dilemma of Amazonian Development* (Boulder, CO, Westview Press, 1983) 891.

Posey, DA, 'Intellectual Property Rights: What Is the Position of Ethnobiology?' (1990) 10(1) *Journal of Ethnobiology* 93.

Posey, DA, 'Intellectual Property Rights: And Just Compensation for Indigenous Knowledge' (1990) 6(4) *Anthropology Today* 13.

Posey, DA, 'Indigenous Peoples and Traditional Resource Rights: A Basis for Equitable Relationships?' in *Workshop on Indigenous Peoples and Traditional Resource Rights at the Green College Centre for Environmental Policy and Understanding* (University of Oxford, 1995) www.iccaconsortium.org/wp-content/uploads/2015/08/example-ip-and-traditional-resource-rights-addison-posey-1995-en.pdf.

Posey, DA, and Dutfield, G, *Beyond Intellectual Property: Toward Traditional Resources Rights for Indigenous Peoples and Local Communities* (Ottawa, International Development Research Centre, 1996).

Posey, DA, 'Commodification of the Sacred Through Intellectual Property Rights' (2002) 83(1–2) *Journal of Ethnobiology* 3.

Posner, RA, *Overcoming Law* (Cambridge, MA, Harvard University Press, 1995).

Posner, RA, *Law, Pragmatism and Democracy* (Cambridge, MA, Harvard University Press, 2005).

Post, G, et al, 'The Medieval Heritage of a Humanistic Ideal: Scientia donum Dei est, unde bendi non potest' (1995) 11 *Traditio* 195.

Proebstl, L, et al, 'Effects of Stimulant Drug Use on the Dopaminergic System: A Systematic Review and Meta-analysis of In Vivo Neuroimaging Studies' (2019) 59 *European Psychiatry* 15.

Rabe, P, and Kindler, K, 'Uber die partielle Synthese des Chinins. Zur Kenntnis der China-Alkaloide XIX' (1918) 51 *Berichte der Deutschen Chemischen Gesellschaft* 466.

Radin, MJ, *Reinterpreting Property* (Chicago, IL, University of Chicago Press, 1993).

Rang, HP, 'Pharmacology: Its Role in Drug Discovery' in HP Rang (ed), *Drug Discovery and Development: Technology in Transition* (Edinburgh, Churchill Livingston/Elsevier, 2006) 163.

Rang, HP, and Dale, MM, *Pharmacology* (Edinburgh, Churchill Livingstone, 1987).

Raviña, E, *The Evolution of Drug Discovery: From Traditional Medicines to Modern Drugs* (Weinheim, Wiley-VCH, 2011).

Rawls, J, *A Theory of Justice* [1971] (rev edn, Cambridge, MA, Belknap Press, 1999).

Rawls, J, 'Some Reasons for the Maximin Criterion' (1974) 63 *American Economic Review* 141.

Rawls, J, 'The Idea of an Overlapping Consensus' (1987) 7(1) *Oxford Journal of Legal Studies* 1.

Rawls, J, *Political Liberalism* (New York, Columbia University Press, 1993).

Reddy, GVP, and Guerrero, A, 'Interactions of Insect Pheromones and Plant Semiochemicals' (2004) 9(5) *Trends in Plant Science* 253.

Reichman, JH, 'Non-voluntary Licensing of Patented Inventions Historical Perspective, Legal Framework under TRIPS, and an Overview of the Practice in Canada and the USA' (UNCTAD-ICTSD Project on IPRs and Sustainable Development, 2003) http://www.ictsd.org/downloads/2008/06/cs_reichman_hasenzahl.pdf.

Resnik, DB, 'A Pluralistic Account of Intellectual Property' (2003) 46(4) *Journal of Business Ethics* 319, 319.

Rich, SM, et al, 'The Origin of Malignant Malaria' (2009) 106 (35) *Proceedings of the National Academy of Sciences* 14902.

Ridker, PM, et al, 'Inflammation, Aspirin, and the Risk of Cardiovascular Disease in Apparently Healthy Men' (1979) 336 *New England Journal of Medicine* 973.

Rifaioglu, AS, et al, 'MDeePred: Novel Multi-channel Protein Featurization for Deep Learning-Based Binding Affinity Prediction in Drug Discovery' (2021) 37(5) *Bioinformatics* 693.

Riesenberg, D, et al, 'High Cell Density Fermentation of Recombinant *Escherichia coli* Expressing Human Interferon Alpha 1' (1990) 34(1) *Applied Microbiological Biotechnology* 77.

Rijpma, SR, et al, 'Atovaquone and Quinine Anti-malarials Inhibit ATP Binding Cassette Transporter Activity' (2014) 13 *Malaria Journal* 359.

Riley, M, (ed), *Indigenous Intellectual Property Rights, Legal Obstacles and Innovative Solutions* (Lanham, MD, Altamira Press, 2004).

Robinson, DF, *Confronting Biopiracy: Challenges, Cases and International Debates* (London, Earthscan, 2012).

Rohden, F, and Scholz, AH, 'The International Political Process Around Digital Sequence Information Under the Convention on Biological Diversity and the 2018–2020 Intersessional Period.' (2022) 4(1) *Plants, People, Planet* 51.

Rousseau, J-J, *Discourse on the Origin and Basis of Inequality Among Men* [1755] (London, Palgrave, 2011).

Russell, B, *History of Western Philosophy* (1946) (London, Routledge Classics, 2004).

Roberts, T, 'CBD and Nagoya – A Rejoinder' (2011) 40(6) *Chartered Institute of Patent Attorneys Journal* 403.

Rosen, AD, *Kant's Theory of Justice* (Ithaca, NY, Cornell University Press, 1993).

Saiki, RK, et al, 'Primer-Directed Enzymatic Amplification of DNA with a Thermostable DNA Polymerase' (1988) 239 (4839) *Science* 487.

Sargent, S, 'What's in a Name? The Contested Meaning of Free, Prior and Informed Consent in International Financial Law and Indigenous Rights' in V Vadi and B de Witte (eds), *Culture and International Economic Law* (Oxford, Routledge, 2015) 87.

John (of Salisbury, Bishop of Chartres), *The Metalogicon: A Twelfth-Century Defense of the Verbal and Logical Arts of the Trivium* (Oakland, CA, California University Press, 1955).

Samaranayake, WR, 'A Critical Evaluation of the Interface Between Intellectual Property Rights and Human Rights with Special Emphasis on Indigenous Intellectual Property' (2022) 25(2) *The Journal of World Intellectual Property* 412.

Sandburg, C, *Good Morning, America* (New York, Harcourt Brace, 1928).

Savaresi, A, 'The International Human Rights Law Implications of the Nagoya Protocol' in E Morgera et al (eds), *The 2010 Nagoya Protocol on Access and Benefit-Sharing in Perspective: Implications for International Law and Implementation Challenges* (Leiden, Martinus Nijhoff, 2012) 53.

Schuffenhauer, A, et al, 'Relationships between Molecular Complexity, Biological Activity, and Structural Diversity' (2006) 46 *Journal of Chemical Information and Modelling* 525.

Schuler, P, 'Biopiracy and Commercialization of Ethnobotanical Knowledge' in JM Finger and P Schuler (eds), *Poor People's Knowledge* (Oxford, World Bank and Oxford University Press, 2004).

Schei, PJ, and Tvedt, MW, '"Genetic Resources" in the CBD: The Wording, the Past, the Present and the Future' (Fridtjof Nansen Institute Report 4, 2010) http://www.fni.no/docandpdf/FNI-R0410.pdf.

Schiebinger, L, *Plants and Empire, Colonial Bioprospecting in the Atlantic World* (Cambridge, MA, Harvard University Press, 2004).

Schwiening, CJ, 'A Brief Historical Perspective: Hodgkin and Huxley' (2012) 590(11) *Journal of Physiology* 2571.

Scott, C, 'Property, Practice and Aboriginal Rights Among Quebec Cree Hunters' in T Ingold et al (eds), *Hunters and Gatherers 2: Property, Power and Ideology* (Oxford, Oxford University Press, 1988).

Sedyaningsih, ER, et al, 'Towards Mutual Trust, Transparency and Equity in Virus Sharing Mechanism: The Avian Influenza Case of Indonesia' (2008) 37 *Annals of the Academy of Medicine Singapore* 486.

Sen, A, 'The Possibility of Social Choice' (1999) 89 *American Economic Review* 178.

Sen, A, *The Idea of Justice* (London, Penguin Books, 2010).

Sheldon, JW, and Balick, MJ, 'Ethnobotany and the Search for Balance Between Use and Conservation' in T Swanson (ed), *Intellectual Property and Biodiversity Conservation: An Interdisciplinary Analysis of the Values of Medicinal Plants* (Cambridge, Cambridge University Press, 1995) 45.

Shiffrin, SV, 'Lockean Arguments for Private Intellectual Property' in SR Munzer (ed), *New Essays in the Legal and Political Theory of Property* (Cambridge, Cambridge University Press, 2001) 165.

Shiffrin, SV, 'The Incentives Argument for Intellectual Property Protection' in A Gosseries et al (eds), *Intellectual Property and Theories of Justice* (New York, Palgrave Macmillan, 2008) 29.

Shiva, V *Biopiracy: The Plunder of Nature and Knowledge* (New York, South End Press, 1997).

Shrinkhal, R, '"Indigenous Sovereignty" and Right to Self-determination in International Law: A Critical Appraisal' (2021) 17(1) *AlterNative: An International Journal of Indigenous Peoples* 71.

Silverman, DJ, *This Land is Their Land: The Wampanoag Indians, Plymouth Colony, and the Troubled History of Thanksgiving* (London, Bloomsbury, 2019).

Simpson, T, 'Indigenous Heritage and Self-determination: The Cultural and Intellectual Property Rights of Indigenous Peoples' (Copenhagen, International Work Group for Indigenous Affairs, 1997).

Schoenfelder, S, et al, 'Preferential Associations Between Co-regulated Genes Reveal a Transcriptional Interactome in Erythroid Cells' (2010) 42 *Nature Genetics* 53.

Singer, P, *Practical Ethics* (Cambridge, Cambridge University Press, 1999).
Singer, P, *Animal Liberation* (New York, Harper Collins, 2002).
Smart, JJC, and Williams, B, *Utilitarianism, For and Against* (Cambridge, Cambridge University Press, 1973).
Sneader, W, *Drug Discovery: The Evolution of Modern Medicines* (Chichester, John Wiley, 1985).
Sneader, W 'The Discovery of Aspirin: A Reappraisal' (2000) 321 *British Medical Journal* 1591.
Sneader, W, *Drug Discovery, A History* (Chichester, John Wiley, 2005).
Snyder, SH, 'Forty Years of Neurotransmitters' in TA Ban et al (eds) *From Psychopharmacology to Neuropsychopharmacology in the 1980s and the Story of CINP as Told in Autobiography* (Budapest, Animula, 2002) 36.
Solovy, EM, and Krishnamurthy, PS, 'TRIPS Agreement Flexibilities and Their Limitations: A Response to the UN Secretary-General's High Level Panel Report on Access to Medicines' (2017) 50 *George Washington International Law Review* 69.
Spinoza, B, *A Theologico-Political Treatise*, in *The Chief Works*, vol 1 (New York, Dover, 1951) 208.
Stack, AJ, et al, 'Accounting of Profits Calculations in Intellectual Property Cases in Canada' (2001) 17(2) *Canadian Intellectual Property Review* 405.
Stamatopoulou, E, 'Taking Cultural Rights Seriously: The Vision of the UN Declaration on the Rights of Indigenous Peoples' in S Allen and A Xanthaki (eds), *Reflections on the UN Declaration on the Rights of Indigenous Peoples* (Oxford, Hart, 2011) 392.
Stephens, LA, *Explorers of the Brain* (London, The Scientific Book Club, 1973).
Stewart, N, *Ethics: An Introduction to Moral Philosophy* (Cambridge, Polity Press, 2009).
Stoeckli, K, and Haag, H, 'High Throughput Screening' in HP Rang (ed), *Drug Discovery and Development: Technology in Transition* (Edinburgh, Churchill Livingston/Elsevier, 2006) 99.
Stokes, JM, et al, 'A Deep Learning Approach to Antibiotic Discovery' (2020) 180(4) *Cell* 688.
Stone, E, 'An Account of the Success of the Bark of the Willow in the Cure of Agues' (1763) 53 *Philosophical Transactions* 195.
Sullivan, DJ, 'Theories on Malarial Pigment Formation and Quinoline Action' (2002) 32 (13) *International Journal of Parasitology* 1645.
Sunstein, CR, 'On Analogical Reasoning' (1993) 106 *Harvard Law Review* 741.
Sunstein, CR, 'Incompletely Theorized Agreements' (1995) 108(7) *Harvard Law Review* 1733.
Sunstein, CR, 'On Legal Theory and Legal Practice' in I Shapiro and JW DeCew (eds), *Theory and Practice NOMOS XXXVII* (New York, New York University Press, 1995).
Sunstein, CR, Legal *Reasoning and Political Conflict* (Oxford, Oxford University Press, 1996).
Svoboda, GH, et al, 'Current Status of Research on the Alkaloids of *Vinca rosea* Linn (*Catharanthus roseus* G. Don)' (1962) 51 *Journal of Pharmaceutical Science* 707.
Swiderska, K, 'What Happened at Nagoya?' (2010) www.iied.org.
Taubman, A, 'Is There a Right of Collective Personality?' [2006] *European Intellectual Property Review* 485.
Taylor, CCW, 'Eudaimonia' in T Honderich (ed), *The Oxford Companion to Philosophy* (Oxford, Oxford University Press, 1995) 252.
Taylor, TC, *An Introduction to Austrian Economics* (Auburn, AL, Ludwig von Mises Institute, 1980) http://mises.org/austecon/chap4.as).
Tenni. B. et al, 'What Is the Impact of Intellectual Property Rules on Access to Medicines? A Systematic Review' (2022) 18(1) *Globalization and Health* 40.
Tohgi, H, et al, 'Effects of Low-to-High Doses of Aspirin on Platelet Aggregability and Metabolites of Thromboxane A2 and Prostacyclin' (1992) 23(10) *Stroke* 1400.
Travis, AS, 'Perkin's Mauve: Ancestor of the Organic Chemical Industry' (1990) 31(1) *Technology and Culture* 51.
Trerise, J, 'Liberty and the Rejection of Strong Intellectual Property Rights' in A Gosseries et al (eds), *Intellectual Property and Theories of Justice* (London, Palgrave Macmillan, 2010) 122.
Tsosie, R, 'Reclaiming Native Stories: An Essay on Cultural Appropriation and Cultural Rights' (2002) 34 *Arizona State Law Journal* 299.

Tuck, R, *Natural Rights Theories, Their Origin and Development* (Cambridge, Cambridge University Press, 1979).

Turnbull, HW, et al (eds), *The Correspondence of Isaac Newton*, vol I (Cambridge, Cambridge University Press, 1959).

Turner, D, 'Vision: 'Towards an Understanding of Aboriginal Sovereignty' in R Beiner and WJ Norman (eds), *Canadian Political Philosophy: Contemporary Reflections* (Oxford, Oxford University Press, 2001) 325.

Tvedt, MW and Fauchald, OK, 'Implementing the Nagoya Protocol on ABS: A Hypothetical Case Study on Enforcing Benefit Sharing in Norway' (2011) 14(5) *Journal of World Intellectual Property* 383.

Tvedt, MW, and Schei, PJ, 'The Term "Genetic Resources": Flexible and Dynamic while Providing Legal Certainty?' in S Oberthür and GK Rosendal (eds), *Global Governance of Genetic Resources: Access and Benefit Sharing after the Nagoya Protocol* (London, Routledge, 2014) 18.

Wilson, L, et al, 'On the Mechanism of Action of Vinblastine' (1974) 63 *Journal of Cell Biology* 373a.

Underkuffler, LS, *The Idea of Property: Its Meaning and Power* (Oxford, Oxford University Press 2005).

Välimäki, E, 'Calculation of Royalties in Compulsory Licensing of Pharmaceutical Patents in Europe – How Much Is Justified?' (2011) *Nordic Journal of Commercial Law Special Edition.*

van Bergen, M, and Snoeijer, W, '*Catharanthus* G.Don. The Madagascar Periwinkle and Related Species' (1996) 96(3) *Wageningen Agricultural University Papers* 1.

van der Heijden, R, et al, 'The Catharanthus Alkaloids: Pharmacognosy and Biotechnology' (2004) 11(5) *Current Medicinal Chemistry* 607.

Vane, JR, 'Inhibition of Prostaglandin Synthesis as a Mechanism of Action of Aspirin-like Drugs' (1971) 231(25) *Nature: New Biology* 232.

Varadi, M, et al, 'AlphaFold Protein Structure Database: Massively Expanding the Structural Coverage of Protein-Sequence Space with High-Accuracy Models' (2022) 50(D1) *Nucleic Acids Research* D439.

Vardy, P, and Grosch, P, *The Puzzle of Ethics* (London, Fount, 1999).

Varese, S, *Witness to Sovereignty: Essays on the Indian Movement in Latin America* (Copenhagen, International Work Group for Indigenous Affairs, 2006).

Venter, JC, *Life at the Speed of Life: From the Double Helix to the Dawn of Digital Life* (London, Abacus, 2013) 250.

Ventose, ED, 'Patent Protection for Second and Further Medical Uses under the European Patent Convention' (2009) 6(1) *SCRIPTed* 57, www.law.ed.ac.uk/ahrc/script-ed/vol6-1/ventose.asp.

Verhaegh, M, 'Kant and Property Rights' (2004) 18(3) *Journal of Libertarian Studies* 11.

Vézina, C, et al, 'Rapamycin (AY-22, 989), a New Antifungal Antibiotic I. Taxonomy of the Producing Streptomycete and Isolation of the Active Principle' (1975) 28(10) *Journal of Antibiotics* 721.

Vogel, JH, et al, 'The Economics of Information, Studiously Ignored in the Nagoya Protocol on Access to Genetic Resources and Benefit Sharing' (2011) 7(1) *Law, Environment and Development Journal* 52.

Waldron, J, 'From Authors to Copiers: Individual Rights and Social Values in Intellectual Property' (1993) 68 *Chicago Kent Law Review* 841.

Waldron, J, *God, Locke, and Equality: Christian Foundations in Locke's Political Thought* (Cambridge, Cambridge University Press, 2002).

Walpole, CSJ, 'The Role of Chemistry in the Drug Discovery Process' in HP Rang (ed), *Drug Discovery and Development: Technology in Transition* (Edinburgh, Churchill Livingston/Elsevier, 2006) 121.

Walsh, G, and R Jefferis, R, 'Post-translational Modifications in the Context of Therapeutic Proteins' (2006) 24 *Nature Biotechnology* 1241.

Walsh, P, 'Well-being' in T Honderich (ed), *The Oxford Companion to Philosophy* (Oxford, Oxford University Press, 1995) 908.

Wani, MH, et al, 'Plant Antitumor Agents. VI. The Isolation and Structure of Taxol, a Novel Antileukemic and Antitumor Agent from *Taxus brevifolia*' (1971) 93(9) *Journal of the American Chemical Society* 2325.

Warburton, N, *A Little History of Philosophy* (New Haven, CT, Yale University Press, 2011).

Watt, JM, 'Magic and Witchcraft in Relation to Plants and Folk Medicine' in T Swain (ed), *Plants in the Development of Modern Medicine* (Cambridge, MA, Harvard University Press, 1972) 68.

Weiner, AB, 'Inalienable Wealth' (1985) 12(2) *American Ethnologist* 210.

Weiss, HJ, and Aledort, LM, 'Impaired Platelet/Connective-Tissue Reaction in Man After Aspirin Ingestion' (1967) 290 *The Lancet* 495.

Whitt, L, *Science, Colonialism, and Indigenous Peoples. The Cultural Politics of Law and Knowledge* (Cambridge, Cambridge University Press, 2009).

Wiessner, S, 'Indigenous Sovereignty: A Reassessment in Light of the UN Declaration on the Rights of Indigenous Peoples' (2008) 41 *Vanderbilt Journal of Transnational Law* 1141.

Wiersum, KF, 'Forest Gardens as an 'Intermediate' Land-Use System in the Nature–Culture Continuum: Characteristics and Future Potential' (2004) 1 *Advances in Agroforestry* 123.

Wilke, M, 'A Healthy Look at the Nagoya Protocol – Implications for Global Health Governance' in E Morgera et al (eds), *The 2010 Protocol on Access and Benefit-sharing in Perspective: Implications for International Law and Implementation Challenges* (Leiden, Martinus Nijhoff, 2012) 123.

Wilson, AGE (ed), *New Horizons in Predictive Toxicology: Current Status and Application* (Abingdon, Royal Society of Chemistry, 2011).

Winnaker, E-L, *From Genes to Clones, Introduction to Gene Technology* (Weinheim, VCH, 1987).

Wood, AW, *Kantian Ethics* (Cambridge, Cambridge University Press, 2008).

Wood, AW (ed), and Nisbet, HB (trans), *GWF Hegel, Elements of the Philosophy of Right* (Cambridge, Cambridge University Press, 2003).

Wood, WB, 'Studies on the Antibacterial Action of the Sulfonamide Drugs. I. The Relation of *p*-Aminobenzoic Acid to the Mechanism of Bacteriostasis' (1942) 75(4) *Journal of Experimental Medicine* 369.

Woodward, RB, and Doering, WE, 'The Total Synthesis of Quinine' (1944) 66(5) *Journal of the American Chemical Society* 849.

Wolfsberg, TG, et al, in J McEntyre and GD Schuler, 'Guide to the Draft Human Genome' (2001) 409 *Nature* 824.

Wright, RW, 'Causation in Tort Law' (1985) 73 *California Law Review* 1735.

Wright, RW, 'Right, Justice and Tort Law' in DG Owen (ed), *Philosophical Foundations of Tort Law* (Oxford, Oxford University Press, 1995) 159.

Wüger, D, 'Prevention of Misappropriation of Intangible Cultural Heritage through Intellectual Property Laws' in JM Finger and P Schuler (eds), *Poor People's Knowledge* (New York and Oxford, World Bank and Oxford University Press, 2004).

You, Y, et al, 'Artificial Intelligence in Cancer Target Identification and Drug Discovery' (2022) 7(1) *Signal Transduction and Targeted Therapy* 156.

Zhai, LH, et al, 'Proteomic Characterization of Post translational Modifications in Drug Discovery' (2022) 43 *Acta Pharmacologica Sinica* 3112.

Zhang, F, et al, 'CRISPR/Cas9 for Gene Editing: Progress, Implication and Challenges' (2014) 23 *Human Molecular Genetics* R40.

Zhavoronkov, A, et al, 'Will Artificial Intelligence for Drug Discovery Impact Clinical Pharmacology?' (2020) 107(4) *Clinical Pharmacology and Therapeutics* 780.

INDEX

A

access and benefit-sharing (ABS) provisions
- affordable treatment, enabling access to 76
- consequentialist arguments 123–126
- Convention on Biological Diversity 9–10, 21–22, 32
- culture, preservation 126
- disclosure requirements 36
- end product differing from TKAGR 74
- environment, preservation 126
- EU ABS Regulation 46
- fair and equitable benefits sharing 9–10, 21–22, 25–26, 27, 39
- mutually agreed terms 73
- Nagoya Protocol 9–10, 22, 23, 24, 25–26, 39, 64–65, 72–74, 75, 76–80; Table 1
- traditional knowledge, protection 161–162, 167
- TRIPs Agreement 32
- utilization of genetic resources 45–46, 64–65, 73

access to TKAGR
- approval of right holder 25, 27–28
- benefit-sharing *See* access and benefit-sharing (ABS) provisions
- consent *See* consensual use
- continued access 38, 70, 71
- control over *See* control rights in TKAGR
- Convention on Biological Diversity 9–10, 19, 21–22
- established right to grant 25
- genetic provider countries 39
- genetic resource, access to 37–41
- initial access 38–39, 70, 71, 72
- justification for rights in *See* justification for rights in TKAGR
- knowledge, access to 70
- legal access 38
- meaning 38–39, 70–72
- mutually agreed terms, establishment 23, 24, 25–26
- Nagoya Protocol provisions 9–11, 21–25, 37–38, 70–72, 75
- secret knowledge 102, 158, 159
- third party use *See* third party use
- veto rights *See* veto right

Alfred, T 156

Allen, B 139

aniline dyes 213–214, 274–275, 283, 286–287

antibacterials 194–195

antibiotics 214, 275, 283

Aristotle 143, 149

artificial intelligence (AI)
- drug development 196
- drug discovery process 1, 192–195, 201, 282
- drug repurposing 194
- homology modelling 193
- network analysis 193–194
- protein structure prediction 193
- target identification 193–194
- target prediction 193

aspirin (acetylsalicylic acid) 18, 203, 205, 206–209, 272, 283

Atkins, P 132, 214, 291

Attas, D 16, 83–84, 99–100, 103, 176, 221, 223

Aubertin, C and Filoche, G 42, 56–57

Ayer, AJ 112

B

Balick, MJ and Cox, PA 187, 213

Barelli, M 168

Barker, J 155, 156–157

Beer, C 215–216

benefit-sharing, right to *See* **access and benefit-sharing (ABS) provisions**

Bentham, J 10–11, 122, 127–128, 132, 133, 242

Bernard of Chartres 13

Bingham, T 87

bioavailability 184

biodiversity and environmental protection *See also* **conservation/sustainable use**
- Convention *See* Convention on Biological Diversity
- cultural diversity and 133, 138–141
- deep ecology 131

Global Framework *See* Kunming-Montreal Global Biodiversity Framework
global health utility 290–291
indigenous culture and 131–136, 138–141, 160–161, 163–164
instrumental value 131, 132–133
international drive for 1, 160–161
intrinsic value 131–133
Nagoya Protocol 39
Rio Declaration 164
through valorisation 126–134
utilitarian approach 126, 131–136, 283–284
Western approach to 131

biological resource
definition 40–41

biomimetics
drug discovery process 191–192
Nagoya Protocol 67–69, 72
utilization 67–69

biopiracy *See* **misappropriation**
bioprospecting 184–187, 198, 220, 282
biosimilar 63–64
biotechnology
derivatives *See* derivative; downstream derivative
genome manipulation 1
meaning 28, 47–54
Nagoya Protocol 42–43, 47–54

Blackburn, S 128
Blankfein-Tabachnick, DH 262
Bonn Guidelines
Convention on Biological Diversity 21–22, 167; Fig.2

Brennan, F 155–156
Brokensha, D et al 161
Bronowski, J 87
Brugnatelli and Fontana 207
Brush, S 164–165
Burns, R 281

C

Calancha, A de la 212
Castan, M 172
causation
analysis 12–13
break in chain of 15, 286–287
but for test 13–14, 59–60, 68, 275
coincidental second uses 274–279, 286–287, 289
competing contributions 2–3, 4, 9–11, 17, 37, 201–202, 282–283
crux point concept 10–11, 15, 17, 179, 200–202, 217, 283
duplicative 14
in fact 2, 13–15, 201, 217, 275, 282
in law 2, 3, 14–15, 201, 217
pre-emptive 14
remoteness 14–15
second/further uses of drug, discovery 1, 3, 4, 274–279, 286
serendipitous discoveries 3, 4, 18, 283

Caventou, J 213
chromatin 44–45, 49, 61
Cieza de Leon, P 209
cocaine 18, 205, 209–212, 278–279, 283, 287
commercialisation *See also* **compensation/reward; valorisation**
biopiracy 6
collective persona, protection 119
enforcement costs 124
incentivising 121, 123, 124, 176–177
indigenous communities' commercial interests 142
innovation, incentivising 114, 121–124, 141, 147–148, 176–177, 262
Nagoya Protocol provisions 22, 23, 38, 43
non-commercial work 76–78, 238
property rights stifling 122–123
right to choose against 32, 190–191
traditional knowledge, of 161, 177
unjust enrichment 141–142
utilitarian justifications 121–124, 126, 135, 138, 141, 142

commons of ideas 12, 122, 274
Lockean theory 95, 97–98, 101, 113, 263

communitarian approach
indigenous self-determination 252–254, 256, 284, 289–290; Tables 12–14
rights in TKAGR 174–176, 178, 252–254, 256, 265, 284, 289–290; Tables 12–14
serendipitous discoveries 252–254, 256, 284; Table 12

compensation/reward *See also* **commercialisation; valorisation**
ABS provisions *See* access and benefit-sharing (ABS) provisions
contribution-based 4, 267, 268–269, 288–289
fair and equitable benefits sharing 9–10, 21–22, 25–26, 27, 30, 39
intellectual labour/property, rewarding 95–96
Locke's theory of property 95–96
Nagoya Protocol model 10
originators of traditional knowledge 5–6
proposals for 165

restorative/corrective justice 148, 256, 263, 265–266; Table 14
serendipitous discoveries 218, 224, 230, 231, 236–237, 240–243, 245–246, 249–256, 285; Tables 7–12
UNDRIP 169–170, 175, 252, 256; Table 14
veto rights, where 290

Comte-Sponville, A 143, 235

confidence, law of 6, 16

confidentiality, breach of 102

consensual use
contingent 12–13
determination of consent 12–13
downstream 12–13
Kunming-Montreal GBF 25, 26–27
Nagoya Protocol 22, 23, 24–25, 26

conservation/sustainable use *See also* **biodiversity and environmental protection**
BBNJ Treaty 28
Convention on Biological Diversity 21, 163
emergency situations 78–80
global health utility 236–239, 255; Table 9
ITPGRFA 30
Kunming-Montreal GBF 26–27
Nagoya Protocol 39, 76–78, 238
UNDRIP 20, 21, 169

contribution
commercial value of, assessment 268
compensation in respect of 4, 267, 268–269, 288–289
competing contributions 2–3, 4, 9–11, 17, 37, 201–202, 282–283, 288–289
dilution/attenuation *See* epistemic dilution
labour-desert theory 220–231, 266, 283, 286
original 220
quantifying 201–202, 267, 268–269, 288–289
researchers' 2–3, 4, 7–8, 9–11, 37
rights based on 266, 267, 268–269, 285, 288
serendipitous discoveries 3, 4, 194, 217, 218, 220–231, 240, 283, 285–286, 288–289
veto rights and 267, 268–269, 274, 285

control rights in TKAGR *See also* **prior informed consent of right-holder; veto right**
access to TKAGR 1, 5–6, 9–11
biomimetics 68–69
collective persona, protection 117, 119–120
communitarian approach 174–176, 178, 252–254, 256, 265, 289–290; Tables 12–14
competing claims 164–165
Convention on Biological Diversity 65–67
digital sequence information 65–67
downstream use 2, 9, 69, 80–81, 229, 246, 272, 274, 281, 284, 285, 287
enforcement 16, 135, 233
generally 1, 3, 4, 5–6, 9–11, 19, 82–89, 91, 99, 102, 116, 117, 133, 143–144, 282, 287–288
global health utility 238–239
indigenous cultures generally 158
indigenous self-determination 154–155, 177, 250–251, 256
Lockean labour-desert theory 95, 101, 218–223, 227, 229, 283
Nagoya Protocol 9–11, 22–26, 37–39, 59, 62, 64, 65, 68–69, 73–75, 80–81, 90, 282; Table 1
reparations 175, 249–250, 265, 284
second uses 254
serendipitous discoveries 232, 236, 237, 241–243, 255; Table 9
TRIPS 31, 32
UNDRIP 20, 169–170, 252
utilitarian argument 119–121, 133, 137–138, 177, 232, 236, 237, 241–243, 254, 255, 266, 283–284, 289–290; Tables 9, 13, 14
valorisation model 136, 232–233, 265

Convention on Biological Diversity (CBD)
Access and Benefit-sharing Clearing-House 19
access and benefit-sharing provisions 9–10, 21–22, 32
adoption 30, 163
biological resources, definition 40–41
Bonn Guidelines 21–22, 167; Fig.2
conservation/sustainable use 21, 163
control over genetic information 65–67
focus 36, 163
functional units of heredity 40–52, 55, 57, 59–61, 64, 72
genetic information 66
genetic resources 9, 39–41, 48, 59
indigenous culture, protection 21, 163–164
ITPGRFA and 30
Nagoya Protocol *See* Nagoya Protocol
synthetic DNA 65–67
TRIPs Agreement and 31–32
utilization of genetic resource 73–74
WIPO GRTKF proposals and 34–35

copyright law
human rights 153

originality requirement 62, 100, 219
traditional knowledge and 142, 165, 167
Correa, CM 41, 42, 45, 54, 56
corrective justice *See* **restorative justice**
Cox, PA 185–187
Craven, L 203, 208, 283
Cromwell, O 213
crux point concept 10–11, 15, 17, 179, 200–202, 217, 283

D

Declaration of Belém 133, 162
Declaration on the Rights of Indigenous Peoples (UNDRIP)
adoption 168–169
compensation 169–170, 175, 252, 256, 284; Table 14
conservation/sustainable use provisions 20, 21, 169
control, right of 20, 169–170, 252
cultural traditions and customs 20, 169
health practices 20, 169
intellectual property 20–21, 169–170, 265
Kunming-Montreal GBF and 27, 171
legal status 21, 168, 171–174
medicinal plants, animals and minerals 20, 169
misappropriation 170, 252, 256, 284
Nagoya Protocol and 171
other approaches compared Table 13
prior informed consent 20, 169–172, 177, 251
provisions 20–21, 169–171; Fig.2
restitution rights 20, 169–170, 252
self-determination, right to 20, 21, 155, 168–169, 171–175, 177–178, 251–252, 284, 289; Table 12
serendipitous discoveries 251–252; Table 12, 256
traditional knowledge 20, 169–170
veto right 170–171, 175; Table 14
Derclaye, E and Taylor, T 129–131, 138, 242
derivative
biomimetics 68, 72
chemical 1, 5, 55–57, 69–70, 72, 189, 192
discovery process 189, 192, 199
downstream *See* downstream derivative
end product differing from TKAGR 74
expanded definition 49–54
genetic expression and 47, 50–51, 69–70, 81
isolated 54–55
Kant's theory of property 107
meaning 47–57
Nagoya Protocol 42–43, 47–57, 60, 65
naturally occurring 54, 55–57, 59–60, 65
utilization of genetic resource 52–70
difference principle
Rawlsian 146–148, 247, 256, 284, 289, 290
digital sequence information 1, 26–27, 65–67, 282
dilution of knowledge *See* **epistemic dilution**
disclosure requirements
access and benefit-sharing provisions 36
TRIPs Agreement 32–33
WIPO GRTKF proposals 34–36
distributive justice *See also* **reparations**
justification for rights in TKAGR 90, 143–148
proportionality 175, 256, 284
Rawlsian 217–218, 244–249, 256, 262
DNA 282
biochemical composition 44–46, 47–48, 56–57
cDNA 58
chemical derivatives 55–57, 69–70, 72
chromatin 44–45, 49, 61
eukaryotic 40, 42, 44, 49, 60, 63, 191, 216, 275
expressed 61–62
extracted from genetic resource 38–39, 40
gene cloning 42, 58–59
gene coding 189–190
gene (functional units of heredity) 40–52, 55, 57, 59–65, 72
genetic composition 44, 48
genetic expression 41–43, 47, 62–65, 81
genetic information 58–69, 80–81
genetic resource 44–45, 80–81
histones 44–45, 61, 64
intergenic 60–61
intragenic 60, 65
mitochondrial 40
mRNA 41, 58
mRNA editing 63
non-coding 60–61, 64, 65
non-DNA components 41–42
pseudo-genes 61
rDNA 189
synthetic *See* synthetic DNA
transgenic organisms 47
Doering, W 215
Doha Declaration 31, 239

downstream derivative
end product differing from TKAGR 74
genetic expression 47, 50–51, 62–65, 69–70, 81
Nagoya Protocol 9–11, 17, 69–70, 79, 80–81, 281
serendipitous discoveries *See* serendipitous discovery
downstream use
causation in fact 13–15, 201, 217, 282
causation in law 201, 217
coincidental second uses 274–279, 286–287, 289
competing contributions 2–3, 4, 9–11, 17, 37, 201–202, 282–283, 286
consensual 12–13
control over 2, 9, 69, 80–81, 246, 272, 274, 281, 284, 285, 287
derivatives *See* downstream derivative
epistemic dilution *See* epistemic dilution
EU ABS Regulation 46
generally 1, 111
genetic information 58–69
information flow 12–13, 282
knowledge ownership 9
Nagoya Protocol rights 9–11, 17, 24, 25, 37, 58, 76–81, 281
origination and 201–202
patent law 3, 202
positive rights in 2, 37
problems arising 7–11
retrospective obviousness 269–272, 274, 276
serendipitous discoveries *See* serendipitous discovery
veto rights 266–274, 284, 285, 289
Drahos, P 158, 168
Drahos, P and Frankel, S 168
drug development 195–197; Table 5
data exclusivity 197
drug discovery process *See also* **biotechnology; research and development**
agonists and antagonists 180–182, 189–191; Table 3
antibacterials 194–195
antibiotics 214, 275, 283
artificial intelligence 1, 192–195, 201, 282
bioavailability 184
biomimetics 191–192
bioprospecting 184–187, 198, 220, 282
causal analysis 12–13
causation *See* causation
chemical derivatives 1, 5, 55–57, 69–70, 72
chemical modification 190
commercialisation *See* commercialisation; valorisation
complexity of passage of TKAGR 4
contributions *See* contribution
control over TKAGR *See* control rights in TKAGR
derivatives *See* derivative; downstream derivative
downstream, control over 2, 9, 69, 80–81, 229, 272, 274, 281, 285, 287
drug development distinguished 195–196
ecological surveying 185
emergency situations 76, 78–80
end product differing from TKAGR 74
epistemic dilution *See* epistemic dilution
ethnobotanical surveying 185
existing information 7–8
extraction process 7–8
fast-throughput screening 183–184
feedback loops 2, 7, 188, 199
follow-on compounds 8
genes coding 189–190
glycosylation 191–192
homology modelling 193
information flow 1, 10, 200–202, 282; Fig.1
isomers 191
lead structure 198–200; Figs.4, 5
ligands 39, 179–192, 193, 196, 198, 203–204, 269, 273, 277
living organisms, compounds derived from 4–5, 179, 182
lock and key hypothesis 180, 183
machine learning 1, 192–195, 201, 282
machine-learning-based target prediction 193
mimicry of natural products 5, 182
mixing with other information 2, 7–8, 9–11, 282
natural products, use of 5
non-commercial work 76–78, 238
originality 62, 64, 65, 72
origination boundaries 179
overlapping or parallel pathways 2, 7, 16, 188, 199
patent law 3
path-dependent 13, 16, 62
path-independent 13, 16, 61–62, 100
pharmacodynamics 190
pharmacological background 179–200
pharmacophore 5, 180
phylogenetic surveying 185

post-translation modifications 191–192
potential pathways 198–200; Fig.1
protein structure prediction 193
rational pharmacology 184
repurposing drugs 194
researchers' contributions 2–3, 4, 7–8, 9–11, 37
safety, predicting 193–194
second/further uses, discovery 1, 2, 3, 4, 194, 204–216, 269–279, 282; Table 6, 286–287, 288–289
serendipitous discoveries *See* serendipitous discovery
side effects 190, 194, 198, 199, 203
in silico modelling 188, 192–195, 198, 282
synthetic DNA *See* synthetic DNA
synthetic drugs 5, 191–192
target prediction 193
testing process 7–8
therapeutic efficacy 190; Fig.3
therapeutic window 190
third parties, interests of 2
traditional knowledge, use generally 5–6
Du Plessis, P 60
DuQuesne, T and Reeves, J 210
Dutfield, G 47, 126, 139, 161, 176, 281
Dutfield, G and Suthersanen, U 100–101, 106, 112, 114, 123, 125, 151–153, 176
Dworkin, R 260

E
ecological surveying 185
Eichengrün, A 207–208
enforcement
costs 124
ease of 135, 233
patents 16
Western-style 141–143
Engle, K 173
environmental protection *See* **biodiversity and environmental protection**
enzymatic reaction
genetic expression 1, 41
enzyme protein
genetic expression 1, 41
Epicurus 127
epigenetic change 1, 44–45, 61, 64, 65, 80–81, 204, 282
epigenetics 282
epistemic dilution
AI and machine learning 201
causation in fact 13–15, 201, 282
contribution, conflict with 288
downstream use and 2, 4, 7–8, 9–11, 37
information flow 1, 10, 200–202, 282; Fig.1
mixing with other information 2, 7–8, 9–11, 37, 282
quantifying 201–202
serendipitous discoveries 18
ethnobotanical surveying 185
eukaryotic material 40, 42, 44, 49, 60, 63, 191, 216, 275
European Union ABS Regulation 46

F
farmers rights, ITPGRFA 30
fast-throughput screening 183–184
Ferguson, N 91, 139, 140
Fichte, JG 86, 110–111, 117, 231–232, 262, 263; Table 13
follow-on compound 8
Food and Agriculture Organization (FAO)
Global Plan of Action on Genetic Resources 29–30
ITPGRFA 29, 30
Liepzig Declaration 29
Freud, S 210
Fromer, JC 262

G
Gaedchke, F 210
Galen 207
gene cloning 42, 58–59
gene coding 189–190
generic copies 196–197
genetic expression
downstream derivatives 50–51, 69–70, 81
enzymatic reactions 1, 41
Nagoya Protocol 41–43, 47, 50–51, 55, 61–64, 69–70, 81
products of 1, 41–43, 47, 69–70, 179
recent developments 204
genetic information
biomimetics 67–69, 72
control over 65–67
Convention on Biological Diversity 66
digital sequence information 1, 26–27, 65–67, 282
downstream use 58–69
genetic resource, treatment as 1, 58–69
Nagoya Protocol 58–69, 282
synthetic DNA 58–67
genetic modification 42, 49, 52–53, 66
genetic mutation, identifying 192–193

genetic resource
access to, control over *See* control rights in TKAGR
access to, meaning 38–39, 59–64, 70–72
biochemical composition 9, 43–46, 47–48
biochemical compounds 54–55
biosimilars 63–64
chemical derivatives 1, 5, 55–57, 69–70, 72
Convention on Biological Diversity 9, 39–41, 48, 59
defining and delimiting 1, 39–41, 59–60, 80–81, 282
dematerialised 66
derivative acquired without access to 54–55
digital sequence information 1, 26–27, 65–67, 282
downstream use *See* downstream use
epigenetic code 80–81
eukaryotic material 40, 42, 44, 49, 60, 63, 191, 216, 275
expressed DNA 61–62
extracted DNA 38–39
fair and equitable benefits sharing 9–10, 21–22, 25–26, 27, 30, 39
FAO Global Plan of Action 29–30
functional units of heredity 40–52, 55, 57, 59–65, 72
genetic information 1, 58–69
genetic material of actual or potential value 40, 41
informational 64–65, 69–70, 71–72, 73, 80–81
invention based on, patenting 33
Kunming-Montreal GBF 26–27
misappropriation *See* misappropriation
mRNA 41, 58
mRNA editing 63
Nagoya Protocol provisions 9–11, 24, 25, 26, 37–39, 42–70, 73, 238
natural epigenetic modifications 1
naturally occurring 54, 55–57, 59–60, 65
non-DNA components 41–42
non-monetary benefits from 26–27
oceans *See* Marine Biological Diversity of Areas Beyond National Jurisdiction Treaty
prokaryotic material 42, 63, 275
protection of traditional knowledge 30
provider countries 39
pseudo-genes 60–61
research and development on 43–46
synthetic DNA 58–67
traditional knowledge associated with *See* TKAGR
transboundary situations 244
utilization, control over *See* control rights in TKAGR
value, actual or potential 40, 41
value, veto right creating 25
veto rights over *See* veto right
genome
biotechnological manipulation 1
epigenetic changes 1, 44–45, 61, 64, 65, 80–81, 204, 282
natural epigenetic modification 1
nuclear transfer cloning 42
Gibson, J 174–176, 178, 219–220, 252–254, 258, 264, 284, 289–290
in-imitativeness 84, 220–223
other approaches compared Tables 13, 14
property, justification for 120
Gibson, PC 208, 283
global health utility 236–239, 242–243, 255, 263, 265–266, 273, 275, 290–291; Tables 9, 13, 14
cultural protection and 290–291
environmental protection and 290–291
Nagoya Protocol, emergency situations 76, 78–80, 238
veto rights and 266, 284, 285, 289, 290–291
Goodland, RJA and Irwin, HS 160–161
Gordley, J 143, 145
Greiber, T et al 43, 54–55
Griffiths, T 158
Gupta, A 120

H
Hanson, NR 13
Harris, JW 114
Harris, S 128
Harsanyi, J 246–248
Hart, HLA 235
Hart, HLA and Honoré, T 14
Hegel, GWF, theory of property
alienation 114–115
intellectual property, justification 113–119, 153, 231–232, 263
justification for property 86, 103, 112–113, 120, 231–232; Table 13
other approaches compared Table 13
subject matter 115–116
Hippocrates 207
histone 44–45, 61, 64
Hobbes, T 139

Hodgkin, A 211
Hoffmann, F 207–208
Hofmann, AW von 213, 214
Hohfeld, WN 85
homology modelling 193
Honderich, T 128
Houssen, W et al 65–66
Hughes, J 219, 270
Hegel's justification for property 112–116
Locke's theory of property 95–98, 101
human rights
conflicting human rights considerations 79–80
copyright law 153
Declaration of Belém 162
ICCPR 151
ICESCR 151–154, 169
intellectual property, rights in 91, 151–154
justifications for rights in TKAGR 89, 91, 150–154, 250–254
Kunming–Montreal GBF 27
moral rights 151, 154
self-determination, right to *See* indigenous self-determination
serendipitous discoveries 250–254
traditional resource rights, proposals for 166, 167
Universal Declaration of 151–152
Huxley, A 211

I
imitativeness
competing contributions 2
intellectual property law 2
incompletely theorised agreement 257, 259–261, 263
indigenous communities and culture *See also* **Declaration on the Rights of Indigenous Peoples**
collective persona 117–120
commercialisation, right to choose against 32, 190–191
control over 250–254
Convention on Biological Diversity 21, 163–164
customary laws and protocols 75–76, 78, 80, 158
Declaration of Belém 133, 162
economic independence 162
environment, preservation 131–136, 138–141, 160–161, 164, 232
Indigenous and Tribal Populations Convention 161, 162
intellectual property 154–155, 157, 158–168
medicinal plants, animals and minerals 21, 169
medicines and health practices 20, 169
Nagoya Protocol 75–76, 78, 79
North America 94
property, concepts of 158–160
protection/preservation 1, 6, 20–21, 125–126, 131–135, 136–137, 138–139, 140–141, 161–167, 290–291
recognition 164–165
religious/spiritual beliefs and property 20, 137, 138, 158, 159, 251–252
Rio Declaration 164
secret knowledge 102, 158, 159
self-determination *See* indigenous self-determination
traditional resource rights, proposals for 166, 167
UNDRIP *See* Declaration on the Rights of Indigenous Peoples
utilitarian approach 125–126, 131–137
Westernisation, threats accompanying 138–141
indigenous self-determination
communitarian justification for property rights 174–176, 252–254, 256, 284, 289–290; Tables 12–14
control rights in TKAGR 154–155, 177, 250–251, 256, 284
Declaration of Belém 162
generally 20, 21, 91, 120, 154–157, 161, 177, 256, 265
human right to 155, 162, 168–169, 250–254, 284, 289–290
ICCPR 173
ICESCR 173
meaning 155–157
prior informed consent 155
serendipitous discoveries, rights in 150–154, 250–254, 256, 284
traditional resource rights, proposals for 166, 167
UN Charter 173
UNDRIP 20, 21, 155, 168–169, 171–174, 177–178, 251–252, 265, 284, 289; Table 12
indigenous sovereignty *See* **indigenous self-determination**
Indigenous and Tribal Populations Convention (ITPC) 161, 162

infringement
- delineating 10–11, 12, 84
- independently developed ideas 16
- remoteness 14–15

in-imitativeness 84, 218, 220–223, 227, 230, 268, 285

innovation
- incentivising 88, 96, 114, 121–124, 145, 147–148, 152, 176–177, 262, 273
- traditional knowledge 123–124
- valorisation 126–138, 141, 145, 147–148, 232–237, 239–242, 255, 258, 264–269, 289

in silico modelling 188, 192–195, 198, 282

intangible property *See also* **intellectual property; knowledge**
- commons of ideas 12, 95, 97–98, 101, 102, 113, 122, 274
- creation of rights in 10–11
- justification for rights in 82–89, 95–120
- originality 83, 99, 100–103
- origination boundaries 83–85
- problem of delineation 10–11, 82–86
- restitution 169–170, 252

intellectual property *See also* **intangible property; knowledge**
- authorial personality 103, 106–111, 153, 176, 231
- clarity and predictability 87–88
- commons of ideas 12, 95, 97–98, 101, 102, 113, 122, 274
- competing contributions 10, 17, 37, 201–202, 282–283
- consequentialist justifications 121–141, 176–177, 220–221, 232–244, 283
- copyright law 62, 100, 142, 153, 165, 167, 219
- data exclusivity 197
- downstream use *See* downstream use
- economic approaches 121, 122, 267
- established forms of legal right 6, 10, 15–17, 154, 161, 162, 165–168, 176–177
- expiration date of right in 196, 270
- Fichtean justification 110–111, 117, 231–232, 262, 263, Table 13
- field of activity, right over 12
- follow-on compounds 8
- generic copies 196–197
- group ownership 101–103, 108–109, 111, 116–120
- Hegelian justification 113–116, 153, 231–232, 263
- human right to 91, 151–154
- imitativeness 2
- incentives-based approach 88, 96, 114, 121–124, 147–148, 152, 176–177, 262
- independently developed ideas 16
- indigenous 91, 154–155, 157, 158–168
- individuation of ideas 83–84, 99–101, 103, 174–175, 176, 218, 221, 227, 229, 252, 263, 266, 283, 288
- international cooperation to protect 141–142
- justification for rights in 11–12, 82–91, 95–141, 142
- Kantian justification 103–110, 117, 231–232; Table 13
- labour-desert (value-added) argument 95–96, 150, 153, 218–236, 255, 263, 273–274, 283; Table 13
- Lockean justification 95–101, 102, 113, 150, 153, 262
- monopoly rights 16
- Munzer and Raustiala's justification 101–103, 117–118, 123–126, 141–142, 177
- origination, problem of 99, 100–103, 176, 283, 288
- origination boundaries 83–85
- patent law *See* patent law
- path-independent discovery 100
- personality-based rights 89, 103–120, 150, 153, 176, 218, 231–232, 255, 262, 263, 283
- problem confronting 82–86
- protection, utilitarian purpose 121
- registered rights 16
- remoteness, questions of 15
- serendipitous discoveries 217–256
- thing incorporating the right 115
- third party rights 90
- TKAGR compared 15–17
- traditional knowledge compared 89–91
- traditional resource rights, proposals for 166, 167
- TRIPs Agreement 31–34, 165
- UNDRIP rights 20–21, 169, 265
- utilitarian justifications 88, 96, 121–141, 232–244
- Western approach to 6, 10, 15–17, 89–91, 154, 161, 162, 165–168, 176–177

International Covenant on Civil and Political Rights (ICCPR) 151, 173

International Covenant on Economic, Social and Cultural Rights (ICESCR) 151–154, 169, 173

International Treaty on Plant Genetic Resources for Food and Agriculture (ITPGRFA)
adoption 29–30
conservation/sustainable use provisions 30
fair and equitable benefits sharing 30
Farmers Rights 30

J
Janke, T 166
Jefferson, T 83, 120
justification for rights in TKAGR
authorial personality 103, 106–111, 153, 176, 231
causation in law 2, 3, 14–15, 201, 217
clarity and predictability 87–88
collective persona 117–120
communitarian 174–176, 178, 252–254, 256, 265, 284, 289–290; Tables 12–14
consequentialist 4, 11, 88, 100, 121–141, 176–177, 220–221, 232–244, 283–284
contradictory approaches 257–263
control *See* control rights in TKAGR
deontological 4, 11, 88, 89, 91–120, 150, 176, 218–232, 262
distributive justice 90, 143–148
downstream *See* downstream derivative; downstream use
economic 88
Fichtean 103, 110–111, 117, 231–232, 262, 263; Table 13
freedom of the individual 89, 104–109, 110, 112–113
generally 18, 82, 176–178
group ownership 101–103, 108–109, 111, 116–120, 176
Hegelian 112–119, 153, 231–232, 263; Table 13
human rights 89, 91, 150–154, 250–254
incentives-based 88, 96, 114, 121–124, 147–148, 152, 176–177, 262
incompletely theorised agreements 257, 259–261, 263
individuation, problem of 99–101, 103, 174–175, 176, 218, 221, 227, 229, 252, 263, 266, 283, 288
intangibles/intellectual property 82–91, 95–101, 102
international cooperation, argument for 141–142
Kantian 103–110, 117, 231–232, 262; Table 13
labour-desert based 89, 91–103, 144–145, 150, 153, 176, 218–236, 255, 263, 266, 273–274; Table 13
limit to 11–12
Locke's theory of property *See* Locke, J, theory of property
moral right argument 117–118, 142
Munzer and Raustiala 101–103, 117–118, 123–126, 141–142, 177
natural rights model 89, 92, 99, 100, 103, 104, 105, 176, 221–231, 255, 283, 288, 289
neo-Lockean just entitlement 95, 99, 101, 102
origination, problem of 99, 100–103, 176, 283
originator's personality right 117, 176
overlapping consensus 257, 259, 260, 261–262, 263, 285
personality-based 89, 103–120, 150, 153, 176, 218, 231–232, 255, 262, 263, 283
pluralistic approach 89, 263
protection of knowledge 82–83, 86–91
Rawlsian distributive justice 217–218, 244–249, 256, 262; Tables 10, 11, 13, 14
remoteness of loss or gain 14–15
reparations 148–150, 177, 249–250, 256, 265, 284; Tables 13, 14
restorative/corrective justice 91, 148–150, 249–250, 256, 284
serendipitous discoveries *See* serendipitous discovery
stability and certainty, ensuring 125
synthesis of findings 257–267; Tables 13, 14
Taubman's 119–120
traditional knowledge 89–91
UNDRIP *See* Declaration on the Rights of Indigenous Peoples
unjust enrichment 141–143
utilitarian 88, 96, 121–141, 232–244, 255, 283–284
value-added argument 89, 91–103, 144–145, 150, 176, 218–236
veto rights of Nagoya Protocol 3, 10, 37, 90
Western philosophical approach 89–91, 154

K
Kamau, EC et al 46
Kant, I 235
authorial personality 103, 106–111, 153, 231–232

freedom, right to 104–109, 110
intellectual property, justification 105–110, 231–232, 262
intelligible possession 104
other approaches compared Table 13
property ownership, justification 86, 103–105, 117, 231–232
Karanja, W 154
Knorr, L 215
knowledge *See also* **ITPGRFA; TKAGR**
BBNJ Treaty provisions 29
clarity and predictability 87–88
commons of ideas 12, 95, 97–98, 101, 102, 113, 122, 274
contribution to *See* contribution
control over *See* control rights in TKAGR
delineating 10–11
dilution *See* epistemic dilution
epistemology 83
group ownership 101–103, 108–109, 111, 116–120, 176
individuation of ideas 83–84, 99–101, 103, 174–175, 176, 218, 221, 227, 229, 252, 263, 266, 283, 288
informational resource, as 71–72
intangible property *See* intangible property
intellectual property *See* intellectual property
justifications for rights in *See* justification for rights in TKAGR
misappropriation *See* misappropriation
not linked to genetic resources 70–71
origination boundary *See* origination boundary
ownership 9
patent law *See* patent law
preservation for own sake 136–137, 232, 283
public good argument 5
reward for, contribution-based justifications 4
TKAGR *See* traditional knowledge associated with genetic resources
traditional, protection generally 5–6, 30, 89–91, 160–168
transgenerational development 15–16, 90, 218–219
veto rights over, Nagoya Protocol 9–11, 24, 25, 26, 37, 90, 238
Western philosophical approach 89–91, 154
WIPO GRTKF proposals 34
Koller, C 210, 212, 278–279, 283, 287
Kubinyi, H 198–200
Kunming–Montreal Global Biodiversity Framework
adoption 26
consent/approval 25, 27
conservation/sustainable use 26–27
digital sequence information 26–27, 66–67
fair and equitable benefits sharing 26–27
goal 26–27
national sovereignty 157
prior informed consent of right-holder 27
target 27
UNDRIP and 27, 171

L
labour-desert theory
contribution 220–231, 266, 283, 286
justification for property rights 89, 91–103, 144–145, 150, 153, 176, 218–236, 255, 263, 266, 273–274, 283; Table 13
serendipitous discoveries 218–236, 255
Laddie J 89
Lenzerini, F 156
Liepzig Declaration 29
ligand
ADME 190
drug discovery process 39, 179–192, 193, 196, 198, 203–204, 269, 273, 277
Linnaeus, C 212
Lipinski's Rule of Five 184
Liu, G et al 195
Locke, J, theory of property
common of ideas 12, 95, 97–98, 101, 102, 113, 263, 274
the Common 92, 93–94, 95, 96–98, 99, 226
enough and as good proviso 92, 95, 97–98
generally 91–95
Hughes' analysis 95–98, 101
individuation, problem of 99–103, 176, 218–219, 221, 229–230, 263, 266, 283, 288
in-imitativeness 220–223, 227, 230
intellectual property, justification 95–101, 102, 113, 262
labour avoidance 95–96
labour-desert (value-added) argument 89, 91–103, 144–145, 150, 153, 176, 218–236, 255, 263, 266, 273–274, 283; Table 13
monetary economy 93
natural law justification 92–93, 99, 100, 103, 105, 177, 221–231, 255, 263, 266, 289
Neo-Lockean school 95, 99, 101–102

non-waste condition 92, 93–94, 95, 98
origination, problem of 99–103, 218–221, 229–230, 263, 266, 283, 288
other approaches compared Table 13
permanent Common 97–98
post-Hughes analysis 99–101
rewarding labour 95–96
self-ownership principle 103–104
serendipitous discoveries 218–231, 255; Table 7
State of Nature 92, 94
traditional knowledge, model applied to 101–103; Table 13

lock and key hypothesis 180, 183

Löwig, KJ 207

Lugo, Cardinal J de 212

M

machine learning (ML)
antibacterial drug discovery 194–195
drug development 196
drug discovery process 1, 192–195, 201, 282
target prediction 193

man-made chemical derivative
generally 1
Nagoya Protocol 55–57, 69–70, 72

Marine Biological Diversity of Areas Beyond National Jurisdiction (BBNJ) Treaty
aim 28
conservation/sustainable use 28
digital sequence information 28, 67
establishment 28
financial benefits of resource use 28
Marine Protected Areas of the High Seas 28
prior informed consent 29
provisions 28; Fig.2
traditional knowledge 29
utilization of resources 28

Marx, K 139

Matthews, D 31

mauveine 18, 206, 213–214, 274–276, 283, 286–287

Mayeda, G 110–111

Merges, RP 261–263, 285

Milius, D 119, 120, 138, 237

Mill, JS 122, 127–128, 129, 132–133, 242

misappropriation
definition 141
discouragement 31
generally 4–7, 141–143
international responses to 6–7, 19
Nagoya Protocol provisions 22
restitution 141, 142
secret knowledge 102
TRIPs Agreement 31
UNDRIP 170, 252, 256, 284
unjust enrichment 141

Monardes, N 209

Moore, A 114, 121, 122

Morgera, E et al
commentary on Nagoya Protocol 24–25, 47, 52–54, 60, 73, 75, 76–79, 171

morphine 205

Munzer, SR 148–150, 249–250, 256, 258, 264, 265, 284, 289; Tables 13, 14

Munzer, SR and Raustiala, K 101–103, 117–118, 123–126, 141–142, 177

N

Nagoya Protocol
affordable treatment, enabling access to 76, 78–80
aim 7, 9, 39
approval and involvement 23, 24–25
benefit-sharing, right to 9–10, 22, 23, 24, 25–26, 39, 64–65, 72–74, 75, 76, 78–80, 281; Table 1
binding nature of provisions 9, 22
biomimetics 67–69, 72
biotechnology, meaning 42–43, 47–54
CBD objectives, implementation 9, 22; Fig.2
chemical derivatives 55–57, 69–70, 72
compensation model 10
conflicting human rights considerations 79–80
conservation/sustainable use provisions 39, 76–77, 78–79, 238
control rights in TKAGR 9–11, 22–26, 37–39, 59, 62, 64, 65, 68–69, 73–75, 80–81, 90, 282; Table 1
customary laws to be considered 75–76, 78, 80
derivative, meaning 42–43, 47–57
digital sequence information 65–67, 282
downstream activities 37, 58–69, 76–81, 281
downstream derivatives 9–11, 17, 69–70, 79, 80–81, 281
emergency situations 76, 78–80, 238
end product differing from traditional knowledge 74
establishment and ratifications 7, 22

genetic expression, products of 41–43, 47, 50–51, 55, 61–64, 69–70, 81
genetic information 58–69, 80–81, 282
genetic resource, access to 37–39, 59–64
genetic resource, meaning 39–41, 59, 80–81
global health utility 76, 78–80, 238
indigenous customary laws and protocols 75–76, 78, 80
isolated derivatives 54–55
justification for veto rights 3, 10, 37, 90
misappropriation of genetic resources 22
misuse of traditional knowledge 22
mutually agreed terms, establishment 23, 24, 25–26
national implementation 19, 23
national laws to be considered 75
naturally occurring compounds 54, 55–57, 59–60, 65
non-commercial work, simplified measures 76, 77–78, 238
patent law compared 16
path-dependent nature of rights 16
positive protection provisions 37–38
positive rights in TKAGR 22–24, 37–81, 281; Table 1
prior informed consent of right-holder 22, 23, 24–25, 38, 46, 70–72, 76, 77, 244; Table 1
research and development on genetic resource 43–46, 76–78
rights not time-limited 103, 219
scope 9–11, 28
sovereign rights over natural resources 23, 157
subsequent applications and commercialisation 22, 23, 38, 43
synthetic DNA, utilization 58–67
UNDRIP and 171
utilization of TKAGR 37–38, 39, 42–70, 73–74
veto rights under 9–11, 24, 25, 26, 37, 90, 238

natural rights
justification for 89, 92–93, 99, 100, 103, 105, 176, 221–231, 255, 266, 283, 288, 289
Locke's theory of 92–93, 99, 100, 103, 105, 221–231, 263, 289

Newman, DJ and Cragg, GM 5, 183
Newton, I 13
Niemann, A 210
Noble, R 215–216, 283
Nozick, R 95, 99, 101–102

O

Ockham, William of 235
Oguamanam, C 120, 168, 172
origination *See also* **origination boundary**
authorial personality 103, 106–111, 153, 176, 231
biomimetics 69–70, 72
copyright law 62, 100, 219
data exclusivity 197
derivative works 107
downstream use and 201–202
drug development 195–197; Table 5
drug discovery process 62, 64, 65, 72
generic copies 196–197
in-imitativeness 84, 218, 220–223, 227, 230, 268–269, 285
intangible/intellectual property 83, 99, 100–103
Lockean labour-desert theory 99–103, 218–221, 229–230, 255, 263, 266, 273–274, 283, 288
originator's personality right 117, 176
patent law 164, 202
problem of 99, 100–103, 176, 283, 288
serendipitous discoveries 220–231
traditional knowledge 99, 100–103, 176
transgenerational development 15–16, 90, 218–219

origination boundary
backward-looking 84–85
crux point concept 10–11, 15, 17, 179, 200–202, 217, 283
delineating 10–11, 12–13, 17, 84, 200–202
forward-looking 84–85
information flow 12–13, 200–203, 282
intangible/intellectual property 12, 83–85

overlapping consensus 257, 259, 260, 261–262, 263, 285

P

Pagenstecher, J 207
Papadopoulou, F 116
patent law
contribution, determining 270
disclosure requirements 32–33, 34–36
downstream use of intellectual property 3, 202
drug discovery process and 3
enforcement 16
European Patent Convention 225–226
expiration date of patent 196, 270
follow-on compounds 8

independently developed ideas 16
in-imitativeness 268–269
justification for 88
monopoly rights 16
Nagoya Protocol compared 16
original discovery requirement 164
patenting plants and animals 32
path-independent nature of rights 16, 100
second/further uses of drug, discovery 3
start date of patent 270
TKAGR compared 15–17, 164–165, 202
TRIPs Agreement provisions 32–33
Pelletier, J 213
Perkin, WH 206, 213–214, 274–276, 283, 286–287
Peters, P 48
pharmaceutically active compound 1
pharmacodynamics 190
pharmacophore 5, 180
philosophical justification for rights *See* **justification for rights in TKAGR**
phylogenetic surveying 185
Pievatolo, MC 106–107
Piria, R 207
Pliny the Elder 207
polymerase chain reaction (PCR) 58–59
Posey, DA 161–163, 165–166, 167
Posey, DA and Dutfield, G 166
Posner, RA 259
prior informed consent of right-holder 35, 60, 175, 253, 281
BBNJ Treaty 29
indigenous sovereignty 155
Kunming–Montreal GBF 27
Nagoya Protocol 22, 23, 24–25, 38, 46, 70–72, 76, 77, 244; Table 1
TRIPs Agreement 32, 33
UNDRIP 20, 169–172, 177, 251
utility through control 137–138
valorisation 135
prokaryotic material 42, 63, 275
Prontosil 214, 275
property *See also* **intangible property; intellectual property; justification for rights in TKAGR**
Fichtean justification for 103, 110–111, 117, 231–232, 262, 263; Table 13
Hegelian justification for 112–119, 153, 231–232, 263; Table 13
indigenous concepts of 158–160
Kantian justification for 103–110, 117, 231–232, 262; Table 13
Locke's theory of 91–103, 262, 263; Table 13
Neo-Lockean school 95, 99, 101–102
rectification of title 95
utilitarian justifications for 88, 96, 121–141, 232–244
Western approach to 89–91, 154, 167–168
public good, knowledge treated as 5, 96

Q
quinine 18, 206, 212–215, 274–277, 283, 286–287

R
Rabe, P 215
Radin, MJ 95
rapamycin (mTOR) 204
Rawls, J 128, 146–148, 174, 217–218, 235
difference principle 146–148, 247, 256, 284, 289, 290
distributive justice 217–218, 244–249, 262
maximin analysis 90, 217–218, 244–249, 256, 265, 290; Tables 10, 11, 13, 14
other approaches compared Table 13
overlapping consensus 259, 260, 261–262, 263, 285
remoteness
causation in fact 14–15, 201, 217, 282
infringement, of 14–15
intellectual property rights and 15
reparations model *See also* **compensation/reward**
generally 148–150, 177, 256, 265, 284, 289; Table 14
other approaches compared Table 13
serendipitous discoveries 249–250, 256
research and development *See also* **biotechnology; drug development; drug discovery process**
aniline dyes 213–214, 274–275, 283, 286–287
aspirin 18, 203, 205, 206–209, 272, 283
biochemical compounds 54–55
chemical derivatives 55–57, 69–70, 72
cocaine 18, 205, 209–212, 278–279, 283, 287
coincidental second uses 274–279, 286–287, 289
commercialisation *See* commercialisation; valorisation
contributions made by researcher 2–3, 4, 7–8, 9–11, 37

degree of wrong 149
emergency situations 76, 78–80
non-commercial 76–78, 238
serendipitous discoveries *See* serendipitous discovery
synthetic DNA *See* synthetic DNA
utilization of genetic resource 43–70
vinca alkaloids 18, 206, 215–216, 278, 283, 287
Resnik, DB 89, 263
restitution 141–143
definition 141
intangible property 169–170
UNDRIP, under 20, 169–170, 252
restorative/corrective justice *See also* **compensation/reward; valorisation**
conditions for 148
control rights in TKAGR 169–170, 175, 249–250, 265
generally 284
justification for rights in TKAGR 91, 148–150, 256
reparations 148–150, 177, 249–250, 256, 265, 284, 289; Tables 13, 14
serendipitous discoveries 249–250, 256
reward *See* **compensation/reward**
rights in TKAGR
control *See* control rights in TKAGR
duration 272–280, 285–286
duties and 85–86
justifiable limit 11–12
justification for *See* justification for rights in TKAGR
veto *See* veto right
Rio Declaration 164
rosy periwinkle 18, 206, 215–216, 278, 283, 287
Rousseau, J-J 139
Russell, B 112

S
Sargent, S 170, 171
Savaresi, A 25, 171
serendipitous discovery
boundary/crux points 217, 283
case studies 204–216, 283; Table 6
causation in law implications 3, 217
communitarian approach to rights in 252–254, 256, 284; Table 12
compensation 218, 224, 230, 231, 236–237, 240–243, 245–246, 249–256, 285; Tables 7–12
contribution 217, 218, 220–231, 240, 285–286, 288–289
deontological justifications for rights in 218–231
determining true nature of 4
fundamental element 227
generally 8, 18, 100, 101, 198, 202, 203–204, 270–272, 283
global health utility 236–239, 242–243, 255; Table 9
human rights justification for TKAGR 250–254
inchoate claims 223–224, 226–231, 273
inherent claims 223, 224–231, 273
justification for rights in TKAGR 217–256
legal treatment, policy options 217–218
Lockean labour-desert theory 218–231, 255, 273–274; Table 7
meaning 204, 269, 285–287
natural law 221–223, 255
personality-based rights 231–232, 255; Table 8
Rawlsian distributive justice 217–218, 244–249, 256; Tables 10, 11
restorative/corrective justice (reparations) 249–250, 256
self-determination rights and 250–254, 256, 284
UNDRIP 251–252, 256; Table 12
utilitarian justifications for rights in 232–244, 255
utility through control 232, 236, 237, 241–243, 255; Table 9
valorisation 232–237, 255; Table 9
veto rights 218, 227, 230, 237–239, 240–256, 267, 269–279, 285, 290; Tables 7–12
Shiffrin, SV 99, 121, 122–123
Shiva, V 6, 94
Signatures, Doctrine of 207
sildenafil citrate 270–271; Fig.7
sine qua non test 13–14, 201
Singer, P 131, 140
Sneader, W 214
Snyder, SH 270–271
Socrates 128
sovereignty *See also* **indigenous self-determination**
Kunming–Montreal GBF 157
Nagoya Protocol 23, 157
Spinoza, B 143
Stamatopoulou, E 171–172

Stoics 127
Stokes, JM et al 194
Stone, E 207
Strathern, M 166–167
Sunstein, C 259–260, 263, 285
sustainable use *See* **conservation/sustainable use**
synthetic DNA
accessing 60–64, 72
cDNA 58
Convention on Biological Diversity 65–67
digital sequence information 65–67
functional units of heredity 59–65
genetic resource, whether classed as 58–67
meaning 58
Nagoya Protocol 58–67, 72
polymerase chain reaction 58–59
utilization 58–69

T
Taubman, A 119–120
Taylor, TC 134, 138
technology, transfer *See also* **biotechnology**
Nagoya Protocol 39
TRIPs Agreement 31
testing process, generally 7–8
therapeutic window 190
third party interests 2
third party use *See also* **infringement**
access to TKAGR generally 71
justifiable limit to use 11–12
patent law monopoly rights 15–16
prevention 11
time-limited right 103
certainty of the originator 219
lack of temporal limitation 4, 219–220, 279
Trade Related Aspects of Intellectual Property Agreement (TRIPS)
ABS provisions 32
adoption 165
biopiracy, discouraging 31
control rights in TKAGR 31, 32
Convention on Biological Diversity and 31–32
disclosure requirements 32–33
flexibilities 238–239, 291
global health 238–239, 291
objectives 31
patentability provisions 32–33
positive rights 31–32; Fig.2
prior informed consent 32, 33
proposed changes 32, 33
traditional knowledge associated with genetic resources (TKAGR)
access to *See* access to TKAGR
biopiracy 6
boundary/crux point delineation 10–11, 15, 17, 200–202, 217, 283
causation *See* causation
commercialisation *See* compensation; valorisation
complexity of drug discovery process 4
conflicting claims 2, 87, 202, 230, 243
consensual use 12–13, 25
contributions *See* contribution
defining and delimiting 1
development across time 90
dilution *See* epistemic dilution
easily reproduced nature 1
end product differing from 74
genetic resource per se and 18
group ownership 101–103, 108–109, 111, 116–120, 176
intellectual property rights compared 15–17
justification for rights in *See* justification for rights in TKAGR
Locke's theory of property 101–103; Table 13
misappropriation *See* misappropriation
mixing with other information 1, 2, 7–8, 9–11, 282
mixing with other TKAGR 9–11, 282
Nagoya Protocol *See* Nagoya Protocol
non-commercial research, enabling 76–78, 238
politicisation 161
positive rights in 1, 5–7
research inspired by 74
secret knowledge 102, 158, 159
transboundary situations 244
transgenerational development 15–16, 90, 218–219
utilization 73–74
value, veto right creating 25
veto rights *See* veto right
traditional resource rights
suggested implementation 166, 167
Tren Maya Project 129
Tsosie, R 117
Turner, D 156
Tvedt, MW and Shei, PJ 60, 62

U
Underkuffler, LS 12
United Nations
BBNJ *See* Marine Biological Diversity of Areas Beyond National Jurisdiction Treaty

CBD *See* Convention on Biological Diversity
Charter 173
Convention on the Law of the Sea 28
Food and Agriculture Organization 29
ITPGRFA *See* International Treaty on Plant Genetic Resources for Food and Agriculture
Kunming-Montreal GBF *See* Kunming-Montreal Global Biodiversity Framework
Nagoya Protocol *See* Nagoya Protocol
rights under 6–7, 19; Fig.2
Rio Declaration 164
Sustainable Development Goals 26
UNDRIP *See* Declaration on the Rights of Indigenous Peoples
UNESCO 163

unjust enrichment 141–143
definition 141
restitution 141, 142

utilitarianism
Benthamite 122, 127–128, 132, 133, 242
commercialisation and 121–124, 126, 135, 138, 141, 142
conflicting goals 236–239
control, utility through 119–121, 133, 137–138, 177, 189; Tables 9, 13, 14, 232, 236, 237, 241–243, 254, 255, 266, 283–284, 289
criticisms of 122–123
culture, preservation 125–126, 131–136, 138–141
economic approaches 121
environment, preservation 126, 131–136, 138–141, 232, 283
global health utility 236–239, 242–243, 255, 265–266, 273, 275; Tables 9, 13, 14
incentivising innovation 121–124, 141, 147–148, 176–177, 262, 273
justifications for intellectual property 88, 96, 121–141, 232–244, 255, 283–284, 289–290
market efficiency 121, 122
Millian 122, 127–128, 129, 132–133, 242
quantifying happiness 127–131, 139, 242
rule-utilitarianism 127, 129–130
serendipitous discoveries 232–244, 255
stability, ensuring 125
traditional knowledge, preservation for own sake 136–137, 232, 283
valorisation model 126–138, 141, 145, 147–148, 232–237, 239–242, 255, 258, 265, 284, 289; Tables 9, 14

V

valorisation
commercialisation *See* commercialisation
control over TKAGR 136, 232–233, 265
determining value 134–135
incentivising innovation 121–124, 141, 147–148, 176–177, 262
other approaches compared 265–266; Tables 9, 13, 14
preservation of the environment 126, 131–136, 138–141, 232
preservation of indigenous culture 131–134, 136–137, 138–141
prior informed consent of right-holder 135
serendipitous discoveries 232–242, 255
utilitarianism 126–138, 141, 145, 147–148, 232–242, 255, 258, 265, 284, 289; Tables 9, 14
veto right creating 25, 284, 289

value-added theory
justification for property 89, 91–103, 144–145, 150, 176, 218–236

Vane, J 209

Varese, S 155

veto right
assessment of contribution 267, 268–269, 274, 285, 288–289
coincidental second uses 274–279, 286–287, 289
compensation for *See* compensation
downstream use of TKAGR 266–274, 284, 285, 289
duration 272–280, 285–286
generally 263, 265; Tables 7–12, 14
global health utility 190–291
limited, workability 267–279
maximin analysis 265
Nagoya Protocol 9–11, 24, 25, 26, 37, 90, 238
retrospective obviousness 269–272, 274, 276
serendipitous discoveries 218, 227, 230, 231, 237, 238, 240–256, 267, 269–274, 285, 290; Tables 7–12
types of 263, 265
UNDRIP 170–171, 175, Table 14
valorisation model 25, 284, 289

Vienna Declaration and Programme of Action 173

vinca alkaloids 18, 206, 215–216, 278, 283, 287

W

Waldron, J 85–86

Warburton, N 112, 146

Weiss, HJ and Aledort, LM 208

Western approach to property 89–91, 154, 155, 167
  Western-style enforcement 141–143
Westernisation
  economic perspective 267
  threats accompanying 138–141
Wiessner, S 155
Wilke, M 78–79
Woodward, R 215
World Intellectual Property Organization (WIPO) 163
  proposed disclosure requirements 34–36
  proposed GRTKF protection 34–36; Fig.2
  relative conservatism 36
  rights under 6–7, 19
  study on protection of traditional knowledge 125, 141–142
World Trade Organisation (WTO)
  rights under 6–7, 19, 31–32; Fig.2
  TRIPs *See* Trade Related Aspects of Intellectual Property Agreement

www.ingramcontent.com/pod-product-compliance
Ingram Content Group UK Ltd.
Pitfield, Milton Keynes, MK11 3LW, UK
UKHW020237290926
15470UKWH00002B/584

9 781509 937530